Globalization and the Colonial Origins of the Great Divergence

Global Economic History Series

VOLUME 11

The titles published in this series are listed at *brill.com/gehs*

Globalization and the Colonial Origins of the Great Divergence

Intercontinental Trade and Living Standards in the Dutch East India Company's Commercial Empire, c. 1600–1800

By

Pim de Zwart

BRILL

LEIDEN | BOSTON

Cover illustration: The island 'Onrust' near Batavia – Abraham Storck (1699). Source: Wikimedia Commons (public domain).

The Library of Congress Cataloging-in-Publication Data is available online at http://catalog.loc.gov
LC record available at http://lccn.loc.gov/2016008174

Typeface for the Latin, Greek, and Cyrillic scripts: "Brill". See and download: brill.com/brill-typeface.

ISSN 1872-5155
ISBN 978-90-04-29965-8 (hardback)
ISBN 978-90-04-29966-5 (e-book)

This book is printed on acid-free paper.

Contents

Appendices

Preface

This book was written over the past few years, while I was working at the International Institute of Social History in Amsterdam and Utrecht University. I am very happy that I have been able to work in these stimulating environments. Financial support for writing this book was given by *Fonds 21*, for which I am grateful. Furthermore, some significant chunks of this book were written while I was visiting Harvard University in the spring of 2014. My gratitude goes to Sven Beckert and Charlie Maier for having me there.

Over the years, I have benefitted from the criticism and support of many colleagues from these institutes, as well as the wider community of social and economic historians: Bob Allen, Catia Antunes, Jean-Pascal Bassino, Bas van Bavel, Christiaan van Bochove, Ulbe Bosma, Sarah Carmichael, Daniel Curtis, Melissa Dell, Selin Dilli, Alberto Feenstra, Peter Foldvari, Johan Fourie, Ewout Frankema, Oscar Gelderblom, Michiel de Haas, Marjolein 't Hart, Leander Heldring, Karin Hofmeester, Herman de Jong, Joost Jonker, Jan Kok, Miguel Laborda Peman, Bas van Leeuwen, Henk Looijesteijn, Jan Lucassen, Debin Ma, Anne McCants, Sevket Pamuk, Sandra de Pleijt, Maarten Prak, Auke Rijpma, James Robinson, Ruben Schalk, Eric Schneider, Daniëlle Teeuwen, Jeroen Touwen, Lotte van der Vleuten, Jan de Vries, Jacob Weisdorf, Jeffrey Williamson, and Richard Zijdeman, the anonymous readers for this series, as well as many others who I have encountered at conferences and workshops. I am especially grateful to Gerrit Knaap and Judith Schooneveld-Oosterling for granting me early access to the VOC's Bookkeeper-General database.

I thank Lex Heerma van Voss and Elise van Nederveen Meerkerk, who read the entire manuscript and provided continuous support for the project, and Jan Luiten van Zanden, who not only read all chapters several times but also gave guidance and direction from the very beginning. In the final stages of getting this book ready for publication, Jennifer Obdam of Brill was very helpful in answering my consistent stream of questions. Ian Cressie of Cressie Communication Services did a magnificent job on improving the English text and he did so within an almost impossible timeframe.

I am indebted to all these people. Of course, I alone am to be held accountable if any inaccuracies, dubious interpretations, or other inadequacies still remain.

Pim de Zwart
Utrecht, January 2016

List of Figures, Tables and Maps

Figures

Tables

Maps

CHAPTER 1

Introduction

1 Trade and Growth

This book is about the long-distance trade of the Dutch East India Company (*Verenigde Oost-Indische Compagnie*; VOC) and the development of living standards in its commercial empire around the Indian Ocean in the early modern era. The relationship between international trade and economic development has been a central theme for economists and economic historians ever since Adam Smith's *Inquiry into the Nature and Causes of the Wealth of Nations* was first published in 1776.[1] Smith was the first to point out the potential benefits of trade through workings of absolute advantage and specialization. Following Smith, advocates of globalization today claim that global free trade promotes economic growth and that growth in turn reduces poverty.[2] Such voices also resonate in the public domain, as in a recent edition of *The Economist*, founded in 1843 to spread and popularize free trade views,[3] it is claimed that capitalism and free trade were the most important factors in the alleviation of poverty in the past decade as they 'enabled economies to grow – and it was growth, principally, that has eased destitution'.[4] At the same time, critics of globalization warn that intercontinental trade widens the income gap both between and within countries.[5]

Both proponents and opponents of globalization have relied on cross-country regressions to investigate the relationship between trade and economic growth. Jagdish Bhagwati and T. N. Srnivasan, prominent advocates of globalization, point out many problems with such regressions, such as poor data quality. As these regressions are greatly dependent on choices regarding period and the

1 Adam Smith, *An Inquiry into the Nature and Causes of the Wealth of Nations* (New York: Bantam Classic, 2003 [Original: 1776]); this section draws on: Pim de Zwart, Daan Marks, Alexandra M. de Pleijt and Jan Luiten van Zanden, 'Trade and Economic Development: Indonesia in the Long-Run', in: Alicia Schrikker and Jeroen Touwen (eds.) *Promises and Predicaments. Trade and entrepreneurship in colonial and independent Indonesia in the 19th and 20th Centuries* (Singapore: NUS Press, 2015) pp. 61–79.

2 See, for example, Jagdish Bhagwati and T. N. Srinivasan, 'Trade and Poverty in the Poor Countries,' *American Economic Review* 92 (2002) pp. 180–183.

3 Dani Rodrik, *The Globalization Paradox. Democracy and the Future of the World Economy* (New York: W.W. Norton & Company, 2011) p. 27.

4 'Towards the End of Poverty,' *The Economist*, June 1, 2013.

5 Dani Rodrik, *Has Globalization Gone Too Far?* (Washington DC: Institute for International Economics, 1997); Joseph E. Stiglitz, *Globalization and Its Discontents* (New York: W.W. Norton, 2002).

 | DOI 10.1163/9789004299665_002

sample of countries, they advise reluctance in using them 'as plausible "scientific" support'.[6] Instead, they suggest that nuanced in-depth case studies are a better tool for analysing the relationship between trade and economic development. At the same time, Dani Rodrik, one of their most conspicuous opponents,[7] takes up a historical perspective in some of his works.[8] Historical research into globalization can shed more light on long-term patterns in the relationship between globalization and economic growth and allows an investigation of the factors that influenced this relationship: when did globalization have negative effects on growth? When were these effects positive? How are these effects distributed between and within countries?

Whereas economists may debate the consequences of current globalization, historians are still discussing the question of when globalization began. As an investigation into the long-distance trade of the VOC, by far the largest of the early modern trading companies, and living standards in its commercial empire (thereby employing a lot of new archival data), this book is well placed to contribute to the debate about globalization's origins,[9] as well as the two other big issues in economic history: the 'Great Divergence' debate and the debate on the colonial origins of development.

1.1 *Globalization*

According to Smith, 'the discovery of America, and then of a passage to the East Indies by the Cape of Good Hope, are the two greatest and most important events in the recorded history of mankind.'[10] In the three centuries after these events, intercontinental trade grew roughly one percent annually. This advance is remarkable when compared with the development of world trade in the centuries before, as well as relative to the growth of other economic indicators: trade grew more than twice as fast as national income.[11]

6 T.N. Srinivasan and Jagdish Bhagwati, 'Outward-Orientation and Development: Are Revisionists Right?' *Center Discussion Paper No. 806* (Yale University, 1999) p. 38; also see: Jagdish Bhagwati, *In Defense of Globalization* (New York etc.: Oxford U.P., 2004).

7 See for example: Rodrik, *Has Globalization?*; ibid., *One Economics, Many Recipes: Globalization, Institutions and Economic Growth* (Princeton: Princeton U.P., 2007); ibid., *The Globalization Paradox*.

8 Rodrik, *The Globalization Paradox*, Chs. 1 and 2.

9 The economic history debate has recently also been picked up by *The Economist*: 'When did Globalisation Start?', *The Economist*, September 23, 2013.

10 Smith, *Wealth of Nations*, p. 793.

11 Ronald Findlay and Kevin H. O'Rourke, *Power and Plenty. Trade, War, and the World Economy in the Second Millennium* (Princeton: Princeton U.P., 2007) p. 305.

In the 1970s and early 1980s scholars like Immanuel Wallerstein and Andre Gunder Frank emphasized the importance of long-distance trade. This trade had been instrumental in bringing about intercontinental specialization and a global division of labour, with Western Europe being pushed towards industrialization and high living standards, whilst the periphery was pushed towards primary production and low levels of per capita income. As such, international trade played an important role in the rise of global economic inequality in this period, it was argued.[12] This process was aided by a decline in international transport costs,[13] which brought markets closer together. This view fell out of grace in the late 80s and early 90s, when it became 'commonplace among economic historians to argue that long-distance trade has been overemphasized by students of the early modern period'[14] as 'the international economy was poorly integrated before 1800.'[15]

In a series of publications in the 2000s, Kevin O'Rourke, Jeffrey Williamson and various co-authors questioned whether growth in early modern trade should be seen as the first stage of globalization.[16] They have suggested that due to war, monopolies, and the limited advance in transport technology there was little room for prices to converge across the globe, a process they see as paramount to globalization. Long-distance trade was focussed on non-competing luxury goods

---

12 Immanuel Wallerstein, *The Modern World System* (New York: Academic Press, 1974) and *The Capitalist World Economy* (Cambridge: Cambridge U.P., 1979), Andre Gunder Frank, *World Accumulation, 1492–1789* (London: Macmillan, 1978) and *Dependent Accumulation and Underdevelopment* (London: Macmillan, 1979); also see: Patrick K. O'Brien, 'European Economic Development: The Contribution of the Periphery', *Economic History Review* 35 (1982) pp. 1–18.

13 Douglass C. North, 'Ocean Freight Rates and Economic Development, 1750–1913', *Journal of Economic History* 18 (1958) pp. 537–555; ibid., 'Sources of Productivity Change in Ocean Shipping, 1600–1850', *Journal of Political Economy* (1968) pp. 953–970.

14 Russel Menard, 'Transport Costs and Long-Range Trade, 1300–1800: Was There a European "Transport Revolution" in the Early Modern Era?' in: J. D. Tracy (ed.) *Political Economy of Merchant Empires* (Cambridge: Cambridge U.P., 1991) p. 228.

15 Ibid.

16 Kevin H. O'Rourke and Jeffrey G. Williamson, 'When did globalisation begin?' *European Review of Economic History* 6 (2002) pp. 23–50; ibid., 'After Columbus: Explaining Europe's Overseas Trade Boom, 1500–1800', *Journal of Economic History* 62 (2002) pp. 417–456; ibid., 'Once More: When did Globalisation Begin?', *European Review of Economic History* 8 (2004) pp. 109–117; ibid., 'Did Vasco da Gama matter to European Markets?' *Economic History Review* 62 (2009) pp. 665–684; ibid: 'From Malthus to Ohlin: Trade, Growth, and Distribution since 1500', *Journal of Economic Growth* 10 (2005) pp. 5–34; Ronald Findlay and Kevin H. O'Rourke, 'Commodity market integration, 1500-2000' in: Michael D. Bordo, Alan M. Taylor and Jeffrey G. Williamson (eds.) *Globalization in Historical Perspective* (Chicago: University of Chicago Press, 2003); Findlay and O'Rourke, *Power and plenty.*

and therefore its effects on the European economy were negligible. As a consequence, O'Rourke and Williamson have dismissed the existence of globalization before the nineteenth century. Only after the Napoleonic wars did the advent of steamships, the construction of canals and the relative lack of large (naval) conflicts lead to an integrated world economy. O'Rourke and Williamson's works have become very influential and it has become textbook knowledge that the nineteenth century was the first era of globalization.[17] Not everyone is convinced of this, however, and a variety of studies have appeared in the past few years that cast doubt on O'Rourke and Williamson's findings.[18]

1.2 *The Great Divergence*

The issue of globalization is related to another large debate in economic history, i.e. regarding the *when* and *why* of the rise in economic inequality between Western Europe and the rest of the world. After the title of a book by Kenneth Pomeranz, this issue is now generally known as the 'Great Divergence' debate.[19]

Until the late 1990s the question of *when* some countries became rich (while others remained poor) was not considered very interesting; it was generally assumed that Western Europe was economically more developed than the rest since at least the late Middle Ages.[20] This interpretation was backed by estimates of GDP per capita indicating that incomes in Western Europe had already exceeded those in the rest of the world long before the Industrial Revolution (Figure 1.1). The question that remained was then *why* this had happened? Next to the role played by international trade, answers to this question emphasized Western Europe's exceptionality in that it had more beneficial

17 See for example the chapter on international trade in a recent textbook: Kevin H. O'Rourke, Leandro Prados de la Escosura and Guilaume Daudin, 'Trade and Empire', in: Stephen Broadberry and Kevin H. O'Rourke (eds.) *The Cambridge Economic History of Modern Europe* (Cambridge: Cambridge U.P., 2010) pp. 96–121.

18 Klas Rönnbäck, 'Integration of global commodity markets in the early modern era', *European Review of Economic History* 13 (2009) pp. 95–120; Rafael Dobado-Gonzales, Alfredo Garcia-Hiernaux, and David E. Guerrero, 'The Integration of Grain Markets in the Eighteenth Century: Early Rise of Globalization in the West', *Journal of Economic History* 72 (2012) pp. 671–707; Paul Sharp and Jacob Weisdorf, 'Globalization revisited: market integration and the wheat trade between North America and Britain from the eighteenth century', *Explorations in Economic History* 50 (2013) pp. 88–98.

19 Kenneth Pomeranz, *The Great Divergence. China, Europe and the Making of the Modern World Economy* (Princeton: Princeton U.P., 2000).

20 See: Robert C. Allen, 'Agricultural Productivity and Rural Incomes in England and the Yangtze Delta, c. 1620–1820', *Economic History Review* 62 (2009) pp. 525–526.

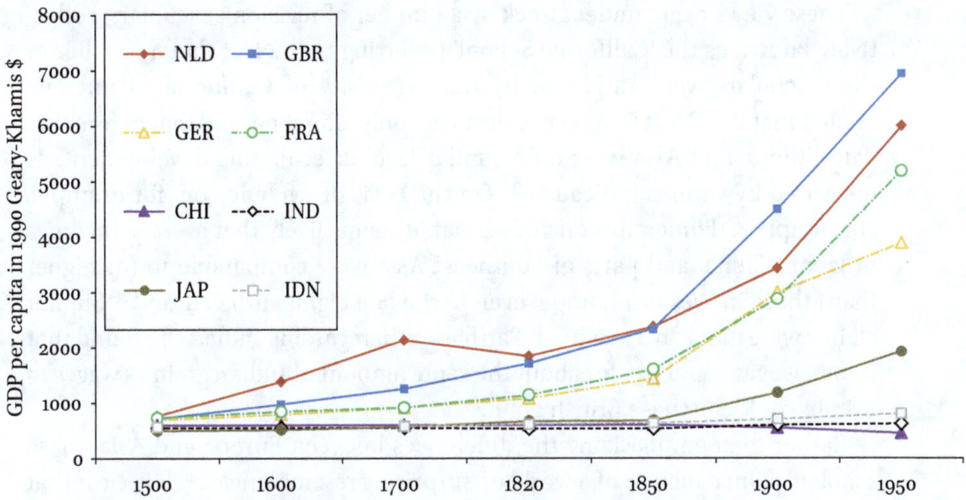

FIGURE 1.1 *The 'Great Divergence': GDP per capita in Europe and Asia, 1500–1950.*
Source: Angus Maddison, 'Statistics on World Population, GDP and Per Capita GDP, 1–2008 AD', *Groningen Growth and Development Centre*: http://www.ggdc.net/.

demographic patterns,[21] more 'inclusive' institutions and secure property rights,[22] a more rational scientific culture,[23] and a more efficient market system.[24]

21 Thomas Malthus, *An Essay on the Principle of Population, as it Affects the Future Improvement of Society with Remarks on the Speculations of Mr. Godwin, M. Condorcet, and Other Writers* (1998 [Original 1798]); J. Hajnal, 'European Marriage in Perspective', in: D. V. Glass and D. E. C. Eversley (eds.), *Population in History* (1965) pp. 101–143; Eric L. Jones, *The European Miracle: Environments, Economies and Geopolitics in the History of Europe and Asia* (Cambridge: Cambridge U.P., 1981) pp. 13–21; Tine de Moor and Jan Luiten van Zanden, 'Girl Power: The European Marriage Pattern and labour markets in the North Sea region in the late medieval and early modern period', *Economic History Review* 63 (2010) pp. 1–33.

22 See for example Douglass C. North and Robert P. Thomas, *The Rise of the Western World: A New Economic History* (Cambridge: Cambridge U.P., 1973), and: Douglass C. North and Barry Weingast, 'Constitutions and Commitment: The Evolution of Institutions Governing Public Choice in Seventeenth-Century England,' *Journal of Economic History* 49 (1989) pp. 803–832.

23 Max Weber, *The Protestant Work Ethic and the Spirit of Capitalism* (1905 [2002]), Joel Mokyr, *The Lever of Riches: Technological Creativity and Economic Progress* (Oxford and New York: Oxford U.P., 1990); ibid., *The Enlightened Economy. An Economic History of Britain 1700–1850* (New Haven and London: Yale U.P., 2009), David S. Landes, *The Unbound Prometheus: Technological Change and Industrial Development in Western Europe from 1750 to the Present* (Cambridge: Cambridge University Press, 1969).

24 For classic works on European exceptionalism see: Jones, *European Miracle*, David S Landes, *The Wealth and Poverty of Nations: Why Some are So Rich and Some So Poor*

These views came under attack by a number of revisionist scholars, collectively known as the 'California School' (referring to the fact that a number of these scholars were employed by the University of California). Pomeranz argued that the Great Divergence occurred only after 1800, and that before that date Europe and Asia were on a similar level of economic development, as measured by various indicators.[25] On the basis of evidence on, for example, consumption, Pomeranz concluded that 'it seems likely that average incomes in Japan, China, and parts of Southeast Asia were comparable to (or higher than) those in Western Europe, even in the late eighteenth century'.[26] Similar claims were made by Prasannan Parthasarathi regarding India, who found that Indian wages could pay for about the same amount of Indian grain as wages in Britain could purchase British grain.[27]

Rather than emphasizing the differences between Europe and Asia, these scholars paint a picture of a world of 'surprising resemblances'.[28] It is clear that if the divergence had occurred much later, different factors than those highlighted by previous historical research must have caused it. Pomeranz claimed that the divergence between China and Europe was not the consequence of the fundamental differences, but rather a fortuitous spin-off of the large colonies of a few Western European countries, combined with the advantage of favourably located coal. Parthasarathi concluded that the challenge of Indian cotton textiles and the shortage of wood provided instrumental pressures that led to Britain's economic ascendance.[29] The past decade has seen contributions that have both disputed and confirmed these claims.[30] A major obstacle

(London: Little/Brown, 1998). This list is not exhaustive, also see: Roman Studer, 'India and the Great Divergence: Assessing the Efficiency of Grain Markets in Eighteenth- and Nineteenth-Century India', *Journal of Economic History* 68 (2008) p. 393.

25 Pomeranz, *The Great Divergence*.

26 Pomeranz, *The Great Divergence*, p. 49.

27 Prasannan Parthasarathi, 'Rethinking Wages and Competitiveness in the Eighteenth Century: Britain and South India', *Past and Present* 158 (1998) pp. 79–109.

28 Pomeranz, *The Great Divergence*, Pt. 1.

29 Prasannan Parthasarathi, *Why Europe Grew Rich and Asia Did Not. Global Economic Divergence, 1600–1850* (Cambridge: Cambridge U.P., 2011) p. 2.

30 Confirming the revisionist views include: Allen, 'Agricultural Productivity' and Sashi Sivramkrishna, 'Ascertaining Living Standards in Erstwhile Mysore, Southern India, from Francis Buchanan's Journey of 1800–01: An Empirical Contribution to the Great Divergence Debate', *Journal of the Economic and Social History of the Orient* 52 (2009) 695–733. Refuting 'revisionist' claims include: Robert C. Allen, 'India in the Great Divergence', in: Timothy J. Hatton, Kevin H. O'Rourke, and Alan M. Taylor, *The New Comparative Economic History. Essays in Honor of Jeffrey G. Williamson* (Cambridge MA: MIT Press, 2007) pp. 111–130; Robert C. Allen, Jean-Pascal Bassino, Debin Ma, Christine Moll-Murata, and Jan Luiten van

to consensus has been the lack of quantitative evidence. This study fills some of this hiatus by presenting extensive, new quantitative data on a number of Asian economies before the nineteenth century.

1.3 *Colonialism and Development*

At the same time as historians became increasingly interested in global comparisons over long periods of time, economists became more aware of the importance of history.[31] From their ranks has emerged a new empirical literature that tests whether historical events, most notably colonialism and associated institutions, still can be found to have effects on current economic development outcomes.

The literature is already too vast to discuss at great length here, but it would be helpful to discuss the most famous studies that have highlighted the different channels through which colonialism has affected economic development outcomes. In a seminal contribution, Rafael La Porta, Florencio Lopez de Silanes, Andrei Shleifer, and Robert Vishny argued that the identity of the colonizer influenced economic development as it determined whether a legal system based on Roman civil law or British common law was established in a colony. As the common law system offered greater protection for investors, it was more conducive to long-term economic growth.[32] Others have stressed the negative effects of colonialism on ethnic fragmentation. High ethnic diversity is closely associated with low levels of education, underdeveloped financial systems, distorted foreign exchange markets, and insufficient infrastructure, which lower economic growth.[33] In another important contribution, Stanley L. Engerman and Kenneth L. Sokoloff argued that the different paths of economic development between Northern and Southern America can be explained by initial differences in factor endowments.[34] Those regions (the

---

Zanden, 'Wages, prices, and living standards in China, 1738–1925: in comparison with Europe, Japan, and India', *Economic History Review* 64 (2011) pp. 8–38; Stephen Broadberry and Bishnupriya Gupta, 'The early modern great divergence: wages, prices and economic development in Europe and Asia, 1500–1800', *Economic History Review* 59 (2006) pp. 2–31; Tirthankar Roy, 'Economic Conditions in Early Modern Bengal: A Contribution to the Divergence Debate', *Journal of Economic History* 70 (2010) pp. 179–194.

31 See also the survey by: Nathan Nunn, 'The importance of history for economic development', *Annual Review of Economics* 1 (2009) pp. 65–92.

32 R. La Porta, F. Lopez-de-Silanes, A. Shleifer and R. Vishny, 'Law and finance', *Journal of Political Economy* 106 (1998) pp. 1113–1155.

33 William Easterly and Ross Levine, 'Africa's Growth Tragedy: Policies and Ethnic Divisions', *Quarterly Journal of Economics* 112 (1997) pp. 1203–1250.

34 Kenneth L. Sokoloff and Stanley L Engerman, 'History Lessons: Institutions, Factor Endowments and Paths of Development in the New World', *Journal of Economic*

Caribbean and Southern America) suitable for growing sugar and other highly valued commodities associated with large-scale production on plantations using slave labour were characterized by significant political and economic inequality that persisted through their institutional development. These institutions and a high degree of inequality negatively affected economic growth.

Closely related to Engerman and Sokoloff's thesis are the works of Daron Acemoglu, Simon Johnson and James Robinson, who claim that those countries colonized by European powers that were relatively rich 500 years ago are now relatively poor, and vice versa, and who argue that this reversal reflects an 'institutional reversal' caused by the colonial powers.[35] In those areas that were relatively prosperous and densely settled in 1500, Europeans introduced (or maintained already existing) extractive institutions to profit from this wealth, whereas in poor and sparsely populated areas, Europeans themselves settled in large numbers and created 'inclusive' institutions that safeguarded private property, thereby encouraging commerce and industry.[36] Acemoglu et al.'s work both stimulated further research by other social scientists as well as attracting a significant amount of criticism. Some critics have questioned the quality of their data,[37] while others have pointed out some methodological shortcomings of the thesis and/or raised theoretical objections.[38] While there is no need to reproduce all these critiques here, for the purposes of my study it is important to discuss what Gareth Austin called the 'compression of history'.[39] He suggests that Acemoglu et al. compare two moments in history, 1500 and 1995, that had so much history in between that fails to take

---

Perspectives 14 (2000) pp. 217–232.

35 Daron Acemoglu, Simon Johnson and James A. Robinson, 'The Colonial Origins of Comparative Development: An Empirical Investigation', *American Economic Review* 102 (2001) pp. 3077–3110.

36 Daron Acemoglu, Simon Johnson and James A. Robinson, 'Reversal of Fortune: Geography and Institutions in the Making of the Modern World Income Distribution', *Quarterly Journal of Economics* 117 (2002) p. 1279.

37 Regarding the 1500 A.D. baseline for Africa, Gareth Austin claims that although some empirical evidence exists, 'it is very limited, and the best of it is not quantitative,' see Gareth Austin, 'The "Reversal of Fortune" Thesis and the Compression of History: Perspectives from African and Comparative Economic History', *Journal of International Development* 20 (2008) p. 998.

38 See for example: Edward Glaeser, R. La Porta, F. Lopez-de-Silanes, A. Shleifer, 'Do Institutions cause Growth?', *Journal of Economic Growth* 9 (2004) pp. 271–303; where it is claimed that human capital rather than institutions have dominant long term effects on economic growth.

39 Austin, 'The "Reversal"'.

sufficiently into account much of the heterogeneity of colonialism over time and by region. Related to this is the critique of the simple contrast between 'settler' colonies that had inclusive institutions and 'non-settler' colonies with extractive regimes.[40] Africanists, for example, argue that this dichotomy clearly distorts the history of colonial Africa. A more common typology used by historians therefore distinguishes between colonies of settlement (where the majority of land was appropriated for European use), colonies of concession (where lands were operated by foreign companies) and colonies of trade (colonies that did not experience large-scale European settlement).[41]

A variation on this tripartite distinction will also be employed in this book as VOC colonization across the Indian Ocean roughly varied according to these three categories (see Table 1.1). Furthermore, rather than linking initial conditions to current outcomes, I will investigate what happened over time in these areas. In doing so, I am able to distinguish various forms of colonialism and its different effects over time and by region.

In this volume I aim to connect these debates through the question of whether or not globalization and colonialism contributed to the Great Divergence in the early modern period and what influenced this connection? In order answer this question I first need to establish whether there is evidence of globalization in the early modern era and what drove this process. Secondly, it needs to be determined when the gap in economic performance between Western Europe and the Rest occurred and what factors may have influenced the unequal development. Third, I investigate how variations in colonialism may have affected living standards at the time and how they relate to globalization. By focussing on these issues, I hope to provide new insights into all three these debates. Finally, I do not wish to suggest that this book will provide conclusive answers to these big questions, but rather that it will make a small, yet significant contribution to the literature on these issues. To do so I will concentrate on the role of the Dutch East India Company in these processes and place a number of different VOC colonies in a global comparative framework.

---

40 Austin, 'The "Reversal"', p. 1008, Anthony G. Hopkins, 'The New Economic History of Africa', *Journal of African History* 50 (2009) pp. 167–169.

41 Austin, 'The "Reversal"', p. 1008. Hopkins, 'The New Economic', p. 168; Sue Bowden, Blessing Chiripanhura and Paul Mosley, 'Measuring and Explaining Poverty in Six African Countries: A long-period approach,' *Journal of Economic Development* 20 (2008) pp. 1049–1079; Hla Myint, *The Economics of the Developing Countries* (London, 1964) and: Jürgen Osterhammel, *Colonialism: a theoretical overview* (Princeton: Princeton U.P., 1999).

2 Linking the Debates: The Dutch East India Company

Established in 1602, the Dutch East India Company existed for almost two centuries until its insolvency at the end of the eighteenth century. The VOC was by far the most important trading company in the Euro-Asian trade between 1600 and 1800: of a total of 9,641 ships in that trade, 4,720 were Dutch,[42] while its nearest competitor, the British East India Company (EIC) employed little over half that number (2,676). Furthermore, Dutch ships were generally larger than those of other European companies and over 60 percent of the total volume of the return trade was transported on Dutch ships.[43] Also in terms of manpower the VOC dwarfed its competitors, as almost a million Europeans were sent to Asia aboard VOC ships,[44] nearly 100,000 more than all its competitors combined.[45] In addition, it hired in total 366,900 Asians over the course of the seventeenth and eighteenth centuries.

In total, these men transported over 2.5 million tons of Asian goods. Furthermore, despite the VOC policy of preferring to pay for goods for the European markets from the sales proceeds of its intra-Asian trade, the Company also poured over half a billion guilders in precious metals into Asian economies (over € 5,500 billion when converted to current prices).[46] To facilitate this trade the VOC opened over 30 trading posts between Cape Town (South Africa) and Nagasaki (Japan).[47] While in some of these places VOC presence was very limited indeed, in others the Company came to establish colonial rule over large stretches of land inhabited by equally large numbers of indigenous peoples. Dutch presence in Ceylon (present day Sri Lanka) and different parts of Southeast Asia are among the earliest examples of European imperialism in Asia.[48] A study of trade and living standards in the Dutch East India Company's commercial empire bears on all three of the major debates.

---

42 F. S. Gaastra and Jaap R. Bruijn, 'The Dutch East India Company's Shipping, 1602–1795, in a comparative perspective', in: ibid. (eds.) *Ships, Sailors and Spices. East India Companies and their Shipping in the 16*th*, 17*th *and 18*th *centuries* (Amsterdam: NEHA, 1993) p. 183.

43 Jan de Vries, 'Connecting Europe and Asia: a quantitative analysis of the Cape-route trade, 1497–1795', in: D. O. Flynn, A. Giraldez, and R. von Glahn (eds.), *Global connections and monetary history, 1470–1800* (Aldershot, 2003) pp. 56–59.

44 F. S. Gaastra, *De Geschiedenis van de VOC* (Zutphen: Walburg Pers, 2002) p. 91.

45 M. W. van Boven, 'Towards a New Age of Partnership (TANAP): An Ambitious World Heritage Project UNESCO Memory of the World', *VOC Archives Appendix* 2 (2002) p.14.

46 Gaastra, *De Geschiedenis*, p. 149; and IISH calculator: http://www.iisg.nl/hpw/calculate2.php/.

47 For a full list of VOC establishments with surviving data see: http://databases.tanap.nl/vocrecords/.

48 Findlay and O'Rourke, *Power and Plenty*, p. 181.

First, while a few recent studies have shown evidence of price convergence in trans-Atlantic trade before the nineteenth century,[49] De Vries reasonably notes that because the institutions in the New World were specifically moulded to serve the interests of export and long-distance trade 'the real test of early modern globalization, by any definition, requires a study of Eurasia.'[50] To Adam Smith, the Dutch East India Company was the epitome of everything that was wrong with state-backed chartered companies.[51] It was, however, a huge company and it transported millions of tonnes of goods between Asia and Europe over the course of two centuries. Despite the impressive amount of research that has been done on the VOC,[52] as well as on the price history of the Netherlands,[53] the data of the Dutch–Asiatic trade that have been brought to bear on the issue of globalization have been meagre: decadal average prices for only three products, namely cloves, coffee and pepper.[54] While pepper and cloves were certainly of great importance to the VOC in the early seventeenth century, by the 1660s they had already been surpassed by textiles in terms of the total invoice value of return cargos.[55] The importance of coffee did increase over the eighteenth century, but the rise of a global market for coffee in the eighteenth century is still subject to debate.[56] Clearly, an elaborate study of

---

49 Dobado-Gonzales et al., 'The Integration'; Rönnback, 'Integration of world'; Sharp and Weisdorf, 'Globalization revisited'.

50 Jan de Vries, 'The Limits of Globalization in the Early Modern World', *Economic History Review* 63 (2010) pp. 715–6.

51 Alex MacGillivray, *A Brief History of Globalization* (London: Constable & Robinson, 2006) p. 102.

52 To mention only a few examples: J. R. Bruijn, F. S. Gaastra and I. Schöffer, *Dutch-Asiatic Shipping in the 17th and 18th Centuries.* Vols. 1–3 (The Hague : Nijhoff, 1979–1987) ; Kristof Glamann, *Dutch-Asiatic Trade 1620–1740* (The Hague : Nijhoff, 1981); Els M. Jacobs, *Merchant in Asia: The Trade of the Dutch East India Company During the Eighteenth Century* (Leiden: CNWS Publications, 2013); Gaastra, *De Geschiedenis.*

53 See the extensive datasets by: N.W. Posthumus, *Nederlandsche Prijsgeschiedenis* (Leiden: Brill, 1943).

54 O'Rourke and Williamson, 'When did globalisation'; Rönnbäck, 'Integration of global'.

55 Om Prakash, *European Commercial Enterprise in India* (Cambridge: Cambridge U.P., 1998) p. 115.

56 David Bulbeck, Anthony Reid, Lay Cheng Tan and Yiqi Wu, *Southeast Asian exports since the 14th century. Cloves, pepper, coffee and sugar* (Leiden : KITLV, 1998) p. 169; Anne McCants, 'Poor consumers as global consumers: the diffusion of tea and coffee drinking in the eighteenth century' *Economic History Review* 61 (2008) pp. 172–200; Steven Topik, 'The Integration of the World Coffee Market', in: William Gervase Clarence-Smith and Steven Topik (eds.) *The Global Coffee Economy in Africa, Asia, and Latin America, 1500–1989* (Cambridge: Cambridge U.P., 2003) pp. 21–49; Rönnbäck, 'Integration of global'.

prices in the Dutch–Asiatic trade is instrumental for formulating answers to questions as to when globalization began and what drove the process.

Second, Pomeranz suggests that, economically speaking, the seventeenth- and eighteenth-century world was one of 'surprising resemblances'. Yet, despite his occasional leaps to other parts of Asia, Pomeranz generally compares the most advanced parts of Asia (the Yangzi Delta) with the most advanced parts of Europe (England). In this book I especially aim to integrate other parts of Asia in these comparisons, as others have already included other parts of Europe.[57] Furthermore, Pomeranz generally makes cross-country comparisons for a few benchmark years, but was unable to show any time trends. My research will trace trends over time, which not only allows the analysis of these trends, thus providing further clues regarding the question of what caused the Great Divergence, but also adding robustness to the comparisons: to what extent are benchmark comparisons representative of 'normal' years, rather than just outliers?

Third, the Great Divergence cannot be properly understood without taking into account that, at the same time as incomes diverged, intercontinental trade took a leap. As Jan de Vries notes, there may be a clear connection between globalization and the Great Divergence:

> When all is said and done, we are presented with two simultaneous developments – the establishment and development of a global maritime trading system under western European direction and the divergent growth of the western European economies – and are asked to believe that a causal link exists connecting the first to the second.[58]

For Pomeranz, a divergence would not have taken place without efficient intercontinental trade, or what may be called 'globalization', as Britain would not have benefitted from the 'ghost acreages' in the New World.[59] Along similar lines, Parthasarathi suggests that Britain would not have felt the need to innovate in textile manufacturing, as it would not have suffered from the competitive pressure of Indian textiles.[60] Others have emphasized the importance of

---

57 Most notably Robert C. Allen, 'The Great Divergence in European Wages and Prices from the Middle Ages to the First World War', *Explorations in Economic History* 38 (2001) pp. 411–447.

58 De Vries, 'The Limits', p. 712.

59 Pomeranz, *The Great Divergence*; also see Kenneth Pomeranz and Steven C. Topik, *The World That Trade Created: Society, Culture and the World Economy, 1400 to the Present* (Armonk: Sharpe, 1999).

60 Parthasarathi, *Why Europe*.

this global trade for Europe's advance through, for example, its effects on institutional change,[61] urbanization,[62] and work ethics.[63] Williamson has connected the debates on globalization and the Great Divergence in some of his work.[64] He suggests that the rise in global inequality between 'core' (Western Europe) and 'periphery' (the rest of the world, minus North America, Australia and New Zealand) in the nineteenth and twentieth centuries can to some extent be explained by the growth of intercontinental trade. While secular increases in the terms of trade (the price of exports over the price of imports) had positive effects on the economic growth of Europe, it had no impact in the periphery. At the same time, the volatility of terms of trade had significant negative effects in the periphery, but had no impact on growth in the core, the result being divergence.[65] But, as Williamson believes that globalization started in the 1820s, his assessment does not stretch back further than the nineteenth century. Yet, considering recent evidence on the occurrence of a Great Divergence already in the early modern period,[66] as well as the possibility of globalization taking off before the 1800s,[67] it is important to investigate the possible connection for the seventeenth and eighteenth centuries.

Finally, there is a connection between globalization and colonialism. While several scholars have argued that empire was a powerful tool for globalization in the nineteenth century,[68] this relationship was different in the early modern period, when colonialism followed trade rather than the other way around.

---

61 Daron Acemoglu, Simon Johnson, and James A. Robinson, 'The Rise of Europe: Atlantic Trade, Institutional Change, and Economic Growth', *American Economic Review* 95 (2005) pp. 546–579.

62 Robert C. Allen, 'Progress and Poverty in Early Modern Europe', *Economic History Review* 56 (2003) pp. 403–443; ibid., *The British Industrial Revolution in Global Perspective* (Cambridge: Cambridge U.P., 2009).

63 Jan de Vries, 'The Industrial Revolution and the Industrious Revolution', *Journal of Economic History* 54 (1994) pp. 249–270; ibid., *The Industrious Revolution: Consumer Demand and the Household Economy, 1650 to the Present* (Cambridge: Cambridge U.P., 2008).

64 Jeffrey G. Williamson, *Trade and Poverty: When the Third World Fell Behind* (Cambridge MA: MIT Press, 2011); ibid., 'Globalization and the Great Divergence: Terms of Trade Booms, Volatility and the Poor Periphery, 1782–1913', *European Review of Economic History* 12 (2008) pp. 355–391.

65 Williamson, *Trade and Poverty*, pp. 191–193.

66 Allen et al., 'Wages, prices'.

67 Flynn and Giraldez, 'Cycles of silver'; Rönnbäck, 'Integration'; Dobado-Gonzales et al., 'The Integration'; Sharp and Weisdorf, 'Globalization revisited'; De Vries, 'The limits'.

68 See for example: Niall Ferguson, *Empire: How Britain Made the Modern World* (London: Allen Lane, 2002).

Nevertheless, the relationship is not straightforward. In some cases global trade was followed by colonialism and 'extractive' institutions, but not in others. A causal connection, or the absence of it, may have been driven by initial factor endowments,[69] geographic conditions and pre-colonial wealth.[70] Clearly, the relationship between trade and economic development differed between areas where different types of institutions were implemented. It is obvious that the European presence was felt throughout many parts of Asia already in the eighteenth century. It is difficult to imagine that while this would have persistent effects on economic development today,[71] it would not have affected economic development and living standards at the time. Furthermore, the economics literature on the long-term effects of colonialism tends to view history as a linear development from roughly 1500 through to today, while a lot of – not always linear – developments occurred in between. Rather than a one-way highway, this historical road was full of bumps and holes, as well as many traffic junctions. In order to chart this bygone route, of which the destination was obviously not then clear in 1500, it is important to trace it back across those years.

In order to contribute to these issues, I follow a quantitative approach. The focus of the data collection will be on wages and prices, the 'DNA of economies'.[72] The price data will be employed to analyze patterns of global trade through the study of price convergence. In addition, prices of basic commodities will be used to calculate consumer price indices for different regions. These indices will be combined with information on wages, using a method that will allow the assessment of living standards over time and across regions. Furthermore, wages provide additional information on the process of human capital formation via an analysis of disparities in the remuneration of skilled and unskilled labour. These figures will be combined with data on demographic developments and labour markets, which are often seen as important factors influencing living standards. Many of the figures unearthed for this study represent the first consistent serial and comparative information about four early modern economies – Bengal, the Cape Colony, Ceylon and Java – in the pre-1800 period.

---

69 Sokoloff and Engerman, 'History Lessons'.

70 Acemoglu et al., 'Colonial Origins' ; ibid., 'Reversal of Fortune'.

71 Ibid.; Nunn, 'The Importance'; Melissa Dell, 'The Persistent Effects of Peru's Mining Mita', *Econometrica* 78 (2010) pp. 1863–1903.

72 Jan Luiten van Zanden, 'The Skill Premium and the "Great Divergence"', *European Review of Economic History* 13 (2009) p. 121.

3 Sources and Data

A common feature of the three major debates introduced in the previous sections is that the results largely rest on shaky data.[73] While we know quite a lot about the development of the economies of Western Europe, reliable quantitative data for most parts of the non-Western world – with the possible exception of Japan – before the later nineteenth century are generally lacking. Here I will contribute to these three related debates through the study of new materials collected from the VOC archives. These archives, which until the later decades of the twentieth century were mainly used to shed light on the institutional history of the VOC as an early modern trading company, form a real treasure trove of information for the economic history of various regions bordering the Indian Ocean,[74] as well as the accompanying histories of globalization, colonialism and divergence before the nineteenth century.

As a commercial company, the VOC employed large numbers of clerks to record sales and purchases, as well as profits and expenses made per establishment. Where the VOC held extensive administrative power, the data are more abundant and may contain more information on demographic developments (such as proto-censuses for taxation purposes) or production figures. At the end of the accounting year, copies of this administration, collected in huge tomes, were sent from the local trading posts to the Asian headquarters in Batavia, as well as to the Company's chambers in Amsterdam and Zeeland. This collection of 'Letters and documents received from the East Indies' (from now on: VOC-OBP)[75] is part of the VOC archives kept at the Dutch National Archives in The Hague. The TANAP project has digitized the content lists of this administration, as well as thematically ordering the documents per establishment, thus making it possible to effectively search for specific data, such as wages and prices, in the different areas of VOC presence.

73 In case of the debate on the long-term effects of colonialism, it is mostly the data for the 1500 AD benchmark that can be questioned. Although some of the GDP figures for 1995 may not be as reliable as often assumed: see for example, Morten Jerven, *Poor Numbers: How We Are Misled by African Development Statistics and What to Do About It* (Cornell: Cornell U.P., 2013).

74 As can also be seen from Om Prakash' influential dissertation *The Dutch East India Company and the Economy of Bengal 1630–1720* (Princeton: Princeton University Press, 1985), as well as the various monographs that appeared under the auspices of the TANAP (Towards a New Age in Partnership in Dutch East India Company archives and research) project; see: http://www.brill.com/publications/tanap-monographs-history-asian-european-interaction.

75 In Dutch: *Overgekomen Brieven en Papieren uit Indië* (OBP), NA VOC: 1.04.02.

In addition to the VOC-OBP, the separate archives of the VOC Bookkeeper-General in Batavia (BGB) constitute an important source of prices in Asia.[76] In the General Ledgers of the BGB, trade in the entire area comprised in the VOC charter was recorded.[77] Fifty-five volumes of the eighteenth century have been preserved, which, for a single financial year, recorded all products and their quantities and values that were shipped between the Dutch Republic and Asia, and among the colonies and trading posts in Asia themselves.

Muster Rolls are another separate series of the VOC archives I have used in my study. The rolls are a well-known source for studying the (European) Company personnel aboard its ships, as well as in the different establishments in Asia.[78] The Muster Rolls were sent to the Chambers of Amsterdam and Zeeland and are still available for the period 1691–1791.[79] Most important for this study is that these rolls state monthly wages of European and Asian company servants employed at the various VOC establishments in the East Indies. Next to the data collected from the primary VOC administration, various published primary sources and secondary literature have been employed to gather additional data. At the same time, some of the published primary sources, such as the memoirs of VOC governors or other European contemporaries, have also been used as qualitative sources to put the observed trends in the quantitative series in their appropriate context. These qualitative sources are also important considering the problems of reliability and representativeness associated with the quantitative materials. Source issues will be dealt with extensively throughout the book.

4 The Case Studies

4.1 *Data Availability*

Ideally, the study would have included an investigation of the development of living standards in all areas where the Company established itself. While comparisons will be made with others parts of the world, as a result of time constraints and limited data availability, the focus of the collection of new data and its analysis will be on four case studies: Bengal, the Cape Colony, Ceylon

---

76 NA BGB 1.04.02.12.

77 BGB: *Generale Journalen*. Recently made available online by the Huygens ING Project Bookkeeper-General Batavia: http://bgb.huygens.knaw.nl/.

78 See F. LeQuin, *Het personeel van de Verenigde Oost-Indische Compagnie in Azië, meer in het bijzonder de vestiging Bengalen* (Leiden, 1982).

79 VOC 5168–5239 (Amsterdam), VOC 11534–11705 (Zeeland).

and Java. These cases were selected on the basis of the availability of data, as well as their position within the larger debates and the differences in the 'type' of colony (as introduced above): Bengal represents a 'peasant export' colony, the Cape Colony a 'settler' colony, and Ceylon and Java exemplify 'concession' colonies (see Subsection 4.5 and Table 1.1). Through these choices I hope to contribute both to the big three debates already mentioned above and to make a valuable contribution to the historiographies of each of these regions.

First of all, data availability played an important role in selecting these case studies. Through the TANAP website, it is possible to create a PDF file with the sorted information related to a specific establishment. The number of kilobytes per PDF inventory provides a rough clue regarding the amount of wage and price evidence available for a specific region. This is only a crude indication, however, as theoretically there might be more wage and price data available for stations with less overall documentation (as, for example, in the case of the Cape Colony). By far the largest volume of documents in the VOC-OBP collection is related to Java and Ceylon, being the largest territories under direct VOC control (see Figure 1.2). The four VOC establishments in India – Coromandel, Malabar, Bengal, and Surat – also left significant documentation. For Bengal, price series were already available through other sources, while the VOC documents on Bengal turned out to be particularly rich in wage data (which have been scarce for India in general). While far fewer documents pertain to the Cape Colony (720 Kb, or 406 pages, of inventory), its function as a provisioning station for ships sailing to and from the East Indies led to the documentation of prices for a number of basic commodities, indispensable data for the calculation of real wages.

Secondly, in studying these different regions the book also includes various 'types' of colonies administered by the VOC. While the VOC was present in over thirty different areas, the form of its presence could differ substantially. In the later eighteenth century the Company had over 5,400 employees permanently stationed in Java, yet only 12 people manned the island of Deshima in Nagasaki.[80] In the next subsections I briefly introduce the four case studies (see Map 1.1).

4.2 *Bengal*

In terms of manpower, Bengal was one of the smaller establishments of the VOC (employing around 200 people in the eighteenth century),[81] yet looking at total turnover Bengal was one of the Company's most important trading

80 Gaastra, *De Geschiedenis*, p. 94.

81 Gaastra, *De Geschiedenis*, p. 94.

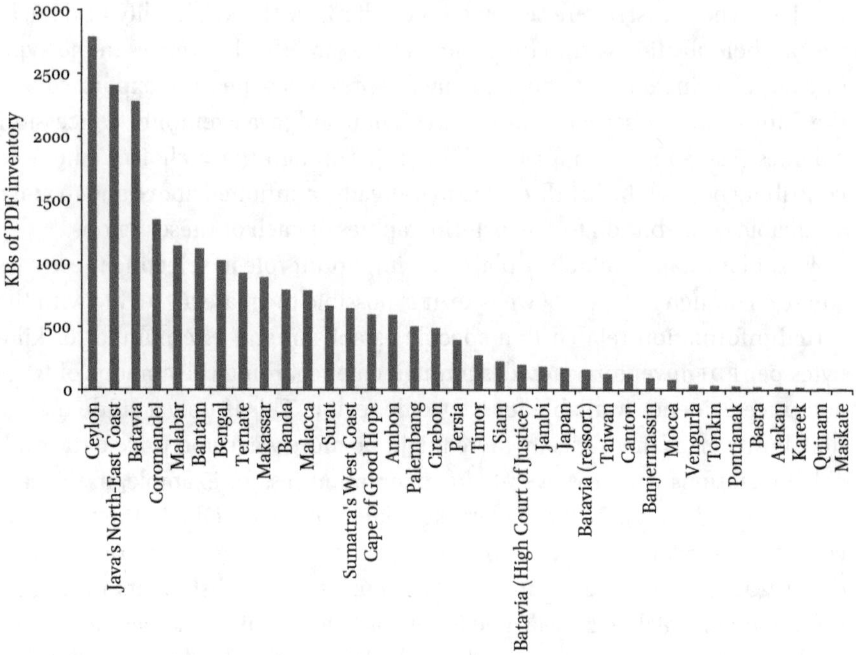

FIGURE 1.2 *Documents pertaining to VOC establishments.*
Source: 'Reconstruction of the archives of the VOC establishments', *TANAP database of VOC documents*: http://databases.tanap.net/vocrecords/
Last visited: 22 October 2014.

establishments during the late seventeenth and early eighteenth centuries. Goods purchased in Bengal accounted for 36 percent of the total Asian cargo exported to the Dutch Republic at the end of the seventeenth century and for 39 percent of cargo exports in the second decade of the eighteenth century.[82]

India in general, and Bengal specifically, have also featured prominently in recent contributions to the Great Divergence debate, yet the evidence that has been put forward so far is ambiguous. While Parthasarathi and Sivramkrishna have suggested that before 1800 living standards were at least comparable with those in the most advanced parts of Europe,[83] Allen, Broadberry and Gupta, as

82 Om Prakash, 'European Trade and South Asian Economies: some regional contrasts, 1600–1800', in: Leonard Blussé and Femme S. Gaastra, (eds.), *Companies and Trade* (Leiden: Leiden University Press, 1981) p. 196.

83 Regarding Southern India: Parthasarathi, 'Rethinking wages'; and Sivramkrishna, 'Ascertaining Living Standards'; Bengal: Prasannan Parthasarathi, 'Agriculture, labour, and

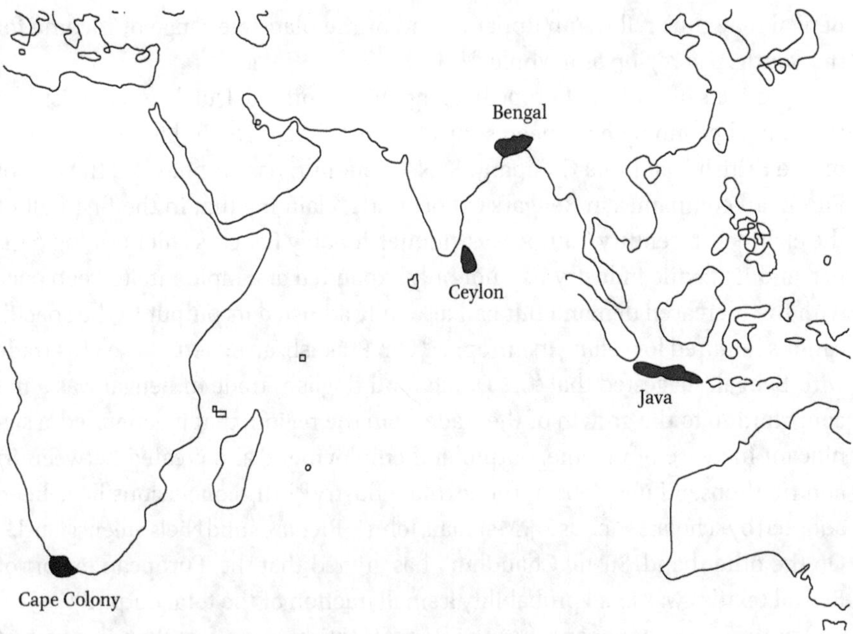

MAP 1.1 *The Indian Ocean with case studies highlighted.*
Sources: Author's own projections.

well as Roy, have provided data suggesting otherwise.[84] Parthasarathi notes that the quantitative data are inconclusive because wages 'obtained from primary sources are radically different from the scattered earnings data found in the secondary literature'.[85] Without pointing out the cause of these differences, he suggests that this indicates the need for more research into primary sources. Roy agrees that the wage evidence is difficult to understand unless we obtain more data on who was paying these wages and for what work'.[86] Bengal is a good case study as it was one of the richest regions of India, 'containing fertile land, plentiful water, and a large cotton textile industry'[87] and incomes in

the standard of living in 18th century India', in: Robert C. Allen, Tommy Bengtsson and Martin Dribe (eds.), *Living Standards in the Past: New Perspectives on Well-Being in Asia and Europe* (Oxford: Oxford U.P., 2005) pp. 99–110; and: ibid., *Why Europe*, pp. 38–46.

84 Allen, 'India in the Great Divergence'; Broadberry and Gupta, 'The early modern'; Roy, 'Economic Conditions'.

85 Parthasarathi, *Why Europe*, p. 45.

86 Tirthankar Roy, *An Economic History of Early Modern India* (Abingdon: Routledge, 2013) p. 137.

87 Roy, 'Economic conditions', p. 180.

Bengal may thus reflect 'an upper bound of the plausible range of income for the South Asia region as a whole'.[88]

The effects of trade by European companies (both the Dutch and English) on the Bengal economy have been subject to further debate. In his seminal work on the British East India Company, K. N. Chaudhuri has emphasized the role of European companies in Bengal's export trade, claiming that in the first half of the eighteenth century Europe was 'unquestionably Bengal's chief trading partner, and its textile industry had not only expanded at a rapid rate to keep pace with the increased demand but had also fully adjusted its output to the specifications required for selling in Europe'.[89] Om Prakash, an expert of the VOC trade with Bengal, suggested that 'the Dutch (and English) trade in Bengal was a net contribution to the growth of the trade from the region', that it generated 'a significant increase of income, output and employment' and created between 87 and 110 thousand new jobs in the textile industry.[90] His conclusions have been adopted by scholars such as P. J. Marshall, John F. Richards and Niels Steensgaard.[91] On the other hand, Sushil Chaudhury has argued that the 'European export of Bengal textiles was in all probability a small fraction of the total output'.[92]

Another important aspect of the Bengal station is the fact that, in contrast to the other case studies, the VOC did not have access to any significant special privileges in matters of trade, nor did it have any political power. The Company therefore operated within existing power structures and did not create institutional changes; its only influence on the Bengal economy was through the increased demand for its goods. After the Battle of Plassey (1757), however, the British East India Company (EIC) took over *de facto* power in Bengal from the independent Nawab. Bengal thereby became the first Indian region where the British introduced direct colonial rule (see Map 1.2). The combined role of Mughal decline, the subsequent period of wars and eventual British

---

88 Ibid.

89 K. N. Chaudhuri, *The Trading World of Asia and the English East India Company, 1660–1760* (Cambridge: Cambridge U.P., 1978).

90 Om Prakash, 'Bullion for Goods: International Trade and the Economy of Early Eighteenth Century Bengal', *Indian Economic and Social History Review* 13 (1976) pp. 159–187; ibid., *The Dutch East India Company*, pp. 242–248.

91 P. J. Marshall, *Bengal – the British Bridgehead* (Cambridge: Cambridge University Press, 1987) pp. 65–7; John F. Richards, 'The Seventeenth-Century Crisis in South Asia', *Modern Asian Studies* 24 (1990) pp. 625–638; and: Niels Steensgaard, 'Asian Trade and World Economy from the 15th to the 18th centuries', in: T. R. de Souza (ed.), *Indo-Portuguese History: Old Issues, new Questions* (New Delhi, 1985) p. 232.

92 Sushil Chaudhury, 'European Companies and the Bengal Textile Industry in the Eighteenth Century: The Pitfalls of Applying Quantitative Techniques', *Modern Asian Studies* 27 (1993) pp. 321–340.

colonial intervention in India's economic decline in the eighteenth and nineteenth centuries has been an important subject in the literature.[93] Both traditional Indian historiography[94] and recent econometric studies[95] have suggested that with the advent of British colonial power, Indian economic fortunes took a turn for the worse. Employing new detailed data for the examination of living standards in Bengal, my study is thus able to contribute to our understanding of the development of the Bengal economy over the eighteenth century in relation to trade, the effects of early British colonial rule, as well as Bengal's comparative position in the Great Divergence debate.

4.3 *Java and Ceylon*

In contrast to Bengal, the VOC came to exert significant power in Java and Ceylon. In Java, the Company expanded its power from its small base in Batavia and immediate surroundings at the beginning of the seventeenth century to govern over two-thirds of the island by the end of the eighteenth, the remainder of the island being occupied by the Mataram Sultanate.[96] In order to gain profit from the island, the VOC stimulated the cultivation of coffee, sugar, cotton and indigo. In Ceylon, the Company came to control an extensive territorial area that was inhabited by (probably) over 800,000 people by the end of the eighteenth century.[97] The island was host to the VOC along its coasts, as well as the Asian kingdom of Kandy in the interior. It was a crucial possession for the Company, both due to its strategic position within the Company's trade network and because it was the only region in the world that produced an exceptionally fine quality of cinnamon.[98]

---

93 C. A. Bayly, *Rulers, Townsmen and Bazaars: North Indian Society in the Age of British Expansion, 1770–1870* (Cambridge: Cambridge U.P., 1983); David Clingingsmith and Jeffrey G. Williamson, 'Deindustrialization in 18th and 19th century India: Mughal decline, climate shocks and British industrial ascent,' *Explorations in Economic History* 45 (2008) pp. 209–234.

94 For a discussion see Tirthankar Roy, 'Economic History and Modern India: Redefining the Link', *Journal of Economic Perspectives* (2002) pp. 109–130, and C. A. Bayly, 'Indigenous and colonial origins of comparative economic development: the case of colonial India and Africa', *World Bank Policy Research Working Paper* 4474 (2008).

95 For example: Abjith Banerjee and Lakshmi Iyer, 'History, Institutions, and Economic Performance: The Legacy of Colonial Land Tenure Systems in India', *American Economic Review* 95 (2005) pp. 1190–1213.

96 After the Treaty of Giyanti in 1755, Mataram was split in two Sultanates: Surakarta and Yogyakarta.

97 See Chapter 5 and Appendix 7.

98 Jurrien van Goor, *Jan Kompenie as schoolmaster. Dutch education in Ceylon 1690–1795* (Groningen: Wolters-Noordhoff, 1978) p. 7.

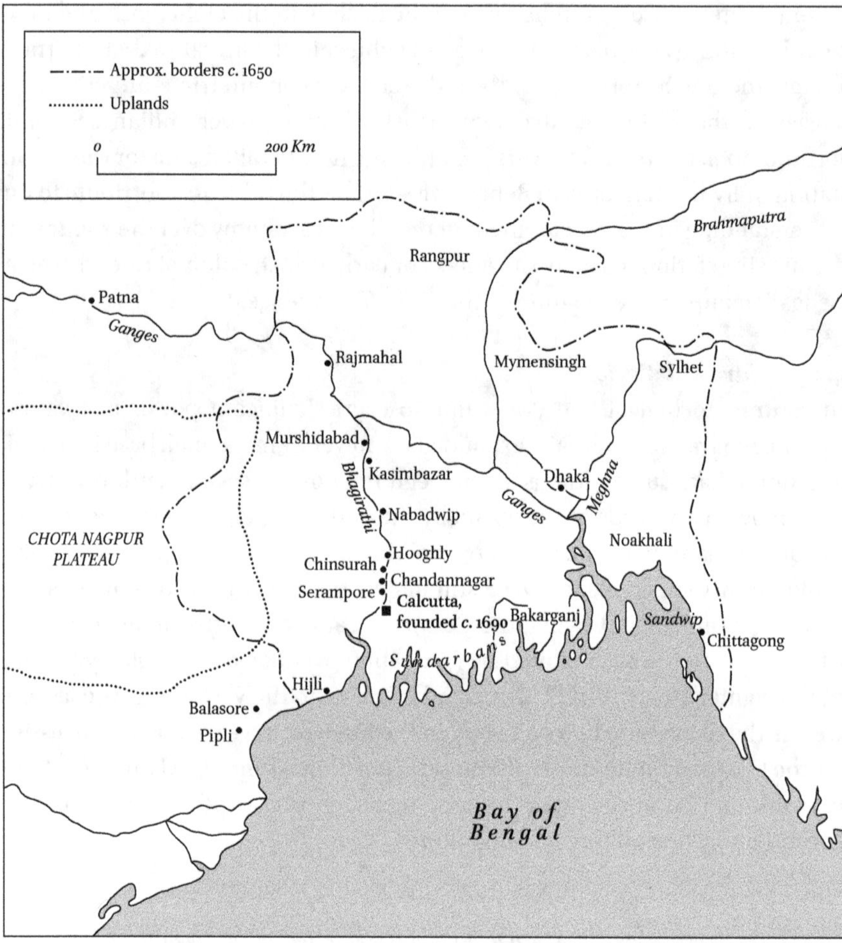

MAP 1.2 *Bengal, c. 1650 borders.*
Based on: Tirthankar Roy 'Where is Bengal?: Situating an Indian Region in the Early Modern World Economy', *Past and Present* 213 (2011) pp. 115–146.

The development of living standards in Java (see Map 1.3), and Southeast Asia in general, has been a subject of scholarly interest for quite some time.[99] Pomeranz occasionally included Southeast Asia in his comparisons, referring mainly to the works of Anthony Reid, who suggests that Southeast Asians' 'lives were no more squalid, their health no more wretched and their physical stature

99 The part on Java has, in part, been published as joint work with Jan Luiten van Zanden: 'Labor, wages and living standards in Java, 1680–1914', *European Review of Economic History* 19 (2015).

no worse than those of eighteenth century Europeans'.[100] At the same time, Acemoglu and Robinson have recently pointed to Southeast Asia as a region where Europeans (mainly the Dutch in this case) introduced extractive institutions that led to 'reversing development'.[101] Their story is also influenced by Reid, who claimed that between 1600 and 1800 Southeast Asian living standards declined dramatically, mostly as a result of changing patterns of trade (brought about by the Europeans, and specifically the Dutch) and climatic changes. While research over the past decades has led to a relative wealth of information on the nineteenth and twentieth centuries,[102] Southeast Asia remains one of the major blind spots in our knowledge on living standards in Asia before 1800. As the development of living standards in Java may have been more or less representative for those in other parts of Southeast Asia,[103] this book fills an important gap in our knowledge. Such information will shed light on the debates on both the Great Divergence and the early effects of colonialism.

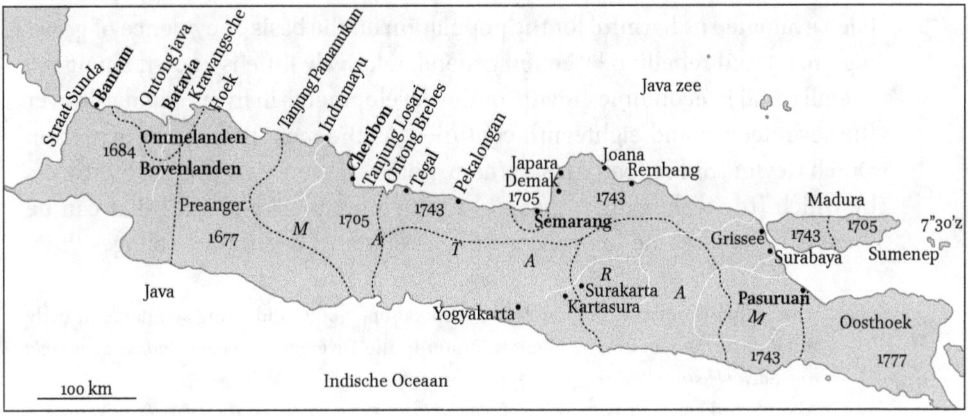

MAP 1.3 *Java, seventeenth- and eighteenth-century borders.*
Based on: Jacobs, *Merchant in Asia.*

100 Anthony Reid, 'Economic and Social Change, c. 1400–1800', in: Nicholas Tarling (ed.) *The Cambridge History of Southeast Asia, Vol. 1. From Early Times to c. 1800* (Cambridge: Cambridge U.P., 1992) pp. 503–4.

101 Daron Acemoglu and James A. Robinson, *Why Nations Fail. The Origins of Power, Prosperity, and Poverty* (2012) pp. 248–273.

102 For example Jörg Baten, M. Stegl, and P. van der Eng, 'The biological standard of living and body height in colonial and post-colonial Indonesia, 1770–2000', *Journal of Bioeconomics* 15 (2013) pp. 103–122; Jan Luiten van Zanden, 'Rich and Poor before the Industrial Revolution, a Comparison between Java and the Netherlands at the Beginning of the Nineteenth Century', *Explorations in Economic History* 40 (2003) pp. 1–23; Jan Luiten van Zanden and Daan Marks, *An Economic History of Indonesia, 1800–2010* (London: Routledge, 2011).

103 In terms of GDP per capita, according to estimates by Maddison. This was suggested by Van Zanden, 'Rich and Poor', p. 4.

Ceylon (Map 1.4) has thus far been neglected in the comparisons between Europe and Asia,[104] yet it provides an interesting case study for this book. Considering its institutional history it is perhaps best compared with Java,[105] while in terms of geography and culture it stands closer to India. Most of the historiography on Ceylon in the VOC period has been concerned with administrative, political, and social changes, however.[106] Some of the traditional literature, as in the case of India and Indonesia, has blamed Dutch and British colonizers for holding back development of the island.[107] The imposition of monopolies on trade in the seventeenth centuries reduced the volume of trade.[108] But, as most monopolies, except that for cinnamon, were a failure, the restrictive policies were relaxed in the later seventeenth century. Nonetheless, the growth of international trade and increased demand for Ceylon's produce in the eighteenth century, especially cinnamon, did not benefit the local population, due to the Company's mercantilist policies.[109] Dutch attempts to increase agricultural production and the cultivation of cash crops have also been evaluated as harmful for the population on the basis of evidence of growing unrest and rebellion.[110] Yet, in general, relatively little is known about the overall trend in economic growth, or the developments in living standards over the seventeenth and eighteenth centuries. As the most prominent expert on Dutch Ceylon, Sinnappah Arasaratnam, noted, 'there are no precise indicators by which [the well-being of people] can be measured' and '[a]ll that can be done is to make some impressionist assessment of qualitative changes'.[111] By

104 Apart from the paper: Pim de Zwart, 'Population, labour and living standards in early modern Ceylon: an empirical contribution to the Divergence debate', *Indian Economic and Social History Review* 49 (2012) pp. 365–398.

105 Alicia Schrikker, *Dutch and British Colonial Intervention in Sri Lanka, 1780–1815: Expansion and Reform* (Leiden and Boston: Brill, 2007) p. 3.

106 K. W. Goonewardena, *The Foundation of Dutch Power in Ceylon, 1638–1658* (Amsterdam: Djambatan, 1958); Sinnappah Arasaratnam, *Dutch Power in Ceylon, 1658–1687* (Amsterdam: Djambatan, 1958); Sinnappah Arasaratnam, 'Elements of social and economic change in Dutch maritime Ceylon (Sri Lanka) 1658-1796', *Indian Economic and Social History Review* 22 (1985) pp. 35–54; Schrikker, *Dutch and British*.

107 See: Schrikker, *Dutch and British*, p. 2.

108 Sinnappah Arasaratnam, 'Dutch Commercial Policy and Its Effects on the Indo-Ceylon Trade (1690–1750)', *Indian Economic and Social History Review* 4 (1967) pp. 109–130.

109 Sinnappah Arasaratnam, 'Ceylon in the Indian Ocean Trade: 1500-1800', in A. Das Gupta and M. N. Pearson (eds.) *India and the Indian Ocean 1500–1800* (Calcutta: Oxford U.P. 1999) p. 238.

110 D. A. Kotelawela, 'Agrarian Policies of the Dutch in South-west Ceylon 1743–1767', *A. A. G. Bijdragen* 14 (1967) pp. 3–34. Schrikker, *Dutch and British*, p. 71.

111 Arasaratnam, 'Elements of social', p. 51.

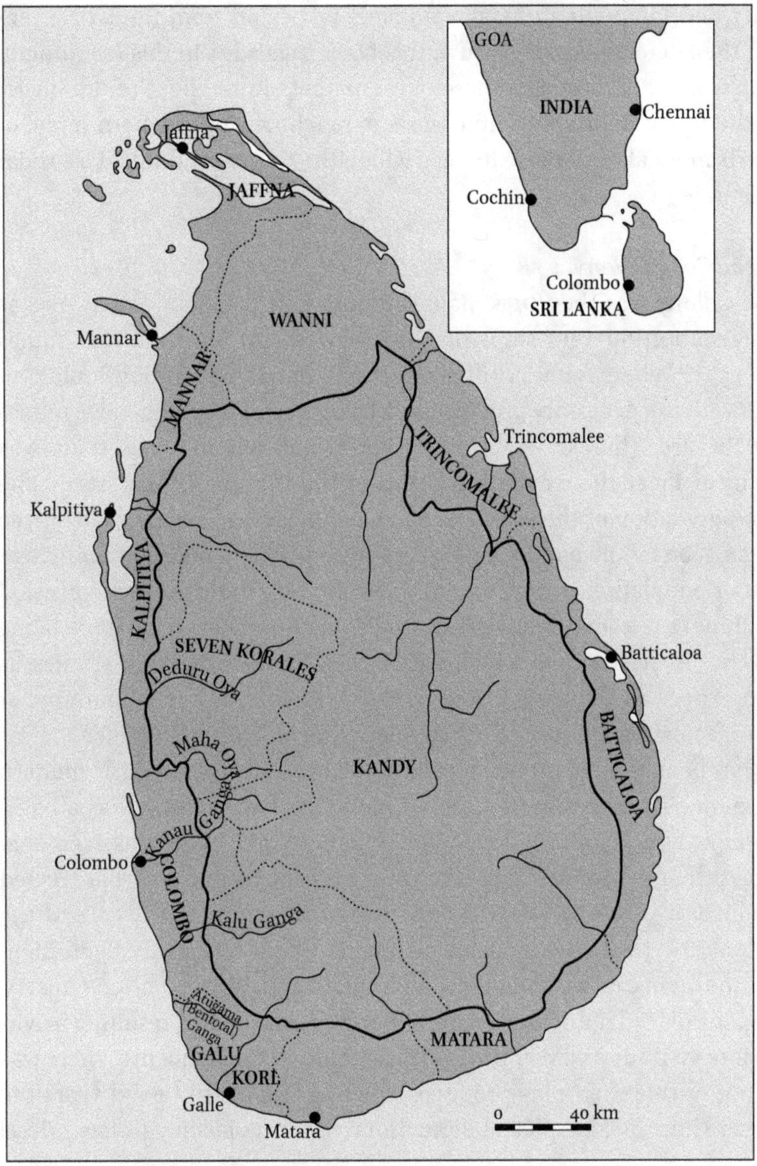

MAP 1.4 *Ceylon, 1766 borders.*
Based on: Nirmal Ranjith Dewasiri, *The Adaptable Peasant. Agrarian Society in Western Sri Lanka under Dutch Rule, 1740–1800* (Leiden & Boston: Brill, 2008) p. xxiii.

estimating developments in living standards in Ceylon from the late seventeenth to the late eighteenth century, this book thus adds to this historiography. Furthermore, it compares these developments in the light of the bigger debates: did living standards mimic those in neighbouring southern India, or were trends more akin to those in Java, where the Company fulfilled a similar imperialist role?

4.4 *The Cape Colony*

The Cape Colony was the VOC's main settlement colony, founded in 1652 as a resupply station for VOC ships on their way to and from the East Indies (see Map 1.5).[112] Whereas it was initially thought that a small station could provide ships with the necessary provisions by trading with the indigenous inhabitants of the area, the Khoesan, it quickly turned out that this trade was insufficient to meet the expanding needs of the Company. As a result, the European population of the colony expanded quickly, from some 1,300 in 1700 to around 22,000 by the end of the eighteenth century. In addition to the free white settler population, a large part of the work force in this colony consisted of slaves imported from eastern Africa, India and Southeast Asia. Were living standards in this settler colony higher than those in the other case studies, as we would expect on the basis of the works by Acemoglu and co-authors, or were other factors paramount in the development of living standards?

There has been significant debate about the condition of the early modern Cape economy. Traditionally, the Cape Colony has been regarded as a backward economy, almost entirely dependent on agriculture.[113] Whereas Acemoglu et al. suggest that in settler colonies institutions were introduced that created the right incentives for investment and economic growth, in the case of the Cape Colony the restrictive policies of the VOC have frequently been highlighted as the main cause of economic retardation and the population's misery. The Company placed numerous restrictions on external trade, resulting in 'virtually no foreign trade and very little internal trade.'[114] Consequently, there was no outlet for farmers' surplus produce, which meant that in good years the farmers were hurt by a surplus of agricultural products leading to low prices,

---

112 The part on the Cape Colony has been published as: Pim de Zwart, 'Real wages at the Cape of Good Hope: a long term perspective, 1652–1912', *Low Countries Journal of Social and Economic History* 10 (2013) pp. 28–58.

113 C. W. de Kiewiet, *A History of South Africa. Social and Economic* (London: Oxford U.P., 1972); Leonard Guelke, 'Frontier Settlement in Early Dutch South Africa', *Annals of the Association of American Geographers* 66 (1976) pp. 25–42; and: Gerrit Schutte, 'Company and colonists at the Cape', in: Richard Elphick and Hermann Giliomee (eds.), *The Shaping of South African Society, 1652–1820* (London: Longman, 1979) pp. 173–210.

114 M. H. de Kock, *Economic History of South Africa* (Cape Town: Juta, 1924) pp. 39–40.

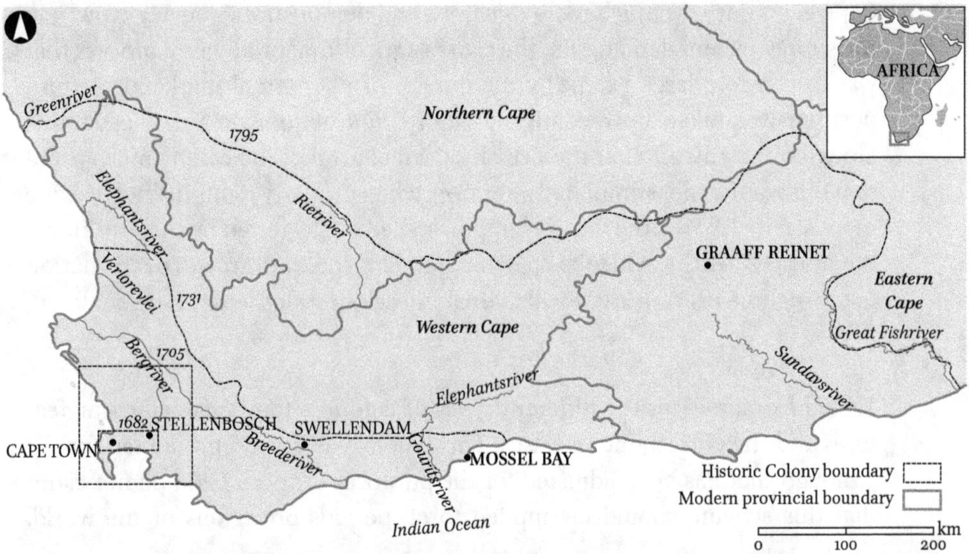

MAP 1.5 *The Cape Colony, seventeenth- and eighteenth-century borders.* Based on: Fourie, 'The Remarkable', p. 421.

while in bad years they suffered from drought and crop failure.[115] Allowing private exports would have raised the prices obtainable by farmers, which would have made it difficult for the VOC to keep prices at the Cape low, thereby jeopardizing the initial purpose of the Cape as a resupply station. In addition, the VOC made no significant capital investments, and lacking an appropriate export crop like in the American colonies,[116] the Cape suffered from the relatively high costs and low quality of its products, as well as its remote geographic location. As recently as 2005, this view was put forward by Charles Feinstein who claimed that before the discovery of diamonds and gold in the late nineteenth century 'markets were small, conditions difficult, and progress slow'.[117]

This view has been contested by a number of scholars. For example, Pieter van Duin and Robert Ross argue that 'any description of the Cape's economic life in terms of "overproduction" must be not only empirically false, but also conceptually absurd, since it is difficult to imagine any entrepreneurs who would continue to produce for a structurally glutted market, on which, presumably, they would continually be operating at a loss'.[118] They suggest that the

115 Charles H. Feinstein, *An Economic History of South Africa. Conquest, Discrimination and Development* (Cambridge and New York: Cambridge University Press, 2005) p. 24.

116 Such as cotton, sugar and tobacco.

117 Feinstein, *An Economic History*, p. 3.

118 Pieter van Duin and Robert Ross, 'The Economy of the Cape Colony in the Eighteenth Century', *Intercontinenta* 7 (Leiden: Centre for the History of European Expansion, 1987) p. 3.

Cape economy was much more dynamic, and demonstrate a steady growth in the supply of, and demand for, the Cape's agricultural products: a process that was driven to a large extent by the growth of its internal market.[119] A third position was taken up recently by Liam Brunt, who claims that economic growth only took off after the British seized control of the colony in 1795, and that this was further stimulated after 1843, when property rights in land became more secure.[120] Was the Cape as impoverished as suggested by the traditional literature? Does the evidence on living standards point to growth or stagnation in the eighteenth century? I will address these questions later in the book.

4.5 *Colony Types*

Table 1.1 summarizes the different types of colonies, their characterizing features and the corresponding cases. This typology is based on the literature,[121] although that has been adjusted for the purposes of this book. I do not claim that this scheme should be applied to all periods or regions of the world.

TABLE 1.1 *Colony types and case studies.*

Type	Features	Case
Peasant Export	The Company as trader, works within pre-existing power structures; large indigenous population.	Bengal
Concession	The Company as 'merchant and king', takes over existing power structures; large indigenous population.	Ceylon and Java
Settler	The Company as trader and political power; builds completely new power structures; large European population.	Cape Colony

Sources: Adaption from Austin, 'The "Reversal"', Hopkins, 'The New Economic', Myint, *The Economics* and Osterhammel, *Colonialism.*

119 Robert Ross, 'The Cape of Good Hope and the world economy, 1652–1835', in: Richard Elphick and Hermann Giliomee (eds.) *The Shaping of South African Society, 1652–1840* (Cape Town: Maskew Miller Longman, 1989) pp. 243–282.

120 Liam Brunt, 'Property rights and economic growth: evidence from a natural experiment', *CEPR Discussion Paper no. 6404* (2007).

121 See above and: Acemoglu et al., 'Colonial Origins'; ibid., 'Reversal of Fortune'; Austin, 'The "Reversal"'; Hopkins, 'The New Economic', Myint, *The Economics*; Osterhammel. *Colonialism.*

Rather, it is merely an attempt to bridge the gap between the theoretical literature and the case studies of this book.

The combination of these four case studies will show how trends in living standards differed in the context of variations in VOC political power, the development of labour markets, demography and long-distance trade. These case studies will also be compared with existing studies on other parts of India, China, Japan and Europe in order to get a better picture of the Great Divergence, globalization and colonialism in the early modern period.

5 Outline

The remainder of this book is set up as follows. Chapter 2 examines whether the early modern period can be assessed as the first age of globalization. After a brief discussion on the definitions of globalization, I suggest that the process of price convergence provides a good indicator of globalization taking place. In order to test whether there was any price convergence in this period, new data on prices have been assembled for the sixteen most important products transported by the VOC between Europe and Asia in the seventeenth and eighteenth centuries. In this chapter I will also attempt to explain the trends in these price series through a discussion of transport costs, piracy, wars and maritime competition. Most of my analysis will focus on conditions in the different commodity markets in Asia: to what extent did various degrees of colonial control influence the patterns of international trade, and what would explain the degree of colonial control in these areas?

Chapter 3 investigates the consequences of this globalization by discussing price developments in Bengal, the Cape Colony, Ceylon and Java. A discussion of different measures of living standards shows the advantages of looking at real wages in order to analyse long-term comparative well-being in the past. To insert all four case studies in the international picture, appropriate consumption baskets will be created that reflect both local consumption patterns and allow international comparison. Issues related to the new price data, regarding, for example, reliability, representativeness, and regional price differentials, are extensively discussed before price levels are compared internationally. Was the cost of living in some areas higher than in others, and, if so, why? Do the trends in prices indicate periods of economic growth or decline? Did globalization lead to inflation, or were local determinants more important drivers of price developments?

Chapter 4 presents new estimates of wage trends over the seventeenth and eighteenth centuries for the regions under discussion. As, due to the relative scarcity of data, the construction of such series is by no means straightforward, the procedures and limitations in doing so are discussed at length. Does the inclusion of real wage figures for Bengal, the Cape Colony, Ceylon, and Java in the global comparisons support 'conventional' or 'revisionist' views in the Great Divergence debate? What do the trends and the comparative real wages in these different types of colonies imply for our understanding of the effects of colonialism? Finally, I also discuss what these figures imply for the historiographies of these regions.

In the penultimate chapter, demographic developments and labour markets are studied in order to both explain developments in real wages and to engage with some of the critiques that have been raised against the real wage approach as an appropriate way to gauge the standard of living in pre-modern (colonial) societies. In order to meet these aims, this chapter presents estimates of total population figures for the case studies in the seventeenth and eighteenth centuries. Furthermore, average household sizes are discussed and some data on the earnings of additional family members are developed in order to assess whether the assumptions of the Allen model for computing real wages hold in these international comparisons. Through a discussion of commercialization, occupational structures, labour relations, and the labour market, I investigate whether real wages reflect the standard of living of an important part of the population at the lower end of the income distribution.[122] I also consider what such numbers entail in a global comparative perspective.

Chapter 6, the final chapter, examines the contribution of this investigation to the three major debates described in this introductory chapter. An extensive collection of appendices set out the procedures followed for estimating series of wages and prices for these early modern societies, for which almost no consistent long-run series of data on their economies were previously available.

122 As suggested in other real wage studies: Allen et al., 'Wages, prices'.

CHAPTER 2

Early Modern Globalization

1 Introduction

Over the past few decades, the discussion on the importance of long-distance trade in the early modern period has grown into one of the major debates in economic history.[1] Kevin O'Rourke, Jeffrey Williamson and their co-authors have addressed in various publications between 2000 and 2009 the issue of whether or not the 'Voyages of Discovery' ushered in the first age of globalization.[2] They define globalization as the integration of markets across regions, with commodity markets reflecting one important dimension of this phenomenon. The best evidence of commodity market integration is 'the extent to which prices of the same commodities converge over time worldwide.'[3] Since they did not find evidence of commodity price convergence before the nineteenth century, they concluded that no market integration took place during the early modern period. Instead, these authors argue that the 1820s should be seen as the starting point of globalization, as after that date technological innovations and declining barriers to trade led to a fall in transaction costs and the integration of global commodity markets. Their work has become very influential and the nineteenth century is now generally referred to as the 'first era of globalization'.[4]

Not everyone is convinced, however. Dennis O. Flynn and Arturo Giráldez have suggested that globalization started in 1571 with the foundation of Manila and direct trade between the Americas and Asia.[5] While they raise serious

1 A modified version of this chapter is published as Pim de Zwart, 'Globalization in the Early Modern Era: New Evidence from the Dutch-Asiatic Trade, c. 1600–1800', *Journal of Economic History* (2016) pp. 520–558. Reprinted with permission.

2 O'Rourke and Williamson, 'When did globalisation?'; ibid: 'After Columbus', ibid: 'Did Vasco da Gama', ibid. 'Once More' ibid: 'From Malthus to Ohlin'; Findlay and O'Rourke, 'Commodity market integration'; Findlay and O'Rourke, *Power and plenty*.

3 O'Rourke and Williamson, 'Once More', p. 109.

4 For example, Martin Uebele, 'National and international market integration in the 19th century: Evidence from comovement', *Explorations in economic history* 48 (2011) pp. 226–242; Moritz Schularick and Solomos Solomou, 'Tariffs and economic growth in the first era of globalization', *Journal of Economic Growth* 16 (2011) pp. 33–70.

5 Dennis O. Flynn and Arturo Giraldez, 'Born with a "Silver Spoon"': The Origin of World Trade in 1571', *Journal of World History* 6 (1995) pp. 201–221; ibid., 'Cycles of Silver: Global Economic

 | DOI 10.1163/9789004299665_003

doubts regarding the narrow definition employed by O'Rourke and Williamson, they also join the same game when they find several 'cycles' in which the price of silver converged globally. Klas Rönnbäck found signs of global price convergence from the late seventeenth century onwards.[6] A study by Paul Sharp and Jacob Weisdorf finds some long-term market integration in the wheat trade between the US and the UK in the eighteenth century. They stress, however, that this is not evidence of globalization *per se*, as they only show market integration between the United States and the United Kingdom.[7] Dobado-Gonzalez et al. recently studied grain prices in the Americas and Europe more generally and concluded that globalization also started in the eighteenth century.[8] In his review of the debate, Jan de Vries takes up a nuanced view, suggesting that globalization in this period faced clear limits, but that it was an era of globalization nonetheless.[9]

As explained in the introductory chapter to this book, I intend to contribute to the debate on the origins of globalization by studying price trends in the Dutch–Asiatic trade. This is not to claim that this is the only important trade of this period. While substantial work has already been done by Chaudhuri,[10] further research is currently being undertaken regarding the Anglo–Asian trade.[11] The collection of more evidence from the Portuguese *Carreira da India* or the French *Compagnie des Indes* and other companies could certainly lead to important insights. Yet there are good arguments for studying the Dutch East India Company's trade, as the VOC was by far the most important trading company operating in the Euro-Asian trade between 1600 and 1800: 49 percent of all ships sailing to Asia in the seventeenth and eighteenth century were Dutch. In the second part of the eighteenth century the English and French were

---

Unity through the Mid-Eighteenth Century', *Journal of World History* 13 (2002) pp. 391–427; ibid., 'Path dependence, time lags and the birth of globalization: A critique of O'Rourke and Williamson', *European Review of Economic History* 8 (2004) pp. 81–108; ibid., 'Born again: Globalization's sixteenth century origins (Asian/Global versus European Dynamics)', *Pacific Economic Review* 13 (2008) pp. 359–387.

6 Rönnbäck, 'Integration of Global'.

7 Sharp and Weisdorf, 'Globalization revisited', p. 96.

8 Dobado-Gonzales et al., 'The Integration'.

9 De Vries, 'The Limits', p. 731.

10 Chaudhuri, *The Trading World*; ibid., *The English East India Company; the Study of an Early Joint-Stock Company, 1600–1640* (London: F. Cass, 1965).

11 For example: Pilar Noques-Marco, 'Euro-Asian globalization in the early modern period (1664–1820s): Trade Boom or Price Convergence?' Paper presented at the conference on *Trade, Poverty and Growth in History* (Madrid 2012).

TABLE 2.1 *Numbers and shares of ships sent to Asia, 1600–1800.*[12]

	1600–1700		1700–1800		Total 1600–1800	
	N	%	N	%	N	%
Dutch	1,770	59	2,950	44	4,720	49
English	811	27	1,865	28	2,676	28
French	155	5	1,300	20	1,455	15
Portuguese	193	6	193	3	386	4
Danish	54	2	234	4	288	3
Swedish	–	–	61	1	61	1
Ostend	–	–	55	1	55	1
Total	2,983	100	6,658	100	9,641	100

Source: Gaastra and Bruijn, 'The Dutch East India Company's Shipping', p. 183.

catching up, but it took until the 1780s before they were able to exceed the Dutch in numbers of Asia-bound ships. At the same time, the average tonnage of goods was also higher on Dutch ships.[13]

This chapter aims to add to the discussion on globalization's origins by exploiting new annual price data on a great variety of goods traded by the VOC in the seventeenth and eighteenth centuries. These data have been examined to find out whether there is any evidence of 'globalization' (defined as price convergence) having taken place in the early modern period. In the next section, Section 2, a discussion of definitions is followed by methodological considerations. Section 3 introduces the sources, while Section 4 kicks off the inquiry into price convergence by exploring some of the data from before the establishment of the VOC, in order to be able to place the influence of the Company in a long-term perspective. Section 5 constitutes the main part of this chapter, as it shows the trends in price convergence for a variety of commodities

12 While one would ideally compare numbers of ships returning to Europe, as it is the trade in goods from Asia that is of most concern for the story of globalization, those data are incomplete. The incomplete figures provide a roughly similar picture as the table presented here. The figures presented in Table 2.1 also differ slightly from De Vries, 'Connecting Europe', pp. 50–53.

13 De Vries, 'Connecting Europe', pp. 46–51.

between ca. 1600 and 1800. After finding in Section 6 that declining transport costs and increased maritime competition may account for a part of the observed trends, in Section 7. I analyse the diverse conditions found in the various commodity markets.

It has been suggested that the customary dichotomy between monopoly goods and goods bought in competitive markets does not suffice to explain the observed trends. In Europe, a clear distinction was indeed made between monopoly goods (the four spices of which the VOC was the sole supplier) and the other products, yet the chapter also emphasizes differences in the extent to which the VOC controlled purchasing markets in Asia. Some markets were largely competitive and the VOC was merely one trader among many, whereas in other markets it had exclusive contracts with local rulers, and in still others it had complete control over production and purchases. Where commodities were traded between competitive markets, price convergence took place. Convergence was, however, not automatic for goods acquired in markets where the VOC had long-term contracts or colonial control over production and trade. Finally, I also attempt to explain differences in the extent of colonial power in these areas by focussing on geography and indigenous institutions.

2 Definitions and Methodology

'Globalization' has become a widely used term, especially since the 1990s. As a result, numerous definitions have arisen, each emphasizing different dimensions (economic, cultural and political) of globalization.[14] In this section, I will focus on the discussion about the term within the field of economic history.

Part of the dispute between Flynn and Giraldez, on the one hand, and O'Rourke and Williamson, on the other, originates from the lack of congruence between their definitions of globalization. Flynn and Giraldez propose that 'globalization began when all heavily populated land masses initiated sustained interaction – both directly with each other and indirectly through other land masses – in a manner that deeply and permanently linked them'.[15] They suggest that a focus on purely economic globalization is 'doomed' and

14 Robert P. Potter, Tony Binns, Jennifer A. Elliott and David Smith, *Geographies of Development* (Harlow: Pearson, 2004) pp. 127–133.

15 Flynn and Giraldez, 'Born again', p. 2.

that globalization contains ecological, demographic, and cultural, as well as economic, elements. Flynn and Giraldez thus emphasize the Columbian exchange of plants and animals across the oceans, especially the adoption of New World crops by the Chinese.[16] One problem with their definition is the question of what qualifies as being deep and lasting impacts of globalization. De Vries notes that Flynn and Giraldez' definition 'evades modelling and testing' and he therefore christened their definition as 'soft globalization'.[17] Their argument is strengthened by their evidence of several phases in which silver prices converged (in the 1640s and around 1750), on the basis of which they argue that a highly integrated global economy emerged in the late sixteenth century.[18]

O'Rourke and Williamson's definition (dubbed 'hard globalization' by De Vries), and consequently their propositions, have the advantage that they can be tested quantitatively. According to them, globalization equals the integration of factor and commodity markets across time and regions. They focus on the integration of commodity markets, and, as noted, suggest that declining price gaps provide the best evidence for this. Figure 2.1 illustrates the mechanism they propose: MM is the home import-demand function. Domestic demand (minus domestic supply) declines if the home price (p) increases; and SS is the foreign supply function: foreign supply (minus foreign demand) rises if the price abroad (p*) increases.

Globalization occurs as a result of falling transport costs or trade barriers, leading to increases in trade volumes, rising export prices and falling import

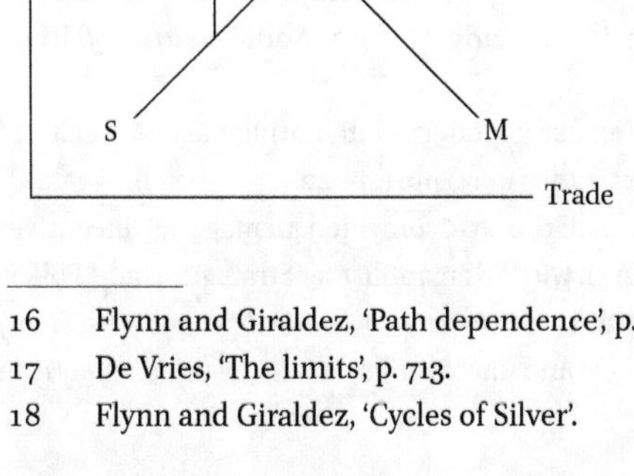

FIGURE 2.1
Trade between home country and the rest of the world.
Source: O'Rourke and Williamson, 'When Did Globalisation?' p. 25.

16 Flynn and Giraldez, 'Path dependence', p. 96.
17 De Vries, 'The limits', p. 713.
18 Flynn and Giraldez, 'Cycles of Silver'.

prices. As trade volumes may also increase as a result of population growth, capital accumulation and/or other factors unrelated to market integration, the best evidence of globalization is thus the decline in the price gap (t) between the foreign export price and the domestic import price; i.e. when price convergence takes place.[19]

Yet, inferring globalization from price gap *t* is not without its problems, as *t* may also be influenced by shifts in the demand curve. Price elasticities of various goods may have changed over time. As a result of growing surplus income in Europe,[20] and the inclusion of luxury goods as standard items in European consumption patterns,[21] the demand curve may have shifted and demand may have become less elastic (larger fluctuations in price would have had smaller effects on quantities). Anne McCants has, for example, demonstrated that the price elasticity of sugar in the Amsterdam Municipal Orphanage declined from −2.05 in the period 1639–1757 to −0.93 in the period 1761–1812,[22] as sugar became a more standard part of diets in north-western European. The result of increased demand and a decline in price elasticity may have been an increase in the price gap over time, as the Company would attempt to benefit from the decreased elasticity by raising prices.[23] As I will show later, there is still significant evidence of price convergence across this period and the issue thus does not alter the general conclusions. However, in the cases of divergence it should be kept in mind that that divergence may be driven by this methodological issue, rather than the lack of globalization.

There are several measures of price convergence. O'Rourke and Williamson study what they call 'mark-ups': the ratio of the selling price to the purchasing price. While this is a straightforward measure, Rönnbäck criticized it as a somewhat unbalanced measure, since 'a quite small absolute change in the

19 O'Rourke and Williamson, 'When did globalisation?' pp. 25–26.

20 O'Rourke and Williamson, 'After Columbus'.

21 McCants, 'Poor consumers', ibid., 'Exotic Goods, Popular Consumption, and the Standard of Living: Thinking about Globalization in the Early Modern World', *Journal of World History* 18 (2007) pp. 433–462.

22 Anne McCants, 'Consumer Behaviour in an early modern Dutch orphanage: A wealth of choice', *Journal of European Economic History* 22 (1993) pp. 121–142.

23 Although Douglas Irwin has suggested that the VOC provided managerial incentives to increase total turnover, see: Douglas A. Irwin, 'Mercantilist as Strategic Trade Policy: The Anglo-Dutch Rivalry for the East India Trade', *Journal of Political Economy* 99 (1991) pp. 1296–1314; ibid., 'Strategic trade policy and mercantilist trade rivalries', *American Economic Review* 82 (1992) pp. 134–139.

price on the selling market translates into a rather big change in the mark-up ratio.'[24] Another disadvantage of the mark-up approach is that it can only measure the price wedge between two different markets. Therefore, the coefficient of variation (CV) is perhaps a more common measure of price convergence.[25] The coefficient of variation allows measurement of price convergence across several markets at the same time and shows the size of the price wedge relative to the mean price between the markets. Rönnbäck suggests a deflated standard deviation should also be included as a measure of price convergence because the CV might show price convergence as a result of a positive demand shock (unrelated to globalization) that drives up the mean price. This chapter will take into account developments in all three measures of price convergence, but Section 7 will only show figures on mark-ups, as these allow easy interpretation. Besides a few exceptions that will be discussed later, the results of the three measures are fairly consistent.

Some scholars have argued that price convergence alone is not 'a sufficient condition for market integration as prices may be determined or influenced by processes outside of the realm of transaction and exchange (e.g. large-scale climatological events).'[26] Therefore these scholars have looked at price adjustment and price volatility, as well as price convergence, as measures of market integration.[27] However, considering the limitations of the data that I present here (they are annual figures with gaps and are therefore not suitable for more advanced testing of market integration), this book looks only at price convergence. This need not be an extreme handicap since we are interested in long-term developments and, as was noted by Giovanni Frederico, an expert on market integration: 'for our understanding of long-term growth, price convergence is much more important than other measures'.[28] He argues that, while it 'may be less glamorous', studying price convergence does not

---

24 Rönnbäck, 'Integration', p. 100.

25 See Giovanni Federico, 'When did European markets integrate?', *European Review of Economic History* 15 (2011) p. 93–126.

26 David S. Jacks, 'Intra- and international commodity market integration in the Atlantic economy, 1800–1913', *Explorations in Economic History* 42 (2005) pp. 381–413, p. 383.

27 Jacks, 'Intra- and international'; Victoria N. Bateman, 'The evolution of markets in early modern Europe, 1350–1800: a study of wheat prices', *Economic History Review* 64 (2011) pp. 447–471; Karl Gunnar Persson, *Grain Markets in Europe, 1500–1900: Integration and deregulation* (Cambridge: Cambridge U.P., 1999) p. 92.

28 Giovanni Federico, 'How much do we know about market integration in Europe', *Economic History Review* 65 (2012) p. 493.

need 'a priori assumptions about the process of adjustment of prices; it is more robust to errors in data; it is highly flexible; and, above all, it focuses on changes in prices which oriented the decisions of millions of producers and consumers'.[29]

3 Sources

The most important contribution of this chapter, Chapter 2, lies in its use of a newly collected dataset. O'Rourke and Williamson admit that their sample of price data is limited and explicitly invite other scholars to challenge or confirm their findings by contributing new data:

> We would be delighted if [...] pre-industrial world economy specialists were to take this empirical challenge seriously, and produce more long-run price data that can speak to the issues of when globalisation started, and what drove the post-Columbus expansion of world trade.[30]

Over 40 years ago, Kristof Glamann pointed out that prices on the commodity exchange in Amsterdam, where products from all corners of the globe competed with each other, provide an excellent source of information on globalization.[31] The prices fetched by various products at auctions in Amsterdam are still available in the VOC archives.[32] While Glamann already assembled a few of these figures for the period between 1650 and 1740,[33] all the data available from this source have now been systematically assembled. In the case of missing data, I have augmented these price series with the data assembled by N. W. Posthumus.[34]

---

29 Federico, 'When did European', p. 95.

30 O'Rourke and Williamson, 'Once more', and: ibid. 'After Columbus', p. 428: 'Of course, our sample of commodities and routes is limited, and we would like to have more and better evidence to see whether other long distance routes, other commodities, and deeper evidence for the fifteenth and sixteenth centuries confirm the conclusions offered here.'

31 Kristoff Glamann, 'European trade 1500–1750', in: Carlo M. Cipolla (ed.) *The Sixteenth and Seventeenth Centuries* (1974) p. 451.

32 VOC 4584–4597. These figures have been assembled by Peter Koudijs, Kariin Sundsback and myself.

33 Glamann, *Dutch-Asiatic*, pp. 279–286.

34 Posthumus, *Nederlandsche prijsgeschiedenis*; these were used to extrapolate the VOC auction series; in general these series do not differ much.

The 'General Ledgers' of the VOC Bookkeeper-General in Batavia constitute the main source of prices in Asia.[35] In these general ledgers, trade across the entire area of the VOC charter was recorded; fifty-five volumes from the eighteenth century have been preserved. In each volume, all products, along with their quantities and values, that were shipped between the Dutch Republic and Asia, and among the 'colonies' and trading posts in Asia themselves, were recorded for a particular financial year. In addition, data were gathered from the *facturas* (export invoices), which are part of the general VOC-OBP.[36] These state the quantities of goods purchased in Asia, as well as the prices for which they were procured, per ship.[37] Additional observations stem from the *rendementen* (returns), which record the purchase and sales prices of various goods at each of the Company's establishments in Asia.[38] These were used as the source of the seventeenth century data (for which no General Ledgers exist) and to fill gaps resulting from missing general ledgers in the eighteenth century. Supplementary to these data from the VOC's accounts, published sources (e.g. the *Nederlandsch-Indische Plakaatboeken, Generale Missiven* and *Daghregisters* of Batavia) were employed to fill remaining gaps.[39] For the period immediately before the establishment of the Company, several

35 NA.BGB 1.04.02.12. *Generale Journalen*. Made available online by the Huygens ING Project Bookkeeper-General Batavia: http://bgb.huygens.knaw.nl/.

36 VOC: *Overgekomen brieven en papieren* (OBP).

37 VOC 603–605; 607; 629; 652; 1067–1074; 1076–1080; 1082; 1087–1088; 1090–1094; 1096; 1098–1100; 1105; 1134; 1152; 1221; 1230; 1232; 1234; 1241; 1245; 1251; 1261; 1269; 1297; 1315; 1395; 1419; 1457; 1501; 1561; 2753; 3819; 3969; 7545.

38 VOC 2683; 2710; 2727; 2730; 2753; 2770; 2810; 2828; 2847; 2892; 2915; 2945; 2974; 3002; 3034; 3127; 3162; 3217; 3223; 3282; 3313; 3366; 3392; 3423; 3440; 3477; 3505; 3535; 3563; 3630; 3635; 3678; 3771; 3781; 3826; 7545; 7552; 7566.

39 J. E. Heeres, H. T. Colenbrander and J. A. van der Chijs (eds.) *Dagh-register gehouden int Casteel Batavia vant passerende daer ter plaetse als over geheel Nederlandts-India.* Vols. 1–31. (The Hague: Martinus Nijhoff, 1887–1931); J. A. van der Chijs (ed.), *Nederlandsch-Indisch Plakaatboek, 1602–1811*. Vols. 1–17. (Batavia: Landsdrukkerij, 1885). W. Ph. Coolhaas, J. van Goor, J. E. Schooneveld-Oosterling and H. K. s' Jacob (eds.) *Generale Missiven van Gouverneurs-Generaal en Raden aan Heren XVII der Verenigde Oostindische Compagnie* (1960–2007); J. W. IJzerman (ed.), *Cornelis Buijsero te Bantam 1616–1618. Zijn brieven en journaal. Met inleiding en bijlagen* (The Hague: Martinus Nijhoff, 1923); W. Ph. Coolhaas (ed.), *Pieter van den Broecke in Azië. 2 Vols.* (The Hague: Martinus Nijhoff, 1962–1963); J. K. J. de Jonge and M. L. van Deventer (eds.), *De Opkomst van het Nederlandsch Gezag in Oost-Indië (1595–1811): verzameling van onuitgegeven stukken uit het oud-koloniaal archief.* 17 Vols. (The Hague, 1862–1888).

descriptions of the first voyages of the Dutch to the East Indies contain price observations.[40]

As the VOC always recorded the purchasing price for the location where it acquired a product, purchasing prices in Batavia actually reflect prices in different parts of Asia; for example, in the case of cloves it reflects the purchasing price on Ambon. The purchasing prices for the products could be reported in different (old) units of measurement, such as the *pond*, the *picol* and the *bahar*. Prices, also, could be expressed in a variety of currencies: for example the *rial*, *rixdollars* or *guilders*. In all cases, I have converted these measures and currencies to guilders per *pond* to enable comparison with auction prices in Amsterdam.[41] It is important to note that the prices in Asia were corrected for differences in the silver values of the guilder in Asia and Europe (also see Chapter 3 and Appendix 2.2).

4 Globalization and Dutch Entry into Asian Markets

Obviously, trade between Europe, Africa and Asia predated the establishment of the VOC, as well as Vasco da Gama's discovery of the Cape route to India. Janet Abu-Lughod, for example, emphasized that the world was globalized in the thirteenth century as the three most populous parts of the world – Western Europe, the Middle East and Asia (South, Southeast and China) – were already intensively connected.[42] This 'world system' was disturbed by the Bubonic

40 J. Keuning (ed.) *De tweede schipvaart der Nederlanders naar Oost-Indië onder Jacob Cornelisz. van Neck en Wijbrant Warwijck 1598–1600: journalen, documenten en andere bescheiden*. Vol. 2. (The Hague: Martinus Nijhoff, 1938); G. P. Rouffaer and J. W. IJzerman (eds.) *De Eerste Schipvaart der Nederlanders naar Oost-Indië onder Cornelis de Houtman, 1595–1597. Journalen, documenten en andere bescheiden*. Vol. 3. (The Hague: Martinus Nijhoff, 1915); W. S. Unger (ed.) *De oudste reizen van de Zeeuwen naar Oost-Indië 1598–1604* (The Hague: Martinus Nijhoff 1948).

41 See Appendices 1 and 2 for details. Following W. G. Wolters, I have assumed for the entire period the following guilder value per coin: *rial* = 3, *rixdollar* = 2.4; *dubbeltje* = 0.10, *stuiver* = 0.05; *duit* = 0.0125. Wolters also discussed the issue of the difference between so-called heavy and light money used by the VOC. See: 'Heavy and light money in the Netherlands Indies and the Dutch Republic: dilemmas of monetary management with unit of account systems', *Financial History Review* 15 (2008) pp. 37–53. Most of the VOC bookkeeping was done in guilders, so the problem is not so big. Furthermore, the issue of 'heavy' versus 'light' guilders had to be dealt with: see Appendix 2. Textiles are, of course, not converted to prices per *pond*, but to prices per piece.

42 Janet L. Abu-Lughod, *Before European Hegemony: the world system A.D. 1250–1350* (New York and Oxford: Oxford U.P., 1991).

Plague in the fourteenth century (while the spread of the Plague itself was a consequence of this early globalization). Findlay and O'Rourke agree that a case for globalization in this period can be made, also as a result of the *Pax Mongolica*.[43] Following in the footsteps of Adam Smith, various scholars have emphasized the immediate effects of the 'Voyages of Discovery' and the Portuguese circumvention of the Venetian spice monopoly in the late fifteenth and early sixteenth centuries on the integration of world markets.[44] Niels Steensgaard argued, however, that a real breakthrough in international trade was accomplished only by the entry of north-western European trading companies, most notably of the Dutch and the English.[45] These companies were an institutional innovation that led 'to more stable prices in the Amsterdam market and a smaller price gap between Europe and Asia'.[46] Similarly, Robert Allen suggests that in the sixteenth century only Portugal benefited from the reduction in transport costs and that it was only with the arrival of the English and the Dutch East India companies in the early seventeenth century that Portugal's maritime monopoly was broken, resulting in a further reduction in the European prices by two-thirds.[47] Two Dutch scholars studying the early trade with the East Indian archipelago have also suggested that the Portuguese had hardly any effect on the Asian trading system.[48] While in this chapter I am mainly concerned with price convergence over the seventeenth and eighteenth centuries, it would be illuminating to get some sense of price gaps occurring before and during the early period of the VOC (even though the evidence is thin) as

---

43 Findlay and O'Rourke, *Power and Plenty*, p. 108.

44 O'Rourke and Williamson, 'Did Vasco'.

45 Niels Steensgaard, *The Asian Trade Revolution of the Seventeenth Century. The East India Companies and the Decline of the Caravan Trade* (Chicago and London: University of Chicago Press, 1973).

46 Niels Steensgaard, 'The Dutch East India Company as an Institutional Innovation', in: Maurice Aymard (ed.) *Dutch capitalism and world capitalism. Capitalism hollandaise et capitalisme mondial* (Cambridge: Cambridge U.P., 1982) pp. 235–258. In: ibid., *The Asian Trade*, pp. 152–153: Steensgaard suggests that '[t]he ultimate proof must await the elaboration of Asian price series, but the information to be gained from available price series is that the gap between the buyers' and the producers' prices was reduced after the rise of the Companies.

47 Robert C. Allen, *Global Economic History: A Very Short History* (Oxford: Oxford U.P., 2012) p. 17.

48 J. C. van Leur, *Indonesian Trade and Society: Essays in Asian Social and Economic History* (The Hague: Van Hoeve, 1955) p. 118; M. A. P. Meilink-Roelofsz, *Asian Trade and European Influence in the Indonesian Archipelago between 1500 and about 1630* (The Hague, 1962) p. 214.

this allows us to put the analysis of price gaps in a long-term perspective. This allows us to analyse the changes caused by the VOC entry into Asian markets: to what extent did the arrival of the Company contribute to the process of globalization, as compared with the developments before?

The answer to this question lies, of course, with Asian price information from the sixteenth century. Unfortunately, such data are scarce and only available for a few products: cloves, cinnamon and pepper. For the fifteenth century, there are two observations of pepper prices from Chinese sources,[49] while a few additional price observations for the sixteenth century could be found in well-known Portuguese documents such as Tomé Pires' *Suma Oriental* and Duarte Barbosa's *Book of Duarte Barbosa*.[50] By combining these prices with those from Dutch sources for the early period and comparing them with the prices for these goods prevailing in Amsterdam, or, when those were not available, Antwerp,[51] a rough sketch of the developments in mark-ups from the fifteenth to the seventeenth centuries can be made (see Table 2.2). When reviewing these data, one must remember that the relatively few observations may not be representative of prices during these decades. However, until new data are unearthed from, for example, Portuguese sources, these data constitute the best evidence currently available.

If one takes these figures at face value, an argument can be made in favour of Steensgaard and Allen's suggestions that the entry of north-western European companies may have led to an initial fall in the mark-up (ratio selling price: purchasing price). The data for cinnamon suggest a decline in the mark-up of somewhat more than 20 in the late sixteenth and early seventeenth centuries to around 12 later in the seventeenth century (and steadily declining until the 1740s; see Figure 2.7). The earliest mark-ups in the 1510s and 1520s for cloves are exceedingly high (140–180), but then drop to remarkably low figures

49 These suggest pepper could be obtained for between 0.32 and 0.62 grams of silver per Dutch *pond*. See: Meilink-Roelofsz, *Asian Trade*, p. 333 n. 57: Ma Huan (1416 or 1425–1432) suggests 100 kati of pepper could be obtained for 1 silver *tael*, according to Fei Hsin (1436) a *bahar* of pepper could be obtained for 6 silver tael. 1 tael = 37.5 grams; 1 bahar = 320 kati; and, 1 *bahar* pepper = 180 kg = 364 *pond*, according to Bulbeck et al., *Southeast Asian exports*, p. 182

50 Tomé Pires, *Suma Oriental: an account of the East, from the Red Sea to Japan, written in Malacca and India in 1512–1515*. 2 vols. (London, 1944); Duarte Barbosa, *The Book of Duarte Barbosa. An account of the countries bordering on the Indian Ocean and their Inhabitants, written by Duarte Barbosa and completed about the year 1518 ad.* [Transl. and ed. by Mansel Longworth Dames] (New Delhi: Asian Educational Services, 1989).

51 Herman van der Wee, *The growth of the Antwerp market and the European economy (fourteenth-sixteenth centuries)*. Vol. 1 Statistics (The Hague: Martinus Nijhoff, 1963).

TABLE 2.2 *Mark-ups (European sales price/Asian purchase price) on cinnamon, cloves and pepper, 1450–1680.*

	Cinnamon	Cloves	Pepper
1420*	–	–	28.9
1510	–	140.0	6.8
1520	–	180.1	–
1530	–	39.7	–
1540	–	4.4	–
1550	–	–	–
1560	21.2	8.2	–
1580	–	–	60.7
1590	–	–	16.2
1600	25.3	25.3	9.1
1610	21.7	21.7	5.3
1620	10.9	19.8	5.2
1630	20.5	18.5	5.9
1640	13.1	13.0	5.6
1650	–	12.1	6.3
1660	13.3	17.8	5.5
1670	12.6	15.3	3.8
1680	11.5	14.4	4.2

Sources: Asia: Barbosa, *The Book*; Bulbeck et al., *Southeast Asian*; Ma Huan *Ying-yai*; Meilink-Roelofsz, *Asian Trade*; Pires, *Suma Oriental*; other data from voc archives see text and Appendix 4.1; Europe: Van Zanden, 'Prices'; Herman Van der Wee, *The growth of the Antwerp market and the European economy (fourteenth-sixteenth centuries)* (Louvain 1963); Posthumus, *Nederlandsche prijsgeschiedenis*.
* 1420 refers to 1416–1436.

(4–8) in the second half of the sixteenth century. Considering these large fluctuations, and the small number of observations, it is hard to interpret these figures. Yet, similar to the mark-ups for cinnamon, a decline in the mark-up for cloves in the first half of the seventeenth century can be discerned from above 20 to around 14–15 later in the century. In both cases, this is despite the VOC acquisition of a monopoly over these spices in the 1650s. This monopoly did, however, prevent a further decline during the remainder of the seventeenth and eighteenth centuries, as I show below.

For a more detailed look at this process of early price convergence, we can focus more specifically on Indonesian pepper prices in the period 1590–1660 (Figure 2.2), for which data are more abundant. It is clear that, starting with the arrival of the first Dutch ships in 1596,[52] the purchase prices of pepper increased rapidly up until roughly 1603. After that, the lack of rivalry among Dutch traders that resulted from the foundation of the VOC may have led to a brief drop in prices.[53] During the 1610s, the price of pepper was driven up again due to fierce competition between, especially, Dutch, English, Chinese (who also often took on the role of intermediary traders) and western Asian merchants in the various pepper ports in the Archipelago (especially in Banten, a major international commercial port). Spearheaded by the infamous Jan Pieterszoon Coen, the VOC's strategy to acquire pepper at low prices became more aggressive. As the Chinese traders and intermediaries were seen as the main cause of high pepper prices, Coen started seizing junks departing for China with cargoes of pepper.[54] Coen also moved the centre of Dutch company activities from Banten to Jayakatra (a vassal of the former), as he thought he would be

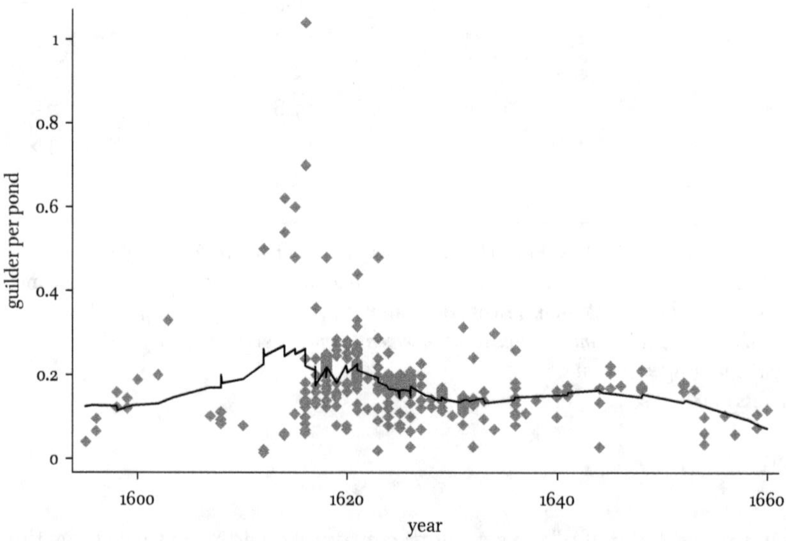

FIGURE 2.2 *Purchasing prices of pepper in the East Indian archipelago, 1590–1660.* Sources: See text and Table 2.2.

52 Rouffaer and IJzerman, *De Eerste Schipvaart.*

53 Meilink-Roelofsz, *Asian Trade.*

54 Much of this section is based on the excellent discussion in: Meilink-Roelofsz, *Asian Trade*, pp. 239–259.

able to exert more influence over the (weaker) ruler of Jayakatra. With the Dutch threatening the position of Banten, tensions led the Sultan of Banten to attack the VOC and Jayakatra in December 1618.[55] The retaliatory raid of the same city by Dutch forces in May 1619, and the rebuilding of it as the VOC headquarters Batavia, however, tipped the balance of power in favour of the Dutch. In succeeding years, the blockade of Banten and the redirection of much its trade through Batavia allowed the Dutch to successfully entrench their position. Banten's steady demise pushed prices down from the 1620s onwards, while the improved Dutch position also allowed the increase of pepper supplies to Amsterdam, leading to a decline in the price of pepper there by 50 percent, from around fl. 1.00 per *pond* to fl. 0.50 in the first half of the seventeenth century, thereby producing the decline in the mark-up in this period.

While future research, especially in Portuguese sources, may bring valuable new data to light for the sixteenth century, from the evidence I present here it can be concluded that the entry of the Dutch probably led an early phase of price convergence. As a result of the increasing hold of the Dutch over purchasing markets (acquired by the use of force), as will be discussed below, the converging trends for pepper and the fine spices did not continue over the remainder of the seventeenth and eighteenth centuries.

5 Price Convergence and the Company

Table 2.3 shows the trends in price differentials for sixteen products traded between Batavia and Amsterdam. In a manner similar to Rönnbäck[56] and O'Rourke and Williamson,[57] I tested whether these trends were statistically significant. These sixteen products together accounted for roughly 90 percent of the total sales in Amsterdam during almost the entire period, meaning that virtually the entire Dutch–Asiatic trade is captured by this analysis. Alas, there were still some gaps in the price series, especially in the seventeenth century. Nonetheless, these series are an improvement *vis-à-vis* the data previously available, and gaps are not detrimental to the analysis since they are assumed to be random (i.e. caused by the loss of source material, not missing because of patterns in trade).[58]

55 Merle C. Ricklefs, *A history of modern Indonesia since c. 1200* (Stanford: Stanford U.P., 2008) p. 33.
56 Rönnbäck, 'Integration', pp. 105–106.
57 O'Rourke and Williamson, 'Did Vasco', p. 670.
58 The series by O'Rourke and Williamson, 'When did globalization?' figure 5 on page 34, or Rönnbäck, 'Integration', figure 2 on page 104, also contain gaps.

The trends in the mark-up are to a great extent similar to those displayed by the coefficient of variation (CV) and the deflated standard deviation (SD). The only difference with the CV trends is that the converging trends for pepper and nutmeg become statistically significant. The dissimilarity with the SD is slightly larger, as prices for nutmeg show a diverging trend, while the price series for coffee are converging. The trends for these three products are thus perhaps less robust than those for the other goods. Although this needs to be kept in mind when looking at the mark-ups in Table 2.3, a number of observations can still be made. By far the majority of price series (9 or 12, if we include coffee, nutmeg and pepper) show convergence, while only 4 (or 6 if nutmeg and coffee are included) display a diverging trend.[59] Furthermore, not only could the trends in price convergence differ between products, the absolute size in the gaps between purchase and sales prices could vary enormously (looking at the y-axes on the right-hand side). Nutmeg made the most handsome profit: at the beginning of the eighteenth century the sales price (fl. 3.72) was over 70 times the purchase price (fl. 0.05).[60] Conversely, if the VOC would only have transported copper and tin from Asia to Europe, its demise would probably have come a lot sooner as the average mark-ups were only 1.4 and 1.7, respectively. Allowing for transport costs, such a route would surely have been operating at a substantial loss. Obviously, this trade constituted only a small proportion of the VOC's total trade.

These examples force us to ask the question of how to asses this array of data? Is price convergence for one product more important than for another? While O'Rourke and Williamson have dismissed early modern globalization on the basis of evidence on, for example, pepper, coffee and cloves, Rönnbäck suggests that globalization cannot be dismissed because of the existence of contradictory evidence on prices for, for example, sugar, tobacco, and tea. Anne McCants notes that as pepper was clearly a much more significant commodity in European consumption than ginger, pepper prices should be given greater weight in any quantitative exercise.[61] De Vries claims that even if mark-ups for most commodities declined only marginally, or not at all, 'overall gross margins faced by the trading companies tended to decline nonetheless because of the additional effect of a continually changing mix of goods in a direction that involved them in progressively greater competition, both in Asia and at home.'[62] He shows that the gross margins on the total trade of the VOC thus declined after 1720 from almost 4:1 to below 2.5:1.

---

59 There are some minor changes in significance of the trends in regressions run with natural logs. See De Zwart, 'Globalization in the Early Modern Era'.

60 Dutch value: Asian price: fl. 0.0625. See appendix for conversion of Asian and Dutch Guilders.

61 McCants, 'Exotic Goods', p. 442.

62 De Vries, 'The limits', p. 724.

TABLE 2.3 *Trends in price convergence for 16 commodities.*

Product	Trends				Average mark-up	Period[63]	N
	Mark-up	CV	SD[64]	Trend			
Cinnamon	0.085 (9.99)	0.001 (8.32)	0.002 (12.12)	Divergence	13.2	1608–1800	145
Cotton yarn	0.012 (4.25)	0.002 (4.72)	0.0002 (3.15)	Divergence	4.1	1660–1789	58
Indigo	0.015 (3.38)	0.003 (3.71)	0.0012 (4.80)	Divergence	2.8	1663–1800	58
Mace	0.031 (4.06)	0.0003 (4.61)	0.0009 (4.41)	Divergence	14.8	1609–1789	143
Nutmeg	−0.037 (−0.86)	−0.0003 (−3.60)	0.0017 (6.20)	None	45.8	1609–1789	129
Coffee	0.034 (4.41)	0.003 (5.71)	−0.0003 (−6.10)	None	5.5	1711–1800	87
Cloves	−0.040 (−6.92)	−0.001 (−7.66)	−0.0006 (−4.74)	Convergence	14.5	1608–1800	164
Copper	−0.005 (−3.39)	−0.002 (−3.20)	−0.0005 (−1.19)	Convergence	1.4	1663–1742	41
Pepper	−0.005 (−1.60)	−0.0003 (−4.10)	−0.0009 (−3.92)	Convergence	5.1	1609–1800	114
Porcelain	−0.016 (−4.01)	−0.005 (−4.62)	−67.17[65] (−2.85)	Convergence	2.0	1729–1792	56
Saltpetre	−0.031 (−8.51)	−0.003 (−9.34)	−0.00005 (−2.79)	Convergence	3.0	1665–1794	86

63 The first and last year for which there were data for both purchase and sales prices. These dates are thus the result of data availability and not the choice of the author.

64 The standard deviation is deflated by the CPI from Jan Luiten van Zanden, 'The prices of the most important consumer goods, and indices of wages and the cost of living in the western part of the Netherlands, 1450–1800', website *Historical Prices and Wages of the International Institute of Social History*: http://www.iisg.nl/hpw/brenv.xls. Last update: December 11, 2009.

65 The high coefficient is the result of the use of a different source, which reflects the gross profit margins rather than the price differential. See Appendix 4.

TABLE 2.3 *Trends in price convergence for 16 commodities.* (cont.)

Product	Trends				Average mark-up	Period	N
	Mark-up	CV	SD	Trend			
Silk	**−0.008 (−3.16)**	**−0.002 (−3.49)**	**−0.001[66] (−1.96)**	Convergence	1.9	1660–1763	44
Sugar[67]	**−0.429 (−9.22)**	**−0.002 (−8.48)**	**−0.0003 (−10.13)**	Convergence	5.2	1623–1786	88
Tea	**−0.031 (−7.73)**	**−0.005 (−7.49)**	**−0.0032 (−11.32)**	Convergence	4.1	1660–1789	84
Textiles	**−0.015 (−8.89)**	**−0.003 (−9.60)**	**−0.0041 (−7.23)**	Convergence	2.2	1660–1792	69
Tin	**−0.003[68] (−2.60)**	**−0.001 (−3.10)**	**−0.0008 (−3.60)**	Convergence	1.7	1668–1789	63

Sources: Porcelain: C.J.A. Jörg, *Porcelain and the Dutch China trade* (The Hague: Martinus Nijhoff, 1982); other products: see text. Significant trends in bold (all at 1 percent level, unless otherwise mentioned).

66 Significant at the 10 percent level.

67 For Asia there are two types of sugar (candy and castor), while the Amsterdam series seem to be for candy (although it is not specified in the source). Only sugar candy is included in this table.

68 Significant at the 5 percent level.

In order to take into account the relative importance of the various goods in the analysis of price differentials, we can weigh the price gaps with the total quantities and values of goods sold at VOC auctions in Amsterdam. Half of all goods brought to Europe by the VOC were sold in Amsterdam and the relative shares of the different goods in the total package are representative for the entire Dutch–Asiatic trade.[69] It is important to use these data to assign relative importance to each of the trends displayed above. Therefore Figure 2.3 shows four series: (1) the mark-up weighted by the sales values in Amsterdam, (2) the mark-up weighted by purchasing values in Asia, (3) the mark-up weighted by the volumes of the goods, and (4) the gross margins of the VOC trade (total sales value / total invoice values).[70] For this exercise it was necessary to interpolate gaps in the mark-ups and price series, therefore Figure 2.3 should be seen as indicative of broader trends, rather than an accurate measure of, for example, year-to-year profitability of the VOC. Due to data constraints, the time frame had to be limited to 1660–1790.

Looking at the average measures of price convergence calculated in this way for the entire package of goods in Figure 2.3, it becomes clear that when taking into account the relative importance of the various products there is mostly convergence. Only the declining trend in the value of sales in Amsterdam is not significant, as it is completely driven by the huge price rises in mace, nutmeg and cinnamon at the end of the period. These rises are a result of the, for the Dutch devastating, Fourth Anglo-Dutch war. Yet, if one considers volumes, Asian invoice values, or gross margins (the more important metric), it is clear that price convergence was taking place in this period, despite the effects of the Fourth Anglo-Dutch war.

The VOC price data thus suggest price convergence for a majority (9 out of 16) of the products being transported between Asia and Amsterdam.[71] In addition, when calculating an average mark-up over time, while taking into account the different weights and volumes of the products transported, price gaps also declined during the seventeenth and eighteenth centuries when taking volumes, invoice values, and gross margins as the appropriate indicators. This evidence thus corroborates Rönnbäck's conclusion that the occurrence of price convergence in the early modern period cannot be dismissed. These data do not corroborate statements that 'there is absolutely no evidence of price convergence'[72] for the Dutch imports from Asia.

---

69 Glamann also notes the Amsterdam figures are representative as 'shown by comparative materials': *Dutch-Asiatic Trade*, p. 14.

70 It is assumed that one piece of textiles weighed 8 pond (the average price difference between a pond of cotton yarn and a piece of textile).

71 This figure increases to 10 out of 16 when running regressions in natural logs as nutmeg becomes significant. See De Zwart, 'Globalization in the Early Modern Era'.

72 Findlay and O'Rourke, 'Commodity Market Integration', p. 26.

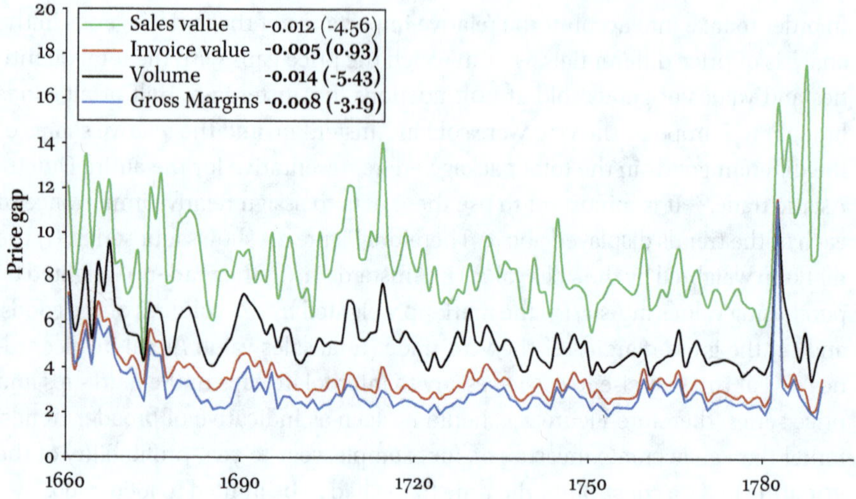

FIGURE 2.3 *Price convergence in the Dutch–Asiatic trade, 1660–1790.*
Sources: see text.

At the same time, Table 2.3 shows that mark-ups on the prices of some commodities could indeed be remarkably high and for some important products we even find divergence during the eighteenth century. Furthermore, with prices in Europe for many of these products still over double those in Asia, even in the late eighteenth century, this is obviously still far from a situation of perfectly integrated markets. The series stop at 1800 or earlier; clearly the trends displayed here could have been disrupted by the Napoleonic Wars. However, this does not alter what can be said about trends during the seventeenth and eighteenth centuries, just as the disruptive effects of the First World War do not invalidate notions of globalization taking place in the nineteenth century.[73]

In addition, my study does not include an analysis of nineteenth and twentieth century price convergence to compare trends. Dobado-Gonzalez et al. demonstrated that market integration in trans-Atlantic grain markets began in the eighteenth century, but also showed that this process gained momentum in the late nineteenth century.[74] O'Rourke and Williamson are probably still right in suggesting that price convergence was much faster and more consistent in the nineteenth century. Their mark-ups for coffee, pepper and cloves

73 Also see the argument made by: Rönnbäck, 'Integration', pp. 99–100.

74 Dobado-Gonzalez et al., 'The Integration'.

seem to be consistently below three in the nineteenth century, clearly far smaller than the mark-ups for those products in the later eighteenth century. Nonetheless, the data presented here can be used to emphasize the earlier origins of this process and to stress the continuity between globalization in the eighteenth and nineteenth centuries, rather than its sudden arrival in the nineteenth century.[75]

Now, of course, we would like to explain both this earlier gradual process of globalization and the variation between the trends for different products. Considering the fact that of those price series that show convergence, one is for a monopoly product (cloves), while of the 4 (or 6) series showing divergence (depending on measure of market integration), only two are for monopoly products (cinnamon and mace), monopolies alone cannot account for the different trends. Since relatively detailed information is available on trends in prices and quantities for almost all products traded by the VOC, as well as the conditions under which these were purchased and sold, we can examine in greater detail what drove the differences in trends and absolute gaps in the mark-ups of these different products.

6 Transport Costs and Conflicts

Price convergence may be caused by two things: declining transport costs and/or reduced barriers to trade.[76] I intend to discuss in this section whether price convergence may have been driven by advances in transport and a decline in piracy and conflicts. From the outset it should, however, be clear that these aspects, which would have affected all trends similarly, do not suffice to explain the variation in trends between the goods. In the next section (7), these differences will be examined by looking at the differences between commodity markets.

6.1 *Transport Costs*

A decline in transport costs may have taken place as a consequence of increased shipping productivity. There has been some discussion on whether shipping productivity increased over the early modern period. While several studies have shown that ocean freight rates declined in the Atlantic trade during this period,[77] others questioned whether these freight rates were properly deflated

75 In line with Dobado-Gonzalez et al.,'s conclusions, 'The Integration', pp. 697–698.
76 O'Rourke and Williamson, 'When did globalisation?'.
77 North, 'Ocean freight rates', and ibid., 'Sources of productivity change'.

and whether the decline in ocean freight rates applied for other trade routes as well.[78]

A survey of the recent literature suggests the possibility of advances in shipping productivity during the early modern period. Jan Lucassen and Richard Unger have shown that labour productivity in ocean shipping rose from the end of the Middle Ages up to 1800 with an (impressive) annual rate of 0.4 percent per year.[79] Milja van Tielhof and Jan Luiten van Zanden recently suggested that only between 1550 and the 1620s did freight rates decline in Dutch shipping.[80] Yet, after the 1650s freight rates increased and did not during the entire eighteenth century fall back to the low levels of the early seventeenth century. Rönnbäck demonstrated that the speed of shipping increased significantly in the trans-Atlantic slave trade,[81] while Peter Solar found that shipping costs between Europe and Asia fell by two-thirds between the 1770s and 1820s as a result of changes in the composition of cargoes, and improvements in ship construction and navigation,[82] as well the increased speed of ships.[83] Another reason for declining transport cost may have been a decrease in piracy and privateering over the eighteenth century, which would have allowed a decline in labour and capital costs for soldiers and armaments.[84]

---

78 C. Knick Harley, 'Ocean freight rates and productivity 1740–1913: the primacy of mechanical invention reaffirmed', *Journal of Economic History* 48 (1988) pp. 851–876; Menard, 'Transport costs'; O'Rourke and Williamson, 'When did globalisation?'.

79 Jan Lucassen and Richard W. Unger, 'Labour Productivity in Ocean Shipping 1500–1850', *International Journal of Maritime History* 12 (2000) pp. 127–142: productivity increases were less impressive in almost all other sectors of the economy.

80 Milja van Tielhof and Jan Luiten van Zanden, 'Productivity Changes in Shipping in the Dutch Republic: the Evidence from Freight Rates, 1550–1800', in: Richard W. Unger (eds.) *Shipping and Economic Growth 1350–1850* (Leiden and Boston: Brill, 2011) pp. 47–80; ibid., 'Roots of growth and productivity change in Dutch shipping industry 1500–1800', *Explorations in Economic History* 46 (2009) pp. 389–403.

81 Klas Rönnbäck, 'The speed of ships and shipping productivity in the age of sail', *European Review of Economic History* 16 (2013) pp. 469–489: Rönnbäck warns that the speed of ships in the slave trade may not be representative for all ocean shipping at the time. However, Peter Solar and Luc Hens also found an increase in shipping in the late 18th century for British East India Company ships: 'The Speed of East India Company Ships', *Mimeo Free University Brussels* (2013).

82 Peter M. Solar, 'Opening to the East: Shipping between Europe and Asia, 1770–1830', *Journal of Economic History* 73 (2013) pp. 625–661.

83 Solar and Hens, 'The Speed'.

84 Rönnbäck, 'The speed of ships', Henning Hillmann and Christina Gathmann, 'Overseas trade and the decline of privateering', *Journal of Economic History* 71 (2011) 730–761.

Focusing on the VOC trade between the Dutch Republic and Asia specifically, the information on transportation costs is more ambiguous. J.R. Bruijn has attempted to estimate shipping costs of the VOC per tonne and finds that shipping costs remained relatively stable over most of the eighteenth century, and only increased during the Fourth Anglo-Dutch War, in the 1780s.[85] Figure 2.4 shows Bruijn's data corrected for general price trends. In addition, he speculated that VOC shipping costs mostly fell in the seventeenth century.[86] Comparing his figures for the eighteenth century with the general inflation in the Dutch Republic,[87] we find a 20 percent decline in freight rates relative to the general price level between 1730 and 1770.

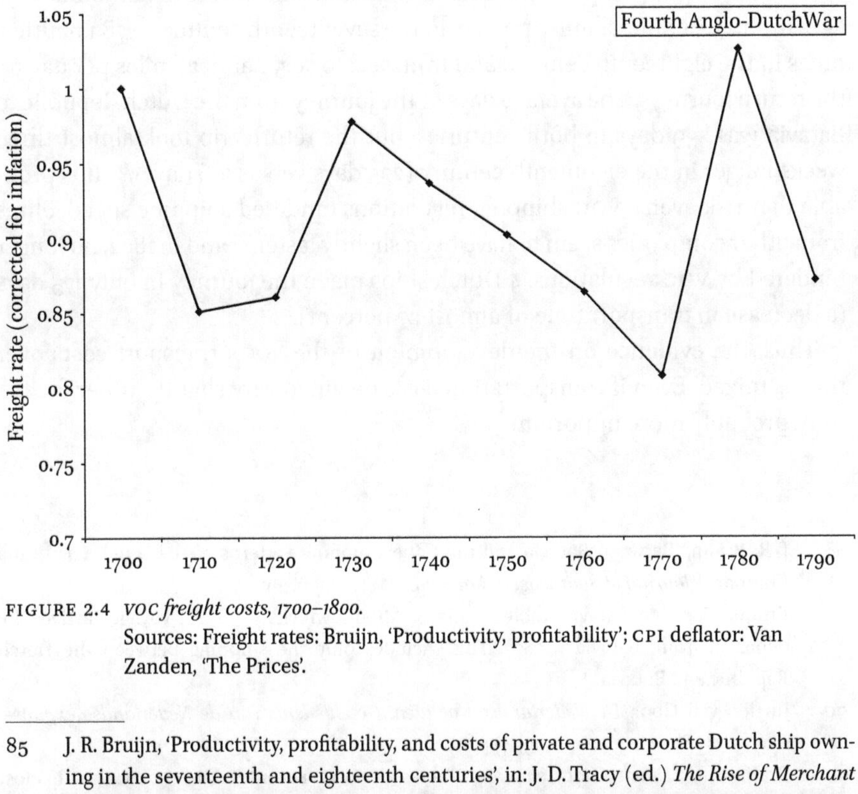

FIGURE 2.4 *VOC freight costs, 1700–1800.*
Sources: Freight rates: Bruijn, 'Productivity, profitability'; CPI deflator: Van Zanden, 'The Prices'.

85 J. R. Bruijn, 'Productivity, profitability, and costs of private and corporate Dutch ship owning in the seventeenth and eighteenth centuries', in: J. D. Tracy (ed.) *The Rise of Merchant Empires. Long-distance trade in the early modern world, 1350–1750* (Cambridge: Cambridge U.P., 1990) pp. 174–194.

86 Bruijn, 'Productivity, profitability'. Similarly, Steensgaard suggested that freight costs in the East India Company trade declined in the first half of the seventeenth century, mostly as a result of decreasing voyage time: Niels Steensgaard, 'Freight Costs in the English East India Trade 1601–1657', *Scandinavian Economic History Review* 13 (1965) pp. 143–162.

87 Using figures from Van Zanden, 'The prices'.

In general, it seems the Company's shipping 'was a rather safe business'.[88] Of all the voyages from the Republic to the East Indies, just over 2.5 percent ended in shipwreck.[89] In addition, piracy was limited: on a total of over 8,000 journeys, only 36 ships to, and 24 ships from, the East Indies were raided. Between 1674 and 1781 not a single returning ship was attacked east of the Cape of Good Hope.[90]

However, Bruijn, Gaastra and Schöffer's shipping statistics do not show improvement in shipping in the eighteenth century compared with the seventeenth. While in the seventeenth century a total of 2.7 percent of all voyages ended in disaster (due to capture or wreckage), this figure increased to 3.2 percent in the eighteenth century.[91] Furthermore, their data suggest that the average speed of Company ships in the Indian Ocean declined on the outbound voyages from 83.5 nautical miles per day in the seventeenth century to 78.1 nautical miles in the eighteenth century, and from 74.2 to 70.5 nautical miles per day on the return journeys. The average days of the journey from the Dutch Republic to Batavia was 239 days in both centuries, but the return trip took almost three weeks longer in the eighteenth century (235 days versus 216 days).[92] It is probable that risk-averse VOC shipping regulations hindered shipping speed. Ships from other companies seem to have been slightly faster,[93] and in 1802, no longer hindered by VOC regulations, 4 Dutch ships made the journey in only 175 days (a decrease in transport time of almost 27 percent).[94]

Thus, the evidence on the development of the VOC's transport costs over time is mixed. Even if transportation costs declined very slightly, other factors were probably more important.

---

88 J. R. Bruijn, 'Between Batavia and the Cape: Shipping Patterns of the Dutch East India Company', *Journal of Southeast Asian Studies* 11 (1980) p. 261.

89 Bruijn, 'Between Batavia', tables 1 and 2. All shipwrecks = 98. All voyages arrived in, departed from, Batavia = 3877. This includes only the shipping between the Dutch Republic and Batavia.

90 Jurrien van Goor, *De Nederlandse Koloniën. Geschiedenis van de Nederlandse expansie 1600–1875* (The Hague: SDU, 1994) p. 50.

91 Bruijn et al., *Dutch-Asiatic shipping*. Tables 3 and 22: seventeenth century: 75 ships lost *vis-à-vis* 2761 journey; eighteenth century 171 ships lost *vis-à-vis* 5317 journeys. In contrast to the figures above, this includes *all* Dutch-Asiatic shipping. Not just those between the Republic and Batavia (but also direct journeys to Ceylon, Bengal, and Canton).

92 Tables 1 and 2 from Bruijn, 'Between Batavia'.

93 Gaastra and Bruijn, 'The Dutch East', pp. 194–195.

94 Bruijn, 'Between Batavia', p. 261. For increased shipping speed in this period, also see Hens and Solar, 'The speed'.

6.2 *Conflict and Competition*

According to O'Rourke and Williamson, as well as Rönnback, international conflict was detrimental to the process of market integration. In terms of the individual series for the products analysed, it is first of all important to note that for, for example, tea, textiles and saltpetre, some of the first observations unfortunately coincide with the Second Anglo-Dutch War (1665–7), which may have driven up sales prices in Amsterdam.[95] Nonetheless, excluding those years from the regressions still produces similar trends.[96] Figure 2.4 already demonstrated the increase in transport cost as a result of the Fourth Anglo-Dutch war (1780–4). As a result, this war seems to have further increased (long-term) mark-ups for mace, nutmeg and coffee, but this did not lead to a structural break in individual trends as there was no convergence for those products to begin with.

The effects of war and conflict for the process of market integration can be tested formally through the use of dummies in a regression framework: the 'war' dummy takes up a value of 1 in case of a year when the Dutch were at war; and a value of 0 in all peace years. Table 2.4 shows the results of trend regressions on the four compound series shown in Figure 2.3 with two 'war' dummies: one for the Anglo-Dutch wars and one for all other wars that include the Dutch as belligerents.[97] It can be assumed that for trade and shipping the Anglo-Dutch wars, which were primarily naval wars, were more disruptive than the others. A glance at Table 2.4 immediately confirms this assumption. In all cases, the effect of the Anglo-Dutch wars is highly significant and leads to a jump in the price gap, while the other wars are never significant. The regressions are very weak for the series weighted by the sales values since the Fourth Anglo-Dutch war not only pushed up price gaps in the short run, but also led to a structural break in the series. In all other cases, however, the effects are not lasting. A possible factor limiting the effect of wars on the price gaps is that the Company could store textiles, but also other goods, for several

95 This can clearly be observed for saltpetre; for textiles, no real peaks can be observed. For tea there are too few observations for surrounding years to conclude whether war time prices were dramatically higher.

96 Trends: Mark-ups: tea −0.027 (−6.83), textiles −0.011 (−7.85), saltpetre −0.028 (−8.34); CV: tea −0.005 (−6.98) textiles −0.0029 (−7.18), saltpetre −0.003 (−8.42); SD: tea −0.003 (−10.41), textiles −0.004 (−6.49), saltpetre −0.00001 (−0.76): All trends are significant at the 1% level except that for saltpetre SD (which is insignificant).

97 The dummy for the Anglo-Dutch wars being assigned a 1 in the years 1665–7, 1672–4 and 1780–4, and 0 in all other years; the dummy for other wars was assigned a 1 in the years 1660, 1672–78, 1688–97, 1701–14 and a 0 in all other years.

TABLE 2.4 *Trend regressions on compound price-gap series, 1660–1790.*

	Regression 1	Regression 2	Regression 3	Regression 4
Panel A: Price gap weighted by sales values				
Constant	16.908* (1.89)	16.005* (1.88)	15.503 (1.17)	14.136 (1.55)
Trend	−0.005 (−0.92)	−0.004 (−0.87)	−0.004 (−0.72)	−0.003 (−0.61)
Anglo-Dutch wars	–	2.039*** (3.06)	–	2.057*** (3.08)
Other wars	–	–	0.1839 (0.42)	0.244 (0.57)
R^2	0.01	0.08	0.01	0.08
F	0.85	5.15***	0.51	3.52**
N	127	127	127	127
Panel B: Price gap weighted by invoice values				
Constant	23.360*** (5.50)	22.636*** (5.90)	24.353*** (5.34)	23.270*** (5.65)
Trend	−0.012*** (−4.56)	−0.011*** (−5.01)	−0.012*** (−4.57)	−0.011*** (−4.84)
Anglo-Dutch Wars	–	1.635*** (5.45)	–	1.629*** (5.41)
Other Wars	–	–	−0.130 (−0.61)	−0.083 (−0.43)
R^2	0.15	0.31	0.15	0.31
F	21.72***	28.22***	10.99***	18.75***
N	127	127	127	127
Panel C: Price gap weighted by volumes				
Constant	29.483*** (6.62)	28.754*** (7.09)	27.943*** (6.02)	27.843*** (6.39)
Trend	−0.014*** (−5.43)	−0.137*** (−5.82)	−0.014*** (−4.97)	−0.013*** (−5.25)
Anglo-Dutch Wars	–	1.646*** (5.19)	–	1.645*** (5.20)
Other Wars	–	–	0.071 (0.32)	0.119 (0.58)
R^2	0.19	0.34	0.19	0.34
F	29.51***	31.28***	14.70***	20.86***
N	127	127	127	127
Panel D: Gross margins				
Constant	17.451*** (3.85)	16.713*** (4.04)	18.900 *** (3.89)	17.797*** (4.01)
Trend	−0.008*** (−3.19)	−0.008*** (−3.36)	−0.009*** (−3.28)	−0.009*** (−3.38)
Anglo-Dutch Wars	–	1.667*** (5.16)	–	1.658*** (5.11)
Other Wars	–	–	−0.190 (−0.83)	−0.141 (−0.68)
R^2	0.08	0.24	0.08	0.24
F	10.18***	19.43***	5.43***	13.05***
N	127	127	127	127

Sources: see text. Note: ***, **, * denote significance at the 1, 5 and 10 percent levels, respectively. T-ratios are in parentheses.

months in its warehouses, thereby being able to absorb initial shocks as supply dried up. At the same time, demand may also have dwindled, as in periods of war and crisis consumers probably give priority to the purchase of more basic commodities.

Wars and conflicts not only had an effect on prices, but also on the quantities imported from Asia. Figure 2.5 sketches the total volume (in Dutch *pond*) of Company commodities sold at auction in Amsterdam (a proxy for importation from Asia, as goods could also be sold from the warehouse and vice versa: goods could be imported, but stored instead of sold) and highlights the wars involving the Dutch Republic. Again the distinction is made between the Anglo-Dutch wars and the other wars. It is clearly visible that volumes dropped during war years and, indeed, especially in those wars involving the English. The Fourth Anglo-Dutch war was an especially disastrous war from the Dutch perspective. The war not only led to an immediate loss of shipping volume,[98] but also to the forfeiture of the VOC's dominant position in the Euro-Asian trade.

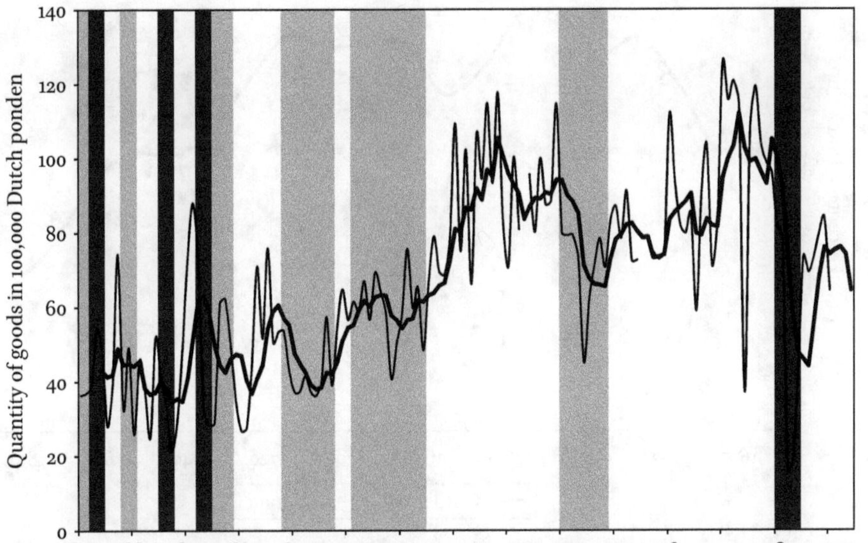

FIGURE 2.5 *Quantity of goods sold in the Amsterdam auctions, 1650–1790.*
Source: VOC auctions Amsterdam: VOC 4584–4597.

98 Also see: Van Zanden and Van Tielhof, 'Roots of growth'.

Related to these wars was the competition among the countries of Europe in the arena of international trade. As Douglas Irwin notes, the Anglo-Dutch wars were instigated by the English 'in an effort to increase their market share in trade by capturing or destroying Dutch shipping'.[99] While the English achieved victory in the First war, the Dutch were able to quickly rebuild their fleet to gain victory in the Second.[100] The Third war (1672–1674) ended with the status quo being maintained and was the last war fought between the Dutch and English for more than a century. Whereas the Dutch were clearly dominant in the seventeenth and early eighteenth centuries, during the course of the eighteenth century English (and French) competition became more pronounced. Figure 2.6 demonstrates that competition increased as from the 1700s, after which the Dutch share in the number of inbound ships declined; after the 1730s the share in outbound ships also began its steady

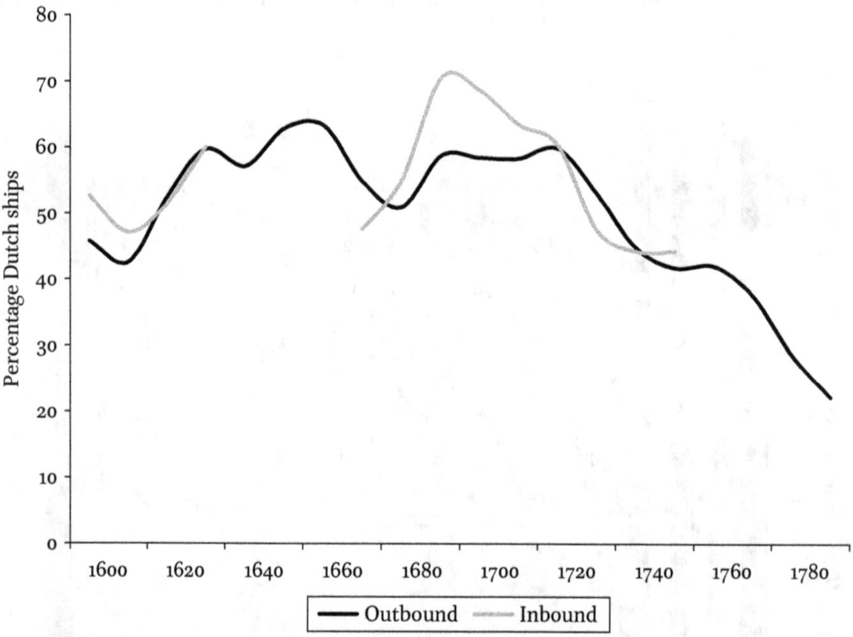

FIGURE 2.6 *Share of Dutch ships in total Euro-Asian trade, 1600–1800.*
Source: De Vries, 'Connecting Europe', pp. 51–53; inbound figures incomplete, years without data on the British East India Company are excluded from this figure.

99 Irwin, 'Strategic trade policy', p. 137.

100 Jonathan I. Israel, *The Dutch Republic: its rise, greatness, and fall, 1477–1806* (Oxford: Oxford U.P., 1995) p. 721.

decay. Yet it was only after the Fourth Anglo-Dutch war, in the 1780s, that the Dutch were finally surpassed in terms of the total number of ships sent to Asia. While the wars themselves may have been disruptive to the globalization process, the associated competition from the French, and especially from the English, probably had a positive effect on the process of price convergence.

In sum, decreases in transaction costs and increased maritime competition allowed for a decline in price differentials in the Euro-Asian trade in the seventeenth and eighteenth centuries. Yet, considering the lack of uniformity in the trends of price convergence among the various products, we need to focus on the differences between the various commodity markets in the remainder of the analysis.

7 Commodity Markets in Europe and Asia

O'Rourke and Williamson suggest that even more than the lack of improvement in transport, 'monopoly, international conflict, piracy and government restriction'[101] were driving up price differentials. While the trading companies (by their charter) held exclusive rights on the wholesale trade of East Indian goods in their home countries, it was only for the four monopoly spices (cinnamon, cloves, mace and nutmeg) that one company controlled the entire world production and was thus genuinely the only seller of these goods on the world markets and as consequence had complete control over prices. In all other cases, the companies sold their goods (at auctions) on their home markets to other merchants, who were in competition with each other on markets throughout Europe.[102]

7.1 *Monopoly and Competition in Europe*

A brief look at the average mark-ups from Table 2.3 immediately shows that price gaps were by far the largest for cinnamon, cloves, mace and, especially, nutmeg. In contrast to the four fine spices, pepper was also brought to Europe by other European trading companies. If markets across Europe were integrated, this would mean that pepper prices in Amsterdam were influenced by those in London, Antwerp, and elsewhere. The integration of European markets has been the subject of many studies in the past years. Using increasingly sophisticated econometric techniques, various scholars have measured

101 O'Rourke and Williamson, 'After Columbus'.

102 De Vries, 'Limits', p. 725.

the extent to which European commodity markets became integrated since the late middle ages. These studies have not led to consistent results as some have shown significant integration of European markets over the early modern period,[103] while others find that integration was domestic, or at most regional, prior to the nineteenth century.[104] Part of this variety may have been caused by differences between various commodity markets. It has, for example, been suggested that while the market for soap underwent integration between 1500 and 1800, the markets for, for example, rice, sugar, honey, and butter did not.[105]

An elaborate examination of the integration of European markets for the goods brought back from the East Indies is outside the scope of this book. Suffice to say that studies on, for example, European pepper markets suggest that these were fairly well integrated by the late sixteenth century.[106] Neither pepper, nor the fine spices, had counterparts outside Asia, yet the other commodities sold by the VOC also had to compete with goods brought to Europe from other parts of Europe or the New World. As Glamann already noted:

> The records show that there was competition...between alternative products, such as East Indian and European textiles; between identical products from different regions enjoying similar climates, e.g., sugar from Java and Bengal, sugar from Madeira and Sao Tome, and Brazilian and West Indian sugar; or between products grown in different climatic regions [...] Chinese, Persian and Italian silk; Japanese, Hungarian, Swedish and West Indian copper; the spices of Asia, Africa and America; coffee from

103 Persson, *Grain Markets*, David S. Jacks, 'Market integration in the North and Baltic Seas, 1500–1800', *Journal of European Economic History* 33 (2004) pp. 285–329. Christiaan van Bochove, *The Economic Consequences of the Dutch. Economic integration around the North Sea 1500–1800* (Amsterdam: Aksant, 2008); David Chilosi, Tommy E. Murphy, Roman Studer, A. Coşkun Tunçer, 'Europe's many integrations: geography and grain markets, 1620–1913', *Explorations in Economic History* 50 (2013) pp. 46–68.

104 Bateman, 'The Evolution'; Federico, 'When did European'; Uebele, 'National and international'.

105 Süleyman Özmucur and Sevket Pamuk, 'Did European commodity prices converge before 1800?', in: T.J. Hatton, K.H. O'Rourke and A.M. Taylor (eds.) *The New Comparative Economic History: Essays in Honour of Jeffrey G. Williamson* (Cambridge, MA: MIT Press, 2007) pp. 59–85; Federico, 'When did European'.

106 O'Rourke and Williamson, 'Did Vasco'; Greg Barrett, 'An exploration of the role of Portugal in the economic integration of Asia and Europe with a focus on the pepper market', paper prepared for the *Asia-Pacific Economic and Business History Conference* 2012 (Canberra, 2012): http://apebh2012.files.wordpress.com/2011/05/apebh-text-of-paper-barrett.pdf.

> Mocha, Java and the West Indies: all of these competed. Study of the volume of trade and the movement of prices at selected locations reveals numerous instances of uniform trends [...] The best barometer, however, is represented by the prices on the commodity exchange of Amsterdam. The yearly prices of colonial goods in this, the most important market place of northern Europe, mirror global market conditions [...] we see a regular flow of traffic through an immense network of trade routes that are linked together to form a European system of redistribution with Antwerp, Amsterdam, London and Hamburg constituting some of its most important centres.[107]

One can further add that indigo from Java competed with that from India and the West Indies. Furthermore, Indian textiles and Chinese porcelain not only competed with cloth and ceramics produced in Europe, they also encouraged the development of European imitations: notable examples are English imitations of Indian calicos,[108] and Dutch Delftware inspired by the Chinese originals. As De Vries argues, '[t]he existence of alternatives and the rise of import substitution influenced the prices at which many Asian goods could be sold in Europe, limiting the "pricing power" of the trading companies'.[109] Thus, the availability of these alternatives could have put downward pressure on the mark-ups of all commodities other than the monopoly spices.

The Company's procedures for selling these commodities in the Dutch Republic changed over time. At the beginning of the seventeenth century, the sale of Asian commodities was mostly through contracts with large buyers or syndicates of buyers. In September 1620, for example, all pepper (the most important import at that time) brought to the Dutch Republic was purchased by a syndicate consisting of only four persons. This is one of many examples given by Glamann in his seminal work on the Dutch–Asiatic trade.[110] If a satisfactory price was not obtained through contracts, commodities were sold at fixed prices. While sale by contract remained the dominant form of sale in the 1630s, there were several disputes surrounding this form of selling

---

107 Glamann, 'European trade', p. 451. See, for example, Topik, 'The Integration' for uniform trends in coffee prices from Java, Mocha and the West-Indies.

108 Stephen Broadberry and Bishnupriya Gupta, 'Lancashire, India, and shifting competitive advantage in cotton textiles, 1700–1850: the neglected role of factor prices', *Economic History Review* 62 (2009) pp. 279–305.

109 De Vries, 'The Limits', p. 722.

110 Glamann, *Dutch-Asiatic*, pp. 29–33.

since the later 1620s.[111] These disagreements eventually led to the sale of Asian commodities at auction from 1642 onwards; only the spices were sometimes exempted, as the Company sought to sell them at a fixed price. Sale by auction led to the distribution of these commodities among a larger number of buyers and prices being determined by the free market. For all of the five products (pepper and spices) for which we have data from the period 1608 to 1650, price convergence can be observed (see Figures 2.7 and 2.9). The change in sales techniques, according to Glamann largely resulting from conflicts of interest within the Company, also may be seen as an institutional innovation (perhaps unintentionally) aiding the process of market integration.

It is therefore clear that, whether or not markets in Europe were perfectly integrated in the early modern period, the behaviour of prices for Asian commodities in Amsterdam – with the exception of monopoly spices – was influenced by prices in other cities, as well as the prices of similar goods brought into Amsterdam from elsewhere. This was especially so after 1642, when these commodities began to be sold by auction, rather than by contract. Another part of the price gap was, of course, influenced by purchasing prices in different parts of Asia.

7.2 *Colonial Control in Ceylon, Java and the Moluccas*

While price gaps were clearly largest for the monopoly spices, and part of the explanation for these large price gaps lies, of course, in the monopoly the VOC had on the sale of these goods in Europe, the story does not end there: Table 2.3 does not provide a single trend for these four products. With regard to cinnamon (which only grew on Ceylon in good quality) it can be seen that, while the data for the period before 1658, when the VOC secured its position on Ceylon, is fragile (only four price observations), mark-ups were not immediately higher after monopolization. Purchasing prices increased from 4 real per *picol* (fl. 0.08 per *pond*) in 1608 to fl. 0.30 per *pond* in 1660,[112] at which level it would remain until 1800.[113] However, the trend in sale prices of cinnamon (which fluctuated) is not only the result of price-setting by the VOC. Rather, these prices were determined to some extent by the forces of demand, but, mostly, by supply (or

111 Many VOC *bewindhebbers* of the various Chambers, and even the Gentlemen XVII, were part of the syndicates that purchased the goods. Shareholders and some *bewindhebbers* from Zeeland protested against these practices. Glamann, *Dutch-Asiatic*, pp. 35–36.

112 VOC 603: This is in fact the price for which the VOC purchased the cinnamon in Banten (Western Java) in 1608. The purchasing price in Ceylon was probably even lower, as otherwise merchants bringing it to Banten would have been operating at a loss.

113 Roughly: the price in the VOC accounts could fluctuate slightly between fl. 0.31 and fl. 0.25.

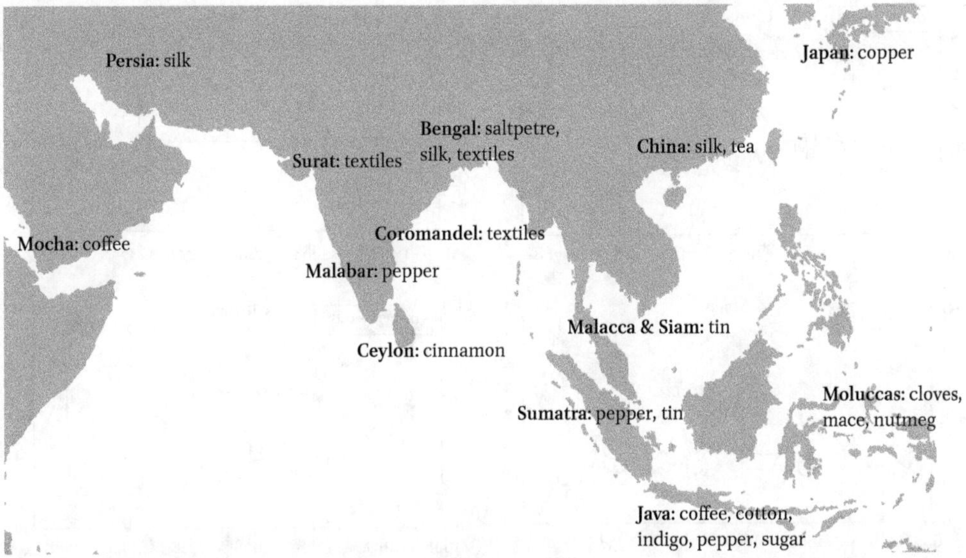

MAP 2.1 *Products and production areas of the VOC in Asia.* Based on: Jacobs, *Merchant In Asia.*

the lack thereof). In contrast to the other spices, the VOC did not actively try to limit supplies, rather supply was restricted by the limited availability of fertile lands and the fact that cinnamon production (peeling) was the task of only one of the (smaller) Sinhalese castes in Ceylon (the *Salagama*). In the 1740s population growth, social unrest and increasing tensions with the Kandyan King (the only remaining indigenous king on the island) led to a dramatic fall in cinnamon supply. Only after victory over Kandy, in 1766, was the VOC able to increase cinnamon production: it broke with the caste system and allowed all Ceylonese to plant and peel cinnamon trees. Furthermore, as sovereign ruler over the entire Ceylonese coast, the Company was better able to secure the monopoly. These developments probably caused the significant rise in the mark-up as from the later 1740s.

Nutmeg and mace came from the tiny Banda Islands in the Moluccas. After unsuccessful negotiations to secure contracts with the local heads (the *orang-kaya*), the VOC used a terrible amount of force to get what it came for. By 1621 the Company had succeeded in killing or expelling the entire indigenous population, as well as destroying all nutmeg trees outside Banda and implementing a plantation system.[114] In the 1650s the Company similarly secured

114 Mace and nutmeg came from the same tree. Interestingly, while mace was very valuable early on, nutmeg, which turned out to be the VOCs main money maker, was not at all

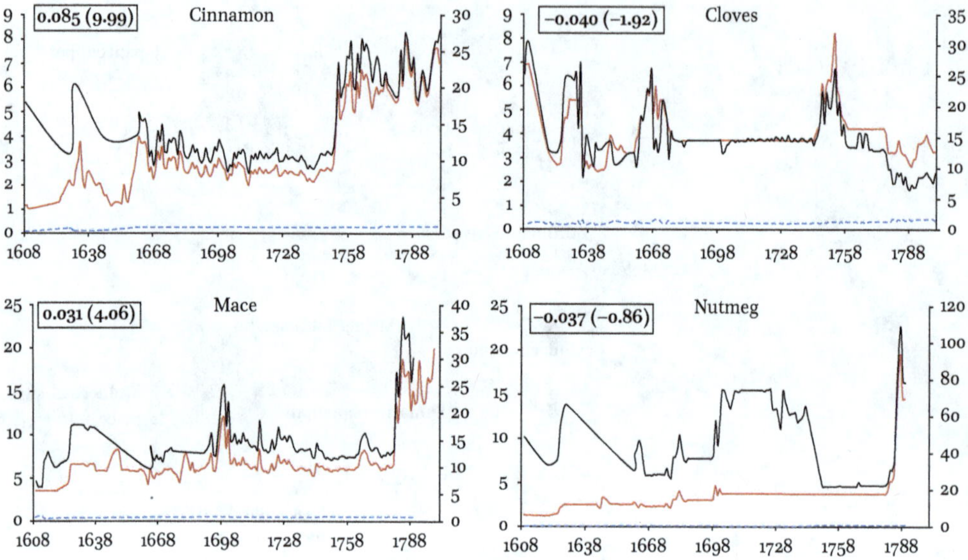

FIGURE 2.7 *Prices and mark-ups for monopoly spices, 1608–1800.*
Sources: see text. Black line: mark-up; Dashed blue line: Purchase price in Asia; Red line: Sales price in Amsterdam. Y-axes left-hand side: *guilders* per pond/piece for prices in Asia and Amsterdam; y-axes right-hand side: mark-ups.

the monopoly over cloves by use of force. The data on cloves provide an interesting case of what happens to mark-ups with and without a monopoly. Bulbeck et al. found that in the sixteenth and early seventeenth centuries there was a significant growth in quantities, as well as local prices, until the VOC monopoly started affecting prices in the 1640s.[115] In the 1770s, French and English traders smuggled clove seedlings from the Moluccas and started growing clove trees elsewhere in Southeast Asia and East Africa.[116] Even though these attempts remained largely unsuccessful until the second half of the nineteenth century, mark-ups declined from a high level of 25 in the 1750s to below 10 by the end of the century.

With the exception of these spices, it has been claimed that all other commodities were bought in competitive markets 'in the sense that rival European

sought after in the sixteenth and seventeenth centuries. Pires, *Suma Oriental*, p. 207 wrote: 'they will not sell you mace and nutmeg except together, that is, if you want a bahar of mace you have to buy seven bahars of nutmeg.'

115 Bulbeck et al., *Southeast Asian exports*, p. 21. This is also confirmed in the seminal work of Meilink-Roelofsz, *Asian Trade*.

116 Bulbeck et al., *Southeast Asian exports*, p. 21.

companies vied with each other to acquire the Asian goods, but also [...] vied with Asian traders for these goods.'[117] This observation is, however, not completely accurate either, as the VOC enjoyed significant control over purchasing markets in other areas as well.

As in Ceylon and the Moluccas, the Company became a colonial ruler over much of Java in the course of the seventeenth and eighteenth centuries. In contrast to these other areas, where the Company more or less actively pursued a policy of expansion against local rulers in order to safeguard its monopoly over the fine spices, in Java the Company was hesitantly drawn into the role of a colonial power as a result of its involvement in conflicts between various competitors for the Mataram throne (in the first half of the seventeenth century much of the island was ruled by the *Susuhunan*[118] of Mataram). Almost every time the company intervened in Javanese power struggles it was able to expand its territory as payment for the supplied military services. The Treaty of Giyanti in 1755 ended the series of wars and the process of territorial expansion. The Company now became sovereign ruler of more than two-thirds of the island, with the remainder of Mataram being split between two equally-sized sultanates: Surakarta and Yogyakarta. In order to compensate for the high overhead costs the Company consequently incurred on the island, it introduced the cultivation of indigo and coffee and further encouraged the cultivation of cotton and, especially, sugar.

Sugar was already cultivated on Java before the Dutch arrived. While initially of little interest to the VOC, around the mid-seventeenth century it was realized that there was a huge market for sugar in Asia. The Company demanded a set quantity of sugar from the sugar millers at a set price each year. If the Company was in control of the purchasing price, then why did prices converge? Due to a loss of markets and exhaustion of the soil, the sugar industry was threatened with extinction in the 1730s, and again the 1770s. In order to save an industry that provided a livelihood for many people on the island,[119] purchasing prices were raised. At the same time, sugar from the West-Indies flooded the European market, resulting in lower sales prices in Amsterdam. Consequently, and as Rönnbäck also demonstrated, global sugar prices converged.[120]

117 De Vries, 'Limits', p. 724.

118 'Honoured lord', title of the ruler of Mataram. Ricklefs, *A History*, p. 47.

119 As well as investments of high VOC officials on the island; Luc Nagtegaal, *Rijden op een Hollandse Tijger. De noordkust van Java en de V.O.C. 1680–1743* (unpublished PhD thesis, Utrecht University, 1988) p. 138.

Both indigo and cotton yarn were purchased in competitive Indian markets in the seventeenth century. At the end of the seventeenth century, in order to circumvent high purchasing prices in India, the Company introduced the cultivation of indigo in Java, as well as encouraging cotton growing. To acquire cotton, the Company imposed forced deliveries at set prices on the Javanese Regents.[121] In order to stimulate indigo cultivation, the VOC initially increased purchasing prices in the early 1730s. Later in the century, however, as indigo did not fetch a good profit in the Dutch Republic, purchasing prices were reduced, and the Dutch started to claim a more active role in overseeing indigo production.[122]

Likewise, coffee cultivation was introduced in Java in the early eighteenth century as a reaction to high prices in Mocha. In the 1710s the company provided the regents in Java with coffee seedlings and offered a high purchasing price of fl. 0.50 per *pond* to stimulate cultivation. As a result, coffee cultivation was so successful that already by the 1720s total deliveries exceeded 4 million *pond*. In 1723 the VOC monopolized the market and forced planters to deliver their entire crop to the Company. In fear of flooding the European market, the purchase price was drastically reduced in the late 1720s and 1730s, while in the 1740s the VOC set quotas for the amount each region was allowed to produce. Nevertheless, the European market turned out to be insatiable and coffee consumption increased from less than 1 million to over 100 million *pond* per year, without significant decreases in prices in the later eighteenth century. Realizing this (rather late), the Company transformed coffee production into a coercive system only in the late 1780s: Javanese peasants were forced to cultivate and deliver a minimum amount of coffee beans each year.[123] Thus, while price differentials between different types of coffee in consumption markets may have declined,[124] the gap between the price paid in Amsterdam and that paid in Batavia most certainly increased as a result of VOC control over production and trade in Java (see Figure 2.8).

120 Rönnbäck, 'Integration'.

121 Robert van Niel, *Java's Northeast Coast 1740–1840: a study in colonial encroachment and dominance* (Leiden: CNWS. 2005) p. 176; Kwee Hui Kian, 'Production, Consumption and Trade of Javanese Cotton Yarn and Textile in the late Seventeenth and Eighteenth Century', Paper presented at *gehn Conference on Cotton Textiles* (Pune 2005), pp. 25–29.

122 Van Niel, *Java's Northeast Coast*, pp. 153–162.

123 Jacobs, *Merchant in Asia*, pp. 260–275. The slave revolt in Santo Domingo and the French Revolutionary wars drove up Amsterdam coffee prices in the 1790s.

124 Emphasized by Topik, 'The Integration'.

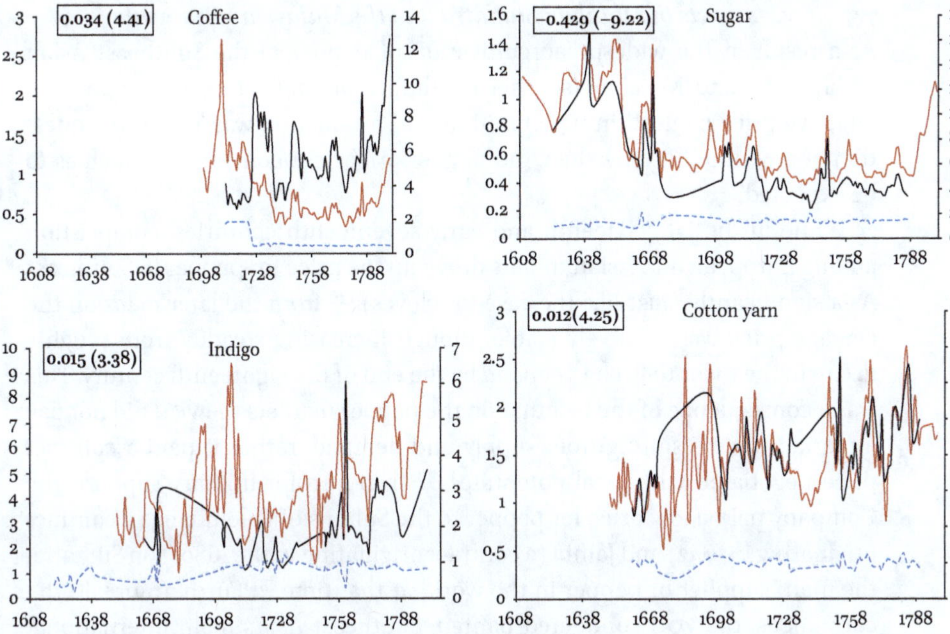

FIGURE 2.8 *Prices and mark-ups for goods obtained in Java, 1608–1800.*
Sources: see text. Black line: mark-up; Dashed blue line: Purchase price in Asia; Red line: Sales price in Amsterdam. Y-axes left-hand side: *guilders* per pond/piece for prices in Asia and Amsterdam; y-axes right-hand side: mark-ups.

De Vries wrote that 'what began as an age of globalization [...] ended as an age of colonialism'.[125] Mostly as a reaction against the forces of globalization (competition and consequentially rising prices in purchasing markets), the Company attempted to control production and purchase prices in its own territories. We can find a colonial system of production on Ambon and the Banda Islands from the middle of the seventeenth century,[126] and in Java and Ceylon from the middle of the eighteenth. Colonialism did not, thus, begin with the English in Bengal in 1757, as claimed by De Vries, but started already with Dutch rule over parts of Java and the Moluccas from the seventeenth century onwards.[127]

125 De Vries, 'The Limits', p. 731.

126 In the sense that the local population was forced to deliver a certain amount of a product each year to the colonial government for relatively low, or no pay.

127 Jacbos also notes the rise of a colonial system in 18th century Java: *Merchant in Asia*, pp. 274–275.

7.3 *Contracts in Malabar, Sumatra and the Malaysian Peninsula*

As a result of the widespread cultivation of pepper in the Southeast Asian archipelago and Malabar (southern India), monopolization of pepper and effective price control through limitation of production was 'out of the question at any time'.[128] Why, then, did pepper prices not converge as much as to be expected?

While in the late sixteenth and early seventeenth centuries, competition among European and Asian traders drove up the price for pepper in Southeast Asia significantly (just like the case for cloves);[129] from the later 1640s on the average price was relatively stable, though increasing steadily from roughly fl. 0.10 in the 1650s to fl. 0.13 per *pond* by the end of the eighteenth century. This was a consequence of the fact that on the pepper markets the VOC did not pay a market price resulting from supply and demand, rather it paid a contract price negotiated with local potentates.[130] In return for military support, the Company paid a low price for pepper to the Sultans of Palembang (a contract originating in 1642) and Jambi (a contract originating in the 1680s) on Sumatra, the main supplier of pepper in the world at that time.[131] Furthermore, in the early 1680s, the VOC conquered Banten, Southeast Asia's main international pepper port, situated only 13 miles east of Batavia.[132] The newly installed Bantenese Sultan was forced to agree to a contract to deliver pepper only to the VOC for a relatively low price, again in return for political and military support. Malabar (south-western India) was another important area of pepper cultivation. In the early 1660s the Company launched an extensive military campaign there and managed to expel the Portuguese from this region. In the process, the Company forced many local sovereigns into involuntary pepper deliveries. Nevertheless, while certainly a dominant actor, the VOC was never able to completely control the Malabar Coast and deliveries remained variable. Especially after 1730, expansionist politics of one of the local kings[133] undermined the Company's power. As a result of this, as well as numerous other

128 J. Kathirithamby-Wells, *The British West Sumatran Presidency (1760–85): Problems of early colonial enterprise* (Kuala Lumpur: Penerbit Universiti Malaya, 1977) p. 180.

129 Also see: Meilink-Roelofsz, *Asian Trade*.

130 As De Vries, 'The Limits', p. 721, notes: 'relations with local rulers sensitively affected the acquisition price of pepper'.

131 In 1666, local chiefs on the west coast of Sumatra (Padang and Aceh) also bound themselves to the Dutch Company.

132 The pepper growing areas of Banten were actually situated in the Lampung region of southern Sumatra.

133 The king of Travancore.

factors,[134] the Company was not able to prevent a decline in pepper supply over the course of the eighteenth century. The declining supply drove up pepper prices in Europe in the second half of the eighteenth century. In fact, if the mark-up is taken as the relevant measure of price convergence, the trend is statistically insignificant (see Figure 2.9).[135]

A more or less similar story applies to tin. The prices for which the VOC purchased tin from the rulers of Palembang, Siam and Malacca were again based on contracts and power play and did not fluctuate much between 1660 and the late eighteenth century. Sale prices in Amsterdam, however, were not only determined by supply from the East Indies, but also by production in Europe. As prices in Amsterdam were as a result relatively low, and hardly any profits were

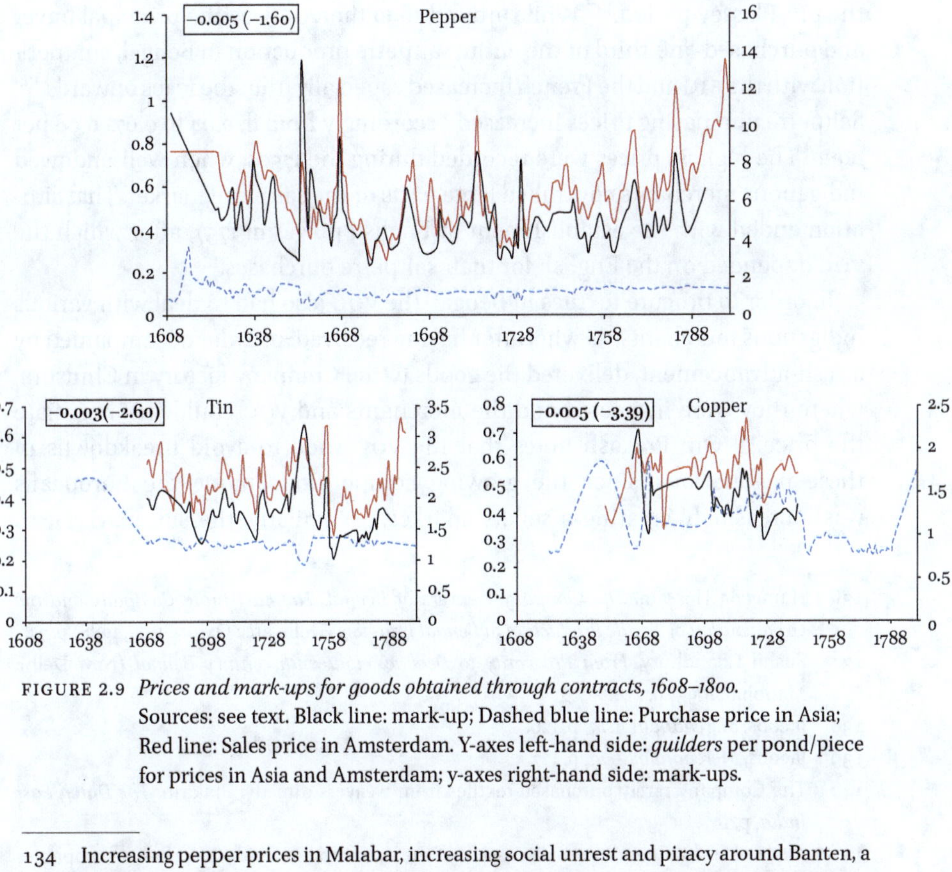

FIGURE 2.9 *Prices and mark-ups for goods obtained through contracts, 1608–1800.* Sources: see text. Black line: mark-up; Dashed blue line: Purchase price in Asia; Red line: Sales price in Amsterdam. Y-axes left-hand side: *guilders* per pond/piece for prices in Asia and Amsterdam; y-axes right-hand side: mark-ups.

134 Increasing pepper prices in Malabar, increasing social unrest and piracy around Banten, a shift from the cultivation of pepper to the production of tin by the Sultan of Palembang. See: Jacobs, *Merchant in Asia*, pp. 70–89

135 Trend: −0.0003; T-statistic: −4.10. Due to increased importance of the purchasing market.

made, tin was much more important in intra-Asian trade. The trends for both these products were, therefore, both weakly converging, despite the contracts. The situation was different again in the other, remaining commodity markets.

7.4 *Competitive Markets in India and China*

My examination of the commodity markets concludes with the markets on which European trading companies and Asian merchants did compete and mark-ups converged accordingly: i.e. those for porcelain, saltpetre, silk, tea and textiles. These were products acquired in Bengal, Surat, on the Coromandel Coast, and in Canton, China (see Map 2.1).

In Bengal, the VOC competed with the Danish, French, the Ostend trading company, and, most significantly, the British East India Company (EIC),[136] but perhaps even more so with Asian merchants who were dominant in Bengal in the pre-Plassey period.[137] While around 1690 the VOC was the principal buyer and purchased one-third of the entire saltpetre production in Bengal, competition with the EIC and the French increased especially from the 1730s onwards.[138] Saltpetre purchasing prices increased accordingly from fl. 0.04 to 0.07–0.08 per *pond*. The highest prices were recorded during the 1750s, when well-endowed indigenous merchants controlled large parts of the saltpetre market. That situation ended with the establishment of English power in 1757, after which the VOC depended on the English for their saltpetre purchases.[139]

In order to procure textiles in Bengal, the VOC also had to deal with various indigenous merchants,[140] who, after having received an order accompanied by a cash-advancement, delivered the goods to the Company factory in Chinsura, where they were inspected and the merchants and VOC could (re-)negotiate the price.[141] Om Prakash notes that the VOC tried to avoid breakdowns in these negotiations 'since the growing competition among the Europeans was increasingly creating a sellers' market'.[142] Similarly, the silk market was

136 Hameeda Hossain, *The Company Weavers of Bengal. The East India Company and the Organization of Textile Production in Bengal 1750–1813* (Delhi etc.: Oxford U.P., 1988) p. 74.

137 Sushil Chaudhury, *From Prosperity to Decline: eighteenth century Bengal* (New Delhi: Manohar, 1995) p. 228.

138 Jacobs, *Merchant in Asia*, p. 126.

139 Jacobs, *Merchant in Asia*, p. 127.

140 The Company rarely purchased textiles from weavers directly: Prakash, *The Dutch East India*, p. 107.

141 Also see Sushil Chaudhury's discussion of the *dadni* system: ibid., 'Merchants, companies and rulers: Bengal in the Eighteenth Century', *Journal of the Economic and Social History of the Orient* 31 (1988) pp. 74–109.

142 Prakash, *The Dutch East India*, p. 105.

extremely competitive, and European companies were unable to control the silk market, and thus silk prices.[143] Purchasing prices were relatively high, while competition with French and Italian silk in Europe meant that mark-ups were generally low, and these declined over the eighteenth century as the VOC lost its leading position to the English.

The Coromandel Coast and Surat were also important production areas of textiles, especially in the seventeenth century. These markets were also characterized by fierce competition and the important position held by middlemen. Various studies on the textile trade and manufacturing have all documented an increase in textile prices in Surat (north-western India),[144] Bengal and Coromandel,[145] while in Europe prices remained roughly constant or declined due to the competition among the European companies.[146] As a result, mark-ups on Indian textiles, arguably the most important of all trades, declined.

Initially the VOC purchased tea from Chinese junks arriving at Batavia, which led to the problem of inconsistent supply. As a result, the purchasing price paid for tea at the beginning of the eighteenth century could be higher than 3 guilders per *pond*.[147] After 1729 the VOC started to buy tea directly in Canton and purchasing prices declined from around fl. 1.30 to around fl. 0.50 per *pond* of *bohea* tea, and they would remain around that level for the rest of the eighteenth century.[148] In Canton, the Company again found itself in competition with the other European companies, as well as private European and Asian merchants, and had to pursue its business through Chinese intermediaries. As a consequence 'prices fluctuated according to the pressures of supply

---

143 Chaudhury, *From Prosperity*, p. 228.

144 For Surat also see: Ghulam Nadri, *Eighteenth-Century Gujarat: The Dynamics of Its Political Economy 1750–1800* (Leiden: Brill, 2008).

145 Chaudhuri, *The Trading World*; Prasannan Parthasarathi, *The Transition to a Colonial Economy: Weavers, Merchants and Kings in South India* (Cambridge: Cambridge U.P., 2001) p. 40; Kanakalatha Mukund, *The Trading World of the Tamil Merchant. Evolution of Merchant Capitalism in the Coromandel* (Chennai: Orient Longman Ltd., 1999) pp. 81–82; S. Hariharan, *Cotton Textiles and Corporate Buyers in Cottonpolis: a Study of Purchase and Prices in Gujarat 1600–1800* (New Delhi: Manak 2002) pp. 298–305.

146 Bishnupriya Gupta, 'Competition and control in the market for textiles: Indian weavers and the English East India Company in the Eighteenth Century', in: Giorgio Riello and Tirthankar Roy (eds.), *How India Clothed the World. The world of South Asian Textiles, 1500–1850* (Leiden: Brill, 2009) p. 286.

147 George B. Souza, *The Survival of Empire. Portuguese trade and society in China and the South China Sea 1630–1754* (Cambridge: Cambridge U.P., 1986) pp. 142 and 145–151.

148 Glamann, *Dutch-Asiatic*, p. 225; Liu Yong, *The Dutch East India Company's Tea Trade with China 1757–1781* (Leiden: Brill, 2006) pp. 212–222.

and demand'.[149] However, as purchasing prices were stable in China in the long run, most of the decline in the mark-up was the result of the spectacular decline in European prices. This price decline was ushered in by a spectacular increase in annual supply: a 100-fold leap from a meagre 30,000 *pond* in the early 1700s[150] to more than 3,000,000 *pond* by the end of the eighteenth century.[151] The fees paid in Canton were based in part on the size of ships and in part on a fixed sum charged for all ships regardless of their size (the 'Emperor's Present'). This system favoured bigger ships (i.e. those sailing in the Euro-Asian trade) and since these charges held no connection with the value of the cargo, the fees declined over the eighteenth century relative to inflation.[152] These duties amounted to around 2 to 4 percent of the value of the cargo.[153] Tariffs in India also seem to have been relatively low before 1750.[154]

Thus, in these cases the VOC competed both with the other European companies and with merchants based around the Indian Ocean. It procured products often through local intermediaries and had to pay a (relatively small) export tax. As the total trade volumes, as well as competition, increased in the eighteenth century, mark-ups fell (as can be seen in Figure 2.10).

8 Conclusion

In this chapter I have examined the notion of 'globalization' in the early modern period, and more specifically what has come to be known as 'hard' globalization in recent years. O'Rourke and Williamson's statements have been put to the test with new price data from the Dutch-Asiatic trade.

149 Paul A. van Dyke, *The Canton Trade: Life and enterprise on the China Coast, 1700–1845* (Hong Kong: Hong Kong U.P., 2006) p. 15. Liu Yong describes how the VOC used various Chinese merchants as middlemen in the purchases of tea in order to create some measure of competition; *The Dutch East India Company's Tea Trade with China 1757–1781* (Leiden: Brill, 2006) pp. 74–89.

150 VOC auctions: VOC 4584–4597.

151 Yong, *The Dutch*, pp. 126–128. See, p. 130 for a dramatic decline in the gross profits on tea sales in the second half of the 18th century.

152 Van Dyke, *The Canton Trade*, pp. 10–11, 103–115.

153 Jacobs, *Merchant in Asia*, p. 187.

154 Suggested by B. Blachandran and S. Subrahmanyam, 'On the History of Globalization and India: Concepts, Measures and Debates', in J. Assayag and C. J. Fuller (eds.) *Globalizing India: Perspectives from Below* (London: Anthem Press, 2005) pp. 17–46; cited in Flynn and Giraldez, 'Born again', p. 364.

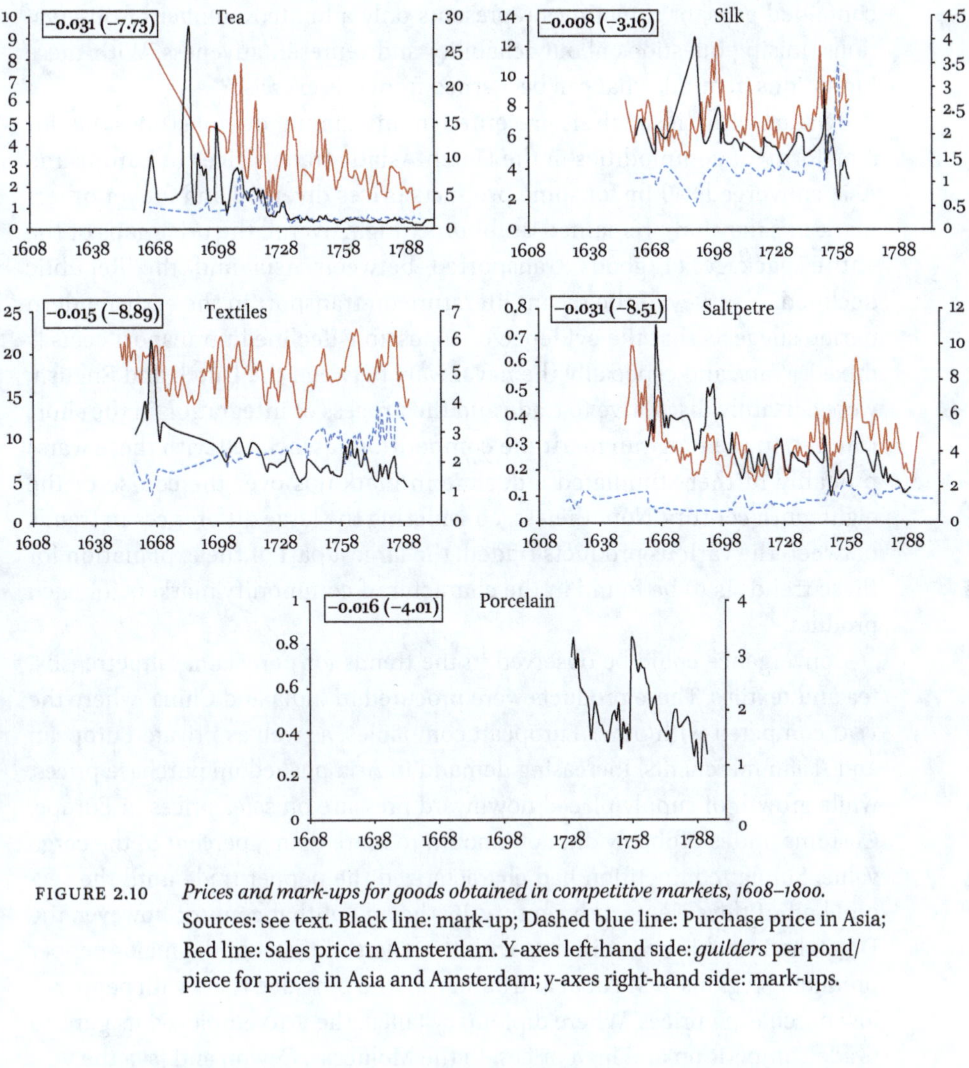

FIGURE 2.10 *Prices and mark-ups for goods obtained in competitive markets, 1608–1800.* Sources: see text. Black line: mark-up; Dashed blue line: Purchase price in Asia; Red line: Sales price in Amsterdam. Y-axes left-hand side: *guilders* per pond/piece for prices in Asia and Amsterdam; y-axes right-hand side: mark-ups.

The discussion of Asian prices and mark-ups between 1450 and 1660 points out that the entrance of the VOC (and the other European companies) in Asian markets possibly led to an initial phase of price convergence. However, power play by the Company hindered the continuation of this trend in later periods.

The main part of my analysis has focussed on the Dutch-Asiatic trade in the period 1608–1800. It examined whether we can find evidence of the process of globalization taking place, as suggested by price convergence, in this particular period and for this particular trade route. This is not the final word in this debate. Evidence from other companies and routes may suggest different patterns, while the data series presented here, despite efforts to the contrary, still contained gaps, or sometimes represents only a limited number of observations, raising questions about reliability and representativeness. With these limitations in mind, what can be learned from this exercise?

To start with, the analysis presented in this chapter demonstrates that for a majority of commodities in the Dutch-Asiatic trade, prices in Europe and Asia converged. While for some products prices diverged and for yet others mark-ups may have remained 'stubbornly high', overall the price gaps of the entire package of goods transported between Asia and the Republic declined. A survey of the recent literature on transport in the early modern period suggests that the evidence on a possible decline in transport costs is mixed. Wars, and especially the naval wars between the Dutch and English, were certainly disruptive to trade and the process of integration in the short run. Yet, in the long run maritime competition (associated with these wars) probably further stimulated a decline in mark-ups over the course of the eighteenth century. Nonetheless, considering the large differences in trends between the various products traded, the largest part of the explanation for these trends is to be found in the character of commodity markets for each product.

Convergence could be observed in the trends for porcelain, saltpetre, silk, tea and textiles. These products were procured in India and China, where the VOC competed with other European companies, as well as private European and Asian merchants. Increasing demand in Asia pushed up purchase prices, while growth of supply placed downward pressure on sales prices in Europe. Customs duties probably did not amount to more than 5 percent of the cargo value. Similar competition had characterized the pepper trade until the second half of the seventeenth century. By the end of that century, however, the Dutch had established contracts with the rulers of many of the major pepper producing regions in Malabar and Sumatra, who provided them with pepper at low purchasing prices. Where diplomacy failed, the VOC employed its guns to evade competition and high prices. In the Moluccas, Ceylon and Java the VOC established itself as a military and political power and gained complete control of the purchasing markets. The VOC was a reluctant imperialist, however, as an extensive military and administrative apparatus dramatically increased overhead costs. Where it did exert such power, it tried to make up for the expense by keeping purchasing prices as low as possible through control over both production and trade.

The discussion above is summarized in Table 2.5. Per product I have noted the average mark-up in the seventeenth and the eighteenth centuries and whether the trend is significant and whether it shows convergence or divergence. Column 5 indicates to which extent prices in the purchasing market were determined by competition (supply and demand), contracts, or complete control of the market.[155] Column 6 shows whether the VOC was the sole supplier of a product in Europe or whether sales prices there were determined by competition.

One can thus conclude that neither claims that the Euro-Asian trade remained effectively monopolized before the nineteenth century, nor the suggestion that besides the monopoly spices all other goods were bought in competitive markets, are entirely accurate. Evidence on early price convergence suggests that the entrance of the VOC (and perhaps the other north-western European companies) in the Asian markets initially had the expected result of rising prices there. Subsequent power struggles and colonialism, however, go a long way in explaining the lack of integration in some markets in the late seventeenth and eighteenth centuries.

Rather than stubbornly high transport costs, tariffs or wars, it was the extent of VOC control over the commodity markets in Asia that determined trends in price convergence. Various scholars have suggested that in the nineteenth century colonialism became one the main drivers of economic globalization as 'empires increased trade by lowering transaction costs and by establishing trade policies that promoted trade within empires.'[156] De Vries also finds that most of the price convergence in the nineteenth century was limited to areas 'brought within colonial and imperial trading structures.'[157] However, in the age of mercantilism, colonialism was in the hands of private companies that had maximizing profits as their most important goal. Territorial control was a means to capture rents and it thereby hindered the process of commodity market integration.

155 Regarding copper, the Dutch were the only buyers of Japanese copper at Deshima, and thus the only seller on the European market. Based on exclusive contracts, purchasing prices in Japan were low, but since Japanese copper had to compete with Swedish, Hungarian and Norwegian copper on the Amsterdam market, selling prices were also low, resulting in low mark-ups in this trade. On the other hand, demand was high for Japanese copper in Asian markets, and in intra-Asian trade copper made a handsome profit, see: Ryuto Shimada, *The Intra-Asian Trade in Japanese Copper by the Dutch East India Company during the Eighteenth Century* (Leiden: Brill, 2006).

156 Kris J. Mitchener and Marc Weidenmier, 'Trade and empire', *NBER Working Paper 13765* (Cambridge 2008) p. 2. Also see: Niall Ferguson, 'no organization in history has done more to promote the free movement of goods, capital and labor than the British empire in the nineteenth and early twentieth centuries', in: Ferguson, *Empire*, p. xxi; Rodrik, *The Globalization Paradox*, p. 26: 'imperialism was a mechanism for imposing trade-friendly rules'.

157 De Vries, 'The limits', p. 719, n. 36.

TABLE 2.5 *Dutch–Asiatic trade, 1600–1800.*

Product	Mean mark-up 17th (N)	Mean mark-up 18th (N)	Trend (entire period)[158]	Determinant of purchasing price	Determinant of sales price
Cinnamon	10.3 (44)	15.9 (100)	Divergence	Control	Monopoly
Cloves	16.1 (63)	13.6 (100)	Convergence	Control	Monopoly[159]
Nutmeg	38.0 (46)	50.2 (82)	None	Control	Monopoly
Mace	13.7 (82)	15.4 (89)	Divergence	Control	Monopoly
Pepper	5.3 (49)	4.9 (64)	None	Contract	Competition
Tin	1.8 (9)	1.7 (51)	Convergence	Contract	Competition
Copper	1.6 (6)	1.3 (30)	Convergence	Contract	Competition
Sugar	9.2 (14)	4.5 (73)	Convergence	Control	Competition
Cotton	3.5 (12)	4.2 (45)	Divergence	Control	Competition
Indigo	2.6 (6)	2.8 (51)	Divergence	Control	Competition
Coffee	–	5.7 (87)	Divergence	Control	Competition
Saltpetre	5.9 (28)	3.2 (53)	Convergence	Competition	Competition
Textiles	3.5 (11)	1.9 (50)	Convergence	Competition	Competition
Silk	2.5 (8)	1.7 (35)	Convergence	Competition	Competition
Tea	5.4 (4)	2.9 (82)	Convergence	Competition	Competition
Porcelain	–	2.0 (56)	Convergence	Competition	Competition

Sources: see text.

Following the literature on colonization, the extent of colonial control was determined by a combination of initial geographic conditions (the area where specific crops could grow),[160] the strength of indigenous institutions (or the level of political centralisation),[161] as well as chance. In regions that grew rare commodities, such as the Moluccas and Ceylon, colonization was a means for establishing a monopoly. In these areas, the effects of globalization could go beyond its impact on supply and demand. Production areas of most other commodities were too extensive to achieve an efficient monopoly, and in order to limit overhead costs associated with territorial control the VOC tried to establish contracts with local potentates in many other areas. In

158 Trend in mark-up.

159 After 1770; competition.

160 Engerman and Sokoloff, 'History Lessons'.

161 Acemoglu et al., 'The colonial origins'.

south-western India (Malabar) and Java the VOC extended its power for strategic reasons. In regions with strong political centralisation, such as Mughal India, Qing China and Tokugawa Japan, VOC power (and thus its probable effects) remained limited. The extent of colonial power not only affected the process of globalization, but also what the effects of this globalization would be for the economies involved. This will be the subject of the remainder of this book.

CHAPTER 3

Prices and Consumption Patterns

1 Introduction

What were the consequences of this globalization for the economies of Europe and Asia? O'Rourke, Williamson and their co-authors' works started out as a contribution to that issue. Some scholars, like Immanuel Wallerstein and Andre Gunder Frank, emphasized the importance of long-distance trade in the period between 1500 and 1800 in the rise in global inequality, claiming that intercontinental trade led to capital accumulation and intercontinental specialization.[1] While the periphery concentrated on the production of primary goods, resulting in low levels of per capita income, the European core could shift part of its production into more productive sectors of the economy, such as manufacturing, thereby pushing Europe towards industrialization and higher standards of living.[2] Others have downplayed the importance of intercontinental trade, for example Patrick O'Brien, who coined the catchy phrase that 'for the economic growth of the core, the periphery was peripheral,'[3] as he estimated that the contribution of intercontinental trade to Western European GNP was at the most 1 percent, and to gross investment at the most 10 percent.[4]

O'Rourke and Williamson are in the same boat as O'Brien, since they suggest that as commodities in intercontinental trade before the nineteenth century were non-competing and luxuries rather than necessities in Europe: 'the vast majority of the "exotic" imports from Asia and the Americas were out of reach of any but the rich.'[5] Therefore this trade did not influence resource allocation and factor prices in Europe and, consequentially, had no 'significant impact on the structure of production or on economic welfare.'[6]

Recent research has re-emphasized the importance of international trade for Europe. Acemoglu et al. found that intercontinental trade induced institutional changes that were central to economic growth in Western Europe between 1500 and 1800.[7] At the same time, Robert Allen has argued that trade led to

1 Wallerstein, *The Modern World*; ibid., *The Capitalist World*; Frank, *World Accumulation*.
2 Also see the discussion by O'Brien, 'European Economic Development', pp. 1–3.
3 O'Brien, 'European Economic Development', p. 9.
4 O'Brien, 'European Economic Development', p. 5.
5 O'Rourke and Williamson, 'After Columbus', p. 434.
6 Ibid., 'When did globalisation', p. 46.
7 Acemoglu et al., 'The Rise'.

 | DOI 10.1163/9789004299665_004

urbanization and larger cities as it offered job opportunities in certain trade hubs. Because larger cities have a more refined division of labour than smaller rural towns, urbanization led to greater efficiency and higher wages, which provided the crucial incentive for industrialization.[8] Research on consumption patterns has produced evidence of the relatively widespread availability and consumption of, for example, coffee and tea in Europe in the eighteenth century.[9] The availability of these products not only raised living standards[10] but also 'enlarged the aspiration to consume and increased the incentive to work and earn high income'[11] thereby inducing a revolution in work ethics.[12]

While many scholars have thus focussed on the impact of intercontinental trade on Europe, equally important is the question of what the consequences were for the various economies of Asia. Findlay and O'Rourke suggest that in China and India the increased inflow of silver, when it did not lead to inflation, had positive effects on commercialization and economic growth.[13] Similarly, O'Rourke et al. suggest that 'an alternative Smithian "vent for surplus" perspective assumes that resources in many 18th century economies were unemployed, or at least, underemployed, and that trade could bring these resources into productive (or more productive) employment at little or no opportunity costs.'[14] Yet, De Vries observes as 'Asia is large and populous', additional European demand for Asian products may have only marginally affected these industries.[15]

However, described in Chapter 2, the effects of this early modern long-distance trade go beyond neo-classical mechanisms of supply and demand in a free market. Where globalization was followed (or hindered) by colonialism (mercantile[16] or otherwise) and monopolization, the effects may have been quite profound. Thus, the effects of what should be considered

8 Allen, *The British Industrial*; ibid. 'Progress and poverty'.

9 McCants, 'Poor consumers', ibid., 'Exotic goods'.

10 Jonathan Hersh and Hans-Joachim Voth, 'Sweet Diversity: Colonial Goods and Welfare Gains from Trade after 1492', *Mimeo* 2011.

11 Allen, *The British Industrial*, p. 22.

12 De Vries, 'The Industrial Revolution'; ibid., *The Industrious Revolution.*

13 Finlay and O'Rourke, *Power and Plenty*, pp. 219–221: following the theory: M (money supply) = kPY. If P (prices) did not increase: k (commercialization) and/or Y (income) did.

14 O'Rourke et al., 'Trade and Empire,', p. 10.

15 De Vries, 'The limits', p. 729.

16 See: Ola Olsson, 'On the Institutional Legacy of Mercantilist and Imperialist Colonialism', *Working Papers in Economics* 247 (March 2007); ibid., 'On the democratic legacy of colonialism', *Journal of Comparative Economics* 37 (2009) pp. 534–551; Potter et al., *Geographies of Development*, pp. 58–73.

'soft' globalization, i.e. when there was no clear-cut evidence of price convergence, were perhaps not so soft at all.

In this chapter, I will make a start with the assessment of the effects of the Dutch East India Company's trade and its related business on living standards on the edges of the Indian Ocean. For various reasons, explained in Chapter 1, the analysis concentrates on Bengal, the Cape, Ceylon and Java. This analysis of living standards links up with the Great Divergence debate, where the controversy over differences in living standards between Europe and Asia holds centre stage. One thing that has become clear from the debate thus far is that evidence about Asian standards of living is generally thin and contradictory. In this study, I intend to make improvements to the evidence available on living standards. Generally one can discern three dimensions when considering standards of living: income, education and health. In the next section, Section 2, the most commonly used measures of living standards are discussed. Most of these measures suffer from problems in terms of data availability or a narrow focus on just one of the dimensions of living standards. In that sense, real wages have some crucial advantages, as wage and price data are available for a wide range of countries for long periods of time, and may contain information on all three elements pertaining to standards of living. From the discussion of the real-wage methodology in Section 3 it becomes clear that the creation of a simple but accurate consumption basket is crucial to the calculation of comparative real wages. For this reason, the evidence on consumption patterns in pre-modern Bengal, the Cape, Ceylon and Java is reviewed in Section 4, before baskets are created that allow for international and intertemporal comparisons. Section 5 then develops the price data and discusses its limitations and representativeness. In Section 6 relative price trends are discussed, and concluding remarks are given in Section 7.

2 Measuring Living Standards

Pomeranz rightly questions what measure is the most relevant to gauge and compare living standards in the past:

> How are we to decide which differences constitute being 'ahead in standard of living'? Why emphasize Europe's probable edge in housing, rather than, say the remarkable supply of safe drinking water in much of Japan, China, and Southeast Asia?[17]

17 Pomeranz, *The Great Divergence*, p. 36.

The body of literature dealing with living standards is vast and many different measures of the standard of living have been put forward. I will discuss the most important of these, before turning to an in-depth discussion of the method adopted in this book, i.e. that of real wages.

GDP per capita is still the most widely used measure of living standards,[18] as well as 'the most acceptable measure of the overall economy and productive capacity'.[19] A number of studies have shown a positive relationship between per capita income and other related aspects of the standard of living, such as life expectancy, infant mortality, education, and, as well, overall 'life satisfaction'.[20] Yet there are a number of problems with GDP per head estimates. First, while improved estimates of GDP per capita for England and Holland are now being extended back to the Middle Ages,[21] such data are relatively difficult to obtain and are subject to large margins of error, especially for the period before 1870.[22] Second, GDP requires a variety of assumptions in order to capture non-market income, such as the work of spouses within the household or food grown for own consumption. Additional problems arise with 'black market' activities, all of which are often substantial in pre-industrial economies.[23] Third, because pre-industrial and developing countries are often highly unequal in their social composition, estimates of average incomes give little information about the standard of living of the majority of the population.[24]

18 Robert C. Allen, 'Real Wages in Europe and Asia: A First Look at the Long-term Patterns', in: Robert C. Allen, Tommy Bengtsson, and Martin Dribe (eds.), *Living Standards in the Past New Perspectives on Well-Being in Asia and Europe* (Oxford: Oxford University Press, 2005) pp. 157–185.

19 Jörg Baten, Debin Ma, Stephen Morgan and Qing Wang, 'Evolution of Living Standards and Human Capital in China in 18–20th centuries: Evidences from real wages, age-heaping and anthrometrics', *Explorations in Economic History* 47 (2010) p. 248.

20 Angus Deaton, 'Income, Health, and Well-Being around the World: Evidence from the Gallup World Poll', *Journal of Economic Perspectives* 22 (2008) p. 69; Charles Kenny, 'Why are We Worried About Income? Nearly Everything that Matters is Converging', *World Development* 33 (2005) p. 1.

21 Stephen Broadberry, Bruce Campbell, Alexander Klein, Mark Overton, and Bas van Leeuwen, 'British Economic Growth, 1270–1870: An output-based approach' *Mimeo* (2012); Jan Luiten van Zanden and Bas van Leeuwen, 'Persistent but not consistent: the growth of national income in Holland, 1347–1807', *Explorations in Economic History* 49 (2012) pp. 119–130.

22 Suleyman Ozmucur and Sevket Pamuk, 'Real Wages and Standards of Living in the Ottoman Empire, 1489–1914', *Journal of Economic History* 62 (2002) p. 294.

23 Stanley L. Engerman, 'The Standard of Living Debate in International Perspective: Measures and Indicators', in: R. Steckel and R. Floud (eds.), *Health and Welfare during Industrialization* (Chicago: University of Chicago Press, 1997) p. 27; Baten et al., 'Evolution', p. 4.

24 Allen, 'Real Wages', p. 158.

Finally, although numerous studies have found a positive link between income and other aspects of the quality of life, this relationship is indirect and does not apply generally.[25] Due to a high degree of social inequality, large parts of a population can be denied decent schooling or healthcare, despite the relatively high GDP per capita of the states in which they abide.

These issues have led to the search for alternative measures of living standards. Consumption of sugar, tea, coffee and other 'everyday luxuries' provide information about the extent to which people were able to buy goods that went beyond ensuring subsistence. Pomeranz suggests that Chinese sugar consumption in 1750 exceeded that in continental Europe, even in 1800.[26] However, such estimates are dependent on other estimates – of trade, production and population – that are of questionable reliability, and most of the luxury consumption may have been driven by elites, thus telling us little about living standards of the masses. Probate inventories also contain much information about luxury consumption and wealth accumulation. As private probate inventories are drawn up by a notary, who did not work without pay, such lists again generally pertain to the better-off families. However, Anne McCants and Johan Fourie have looked at probate inventories drawn up by orphanages after the death of parents that are more likely to reflect the poorer parts of society. Fourie has used such inventories to show that farmers in the Cape Colony during the eighteenth century were remarkably wealthy, also in comparison with north-western Europe.[27] Such sources have yet to be presented for most parts of the non-western world – if at all available.

Following new growth theory, which claims that the formation of human capital is one of the main determinants of long-term economic growth,[28] some studies have focused on measuring levels of human capital. Traditionally, research looked at literacy rates that were estimated by looking at the share of the population able to sign legal documents or marriage registers. A more recent method uses book production, which 'measures the size of the market for books and therefore represents actual use of reading skills',[29] and a recent

25 Kenny, 'Why Are We', p. 2.

26 Pomeranz, *The Great Divergence*, p. 122.

27 Johan Fourie, 'The remarkable wealth of the Dutch Cape Colony: measurements from eighteenth-century probate inventories', *Economic History Review* 66 (2013) pp. 419–448; McCants, 'Poor consumers'.

28 Oded Galor, 'From Stagnation to Growth: Unified Growth Theory', in: P. Aghion and S. Durlauf (eds.), *Handbook of Economic Growth* (Amsterdam 2005) pp. 172–293; Glaeser et al., 'Do institutions'.

29 Jörg Baten and Jan Luiten van Zanden, 'Book production and the onset of modern economic growth', *Journal of Economic Growth* 13 (2008) p. 221.

study has shown that book production per capita correlates with both literacy and per capita GDP growth.[30] Another technique is to quantify numeracy by looking at the use of 'age heaping' in population censuses or legal documents: poorly educated people in the past tended to report their age in 'attractive' numbers, for example ending in a 5 or a 0, whilst better educated individuals were more likely to report their exact age.[31] Numeracy is an indispensable skill for many commercial and technical activities and is therefore an important indicator of human capital. A strong relationship has been found between age heaping and illiteracy. An obvious weakness of all these approaches (when examining living standards) is, however, that they do not capture the aspect of health.

Anthropometric methods (the study of heights, for example) have therefore been employed extensively in the last three decades since they are good indicators of biological components of welfare, such as health, life expectancy and the quality of nutrition.[32] Height is positively affected by the quantity and quality of nutritional inputs, whilst disease and physical activities absorb nutrients, thus affecting growth negatively. Early studies have demonstrated a strong correlation between height and per capita income, and between height and mortality.[33] Average height is particularly sensitive to nutritional deficit and therefore a good measure for observing economic inequality and, thus, the standard of living of the poorer classes in societies.[34] Another advantage is that data on heights can be found in a wide variety of sources that go far back in time and are available for more places than the data needed for estimating per capita income.[35] Even in the absence of consistent population data, authors have made claims regarding height that were based on observations of contemporaries: Reid, for example, suggests that Southeast Asians were roughly as tall as Europeans since travellers declared them as 'being of "average" height'.[36] Height, however, does not measure the educational aspect of the standard of living and therefore complements, rather than substitutes for other welfare

30 Ibid., p. 235.

31 Brian A'Hearn, Jörg Baten, and Dorothee Crayen, 'Quantifying Quantitative Literacy: Age Heaping and the History of Human Capital', *Journal of Economic History* 69 (2009) 783–808; Baten et al., 'Evolution', p. 14.

32 Richard H. Steckel, 'Stature and the Standard of Living', *Journal of Economic Literature*, 33 (1995) 1903–1940. Baten et al., 'Evolution', p. 6.

33 Engerman, 'The Standard of Living', p. 35.

34 Baten et al., 'Evolution', p. 6; Steckel, 'Stature', p. 1918.

35 Engerman, 'The Standard of Living', p. 34.

36 Anthony Reid, 'The Origins of Southeast Asian Poverty', in: W. E. Willmot (ed.) *Scholarship and Society in Southeast Asia* (Christchurch, 1979) pp. 33–49.

indicators. And, in a recent paper, Howard Bodenhorn et al. have shown that many heights studies suffer from serious issues concerning sample-selection bias.[37] Another way to look at the health aspect of standard of living is by looking at life expectancies.[38] For many areas or locations data for such estimates from before the twentieth century are scarce;[39] they are either based on genealogies, an exercise fraught with serious difficulties, or are available for only a few villages, raising issues of representativeness.

The Human Development Index (HDI) has become a fashionable welfare indicator in recent years, because it captures the three different dimensions of standard of living – education, income and health – in a single index.[40] Education is dependent on both enrolment and literacy rates; income is measured by log GDP per capita; and health is measured by life expectancy at birth. The three components are given equal weight and have a value between zero and one, as does HDI, which makes international comparisons possible. The obvious advantage of the HDI is that it captures three important welfare indicators in one number that can be easily compared across countries. One shortcoming is that the HDI does not provide any indication about the distribution of welfare within countries. Furthermore, the equal weights for the three components have attracted criticism and can, indeed, be considered arbitrary.[41]

A general problem of these methods for historical studies is that they are dependent on data that are often unavailable for the period before 1800 or suffer from a narrow focus on only one of the dimensions of the standard of living. Compared with the methods discussed above, focussing on wages and prices has a number of advantages. The data are available for a much wider range of countries and go much further back in time. Also, real wages can be calculated at the individual household level for ordinary workers. Furthermore, wage and price data can contain information about all three of the elements (income,

---

37 Howard Bodenhorn, Timothy W. Guinnane, and Thomas A. Mroz, 'Sample-selection Bias in the Historical Heights Literature', *Mimeo* (2012).

38 William Lavely and R. Bin Wong, 'Revising the Malthusian Narrative: The Comparative Study of Population Dynamics in the Late Imperial China', *Journal of Asian Studies* 57 (1998) pp. 714–648.

39 The big exception is of course England, for which E. A. Wrigley and R. S. Schofield have conducted meticulous research: E. A. Wrigley and R.S. Schofield, *The Population History of England 1541–1871. A Reconstruction* (London: Edward Arnold, 1981).

40 Nicholas Crafts, 'The Human Development Index 1870–1999: Some Revised Estimates', *European Review of Economic History* 6 (2002) pp. 395–405.

41 Richard H. Steckel and Roderick Floud, 'Introduction', in: ibid. (eds.) *Health and Welfare during Industrialization* (Chicago: University of Chicago Press, 1997) p. 12.

health and education) contributing to the standard of living.[42] At the same time, using real wages as a method of measuring living standards does have drawbacks. These are are discussed in Chapter 4.

3 Calculating Real Wages

For the reasons discussed in the previous section, many studies rely on real wages – the purchasing power of an labourer (often unskilled) – as an indicator of the economic well-being of a large part of a population. After pioneering work by, for example, Thorold Rogers and Auguste Hanauer in the late nineteenth century,[43] important advances were made in the 1930s by members of the International Scientific Committee on Price History. These scholars had been compiling databases of wages and prices for European cities from the Middle Ages onwards and, as a result, the data on Europe are relatively complete. These early real wage studies showed that European real incomes declined between the fifteenth and the late eighteenth centuries and that only in the early twentieth century did (English) real wages surpass their late medieval levels.[44] These studies suggested that there was no economic growth in early modern Europe, which seemingly had become stuck in a Malthusian cycle until the Industrial Revolution.

In the case of Britain, workers' living standards during the Industrial Revolution became a particular subject of debate.[45] While the participants in

42 The health aspect is addressed by standardizing consumption on the basis of kcal, while the educational aspect is covered by the wage differentials between skilled and unskilled workers.

43 J. E. T. Rogers, *A History of Agriculture and Prices in England.* 7 vols. (Oxford: Clarendon Press: 1866–1892); A. C. Hanauer, *Etudes economiques sur l'Alsace, ancienne et moderne* (Strasbourg: Hagemann, Librairie. 1878).

44 See E. H. Phelps-Brown and S. V. Hopkins, 'Seven Centuries of the Prices of Consumables, compared with Builders' Wage-rates', *Economica* 22 (1956) pp. 195–206.

45 See for example M. W. Flinn, 'Trends in Real Wages, 1750–1850', *Economic History Review*, 27 (1974) pp. 395–413. P. H. Lindert and J. G. Williamson, 'English Workers' Living Standards During the Industrial Revolution: A New Look', *Economic History Review* 36 (1983) pp. 1–25; Charles F. Feinstein, 'Pessimism perpetuated: real wages and the standard of living in Britain during and after the Industrial Revolution', *Journal of Economic History* 58 (1998) pp. 625–58; Gregory Clark 'The condition of the working class in England, 1209–2004', *Journal of Political Economy* 11 (2005) pp. 1307–1340; and Robert C. Allen, 'Pessimism preserved: Real wages in the British Industrial Revolution', *Oxford University Department of Economics Working Paper* 314 (2007).

this debate have all used real wages as an indicator of living standards, they still come to very different conclusions. It thus became clear that (relatively small) differences in methodology can lead to significantly different conclusions. Most of these differences stem from dissimilarities in consumer price indices (CPI), which require a basket of goods reflecting the actual consumption pattern of the workers. Calculating a CPI over time gives rise to index number problems as changes in relative price differences between complementary goods and the introduction of new goods (e.g. due to technological progress or international trade) can cause overstatement or understatement of price increases. Contributors to the British standard of living debate have used different formulae (Laspeyres, Paasche, geometric, etc.) to construct their indices, employed different weightings (and/or shifting weights) and used different price series, or included different products, in their consumption baskets.

The Laspeyres index tends to overstate inflation as it does not take into account that consumers will substitute more expensive goods with less expensive ones. The Paasche index understates inflation because it does not reflect the reduction in consumer welfare due to substitution, while a geometric index allows consumption to vary with price. The Laspeyres index, in which the quantity of each good is specified, is preferred because the consumption basket can then be taken to represent the level of subsistence. For a Paasche Index one needs data on product quantities on a yearly basis, which is often unavailable. Allen has shown that the differences between the Laspeyres index and geometric indices are small.[46]

The introduction of new goods likewise influences price indices. William Nordhaus has demonstrated that in the case of lighting, traditional price indices (that do not take into account new products as a result of technological change) dramatically overstate the true increase in prices.[47] Gregory Clark did include new products in his CPI for England that indeed led to a lower price index and, thus, higher real wages during the early Industrial Revolution, when technological change was rapid.[48] However, the introduction of new goods requires extremely detailed budget information.[49] While this is now perhaps

46 Allen, 'The Great Divergence'; ibid., 'Pessimism preserved'. Feinstein also suggests that the Laspeyres index is the most suitable procedure for measuring long-term changes in living standards; 'Pessimism perpetuated', p. 634.

47 William D. Nordhaus, 'Do Real Output and Real Wage Measures Capture Reality? The History of Light Suggests Not', in: Robert J. Gordon and Timothy F. Bresnahan (eds.), *The Economics of New Goods* (Chicago: University of Chicago Press, 1997) pp. 29–66.

48 Clark, 'The condition'.

49 Allen, 'Pessimism Preserved'.

possible for England, such information is unavailable for most other countries in the world. This procedure is thus not feasible for comparing historical living standards across the globe before the nineteenth century.

Even if one decides not to introduce new products into the price index, it has to be determined what products to include and what proportion each item takes up in the basket of goods. This has differed substantially across various studies. For example, in the basket constructed by Clark the share of spending on carbohydrates is 27 percent,[50] while, for the same country and time period, this share is 39 percent in the basket compiled by Feinstein. Furthermore, Feinstein used three sets of quantity weights to 'reflect changes in the pattern of consumption.'[51] Again, these weights are often based on detailed household budget information, and such information is not abundantly available for most parts of the world.

Allen proposed, therefore, a consumer basket based on a standard amount of caloric and protein intake, as well as some other basic commodities.[52] The ambitions of his methodology were twofold. First, to measure not only the development of wages over time (as most studies set out to do), but also to create an absolute benchmark, in the form of a 'subsistence basket', to find out if workers could afford the expenditures needed for the subsistence of themselves and their families. In this way a kind of absolute 'poverty line' was introduced in the literature of economic history that represented something like the contemporary World Bank Poverty Line (currently US $1.25 per day).[53] By expressing annual wages in the quantity of subsistence baskets that could be bought, wages were turned into an absolute measure of welfare.

The second aim of the Allen method was to use these 'absolute' real wages to make international and inter-temporal comparisons. Standardized baskets provide a minimum amount of calories per day, mainly from the cheapest available carbohydrate in a specific region, e.g. rice in many parts of Asia and oats in north-western Europe. The diet also includes small quantities of meat or fish and butter or oil, and provides at least the recommended daily intake of protein. In addition, some non-food items such as cloth and fuel are included in baskets.[54] Substitutions are permitted between complementary products,

50 Clark, 'The condition'.

51 Feinstein, 'Pessimism perpetuated', p. 634.

52 Allen, 'The great divergence'.

53 Robert C. Allen, Tommy E. Murphy and Eric B. Schneider, 'The Colonial Origins of the Divergence in the Americas: A Labor Market Approach', *Journal of Economic History* 72 (2012) pp. 863–894.

54 Allen et al., 'Wages, prices', pp. 19–20.

which makes it possible to allow for differences in national tastes, cuisines and climates. This approach for calculating comparative real wages is now widely accepted as a robust measure of welfare and has recently been employed in a range of studies for various regions across the globe. Table 3.1 gives an example of a standardized basket providing over 1940 kcal with wheat as the main staple (used for example for the Cape Colony).

Because of the relatively widespread availability of wage and price data and Allen's innovations, there has been a surge in comparative real wage studies over the past decade.[55]

TABLE 3.1 *Barebones subsistence basket at the Cape.*[56]

	Unit	Quantity per person per year	Nutrients per kg		Nutrients per day	
			Calories	Grams of Protein	Calories	Grams of Protein
Wheat	kg	179	3400	132	1667	65
Beans	kg	20	3383	213	185	12
Meat	kg	5	2500	200	34	3
Butter	kg	3	7268	7	60	0
Soap	kg	1.3	–	–	–	–
Candles	kg	1.3	–	–	–	–
Lamp oil	litre	1.3	–	–	–	–
Cotton	m^2	3	–	–	–	–
Fuel	MBTU	3	–	–	–	–
Total	–	–	–	–	1946	86

Sources: Based on Allen et al., 'Wages, prices'; see also De Zwart, 'Real wages'.

55 Allen, 'India', Allen et al., 'Wages, prices'; Allen et al., 'The Colonial Origins'; Leticia Arroyo Abad, Elwyn Davies and Jan Luiten van Zanden, 'Between Conquest and Independence: Real wages and demographic change in Spanish America, 1530–1820', *Explorations in Economic History* 49 (2012) pp. 149–166; Jean-Pascal Bassino and Debin Ma, 'Japanese Unskilled Wages in International Perspective, 1741–1913', *Research in Economic History* 23 (2006) pp. 229–248; Ewout Frankema and Marlous van Waijenburg, 'Structural Impediments to African Growth? New Evidence from Real Wages in British Africa, 1880–1965', *Journal of Economic History* 72 (2012) pp. 895–926.

56 For wheat, caloric values were taken for wheat flour from the USDA National Nutrient Database http://ndb.nal.usda.gov. Other caloric values have been taken from Allen et al. 'Wages, prices.'

4 Consumption Baskets

In order to maintain comparability, I have taken the baskets created by Allen et al. for China and Europe as benchmarks, but made slight adjustments to the baskets for Bengal, the Cape, Ceylon and Java on the basis of evidence regarding differences in consumption patterns. Table 3.2 shows the consumption baskets for the various regions. In this section, some of the evidence available on differences in consumption patterns will be reviewed, and the delicate balance in the basket between an accurate reflection of the prevailing consumption pattern, on the one hand, and comparability, on the other, is discussed.

TABLE 3.2 *Consumption baskets, subsistence life style, in Europe, the Cape Colony and Asia.*

	Unit	Europe & Cape[57]	China[58]	India (Bengal)[59]	Ceylon	Java
Main staple[60]	kg	155–179	171–179	164–209	165[61]	168
Beans/peas	kg	20	20	20	20	25
Meat/fish	kg	3	3	3	–	6[62]
Butter/oil/ghee	kg	3	3	3	5	–
Sugar	kg	–	–	2	2	2
Soap	kg	1.3	1.3	–	1.3	1.3
Salt	kg	–	–	–	–	2
Linen/cotton	m²	3	3	3	3	3
Candles	kg	1.3	1.3	–	1.3	2.6
Lamp oil	litre	1.3	1.3	–	1.3	–
Fuel	MBTU	3	3	–	–	3

Sources: Allen, 'India'; Allen et al., 'Wages, prices'.

57 Allen et al, 'Wages, prices and living standards', 21: 176 kg oats or 186 kg rye for northwestern Europe, 179 kg wheat for the Cape.

58 Ibid.: 171 kg rice in Suzhou and Canton; 179 kg sorghum in Beijing.

59 Allen, 'India': 164 kg rice/209 kg millet.

60 Europe: rye, wheat, oats; Cape: wheat; China: rice or sorghum; India, Ceylon and Java: rice.

61 Whereas in previous work 'paddy' was used in the basket, as it was cheaper than rice and thus better reflects the barebones level of consumption (De Zwart, 'Population, labour'). Yet, considering notations that paddy was used as fodder (VOC 2336, f. 444) this is changed to rice here (fed to slaves according to VOC 2336, f. 444), which was somewhat more expensive.

62 Fish.

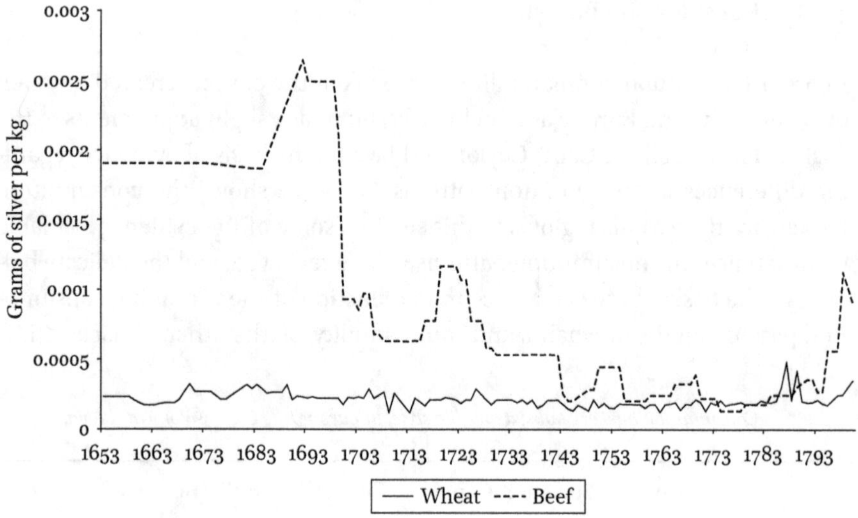

FIGURE 3.1 *Cost per kcal of wheat and meat at the Cape.*
Sources: see text.[63]

The Cape basket is very similar to the basket created for Europe. Consumption patterns are to a large extent determined by culture and environmental conditions. As the Cape was a society formed by VOC personnel and settlers of north-western European descent – mostly Dutch, English, German and French – it is likely that the consumption patterns of these settlers in the Cape Colony were more or less similar to those of north-western Europe. Furthermore, the climate and geography of the Cape was not much different from Spain, allowing the cultivation of crops also available in Europe: 'the meat from livestock farming and vegetables from the Company's gardens made possible the continuation of basic European food practices like the Dutch *hutsepot*'.[64] The only difference is that wheat is the main staple at the Cape, while the English and Dutch baskets are based on oats and rye, respectively.

This consumption basket for the Cape differs from the one employed by Sophia and Stan du Plessis in their study on Cape living standards, as their

63 In 1676 and 1681 very low prices of meat were reported (VOC 4012 f. 426; VOC 4017 f. 425) of 5 and 3 cents per *pond*, respectively, versus 30 cents in the surrounding years. It is therefore assumed that these are errors. For this comparison these numbers have been left out and missing values were linearly interpolated.

64 Stacey C. Jordan, 'Coarse Earthenware at the Dutch Colonial Cape of Good Hope, South Africa: A History of Local Production and Typology of Products,' *International Journal of Historical Archaeology* 4 (2000). 141.

basket contains much larger amounts of meat. They emphasize that commentators on the colonial diet at the Cape underlined the importance of meat in a generally rich diet.[65] An example is the diet of Joachim von Dessin, a soldier (lowest ranking official) in VOC service, who arrived at the Cape in 1727. His inventory includes wheat and rice, a variety of beans, spices (mustard, cumin, pepper, tamarind), sugar and coffee, oil and lard, wines, soap, wood and candles, as well as pork and beef.[66]

Furthermore, they argue that 'more persuasively from an economic perspective'[67] the relative price of meat at the Cape encouraged meat consumption relative to bread. Thus in some years, depending on prices, their basket contains up to 100 kg of meat per year.[68] Using price data that will be introduced in Section 5, the price per kcal can be calculated for wheat and meat at the Cape. Figure 3.1 shows that only for a few years, i.e. 1774/7 and 1786/7, meat was actually cheaper per kcal than wheat. For much of the remaining period it was still a luxury product. Besides, even if more meat may reflect consumption at the Cape more accurately, it limits the extent to which one can make international comparisons.[69] Therefore, it seems reasonable to keep the amount of meat similar to that of the other baskets.

For India, much of the evidence points to a simple diet. From contemporary accounts it becomes clear that the diet 'of the common people in most parts of India consisted mainly of rice, millets and pulses.'[70] Francisco Pelsaert, a VOC employee at Agra and Surat in the early seventeenth century, says that common workmen:

> know little of the taste of meat. For their monotonous daily food they have nothing but a little *khichri*,[71] made of 'green pulse'[72] mixed with rice,

65 G. Botha, *General history and social life of the Cape of Good Hope* (Cape Town: Struik, 1962).

66 Sophia du Plessis and Stan du Plessis, 'Happy in the service of the Company: the purchasing power of VOC salaries at the Cape in the 18th century', *Economic History of Developing Regions* 27 (2012) p. 132; H. W. Claasens, *Die geskiedenis van boerekos, 1652–1806* (Pretoria: Protea Boekhuis , 2006) p. 118.

67 Du Plessis and Du Plessis, 'Happy in the service', p. 133.

68 Ibid., p. 134.

69 Their basket contains between 26 and 100 kg meat.

70 Allen, 'India', p. 22.

71 In the text: *kitchery*; W. H. Moreland and P. Geyl (transl.), *Jahangir's India. The Remonstrantie of Francisco Pelsaert* (Cambridge: W. Heffer & Sons Ltd., 1925) pp. 60–1.

72 In the original: 'groene ertjens', which could be translated as green peas. Moreland and Geyl note that probably *moth* is meant here, the cheapest pulse.

> which is cooked with water over a little fire until the moisture is evaporated, and eaten hot with butter in the evening; in the day time they munch a little parched pulse or other grain, which they say suffices for their lean stomachs.[73]

In Bengal, rice was the major agricultural crop and thus formed the staple diet of the masses;[74] wheat was not a common part of the diet, even in wheat producing regions. Fish was relatively popular in coastal regions such as Bengal, but 'fish, too, was not taken either very often or in large quantities, especially by those who lived inland or far from rivers.'[75] Furthermore, 'there was a taboo on beef and pigmeat which extended to hens, eggs and most of the domesticated animals'.[76] According to Satish Chandra, butter (*ghi*) and sugar, on the other hand, were a common part of the diet for many, while spices were too expensive.[77] From this evidence, it seems that the basket created by Allen for India as a whole[78] may to some extent reflect the actual diet of workmen in early modern Bengal (see Table 3.2). This very basic basket may have even been too luxurious for the very poor, whose food is described as 'boiled rice, nichany, millet and grass roots', while in Bihar they ate 'pea-like grain'.[79] Rajat Datta quotes a budget for a common artisan in Rangpur (Bengal) in c. 1807 that is made up for over 80 percent of rice.[80]

As in India, rice was the main food staple consumed in Ceylon. On the basis of observations by European travellers in the seventeenth century, as well as due to data constraints, a few alterations were made as compared with the Indian consumption basket. Meat and fish were left out of the basket for Ceylon, both due to a lack of price data and because Robert Knox, an English prisoner in Kandy in the seventeenth century, wrote:

---

73 Moreland and Geyl, *Jahangir's India*.

74 Satish Chandra, 'Standard of Living', in: Tapan Raychaudhuri and Irfan Habib (eds.) *The Cambridge Economic History of India. Volume I: c. 1200 – c. 1750* (Cambridge Cambridge University Press, 1982) p. 461.

75 Chandra, 'Standard of Living', p. 462.

76 Ibid.

77 Ibid.

78 Allen, 'India in the Great Divergence'.

79 Chandra, 'Standard of Living', p. 462; Radhakamal Mukerjee, *The Economic History of India* (London: Longmans, 1945) p. 57.

80 Rajat Datta, *Society, economy and the market: commercialization in rural Bengal, c. 1760–1800* (Delhi: Manohar, 2000) p. 193.

> Beef here may not be eaten; it is abominable: Flesh and Fish is somewhat scarce. And that little of it they have, they had rather sell to get money to keep, then eat it themselves: neither is there any but outlandish men, that will buy any of them.[81]

The meat and fish have been replaced by extra kilograms of butter and rice, as the Dutch seventeenth century traveller, and reverend, Philippus Baldaeus noted that the Ceylonese 'have a taste for butter'.[82] Sugar is included in the basket because there is evidence of the use of *jaggory* (palm sugar) in a number of dishes.[83] In addition, whereas soap, candles and lamp oil were omitted from the Indian basket due to a lack of price series, these have been included in the Ceylonese basket for three reasons: (1) these prices were available; (2) it makes the CPI dependent on the movement of a greater variety of prices, thereby enhancing its quality; and (3) there are no reasons to assume that while people living in the rest of the world were consuming 1.3 kg/litres of soap, candles and lamp oil per year, people living in Ceylon were not.[84] Finally, unlike the European and Chinese baskets, firewood/fuel has been left out of the basket. Again, there are three arguments for this: (1) the lack of price series; (2) the fuel used for heating was minimal, due to the warm climate; and (3) Knox describes that it was one of the women's tasks to gather firewood in the woods (Ceylon was densely forested),[85] implying that firewood was not bought on the market.

Rice was also the main staple and the dominant source of calories in Java.[86] Anthony Reid cites numerous European commentators who observed that Southeast Asians ate very little meat. Instead of meat, it is therefore more likely that greater amounts of fish were consumed.[87] Luc Nagtegaal notes that the

---

81 Robert Knox, 'An Historical Relation of Ceylon', *Ceylon Historical Journal* 6 (1956–57) p. 138 [Original published in 1681].

82 Philippus Baldaeus, *Naauwkeurige beschryvinge van Malabar en Choromandel, der zelver aangrenzende ryken, en het machtige eyland Ceylon* (Amsterdam, 1672) p. 177.

83 Dewasiri, *The adaptable peasant*, p. 87; Knox, *Historical relation*, p. 141. The price evidence is, however, for cane sugar, which serves as a proxy.

84 Knox describes the Sinhalese habit of washing both before and after meals: *Historical relation*, p. 140.

85 Knox, *Historical relation*, p. 147.

86 Peter Boomgaard, *Children of the colonial state. Population growth and economic development in Java 1795–1880* (Amsterdam: Free University Press, 1989) pp. 222–228; Anthony Reid, *Southeast Asia in the age of commerce 1450–1680. Vol. 1: The lands below the winds* (New Haven and London 1988) p. 28; Nagtegaal, *Rijden*, p. 35.

87 Due to the lower caloric values of fish vis-à-vis meat, the amount is doubled to 6 kg per year.

majority of animal protein in the Javanese diet stemmed from fish.[88] While fish may have been harder to obtain inland, Reid suggests it was an important article of internal commerce: cities in Java were supplied with dried fish by Banjarmasin,[89] for example. A sixteenth-century commentator noted regarding the Visayan Islands in the Philippines:

> The inhabitants of the mountains cannot live without the fish, salt, and other articles of food…of other districts; nor, on the other hand, can those of the coast live without the rice and cotton of the mountaineers.[90]

While the sources cited by Reid suggest 'a relative paucity of vegetables', this was compensated for by the abundance of fruit. No price data on fruit are currently available, but it can be kept in mind that Javanese may have augmented their consumption basket with fruit.[91] Similarly, Nagtegaal notes the consumption of maize (*jagung*), although it was not traded and does not, therefore, turn up in VOC sources.[92] In addition, due to the absence of price series, butter or olive oil included in the other baskets has been replaced with some extra sugar and beans. Sugar was widely consumed, while beans (*kacang*) also seem to have been widely produced (and thus consumed for additional protein).[93] Finally, some additional salt was included in the Javanese basket; this fits both notes by early modern observers about the great importance of salt as an article of everyday consumption in Southeast Asia,[94] as well as studies on nineteenth-century living standards.[95]

---

88 Nagtegaal, Rijden, p. 39.

89 Reid, *Southeast Asia* I, p. 29.

90 Michael de Loarca, 'Relation of the Filipinas Islands' (1581), cited in Reid, *Southeast Asia* I, p. 28.

91 But so have the Europeans studied in the other real wage studies: Allen, 'The Great Divergence'.

92 Nagtegaal, *Rijden*, p. 35.

93 Nagtegaal, *Rijden*, p. 35; he also notes the widespread consumption of maize (*jagung*), but as there was no trade in maize, it is rarely mentioned in the VOC sources.

94 Gerrit Knaap and Luc Nagtegaal, 'A Forgotten Trade: Salt in Southeast Asia 1670-1813', in: Roderich Ptak and Dietmar Rothermund (eds.) *Emporia, commodities and entrepreneurs in Asian maritime trade, c. 1400–1750* (Stuttgard: Franz Steiner, 1991) pp. 127–8; Reid, *Southeast Asia* I, pp. 28–9; Peter Carey, *The power of prophecy: Prince Dipanagara and the end of the old order in Java, 1785–1855* (Leiden: KITLV Press, 2007) pp. 44–45.

95 Van Zanden, 'Rich and poor'. While the consumption of salt may have been higher, most coastal people may have been able to procure salt themselves.

Two things stand out in this discussion. First, evidence on consumption patterns in these areas suggests a relatively simple diet (with the possible exception of the Cape, where more meat may have been consumed). Second, the discussion highlights the tensions between the aim to calculate real wages in relation to a poverty line and the ambition to calculate real wages that are comparable over time and space. For the first aim, it is important to include all available information on consumption patterns and how these changed over time in any one particular society. Doing so does, however, hinders international comparisons, especially since information on such details are lacking for many pre-modern societies. International and inter-temporal comparison requires a certain simplification and standardization of consumption baskets, otherwise the figures that emerge from the comparison would reflect different styles of living.[96] In my study, I have employed the simplified basket because of data constraints (there simply are no detailed data on household consumption, or enough price data to calculate the costs of more complicated consumption baskets), and because international comparisons are at the cornerstone of this study.

5 Price data

Having defined consumption baskets, price data of the products included in the basket are needed to calculate the cost of the baskets across time. In this section I compute, on the basis of new primary material, a time series of the price of the consumption baskets. First, however, the sources and the problems involved in this exercise are discussed, before a comparative analysis of price levels can be made.

5.1 *Sources*

As noted in the introductory chapter to this book, the VOC accounts are a rich source of prices in the regions studied. As I have explained in Chapter 2, the archives of the VOC Bookkeeper-General in Batavia constitute a major source of prices.[97] In addition, three types of documents containing price data are to be found in the VOC-OBP that are organized per Company establishment.[98] First, there are bills or specifications of expense, which state the costs ships

96 As real wages based on a more luxurious basket will lead to a lower standard of living compared with real wages calculated with simpler baskets.

97 NA BGB: Inv. no. 1.04.18.02. Ref. nos. 10751–10801.

98 NA VOC: 1.04.02. *Overgekomen Brieven en Papieren* (OBP). See introduction.

made to restock supplies for the ship (when at the Cape of Good Hope) as it was sailing to the Indies, or returning to the Dutch Republic. Second, there are books of accounts that contain statements of the expenditures of a VOC establishment in a certain year, as well as describing the goods and their value stored in the establishment's warehouse. A third source of prices is the so-called *rendementen*, which are lists presenting evidence of the profits that were made on the sale of goods.[99]

In addition, data could also be found in the *Scheepssoldijboeken*, i.e. Ship's Pay-Ledgers, which form a separate section of the VOC archives.[100] For each ship sailing to the East a pay-ledger was created that bore the name of the ship.[101] It is essentially a record of staff administration as it contains a list of all the personnel on board the ship, their rank, wages, possible debts, etc. However, in some cases, lists of the expenditures made replenishing supplies at Batavia or Cape Town (and in a few cases for Bengal and Canton) for the return trip to Europe were bound into the back of the volume. These are essentially the same as the bills of expense described above, but bound into a different source.

For Bengal, prices were found in lists of the prices for which some necessities could be obtained in Chinsurah[102] that are part of the series 'Proceedings of the Political Council' in Bengal (in turn part of the VOC-OBP).[103] These data supplement the price series constructed for Bengal by Allen and Roman Studer.[104] Additional price data for the Cape were collected from the inventories of the Orphan Chamber at the Cape of Good Hope (MOOC 8 and 10). This institution registered all deaths and wills, as well as inventorying and acting as executor in various cases.[105] When no relatives could be found, the goods and

99 For Ceylon, Christiaan van Bochove already collected data from the *rendementen*: 'Prices in Sri Lanka and Southern India during the pre-Industrial period': http://www.iisg.nl/hpw/voc-srilanka-southernindia.pdf

100 *Scheepssoldijboeken*: VOC 5269–6842.

101 Remco Raben and H. Spijkerman (eds.), *De archieven van de Verenigde Oostindische Compagnie / The Archives of the Dutch East India Company* (The Hague: SDU, 1992) pp. 61–62.

102 Refers to the main establishment of the VOC in Bengal; also often named Hooghly-Chinsurah, or just Hooghly. Since Hooghly is also the name of the river, I consistently refer to the establishment as Chinsurah in this book.

103 'Notitie waar voor d'ondervolgende benodigtheden inde dispens d'eerst komende ses maanden konnen gelevert werden': VOC 2872 f. 180; 3037 f. 2641; 3168 f. 487; 3343 f. 20; 3371 ff. 318–9; ff. 551–2; 3427 ff. 572–573; 3452 f. 796; 3481 f. 203; 3481 ff. 16–7; 3510 f. 464; 3538 f. 189; f. 456; 3565 f. 308; 3660 ff. 241–2; 3716 f. 145; f. 636; 3747 f. 395, f. 615; 3529 f. 25; 3830 f. 434; 3919 f. 683; 3953 f. 448.

104 Available at http://gpih.ucdavis.edu.

105 Fourie, 'The remarkable'.

property were sold by public auction. These inventories have been made available online via the TEPC and TANAP project.[106] Some prices for wheat, cotton, soap and butter were taken from this source. Furthermore, a few prices for the latter eighteenth century were found in the Western Cape Archives in Cape Town.[107] Finally, some price data for the Cape and Java could also be obtained from various sources in secondary literature.[108]

5.2 *Issues*

Creating historical price time series from these sources is fraught with difficulties. The price data available for earlier time periods are often the prices paid by important institutions, which raises issues of reliability and representativeness. Grain prices are often wholesale, while the prices of other products, such as soap and textiles, may have been fixed in long-term contracts. Prices of raw materials are sometimes used if those for the finished product are unavailable, e.g. the price of tallow as a proxy for candles.[109] Critics of institutional prices have suggested that a divergence in the movement of wholesale and retail prices may have taken place: 'for example, the costs of transport and distribution might move differently from those of commodities, local prices might deviate from those set in national markets and shopkeepers might attempt to even out the larger fluctuations in wholesale prices'.[110] Through a comparison of various English wholesale, contract and retail prices between 1780 and 1880, Feinstein shows that there is no significant divergence in the long-term trend or short-run fluctuations between these series. It is unclear to what extent this also applies to other periods and regions. However, even if consumer retail prices are unavailable it is 'important to see what story the institutional prices tell, for they are the only game in town'.[111]

In other studies, the difference between wholesale and retail prices is often resolved by employing constant mark-ups based on a number of

106 Inventories of the Orphan Chamber: http://databases.tanap.net/mooc/.

107 Western Cape Archives: Council of Policy (C): 2739 and 2734.

108 The Cape: A. J. du Plessis, *Die geskiedenis van die graankultuur in Suid-Afrika, 1652–1752* (Cape Town, 1933); Van Duin and Ross, 'The economy', Du Plessis and Du Plessis, 'Happy in the service'; I thank Sophia and Stan du Plessis for making their price data available to me. Java: Van Niel, *Java's Northeast Coast*; Nagtegaal, *Rijden.*

109 Feinstein, 'Pessimism perpetuated', 636.

110 Charles Feinstein, 'Changes in nominal wages, the cost of living and real wages in the United Kingdom over two centuries, 1780-1990', in: Peter Scholliers and Vera Zamagni (eds.) *Labour's Reward. Real wages and economic change in 19th and 20th century Europe* (Aldershot: Edward Elgar, 1995) p. 10.

111 Allen, 'The Great Divergence', p. 418.

observations for retail prices. The issue requires some additional attention in this study, as the prices taken from the VOC administration are mostly the wholesale prices paid by a large trading organization that also wielded considerable political power. For Bengal and Ceylon the problems are limited as we can rely on the prices gathered by Allen and Studer for Bengal and the sales prices from the *rendementen* for Ceylon. In the cases of Java and the Cape Colony, however, I had to rely to a greater extent on VOC purchasing prices.

As principal buyer of agricultural produce at the Cape, the VOC fixed prices paid for wheat through long-term contracts. According to Robert Ross, 'the free market price in Cape Town did not drop much below the VOC's figure even in years of abundant harvests, but could rise well above it in years of scarcity, despite the best efforts of the VOC and the Cape Town *Burgerraad* (which in this represented the consumers) to hold it steady'.[112] Bearing in mind its role as a station for replenishing VOC ships sailing to and from the East Indies, and considering farmers' complaints regarding the low prices obtained for their products,[113] a downward bias in VOC prices at the Cape is to be expected.

From the comparison in Figure 3.2 of official VOC prices found in *Scheepssoldijboeken* and bills of expenses with those from other sources (e.g. MOOC auctions) it seems the 'free market' price was often lower than the official price. Furthermore, a comparison of Cape prices with those in the other cases and in Amsterdam shows that they were on the same high level as in Amsterdam during the seventeenth and early eighteenth centuries (see Figure 3.7). This evidence casts some doubts on the legitimacy of the Cape farmers' complaints.[114] As Van Duin and Ross have already noted 'it has been too commonly assumed that the farmers' own complaints on their poverty and on the absence of markets reflected economic reality'.[115]

Thus, when creating the CPI for the Cape, no mark-ups were employed on VOC prices. Instead, I have taken the arithmetic mean of multiple notations,

---

112 Robert Ross, 'The Cape', p. 247.

113 Johan Fourie, *An Inquiry into the Nature, Causes and Distribution of Wealth in the Cape Colony, 1652–1795* (unpublished PhD thesis, Utrecht University, 2012) pp. 80–81.

114 In fact, it seems that the Cape farmers were relatively well off: see Fourie, *An Inquiry*, and Fourie, 'The remarkable', and Johan Fourie and J. Uys, 'Luxury product consumption in eighteenth-century Cape Colony households', *Low Countries Journal of Social and Economic History* 9 (2012) pp. 29–60. This also suggests that one should be cautious with the interpretation of qualitative sources; statements of contemporaries have obvious biases.

115 Van Duin and Ross, 'The economy'.

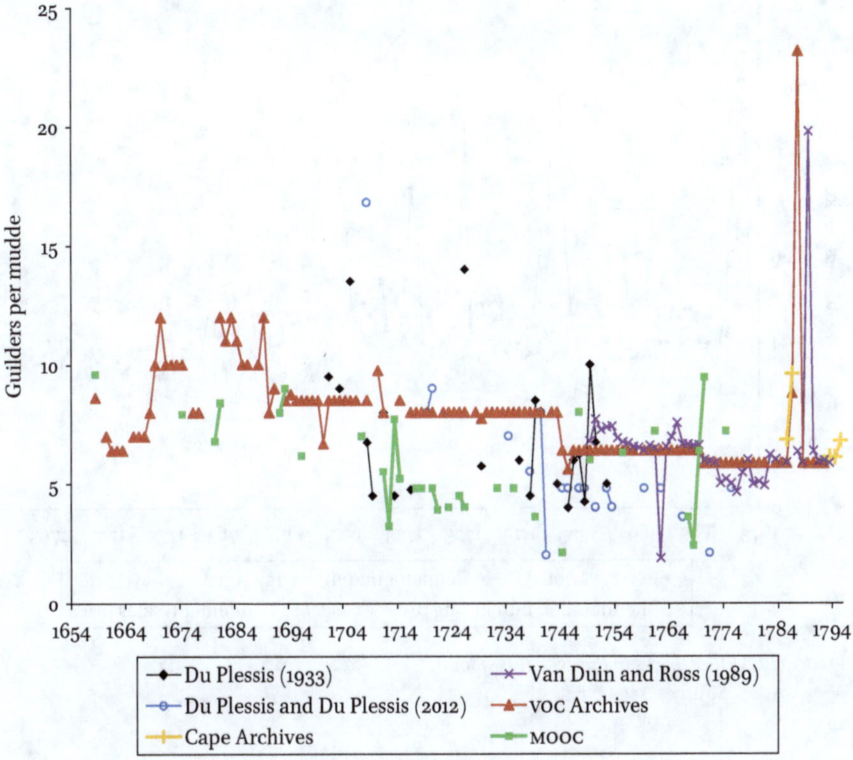

FIGURE 3.2 *Wheat prices in Cape Town, 1654–1795.*
Sources: see text.

as it is unclear whether Cape consumers were always able to purchase their wheat at auctions, which were held on the countryside estates of the deceased.[116]

In the case of Java, the Company could obtain shipments of rice and other products below the market prices.[117] Especially when the Company consolidated its power over Java's north-east coast (the main supplier of rice to Batavia) in the 1740s and 1750s, one might fear that the VOC would be able to procure greater quantities of rice at a lower cost.[118] Fortunately, the *rendementen*

116 Taking the average also means that two smaller crises in wheat farming will now appear, rather than one big one, since the sources (the VOC, on the one hand, and Van Duin and Ross on the other) date the increase in wheat prices differently.

117 Robert van Niel, 'Economic and population changes in Java, 1750–1850', in: A. Hayami and Y. Tsubouchi (eds.) *Economic and demographic development in rice producing societies: some aspects of east Asian economic history, 1500–1900* (Leuven: 1990) p. 294.

118 Jacobs, *Merchant in Asia*, p. 244.

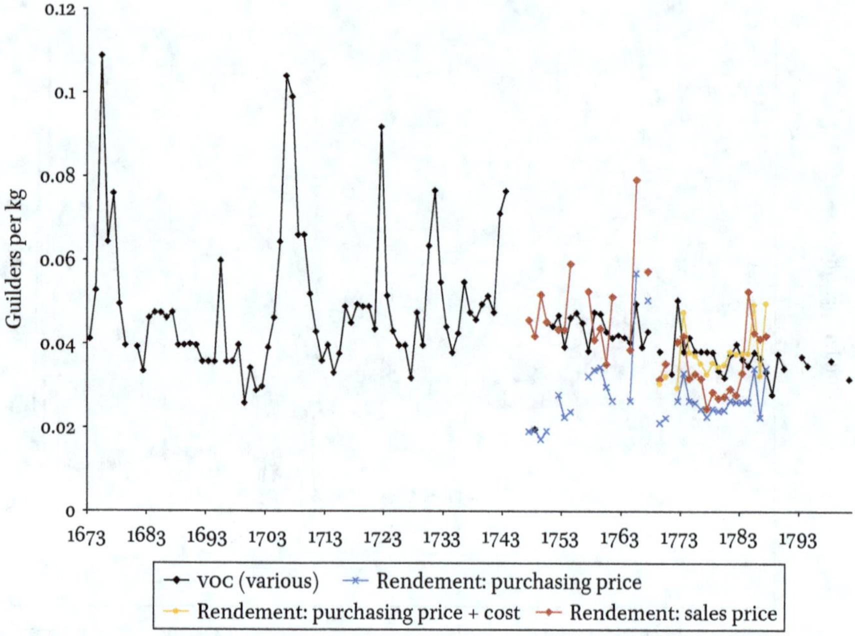

FIGURE 3.3 *Rice prices in Batavia, 1673–1801.*
Sources: see text.

(returns) for Batavia for the period 1747–1787 contain data on purchasing and sales prices, while those between 1769 and 1787 even show the costs for transport, storage, personnel and risk.

Figure 3.3 plots these prices against the prices of rice found in other VOC documents. Interestingly, if costs are taken into account, the VOC was mostly making a loss on its rice sales in Batavia. This suggests that the VOC was primarily interested in feeding its workers in Batavia, while profits were to be made through the sale of other crops.[119] The figure shows that the prices taken from the other VOC sources more closely resemble sales prices recorded in the *rendementen* than the purchasing price. These data thus confirm Van Niel's observation that 'the private rice market, however, came increasingly to operate outside Company control and was mainly in the hands of wealthy Chinese and Europeans'.[120] This also corroborates Nagtegaal's impression that 'the prices paid by the VOC did not deviate drastically from the general market prices as

119 Van Niel, *Java's Northeast Coast*, p. 123.

120 Van Niel, *Java's Northeast Coast*, p. 128.

they prevailed for others'.[121] Furthermore, the amounts of rice contracted seem to have been generally less than 10 percent of local production.[122] While Van Niel notes that the price of rice increased over the eighteenth century,[123] my newly collected VOC data suggest otherwise.[124] Therefore no mark-ups on rice have been used for prices from the period before 1747 as this would unfairly depress living standards. At the same time, the evidence from the *rendementen* does suggest minor mark-ups on salt, sugar and textiles (see Appendix A4.5).

In addition, these patterns make sense in the context of other information we have on the economic history of Java. Peaks in prices in the late seventeenth and early eighteenth centuries coincide with periods of warfare.[125] After 1755 a long period of peace seems to have allowed the expansion of agricultural production,[126] which is also suggested by evidence on the expansion of trade. Maddison finds an increase in per capita export production between 1700 and 1780.[127] That this did not occur at the cost of reduced food production is suggested by the fact that the total value of goods (in guilders, at VOC purchasing prices) and total amounts of rice shipped from Semarang (on Java's north-east coast) to Batavia increased over the eighteenth century (also when accounting for population growth).[128] While we only have evidence from VOC trade, Gerrit Knaap has shown that, in contrast to suggestions by, for example, Reid, the role of Javanese merchants remained substantial up until the latter eighteenth

121 Nagetgaal, *Rijden*, p. 176. Own translation of: 'mijn indruk is dat doorgaans de prijzen die de VOC betaalde niet sterk afweken van de algemene marktprijzen zoals die ook voor anderen golden'.

122 Van Niel, 'Economic and population change', p. 297.

123 Van Niel, *Java's Northeast Coast*, pp. 127–8.

124 In fact, his own data (Van Niel, *Java's Northeast Coast*, appendix 13) do not point to an increase in prices either.

125 Nagtegaal, *Rijden*, pp. 176–7.

126 Peter Carey, 'Waiting for the "Just King": The Agrarian World of South-Central Java from Giyanti (1755) to the Java War (1825–1830)', *Modern Asian Studies* 20 (1986) pp. 89–91; Alberto Feenstra, 'Dutch Coins for Asian Growth. VOC-Duiten to Assess Java's Deep Monetisation and Economic Growth, 1724-1800', *Low Countries Journal of Social and Economic History* 11 (2014); Jacobs, *Merchant in Asia*, p. 241; Victor Lieberman, *Strange Parallels: Southeast Asia in Global Context, c. 800–1830* (Cambridge: Cambridge U.P., 2009) pp. 870–1; Merle Ricklefs, 'Some statistical evidence on Javanese social, economic and demographic history in the later seventeenth and eighteenth centuries', *Modern Asian Studies* 20 (1986) p. 30; ibid., *A History of Modern Indonesia since c. 1200* (Stanford CA: Stanford University Press, 2008) p. 121.

127 Angus Maddison, 'Dutch Income in and from Indonesia 1700–1938', *Modern Asian Studies* 23 (1989) pp. 645–670.

128 Van Niel, *Java's Northeast Coast*, p. 131; Nagtegal, *Rijden*; De Zwart and Van Zanden, 'Labor, wages'.

century, although they were clearly surpassed in importance by the VOC and the Chinese.[129] While the VOC may have dominated long distance trade, Javanese traders were specialized in local and inter-insular connections. In recent work, Knaap estimates that in the port of Semarang (the VOC capital on Java's north-east coast) VOC trade represented only 6 percent of the total trade in the 1770s.[130] Finally, various colonial officials have suggested an increase in production and consumption in Java in the latter eighteenth century.[131]

It can be concluded that while these data are perhaps not ideal, they do not seem to be more problematic than, for example, those for seventeenth-century England, where, according to Christopher Hill, a man lived:

> in a house built with monopoly bricks, with windows [...] of monopoly glass; heated by monopoly coal [...], burning in a grate made of monopoly iron. He washed himself in monopoly soap, his clothes in monopoly starch. He dressed in monopoly lace, monopoly linen, monopoly leather, monopoly gold thread... His clothes were held up by monopoly belts, monopoly buttons, monopoly pins. They were dyed with monopoly dyes. He ate monopoly butter, monopoly currents, monopoly red herrings, monopoly salmon, and monopoly lobsters. His food was seasoned with monopoly salt, monopoly pepper, monopoly vinegar. He wrote with monopoly pens, on monopoly writing paper; read (through monopoly spectacles, by the light of monopoly candles) monopoly printed books.[132]

It can, thus, be argued that price developments unearthed from the VOC archives and presented in this chapter can be meaningfully compared with data from other parts of the world.

---

129 Gerrit Knaap, 'Shipping and trade in Java, c. 1775; A quantitative analysis', *Modern Asian Studies* 33 (1999) pp. 405–420.

130 Gerrit Knaap, 'Semarang. A colonial provincial capital and port city in Java, circa 1775', in: U. Bosma and T. Webster (eds.), *Commodities, Ports and Asian Maritime Trade, c. 1750–1950* (Palgrave/Macmillan 2015).

131 Waterloo to Engelhard (1804): 'one only has to direct one's eyes to those lands which [now] produce rice and which just twenty years ago were still waste and uncultivated' (cited in: Carey, *Power and prophecy*, p. 35), Engelhard to High Government Batavia: 'rice consumption in everyone's household is greater than formerly. [...] the condition of the Javanese is very different from 50 to 60 years ago when they lived in ignorance and were depressed and suppressed by the continual wars' (cited in: Van Niel, *Java's Northeast Coast*, p. 131) and Crawfurd (1812): 'a traveler could now pass a hundred miles in Java without encountering an uncultivated spot' (cited in: Carey, 'Waiting for the "Just"', p. 91).

132 Christopher Hill, *The Century of Revolution, 1603–1714* (New York: W. W. Norton, 1966) p. 32.

5.3 *Regional Price Variation*

One of the assumptions underlying the real wage methodology described in previous subsections is that real wages in a capital or another major city can to some extent be seen as representative for welfare in the wider region or even the entire country.[133] Critics may suggest that price developments in capitals are not representative and that generalizations cannot be made on the basis of such data. However, regarding the standard of living debate of English workers, Feinstein suggested that London price series 'accurately reflect national movements in prices'.[134] While regional commodity markets may have been relatively well-integrated in nineteenth-century England, this need not be the case for the eighteenth-century territories examined here. This subsection reviews some of the evidence regarding regional variation in prices. The focus is again on main staple crops as the data were generally most abundant for these and the effects on living standards the strongest. In Section 6 more will be said about price developments of the other products.

In the early modern Cape Colony, Cape Town was the major town, the only port and the main market. Large wine and wheat farms dominated the area around Cape Town, while further into the interior pastoral livestock farmers occupied an ever expanding territory. Figure 3.2 may suggest that prices in the countryside were somewhat lower than in Cape Town. However there is no additional information on prices in, for example, Stellenbosch or Franschhoek.

For the other regions under discussion, information is somewhat more abundant (even if still scarce). For Bengal, the issue of regional price variation has been analysed by Roman Studer.[135] According to his study, local rice markets in India in the period 1750–1830 were fairly well integrated (correlation coefficient 0.91): 'neighbouring villages or cities less than 35 km apart clearly exhibit a common price regime'.[136] However, the correlation is much weaker (0.46) between prices in markets that were between 35 and 70 km distance from each other. For markets over 70 km from each other the relationship between markets becomes very weak, while beyond a distance of 300 km there is no discernible relationship between prices. Rajat Datta shows price series for the neighbouring Bengali districts of Burdwan and Birbhum between 1784 and 1813, claiming that the synchronicity between these prices is a clear indication

133 Allen et al. 'Wages, prices'; Arroyo Abad et al., 'Between conquest'.

134 Feinstein, 'Pessimism perpetuated', p. 636. Supported by Nicholas Crafts, 'Regional price variations in England in 1843: an aspect of the standard-of-living debate', *Explorations in Economic History* 19 (1982) pp. 51–70.

135 Studer, 'India and the Great Divergence'.

136 Studer, 'India and the Great Divergence', p. 403.

of market integration.[137] At the same time, Datta also shows a few observations of price differentials between town and countryside in Bengal. While these observations are very erratic, it seems that prices in towns were on average 46 percent higher.[138] However, since I also look at urban wages, these prices are more suitable for calculating real wages for Bengal.

Figures 3.4, 3.5 and 3.6 show rice prices for a number of towns in Bengal, Ceylon (and Southern India: Tutucorin) and Java. A brief glance at the three figures shows that prices exhibit more or less similar trends in the same region, but that the developments differ between the regions. Although Bengal displays a slightly rising trend in the first half of the eighteenth century, the trend is largely flat after the crisis of 1769–70. At the same time, prices in Java were

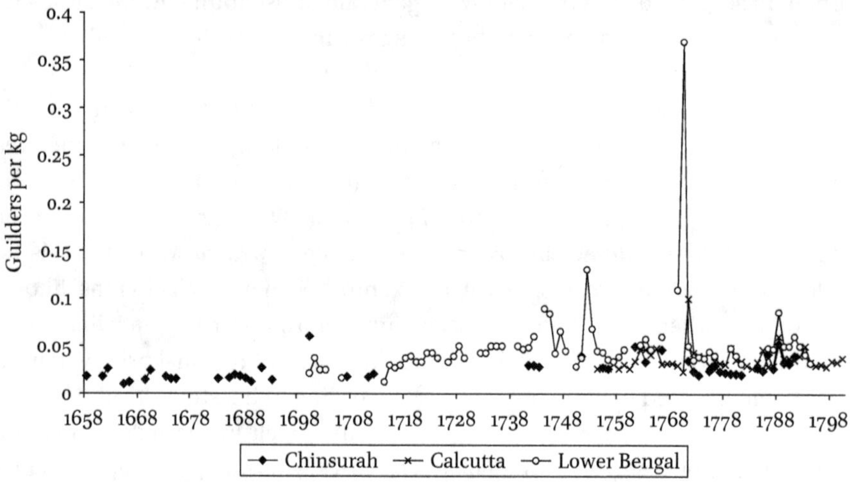

FIGURE 3.4 *Rice prices in Bengal, 1688–1790.*
Sources: see text and Allen and Studer, 'Prices and Wages'.[139]

---

137 Datta, *Society, economy*, p. 198 and p. 229.

138 Ibid., p. 199.

139 The data were taken from the excel sheets as provided by Allen and Studer, who took the data from A. S. M. A. Hussain, 'A quantitative Study of Price Movements in Bengal during Eighteenth and Nineteenth Centuries', (PhD thesis, University of London, 1976). However, as some of the data were interpolated by unknown methods, I went back to the original sources to see which data had been interpolated and which were actual observations: G. Herklots, 'Table showing the market price of Grain &c. in lower Bengal from the year 1700 to 1813, extracted from authentic documents of one month in each year, for which generally the month of August was selected', *Gleanings in Science* 1 (1829) pp. 368–369; W. B. Baily, 'Statistical Account of Burwan', *Asiatick Researches* 12 (1818) pp. 567–573. Interpolations by Allen and Studer were deleted from this figure.

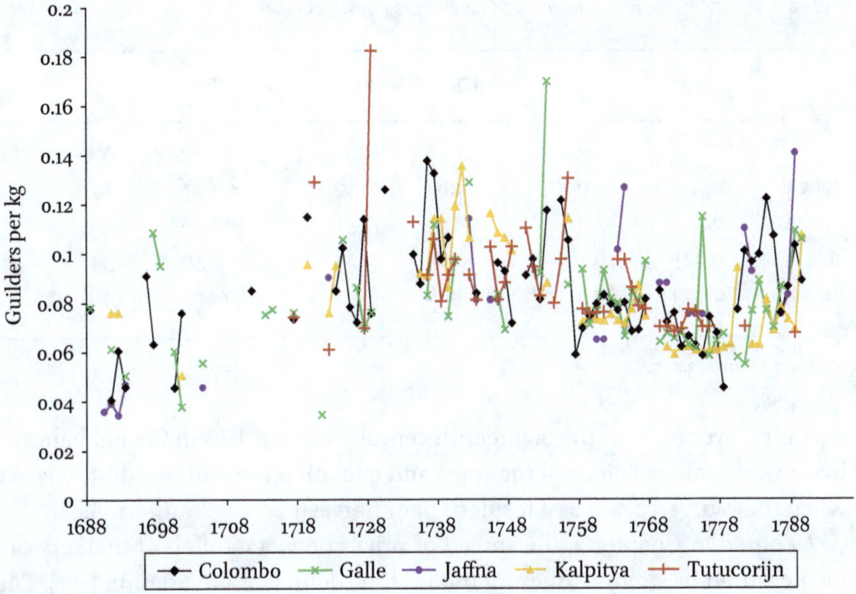

FIGURE 3.5 *Rice prices in Ceylon and Southern India, 1688–1790.*
Sources: see text.

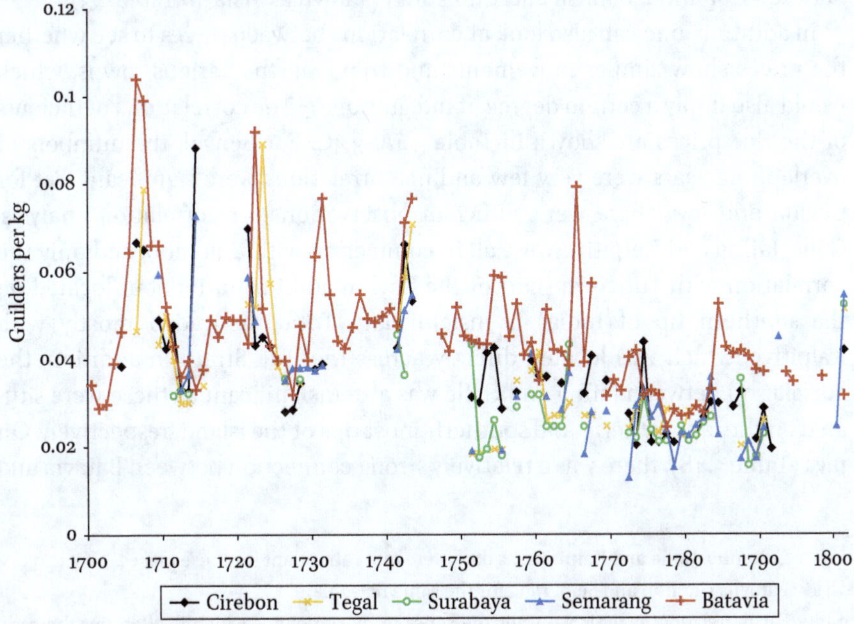

FIGURE 3.6 *Rice prices in Java, 1700–1801.*
Sources: see text.

TABLE 3.3 *CV in rice prices within and between regions, 1700–1800.*

	1700–49		1750–99		1700–99	
	CV	*N*	CV	*N*	CV	*N*
Bengal	n/a	0	0.281	17	0.281	17
Ceylon	0.225	5	0.139	31	0.149	36
Java	0.225	13	0.265	21	0.250	34
Asia	0.471	18	0.486	31	0.485	49

Sources: Figures 3.4–3.6.

declining over most of the eighteenth century, while prices in Ceylon behaved like a wave: increasing until the 1740s and declining thereafter until the 1780s, when they surged again as a result of poor harvests across southern Asia.

As noted in Chapter 2, the spread of prices between different markets can be measured by, among other methods , the coefficient of variation (CV). The data contains many gaps, but it may still be illuminating to show some information on average price dispersion. Table 3.3 therefore shows the average CV for three towns each in Ceylon,[140] Java,[141] and Bengal, as well as the average CV between Colombo, Batavia and Chinsurah (shown as 'Asia' in Table 3.3).

In addition, one can also look at correlations between prices to see whether the prices show similar movements and trends in the various towns, which would also imply a certain degree of integration.[142] The correlation coefficients of the rice prices are shown in Table 3.4A–3.4C. For Bengal, the numbers of overlapping years were very few and no correlations were significant. Yet for Ceylon and Java there were sufficient observations for correlation analysis. Galle, Jaffna and Kalpitiya were all in connection with Colombo, and only the correlation with Tuticorin (part of the Ceylon administration, but located on the southern tip of India) is insignificant. Tuticorin traded mostly with Kalpitiya, which was located directly across the Palk Strait. In addition, the correlation between Jaffna and Galle was also insignificant as these were situated on the far northern- and southern-most tips of the island, respectively. On Java (Table 3.4B), there was a relatively strong connection between Batavia and

140 Colombo, Galle and Kalpitiya, as data were most abundant for these places.

141 Batavia, Cirebon and Semarang for the same reason.

142 For correlation analysis we want the series to be stationary, which is often not the case. Therefore the data are usually differenced. Due to the limited observations this is not feasible in this case (as we would again lose many observations). The correlations shown here are only indicative and should not be considered robust evidence of market integration.

TABLE 3.4A *Correlation coefficients for rice prices in Ceylon, 1688–1789.*

	Colombo	Galle	Jaffna	Kalpitiya	Tutucorin
Colombo	1.00	–	–	–	–
Galle	0.41	1.00	–	–	–
Jaffna	0.61	0.33	1.00	–	–
Kalpitiya	0.49	0.44	-0.00	1.00	–
Tutucorin	0.26	0.18	0.09	0.62	1.00

TABLE 3.4B *Correlation coefficients for rice prices in Java, 1700–1801.*[143]

	Batavia	Cirebon	Semarang	Surabaya	Tegal
Batavia	1.00	–	–	–	–
Cirebon	0.51	1.00	–	–	–
Semarang	0.32	0.82	1.00	–	–
Surabaya	0.12	0.50	0.58	1.00	–
Tegal	0.55	0.69	0.80	0.64	1.00

TABLE 3.4C *Correlation coefficients for rice prices around the Indian Ocean, 1688–1789.*

	Bengal	Colombo	Batavia
Bengal	1.00	–	–
Colombo	0.01	1.00	–
Batavia	-0.11	0.33	1.00

Sources: Tables 3.4a–3.4c; Figures 3.4–3.6.

cities that were close: Batavia, Cirebon and Tegal; the relationship is a little weaker for Semarang (which is slightly further east) and the correlation with Surabaya (even further east) was insignificant. As all the cities were positioned between Batavia and Surabaya, the other correlations were all significant. Finally, Table 3.4C shows that, despite the gap in price levels, there was a

143 While there were also observations for Gresik, Pekalongan and Joana these referred only to the second half of the eighteenth century and were omitted from the analysis.

relationship between prices in Batavia and Colombo, which also fits the evidence of rice shipments from the former to the latter.

Due to the limitations of the data, these figures should not be interpreted as robust information on the integration of markets. However, in general one can conclude that price developments exhibit similar trends and price gaps are relatively limited within the same region (relatively low CVs), but not across regions (higher CVs for 'Asia'). This corroborates research by Studer, as well as that of Dobado-Gonzales et al., suggesting limited market integration across greater distances in Asia.[144] From the correlation coefficients in Table 3.4 a similar picture emerges: among most Ceylonese and Javanese towns the CV for rice prices was relatively large and significant (although declining with distance). For the purpose of this chapter (Chapter 3) in mind, one can conclude that the developments being compared between the major cities (Batavia, Cape Town, Chinsurah and Colombo) may in fact be representative for developments in the wider regions (Java, Cape Colony, Bengal, and Ceylon).[145] Yet between regions across Asia, trends could differ more profoundly, which reinforces the argument that comparisons in the Great Divergence debate should not be based only on the levels of continents (i.e. Europe vs. Asia) but have to take into account differences within these continents as well.

Thus, Figures 3.5–3.7 already hint that prices were higher – much higher – in Ceylon than in both Bengal and Java. Whereas in Bengal and Java prices for a kilogram of rice were higher than 10 cents for only a few exceptional years (of crisis), Ceylonese prices were generally around that level, and often above. The comparative cost of living in these regions will be analysed further in the next subsection.

5.4 *Global Price Comparisons*

Before proceeding with this analysis, some smaller practical issues that can further frustrate the creation of historical time series should be considered. Prices in the period of interest were recorded in different coinages: for example, *rixdollars*, *guilders*, *stuivers*, or sometimes *rupees*. In order to make global comparisons one needs to know market exchange rates to be able to convert these prices from one coinage to another. Such rates are, however, missing in many cases. Because silver coins were the principal medium of exchange in most early modern states, the solution is to convert the coins to the weight of silver

144 Rafael Dobado-Gonzalez, Alfredo Garcia-Hiernaux and David E. Guerrero, 'West versus East: Early Globalization and the Great Divergence', *Mimeo* 2013.

145 At least in terms of prices, regional wage dispersion is discussed in the next chapter.

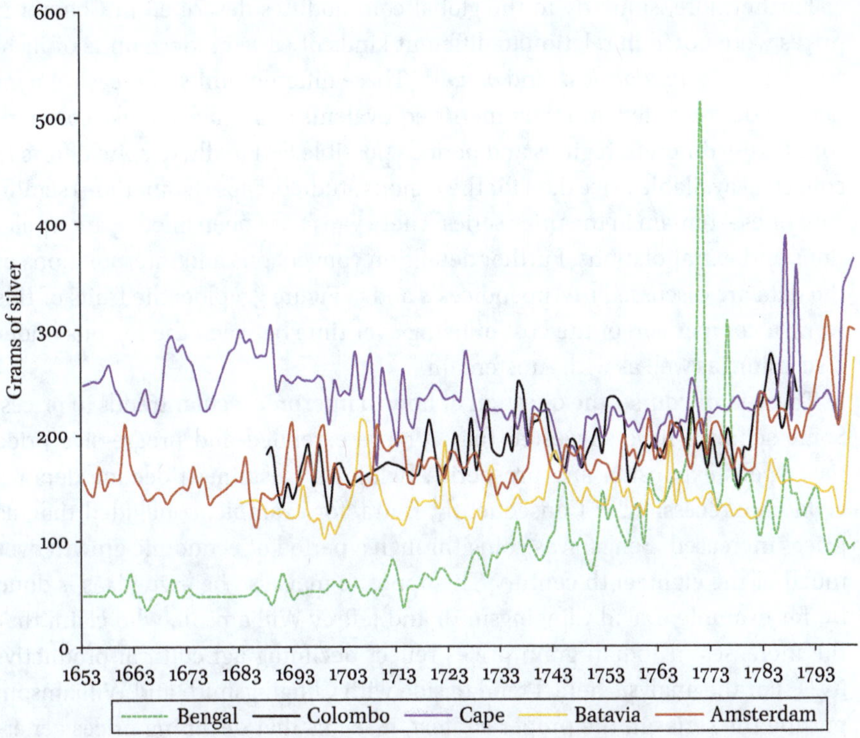

FIGURE 3.7 *Price of a subsistence basket in Europe and Asia, 1650–1800.*
Sources: see text and Allen, 'India in the Great Divergence'; Allen et al., 'Wages, prices'.

they could buy per unit.[146] The Dutch guilder contained 9.8 grams of silver up to 1680 and 9.61 grams of silver from 1681 onwards.[147] For some time, the value of the guilder used by the VOC in Asia was lower than the guilder in the Dutch Republic and this Asian currency was therefore referred to as 'light money'. Yet, the value of the Asian relative of the Dutch guilder fluctuated throughout the seventeenth and eighteenth centuries. According to Els Jacobs, one Asian guilder was worth 20 percent less than the Dutch guilder prior to 1743; 16.35 percent less between 1743 and 1768; while after 1768 the differences disappeared.[148]

146 Allen, 'Real Wages', p. 158.

147 Jan Luiten van Zanden, 'Prices and wages and the cost of living in the western part of the Netherlands, 1450–1800', website *Historical Prices and Wages* of the *International Institute of Social History*: http://www.iisg.nl/hpw/brenv.xls. Last update: December 11, 2009.

148 Jacobs, *Merchant in Asia*, pp. 300–304; Wolters, 'Heavy and light'; and Gaastra, *De geschiedenis*, pp. 144–5. See Appendix A2.2.

Furthermore, similarly to the global commodities described in Chapter 2, prices were noted in relation to different kinds of early modern units of measurement: e.g. *mudde*, *last*, and *pond*.[149] These different units of measurement need to be converted into their metric equivalents to be able to make comparisons across different regions and periods possible.[150] Finally, despite efforts to collect all available price data for the regions studied, gaps – sometimes significant ones – remain in the price series. These gaps have been filled by interpolations and extrapolations. Further details on conversions and interpolations of the data are discussed in Appendices 4 and 5. Figure 3.7 plots the fruits of this work: a comparison of the cost of living over time between the regions under discussion, as well as with Amsterdam.

There is, of course, the question of how to interpret secular trends in prices. Some scholars have suggested that 'a more extended and progressive price rise…spells expansion and prosperity, [while] a [sustained] decline denotes economic recession.'[151] Consequently, Datta, for example, concluded that, as prices increased, Bengal was going through a period of economic growth over much of the eighteenth century. The opposite may also be argued, as is done by, for example, David Clingingsmith and Jeffrey Williamson, who claim that the increases in Indian grain prices reflect declining agricultural productivity.[152] For the analysis here, I tend to side with Clingingsmith and Williamson: putting the series in the proper context, it seems that declining prices generally reflect increasing productivity (supply increases more than demand – i.e. population), while increasing prices reflect declining productivity or more pressure on supplies (due to population growth). As wages are usually rather sticky (as discussed in Chapter 4), increasing prices generally imply declining living standards.

Thus, a number of observations can be made on the basis of Figure 3.7. First of all, especially in the late seventeenth and early eighteenth centuries, prices seem to have been very high at the Cape, perhaps as a result of its remote location and its extensive system of agriculture. In the seventeenth century, it was difficult to grow enough food at the Cape, and additional rice had to be

149 For the old Dutch units of measurement and their metric value, see: J. M. Verhoeff, *De oude Nederlandse maten en gewichten* (Amsterdam: P. J. Meertens Instituut, 1982) and Appendix 1.

150 Drawing, for example, on the work by Verhoeff, *De oude Nederlandse;* and the VOC *Glossarium*: http://resources.huygens.knaw.nl/vocglossarium.

151 Datta, *Society, economy*, p. 195: citing C. E. Labrousse, 'Economic Fluctuations and the Individual', in: M. Aymard and H. Mukhia (eds.), *French Studies in History, vol. 1: the Inheritance* (Delhi, 1989) p. 271.

152 Clingingsmith and Williamson, 'Deindustrialization'.

imported from Java to feed its growing populace. The Cape therefore struggled to supply all bypassing ships with the necessary goods.[153] Over the course of the eighteenth century, wheat production expanded and prices slowly declined. A positive effect of VOC pricing policies was to avert many subsistence crises caused by harvest failures, while the farmers were ensured a guaranteed minimum price for their produce, even in years of abundant harvests. The crisis in the 1780s shows that the VOC could not defy the forces of the market entirely (see Figure 3.2).[154]

A second observation is that prices were also relatively high in Ceylon (as also noted in Subsection 5.3). Ceylon was generally unable to produce enough food for the entire population, making imports of large quantities of rice from Bengal, Coromandel (south-eastern India) and Java necessary (and therefore relatively expensive).[155] Thus one can observe a spike during, for example, the 1780s, when rice prices increased as it became harder to obtain rice from abroad (due to political turmoil in Coromandel, a shortage of sailors, and greater priority given to rice imports for Surat and Malabar).[156]

Third, prices seem to have been generally somewhat lower in Java. Only rice prices during the first half of the eighteenth century display serious spikes, mostly as a consequence of wars fought in that period. As I note in Chapter 2, the Company expanded its control over Java as it was drawn into various power struggles over the Mataram throne. In addition to the rebellion against the Susuhunan in the 1670s and 1680s, and the successful Company's campaigns against Banten in the early 1680s, the VOC intervened in three Javanese wars of succession (1704–07, 1719–23, and 1746–57), while Mataram, in turn, intervened in the Chinese war of 1741–1743.[157] These wars pushed up prices not only because of the destruction of crops, but also by limiting the possibilities of transporting rice from, for example, Java's north-east coast (the main area of rice production) to Batavia. As noted in earlier subsections, the peace that established after 1755 allowed relatively low price levels in the second part of the eighteenth century.[158] While perhaps hard to discern from Figure 3.7, these

---

153 Monica Wilson and Leonard Thompson, 'White Settlers and the Origin of a New Society, 1652–1778', in: ibid. (eds.), *The Oxford History of South Africa. Vol. 1.* (Oxford: Clarendon Press, 1971) p. 191.

154 Ross, 'The Cape'.

155 Sinnappah Arasaratnam, 'The Rice Trade in Eastern India 1650–1740', *Modern Asian Studies* 22 (1988) pp. 533–542; ibid., *Dutch power in Ceylon*, p. 130; K. M. de Silva, *A history of Sri Lanka* (London: Hurst, 1981) p. 171.

156 De Silva, *A history*, p. 172.

157 See: Ricklefs, *A History.*

158 See next chapter for more information.

prices show a slightly declining trend over most of the eighteenth century. Only at the end of the eighteenth and beginning of the nineteenth centuries, can a spike in Batavia prices be observed, this being the consequence of a series of bad harvests between 1795 and 1803[159] and the British blockade of Batavia.

Fourth, until the 1740s prices were lowest in Bengal. According to, for example, Parthasarathi, this may suggest the relatively high productivity of agriculture in this region. Clingingsmith and Williamson provide several reasons for why prices rose and agricultural productivity declined over the course of eighteenth century.[160] First of all, the waning of Mughal power led to increased occurrence of local wars, which not only led to destruction of crops and capital by marauding armies but also pulled important resources (men and animals) away from agriculture into military pursuits. Furthermore, there are indications that the revenue burden was higher among Mughal successor states and under British colonial government than under the Mughals. Finally, Clingingsmith and Williamson claim that the increased occurrence of droughts during the later eighteenth century lowered agricultural productivity and put further pressure on grain prices. Severe drought in 1769–1770 led to a famine that drove up prices dramatically. All of this occurred at the same time as the population (and thus demand) was growing relatively rapidly (see Chapter 5).

To conclude this subsection, the cost of living in these areas can be compared to that in Amsterdam. In terms of levels, the comparison confirms the observation by Allen et al. that prices were not generally higher in Europe than in Asia (which was suggested by, for example, Adam Smith). They found that in the eighteenth century the silver price of a subsistence basket in China (in Beijing and Shanghai) was roughly on a par with the cost of the subsistence in London and Leipzig. Similarly, prices in Amsterdam were on the same level as those in Ceylon, but slightly below those at the Cape. Only in Bengal and Java were prices lower.

At the same time, looking at the trends in this global comparison it seems that the price levels in these areas converged until the 1760s, after which they diverged. As this may be difficult to discern from Figure 3.7, I have plotted the coefficients of variation (CVs) of these series between 1688 and 1789 (when there is data for all series), which is shown in Figure 3.8. This convergence of CPIs (expressed in silver values) confirms Flynn and Giraldez' suggestion of a period of silver price convergence during the first half of the eighteenth century.[161]

---

159 Peter Boomgaard, 'From Subsistence Crises to Business Cycle Depressions, Indonesia 1800-1940', *Itinerario* 26 (2002) pp. 35–51.

160 Clingingsmith and Williamson, 'Deindustrialization'.

161 Flynn and Giraldez, 'Cycles of Silver'; ibid., 'Path Dependence'.

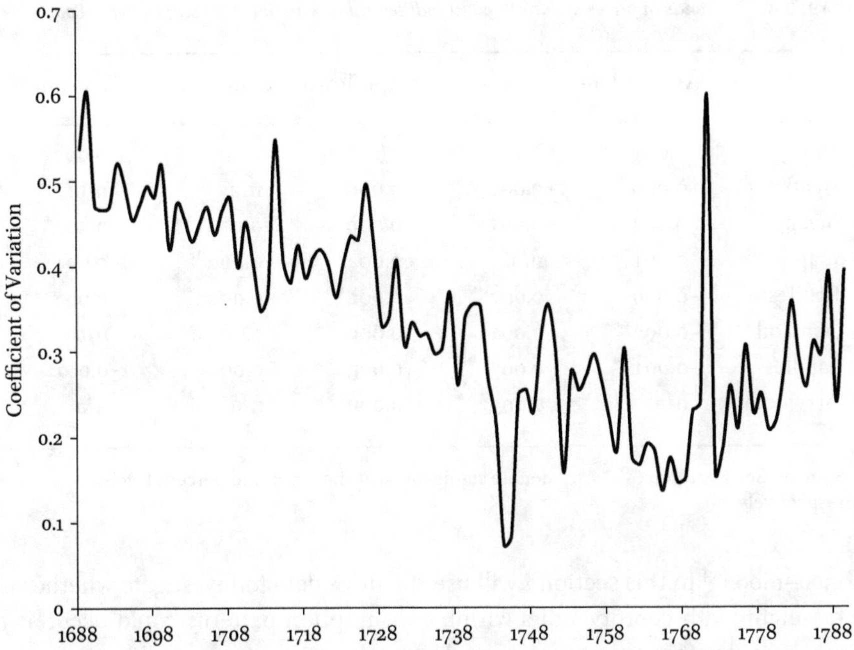

FIGURE 3.8 *Coefficients of variation (CVS) for CPIS of Amsterdam, Batavia, Chinsurah, Colombo and Cape Town.*
Sources: Figure 3.7.

6 Relative Prices and Luxury Consumption

The discussion has so far focussed on the development of prices of a single consumption basket over time. These series do not capture possible shifts in relative prices, which may have instigated a change in consumption patterns. Yet, Pomeranz suggested that:

> Europeans certainly ate more meat and far more dairy products than most peoples in Asia. But this advantage was declining, not growing, in the early modern period, and doing so rapidly: meat consumption in Germany, for instance fell by about 80 percent between the late Middle Ages and 1800.[162]

A recent study by Philip T. Hoffman et al., on the other hand, has shown that in Europe the prices of luxuries generally declined *vis-à-vis* grains in the period

162 Pomeranz, *The Great Divergence*, p. 35.

TABLE 3.5 *Trends in prices of various commodities, relative to the main staple, 1650–1800.*

	Amsterdam	Batavia	Cape Town	Colombo	Chinsurah
Butter	−0.001*	n/a	n/a	−0.002***	−0.002***
Meat[164]	−0.000	−0.002***	−0.006***	n/a	n/a
Sugar	0.004***	−0.001**	0.000	−0.003***	−0.005***
Soap	0.001**	n/a	0.004***	−0.002***	−0.001
Textiles	−0.000	0.002***	0.002**	−0.002***	−0.008***
Lamp oil	−0.002***	0.001	0.009***	0.001	n/a
Candles	−0.001**	0.003***	0.005***	0.001	−0.001
Firewood	n/a	0.003***	0.009***	n/a	n/a

Sources: See text. Note: ***, **, * denote significance at the 1, 5 and 10 percent levels respectively.

1500–1800.[163] In this section I will use the price data to investigate whether in the eighteenth century shifts within consumption patterns could occur as a result of declining relative prices of more luxurious items such as butter or textiles.

Table 3.5 shows the trends in prices of a variety of commodities relative to that of the main staple in Amsterdam, Batavia, Cape Town, Colombo and Chinsurah. As in Chapter 2, the trends were tested upon their level of significance. This table provides a mixed picture for the period 1650–1800. Whereas Jan de Vries has suggested that 'especially in the century following 1650'[165] there was a substantial shift in consumer patterns, Hoffman et al.'s figures show that most of the relative price decline of luxuries in Europe occurred in the period before 1650.[166] In Amsterdam after 1650 the relative prices of butter, lamp oil, and candles were declining, but not spectacularly so (butter and candles less than 0.1 percent per year and significant only at the 10 and 5 percent levels, respectively), while the relative price of soap showed increases of a similar order of magnitude, and that for sugar increased by a more impressive 0.4 percent annually.

Figure 3.1 already showed that the relative price of meat declined more spectacularly in the Cape Colony. The declining trend in meat prices makes it

163 Phillip T. Hoffman, David Jacks, Patricia A. Levin, and Peter H. Lindert, 'Real Inequality in Europe since 1500', *Journal of Economic History* 62 (2002) pp. 322–355.

164 In the case of Batavia, fish was used in the basket, but it shows the same trend as meat.

165 De Vries, 'The limits', p. 722, footnote 45.

166 See their Figure 1: Hoffman et al., 'Real Inequality', pp. 332–333.

likely that inhabitants at the Cape increased their meat consumption over the eighteenth century, as qualitative evidence on consumption patterns also suggests. All other products, however, became relatively more expensive over the period 1650–1800. While they may have enjoyed cheaper meat, cooking and eating it, especially when it was dark and cold outside, became more expensive. For Batavia, a similarly mixed picture emerges as meat and fish became relatively cheaper, while clothing, heating and lighting came to occupy a substantial part of the budget. The fact that textiles became more expensive over this period may account for the decline in textile imports observed by Reid. Only for Ceylon and Bengal did the prices of the other products included in the basket either decline relative to rice or show a similar trend (leading to an insignificant relative price trend). Remarkable for the relationship between trade and prices is that the relative price for clothing declined in Bengal. Cotton textiles were in demand (leading to higher prices) for long-distance trade, yet the price of grains increased faster. This suggests that increased local demand (due to population growth) relative to local supply (a possible decline in agricultural productivity), rather than international trade, was driving inflation over this period.

It is difficult to reach a straightforward conclusion on the basis of such mixed trends. Perhaps the best conclusion to make is that in the one-and-a-half centuries up to 1800 trends in relative prices within the basket do not point to dramatic changes in consumption patterns; some workers may have increased their meat or sugar consumption somewhat over this period, but this went at the expense of more costly fuel and lighting. Only in Bengal and Ceylon did most of the other commodities become consistently cheaper than rice over time, although this probably did not induce a change in consumption patterns as rice still represented the cheapest source calories, and, as shown in Chapter 4, these workers could not afford consumption above subsistence levels.

7 Conclusion

This chapter takes the first step needed to be able to meaningfully compare living standards between different regions in Asia, southern Africa and the rest of the world. Such comparisons are at the heart of the Great Divergence debate; while scholars of the 'California School' have suggested that living standards in many parts of Asia were on a par with Europe, various others have disputed such claims.

I have examined various measures of the standard of living, concentrated around three dimensions: income, health and education. Some of these measures require data that are usually unavailable before the 1800s, or suffer from issues of sample bias or their narrow focus on only one of the dimensions of the standard of living. Wage and price data, however, are available for a larger number of countries much further back in time and can contain information on the three elements of the standard of living. In recent years, a methodology has been developed that allows comparisons of real wages over time and space by creating baskets standardized on caloric values. These baskets reasonably reflect consumption patterns in the regions studied, as diets were relatively simple. This methodology is now widely used for global comparisons of living standards. Furthermore, the discussion of relative price trends in Section 6 suggests that shifts within consumption patterns between 1650 and 1800 were probably not very dramatic.

Figure 3.7 clearly shows that prices were relatively high at the Cape, even though agricultural expansion allowed a slight decline in prices during the eighteenth century. Prices in Ceylon were also relatively high and comparable to prices in Amsterdam (Ceylon remained dependant on imported rice for the entire period under discussion), in contrast to Bengal and Java, where the cost of living was generally lower than in north-western Europe. Bengal initially profited from a relatively productive agriculture sector, producing surpluses that were sent not only to Ceylon but also to towns along the coast of India, as well as the rest of Southeast Asia.[167] In Java, besides the war-time peaks in the late seventeenth and early eighteenth century, prices were comparatively low over most of the eighteenth century. The peace and stability that followed the 1740s led to an expansion of agriculture and declining prices, a trend that was only reversed in the early 1800s, the result of a series of bad harvests and the British blockade of Batavia.

What about the relationship between international trade and the price developments sketched above? Recent research on the Cape Colony has demonstrated that agricultural production responded to the arrival and departure of ships sailing to and from the East Indies.[168] Figure 3.7 shows that as this trade did not lead to inflation in the long run it may have had beneficial effects on the economy. In Ceylon and Java there was also no consistent rise in prices. As noted, prices in Ceylon were generally high throughout the period. Considering the relatively low and declining prices in Java at a time of expanding monetization and production (see Chapter 5), it is more likely that trade may have had a

167 Parthasarathi, *Why Europe*, p. 69; Arasaratnam, 'The Rice Trade'.

168 Willem H. Boshoff and Johan Fourie, 'The significance of the Cape trade route to economic activity in the Cape Colony: a medium-term business cycle analysis', *European Review of Economic History* 14 (2010) pp. 469–503.

beneficial impact. Only in the case of Bengal should we reckon with the possibility that the 'bullion for goods'[169] trade led to inflation as prices more than tripled over the eighteenth century, which must have put downward pressure on living standards. However, one cannot be sure that this increase was primarily caused by trade, rather than by lower agricultural productivity due to changing climate and increased rent-seeking under Mughal successor states and English rule, as suggested by Clingingsmith and Williamson.[170] Considering the relative price decline of cotton textiles, the major commodity in the 'global trade carousel',[171] Clingingsmith and Williamson's hypothesis seems more plausible than inflation caused by trade. These price trends were thus to a great extent determined by local developments. At the same time, it cannot be ignored that the CPIs expressed in silver equivalents in Europe, southern Africa and Asia show a converging trend over the eighteenth century, with the coefficient of variation declining from 0.5 in the late seventeenth to 0.2 in the mid-eighteenth century. This confirms Flynn and Giraldez' argument about converging silver prices in this period[172] and provides another clue that some degree of globalization was already underway in this period.

While these price series alone are already very informative about the economies under study, prices only contain information about the standard of living if they are combined with reliable data on wages. In the next chapter, wage data will be discussed and combined with these prices in order to estimate standards of living.

---

169 Prakash, 'Bullion for Goods'.

170 Clingingsmith and Williamson, 'Deindustrialization'.

171 To paraphrase Andre Gunder Frank: *ReORIENT: global economy in the Asian age* (Berkely: University of California Press, 1988), p. 52.

172 Flynn and Giraldez, 'Cycles of Silver'.

CHAPTER 4

Wages and the Standard of Living

1 Introduction

The second step in the calculation of living standards (the first being taken in Chapter 3) requires an estimation of the wages in these case studies. Adam Smith already suggested in the eighteenth century that there was a clear global division of wages, with higher wages in Europe than anywhere in Asia.[1]

A variety of recent studies have investigated comparative real wages in the light of the Great Divergence debate. Whereas Pomeranz and Parthasarathi claimed that incomes and wages were on a par or higher than in Europe in the eighteenth century, these studies have shown that real wages in Japan, China and India were lower than in England or the Dutch Republic. They were on a par with cities in other parts of Europe, however. Allen et al. therefore conclude that 'it was only England and the Low Countries that pulled ahead of the Rest. The Rest, in this context, includes not only Asia, but also much of Europe'.[2] In this chapter, new wage evidence will be combined with the prices for the consumption baskets discussed in the Chapter 3. This exercise will reveal where Bengal, the Cape Colony, Ceylon and Java are on this eighteenth-century wage ladder, thereby providing new insights for the Great Divergence debate.

Moreover, as Jean-Laurent Rosenthal and R. Bin Wong note 'we know that when economies are growing rapidly, wages rise, and when economies run into trouble, wages fall'.[3] This chapter will thus reveal more about trends in economic development over the seventeenth and eighteenth centuries, trends that have been the subject of some discussion in the historiographies of these different areas.

First of all, in the case of Bengal, the eighteenth century has traditionally been seen as 'an epoch of decay, chaos, greed and violence'.[4] British imperialism, beginning with the Battle of Plassey in 1757, and globalization have often been blamed for the economic malaise,[5] although climatic factors and the

1 See: Allen, 'India in the Great Divergence', p. 9.

2 Allen et al., 'Wages, prices', p. 31.

3 Jean-Laurent Rosenthal and R. Bin Wong, *Before and Beyond Divergence. The Politics of Economic Change in China and Europe* (Cambridge MA: Harvard U.P., 2011) p. 43.

4 David Washbrook, 'Eighteenth Century Issues in South Asia', *Journal of the Economic and Social History of the Orient* 44 (2001) p. 372.

5 Tirthankar Roy, 'Beyond divergence: rethinking the economic history of India', Economic History of Developing Regions 27 (2012) pp. 57–65; ibid., 'Economic History and Modern India'.

 | DOI 10.1163/9789004299665_005

disintegration of the Mughal Empire have also been put forward as reasons.[6] At the same time, a number of relatively recent studies have argued that rather than an age of decline, there are also indications of economic blossoming over the eighteenth century. Tilottama Mukherjee remarked in 2011 that 'Bengal experienced a long-term elaboration and expansion of the economy in the eighteenth century, marked by urbanisation and commercial growth.'[7] Similar revisionist claims have also been made regarding eighteenth-century Gujarat,[8] and northern India.[9] Nonetheless, the latest GDP per capita estimates for India as a whole clearly point to a decline,[10] in line with earlier estimates of real wages and other measures of the standard of living.[11]

The view of destitute inhabitants of the Cape Colony, put forward in much of the older literature, has mostly been based on farmers' letters describing their own impoverishment.[12] As noted in Chapter 3 (Subsection 5.2), such qualitative and biased observations should be treated with great caution. The study of living standards in the Cape Colony has experienced a revival in the past few years and the results from that research have altered this picture. Du Plessis and Du Plessis have shown that VOC officials at the Cape enjoyed rising living standards over the eighteenth century as a result of declining prices.[13] Johan Fourie used evidence from probate inventories to show that the possession of luxury goods by Cape farmers compared favourably with England and Holland, and that the poorer farmers became wealthier over the course of the eighteenth century.[14] Recent estimates of GDP per capita also point to a society where the average inhabitant enjoyed an income comparable to those in north-western Europe. Per capita income declined over the eighteenth century, however, pointing to stagnation rather than growth.[15]

---

6 Clingingsmith and Williamson, 'Deindustrialization'.

7 Tilottama Mukherjee, 'Markets in eighteenth century Bengal economy', *Indian Economic and Social History Review* 48 (2011) p. 144. Similar suggestions were made by Datta, *Society, economy*.

8 Nadri, *Eighteenth-Century Gujarat*.

9 Bayly, *Rulers, townsmen*.

10 Stephen Broadberry, Johann Custodis and Bishnupriya Gupta, 'India and the Great Divergence: An Anglo-Indian Comparison of GDP per capita, 1600–1871', *Explorations in Economic History* (2015) pp. 58–75.

11 Allen, 'India in the Great Divergence'.

12 Johan Fourie and Jan Luiten van Zanden, 'GDP in the Dutch Cape Colony: the national accounts of a slave-based society', *South African Journal of Economics* 81 (2013) p. 471.

13 Du Plessis and Du Plessis, 'Happy in the service'.

14 Fourie, 'The remarkable wealth'. Fourie and Uys, 'Luxury product consumption'.

15 Fourie and Van Zanden, 'GDP in the Dutch Cape'.

Regarding Southeast Asia as a whole, Reid stresses that he could find no evidence of famines, starvation or misery in the accounts of early European travellers (as was the case for India and China), and he gives examples of daily wages in c. 1600 that were on average 25 times the daily rice requirements of one person.[16] Experts on Javanese economic history have pointed to declining living standards over time. Peter Boomgaard found a declining trend in real wages over the eighteenth century.[17] Merle Ricklefs concluded that 'on balance, Dutch involvement in Java was to a great extent a catastrophe for all concerned'.[18] Luc Nagtegaal, however, notes that while the thesis of the underdevelopment of Java over the seventeenth and eighteenth centuries is not implausible, the opposite could also have been the case.[19] Following Smithian theory, he suggested that increasing trade may have led to more effective use of land and labour.[20]

For Ceylon, little is known about the trends in living standards over the seventeenth and eighteenth centuries. As in the case of Java, most of the historiography has generally assumed that, due to its mercantilist policies, the Company contributed to the underdevelopment of the island.[21] At the same time, Arasaratnam has noted that in Jaffna prosperity increased and that some groups of workers could benefit from the increased demand for labour by the VOC, especially in the construction and commercial sectors. For this period, so far no consistent data on any indicator of economic development has been put forward that could shed light on this.

The remainder of this chapter will proceed as follows. In Section 2 I introduce the sources I have used for the wage data and extensively discuss the problems associated with those data. Section 3 uses these data, in combination

16 Reid, *Southeast Asia*, p. 130: his range varies between 2.7 (for a slave) and 650 (caulker) times the daily rice requirement. The average of 25 is taken from Peter Boomgaard, 'Why work for wages? Free labour in Java 1600–1900', *Economic and Social History in the Netherlands* 2 (1990) p. 44.

17 Boomgaard, 'Why work'.

18 Merle C. Ricklefs, *Modern Javanese Historical Tradition. A Study of an Original Kartasura Chronicle and Related Materials* (London: SOAS, 1978) p. 3.

19 Nagtegaal, *Rijden*, p. 197.

20 Although in the English version of his dissertation, published a few years later, he clearly sides with the view that the VOC caused underdevelopment: Luc Nagtegaal, *Riding the Dutch tiger: the Dutch East Indies Company and the northeast coast of Java, 1680–1743* (Leiden: KITLV Press, 1996).

21 See, for example, Sinnappah Arasaratnam, Dutch Commercial Policy in Ceylon and its effects on the Indo-Ceylon Trade (1990–1750)', *Indian Economic and Social History Review* 4 (1967) pp. 109–130; Schrikker, *Dutch and British*, p. 2.

with the prices from the previous chapter, to calculate real wages and compares these with real wages with those in China, Japan and Europe. In Section 4 wage differentials between skilled and unskilled workers are analysed in order to discuss differences in human capital formation across the globe. Section 5 sums up the findings presented in the chapter.

2 Wage Data

In this section, I present a time series of nominal wages that is based on wage observations taken from a variety of sources. Because wage data are generally much scarcer than price data, significant gaps had to be filled by estimating the trend of wages over time.[22] The various sources for the wage observations are introduced and several problems related to the creation of a nominal wage series are discussed.

2.1 *Sources*

The most 'ideal' source of wages are statements of the expenses incurred for the construction and repairs of VOC buildings and ships in the various regions. These documents could be scattered individually throughout the general VOC-OBP series or were inserted among the 'Proceedings of the Political Council' that are part of the OBP; the latter was generally the case for Bengal. These documents state the costs of materials for building projects, as well as the various types of workers hired, the number of days they were employed.[23] As real wage studies for other areas, such as Europe, have often used wages of building craftsmen and labourers, wages taken from these documents are quite comparable with those in other studies. Furthermore, most of the wages registered in these documents were reported as daily rates, which are generally preferred over monthly or annual rates. Especially for Bengal, this turned out to be a rich source of information on wages.

A second source of wage data is the separate VOC archive series of the 'General Land and Sea Muster Rolls'. Rolls for almost the entire eighteenth century are still available in The Hague, while separate rolls for different

22 As done by Allen, 'India in the Great Divergence', and Allen et al., 'Wages, prices'.

23 Unfortunately, in some cases, especially for those on Java and Ceylon, no mention was made of the number of days that the workers were hired for, or all the figures were aggregated, which makes it impossible to calculate daily wages. These could, thus, not be used in this research. The availability of even more of such documents than those employed in this study does suggest that labour for wages may have been widespread.

establishments are also available for the seventeenth century. These rolls are well-known sources for studying Company servants serving on ships and at various establishments in Asia. For our purposes, it is important that these rolls state the monthly wages of Company servants employed at the different VOC establishments in the East Indies. These sources, however, generally cover only European personnel, which make them less interesting for this book. For the Cape Colony, wages from five of these rolls were already collected for a number of benchmark years between 1699 and 1790 by Sophia and Stan du Plessis.[24] I have supplemented their data by adding wages from the earliest muster rolls from the years 1657 and 1658.[25]

For Ceylon specifically, the Colombo account books, which have survived for the years 1759–1790, constitute the most important source of information.[26] Quantitatively these books of accounts are a treasure trove for studies on the VOC's business in Ceylon.[27] For this book, the monthly statements of wages paid to European and indigenous servants of the Company are the most interesting: the monthly wages paid to a great variety of servants on the payroll, ranging from washers to village heads, are at our disposal.[28] In addition to these data, wages were assembled for a few earlier years from scattered 'lists' or 'rolls' of the indigenous servants employed,[29] as well as from statements on the costs of building repairs.[30]

In the case of Java, next to wages taken from statements of the costs of building construction, ship-building and ship's repairs, the *Nederlandsch-Indische Plakaatboeken*, i.e. the collection of proclamations by the Governor and Council of the Indies, contained numerous decrees setting the wages of coolies and craftsmen working for the Company. Additional wage observations were taken from other published sources, such as the *Dagh-register* and the

---

24 Du Plessis and Du Plessis, 'Happy in the service'. I thank Stan and Sophia for kindly sharing these data with me.

25 VOC 3991, 3992 and 4038. Furthermore, I collected data from muster rolls for 1778 and 1786 to trace the beginnings of the wage increases occurring in the late eighteenth century: VOC 12575 and 12602.

26 VOC 2985–3979.

27 See also Albert van den Belt, *VOC bedrijf op Ceylon. Een voorname vestiging van de Oost-Indische Compagnie in de 18de eeuw* (Zutphen: Walburg Pers, 2008).

28 These wage lists were available per month. I have assembled those from the months September or October, depending on the readability of the documents. A comparison with similar data collected for April suggested no wage changes across different months.

29 VOC 1340 f. 1416–1422; VOC 1351 ff. 2527–2531; VOC 1643, ff. 606–613; VOC 1544, f. 1218; VOC 2541, ff. 3149–3193; VOC 8902 ff. 540–566; VOC 839 f. 767; VOC 8978 ff. 446–449.

30 VOC 1351 f. 2514–2515; VOC 8974 f. 2011–2013.

Verhandelingen van het Bataviaasch Genootschap,[31] as well as various secondary sources.[32]

2.2 *Representativeness*

A potential problem with wages taken from VOC sources can be caused by a bias in the reported rates. Such a bias may have occurred in two ways. First, there could be an upward bias as an additional premium was possibly paid to ensure the efficiency and loyalty of the local workers. Second, the opposite may have been the case, as the dominant position of the VOC in many places may have allowed it to "squeeze" these workers into accepting lower wages. I will investigate this problem of bias by comparing VOC wages with those found in other sources, in order to say something about the representativeness of wages paid by the VOC against wage levels generally prevailing in a society.

This issue is probably the least problematic in the case of Bengal, where the Company had relatively little power to influence the labour market. Here, the VOC, like the EIC and other European companies, entered a mature labour market and had to pay market rates.[33] This also becomes clear when comparing wages from VOC sources with wages from other literature. At the beginning of the eighteenth century, between 1703 and 1711, the EIC paid a peon at Fort William (in Calcutta) between 1.5 and 2 rupees per month,[34] while the VOC paid between 1.69 and 2.25 rupee in 1699,[35] and 2.5 rupee in 1709, only slightly higher. In the 1750s the literature reports wages of around 2.5 rupees per month for a peon employed by the English,[36] while Dutch sources suggest 2.44 rupees

---

31 The *Dagh-Register* is a diary of events that took place in Batavia and other important news for the VOC reported on a daily basis. The years between 1624 and 1682 have been published. The *Verhandelingen* is a journal that was distributed by the Batavian Society for Arts and Sciences between 1779 and 1922. Van der Chijs (ed.) *Nederlandsch-Indisch*; De Jonge (ed.), *Opkomst*; Heeres et al. (eds.) *Dagh-register*; Hooyman, 'Verhandelingen'.

32 Boomgaard, *Children*; ibid., 'Why work'; Feenstra, 'Dutch Coins'; Frederik de Haan, *Priangan: de Preanger-regentschappen onder het Nederlandsch bestuur tot 1811* (Batavia: 1910–12); Nagtegaal. *Rijden*.

33 More on this in Chapter 5, but see also Jan Lucassen, 'Working at the Ichapur Gunpowder Factory in the 1790s (Part I)', *Indian Historical Review* 39 (2012) pp. 19–56; ibid., 'Working at the Ichapur Gunpowder Factory in the 1790s (Part II)', *Indian Historical Review* 39 (2012) pp. 251–271; Parthasarathi, *Why Europe*, p. 59.

34 Mukerjee, *Economic History*, p. 49.

35 VOC 8734, f. 109: 2 peons were paid 2.25 rupees per month, 2 got 2 rupees, 1 received 1.75 rupees, while 4 peons earned 1.69 rupees per month.

36 See Allen and Studer, 'Prices and Wages': 1751–1752; Calcutta: Mukerjee, *Economic History*, p. 49.

per month in the period 1745–1755.[37] In the late 1780s wages for coolies at Fort William had increased to 3 rupees,[38] whereas the Dutch paid coolies even 3.3 rupees per month in Chinsurah. However, the data are not always consistent with this picture: in the late 1730s the English paid a wage of 2.5 rupees per month in 'Bengal' and Kasimbazar,[39] while in 1738 the Dutch paid 3.75 rupees to a peon in Chinsurah, and a similar wage in Kasimbazar in 1743, although this wage fell again to 2.0–2.5 rupees in the late 1740s.[40] Furthermore, we find a wage of 3 rupees paid to peons by the English in Dhaka in 1774, while in the same year the VOC reports a wage of only 1.98 rupees there. Nonetheless, one may conclude that these wages – exceptions apart – are on roughly the same levels, and that there seems to be no consistent downward or upward bias in VOC wages.

In the Cape Colony, although the evidence is limited, there we do see a consistent discrepancy between the wages earned by workers still under VOC contract and those *knechts* working without a long-term contract as, for example, farmhands. The Company's *knechts* could also be VOC soldiers or sailors hired out to a settler. They signed a renewable one-year contract with the head of a household and received a monthly cash wage. After 1692 all contracts between Company *knechts* and settlers had to be in writing and wages were fixed until 1795. The free *knechts* (among them a number of free blacks) did not enjoy institutional and contractual protection from the VOC, but their wages were significantly higher.[41] Zacharias Wagenaar, Commander of the Cape, noted in 1666 that free Dutch servants received 'besides their gratuitous subsistence, ten and twelve, aye! fourteen and fifteen guilders monthly'.[42] Ad Biewenga suggests that the average wage of a building labourer around 1700 was 13 to 14 guilders per month (roughly 1.5 times the wage of the lowest ranking VOC employee).[43] Skilled work was even more lucrative, as G. W. van Imhoff,

37 VOC 8796, 8798, 8800, 8802, 8804, 8805.

38 Data from ongoing work by Jan Lucassen, collected from the *British Military Board Proceedings* at the National Archives of India in New Delhi. I thank Jan for sharing these with me.

39 See Bengal: Allen and Studer, 'Prices and Wages': 1737; Bhattacharya, *East India Company*, p. 205; Kasimbazar: A. S. M. A. Hussain, 'A Quantitative Study of Price Movements in Bengal during eighteenth and nineteenth centuries', (London: unpublished PhD thesis, 1976) p. 33.

40 Kasimbazar is situated c. 175 km north of Chinsurah.

41 R. C. -H. Shell, *Children of Bondage. A social history of a slave society at the Cape of Good Hope, 1652–1838* (Johannesburg: Wits University Press, 1997) p. 13.

42 D. Moodie (ed.), *The Record, or a Series of Official Papers Relative to the Condition and Treatment of the Native Tribes of South Africa* (Cape Town: Balkema, 1960) p. 293.

43 Ad Biewenga, *De Kaap de Goede Hoop: Een Nederlandse vestigingskolonie, 1680–1730* (Amsterdam: Bert Bakker, 1999) p. 101. A VOC soldier earned 9 guilders per month.

Governor-General of the VOC in Batavia, noted that free masons and carpenters earned between 8 and 9 *schellingen* per day in 1743, twice the wage of a VOC craftsman.[44]

Since there are detailed data available on the population and the labour market in the Cape Colony,[45] it is possible to correct for this bias. While these data will be further discussed in Chapter 5, for now it suffices to note that there are data available on the number of free *knechts* and the number of VOC servants. Using these data, VOC wages taken from the muster rolls could be corrected for underestimation by assuming 'free' unskilled wages were constantly 1.5 times, and that 'free' skilled wages were constantly 2 times higher than the VOC rates, and then adding shifting weights to these different wages on the basis of the information in Figure 5.7.[46]

One may expect that the issue could be more problematic in Ceylon and Java, where the VOC also held significant political power next to its role as a trader. However, as I shall discuss below in Chapter 5, it seems that next to the 'un-free' labour market, there was a 'free' labour market in operation, where the Company hired labourers at market rates. For Ceylon, wage evidence other than that from the VOC books is very limited, yet it suggests that even in the provinces of Ceylon where the Company wielded considerable political power, it still had to pay wages that were more or less in conformity with the market. In his description of Ceylon in 1672, the Reverend Baldaeus wrote that carpenters and masons earned five to six *stuivers* per day.[47] This is similar to the wage found for a carpenter and mason in VOC service in Mannar, earning 3 3/8 rix-dollars per month of 27 working days, which converts to six *stuivers* per day.[48] While in the memoir of Governor Julius Stein van Gollenesse (1743–1751) a monthly wage of 1 pagoda and a *parra* of rice, which translates into about 7 guilders, is noted for a craftsman working in a blacksmiths' shop (the wage noted in the VOC accounts is 7.2 guilders per month in 1769).[49]

44 J. X. Merriman (ed.), *The Reports of Chavonnes and his Council, and of Van Imhoff, on the Cape. With incidental correspondence* (Cape Town: The Van Riebeeck Society, 1918).

45 Van Duin and Ross, 'The economy', also see next chapter.

46 Employing the shares of VOC employees and *knechts* as weights for minimal and maximum wage rates. No data on these shares were available for the period between 1652 and 1700, therefore a linear time-trend was fitted to the share of VOC employees on the available data for 1701–1790: VOC = 0,1484t + 77,798 ($R^2 = 0.84$).

47 Baldaeus, *Naauwkeurige beschryvinge*, p. 188.

48 VOC 1544, f. 1218: 3 3/8 rix-dollar divided by 27 days is 0.13 rix-dollar (consisting of 48 *stuivers*) is 6 *stuivers* per day.

49 Julius Stein van Gollenesse, *Memoir of Julius Stein van Gollenesse, Governor of Ceylon. For his successor Gerrit Joan Vreeland on February 28, 1751*, translated by S. Arasaratnam

The only wages found in the secondary literature are those reported by Arasaratnam, who remarks that unskilled labourers earned fl. 6 guilders per month.[50] While this seems to be high compared with most of the other data gathered during my research, his observation stems from 1740, when a similar wage for a coolie was reported in the VOC accounts for that year.[51] His suggestion that wages of skilled craftsmen were around fl. 18, however, seems unlikely in the face of the other evidence. Perhaps he is accidently referring to a European craftsman.

For Java, comparisons between wage observations from different sources is more difficult, as the wages from the costs of building and repairs mostly refer to craftsmen in a variety of cities along Java's north-east coast, while those from the *Plakaatboeken* mostly relate to Batavia. However, perhaps the fact that there were at least 65 decrees concerned with setting wage levels of various labourers,[52] at least thirteen of which were specifically issued to increase the level of wages,[53] might suggest that the Company was adjusting wages to prevailing market rates. For example, an edict raising the wages of coolies working in the Chinese hospital in Batavia on January 5th, 1807 stated that the salary had to be raised to 5 *rix-dollars* per month, as no one could be found to work for only 3 *rix-dollars*.[54] An edict issued a couple of weeks later raised the wages of Chinese blacksmiths from 40 *stuivers* to one *rix-dollar* per day, because that was what they could earn on the free market.[55]

(Colombo, 1974) pp. 91 and 144: one pagoda was about 6 guilders, while a *parra* of rice cost about 1 guilder.

50 S. Arasaratnam, 'Historical foundation of the economy of the Tamils of north Sri Lanka', *Chelvanavakam Memorial Lectures* (Jaffna 1982) p. 17.

51 VOC 8978, f. 446.

52 Plakaatboek VIII: 30.5.1765; 9.8.1765; 27.9.1765; 25.5.1766; 8.9.1768; 16.3.1773; Plakaatboek X: ?.6.1776; 16.6.1778; 8.12.1778; 12.8.1779; 27.8.1779; 7.9.1779; 24.11.1783; 16.3.1784; Plakaatboek XI.: 29.6.1792; 20.9.1794; 27.9.1794; Plakaatboek XII: 26.12.1795; 26.12.1795; 16.1.1796; 16.1.1796; 16.1.1796; 23.1.1796; 11.2.1797; 24.3.1797; 1.7.1797; Plakaatboek XIII: 1.7.1800; Plakaatboek XIV: 12.10.1804; 2.5.1805; 28.6.1805; 17.5.1807; 29.9.1807; 14.1.1808; 22.1.1808; 27.1.1808; 11.2.1808; 26.2.1808; 19.6.1808; Plakaatboek XV: 8.7.1808; 20.9.1808; 8.10.1808; 2.11.1808; 30.11.1808; 9.6.1809; 19.5.1809; 8.5.1809; 8.5.1809; 9.3.1809; Plakaatboek XVI :27.6.1810; 19.7.1810; 3.2.1811.

53 Plakaatboek VIII: 25.8.1769; Plakaatboek X: 12.1.1780; 18.9.1781; 11.3.1785; Plakaatboek XII: 26.6.1795; Plakaatboek XIII: 6.9.1800; 4.11.1803; 9.12.1803; Plakaatboek XIV: 26.8.1806; 7.8.1806; 5.1.1807; 23.1.1807; 3.5.1808; Plakaatboek XV: 14.1.1809; 17.1.1809; 21.4.1809; 27.9.1809; Plakaatboek XVI: 9.1.1810; 14.2.1810; 27.6.1811; 7.7.1811.

54 Plakaatboek XIV: 18.1.1807. A rix-dollar or *rijksdaalder* was a coin worth 48 *stuivers*, equal to 2.40 guilders.

55 Plakaatboek XIV: 23.1.1807.

To summarize, there seems to be no consistent bias in the wage data for Bengal, while those for the Cape Colony have to be corrected for underestimation. For Ceylon and Java the evidence is limited, but, as will also be discussed in more detail below, a free labour market existed, where the VOC presumably paid wages at market rates. This last point shall be further investigated in Chapter 5.

2.3 *Regional Variation*

Another issue with the wage data is related to the difference between wages within each of the case studies. One of the assumptions in the real wage methodology is that the real wages computed for a major city in a country (often the capital) is somehow representative for developments for the wider region, or even the entire country. In Chapter 3, I showed that, although regional commodity markets may have been relatively well integrated and the prices showed similar trends across different cities, this may not have been the case for labour markets. In fact, most labour markets before the twentieth century seem to have been poorly integrated. For example, M. W. Flinn concludes that in England there were 'very clearly substantial regional variations in wages' in the eighteenth and nineteenth centuries.[56] Even by the early twentieth century the integration of labour markets in England was far from complete.[57] At the same time, De Vries notes the difference between nominal wages in the Eastern and Western Netherlands in the seventeenth and eighteenth centuries.[58]

As in the case of prices, the Cape will not be included as that case was dominated by one city. While wages for free *knechts* may have fluctuated further back in the hinterland (see also Subsection 2.2), there are simply no data at this time on which to base any conclusions.

More information is available for Bengal (and Bihar). While most data refer to the main establishment in Chinsurah, there are also documents pertaining

56 M. W. Flinn, 'Trends in Real Wages, 1750-1850', *Economic History Review* 27 (1974) p. 404. For studies on wage differentials in Britain: E. H. Hunt, *Regional wage variations in Britain 1850–1914* (Oxford: Oxford U.P., 1973); ibid., 'Industrialisation and regional inequality: wages in Britain, 1760-1914', *Journal of Economic History* 46 (1986) pp. 935–966; F. W. Botham and E. H. Hunt, 'Wages in Britain during the Industrial Revolution', *Economic History Review* 40 (1987) pp. 380–399; Elizabeth W. Gilboy, *Wages in Eighteenth Century England* (Cambridge: Harvard U.P., 1934).

57 George R. Boyer and Tim Hatton, 'Regional Labour market integration in England and Wales, 1850-1913', in: G Grantham and M MacKinnon (eds.), *Labour Market Evolution* (London, 1994) p. 103.

58 Jan de Vries, 'How did pre-industrial labour markets work?', in: George Grantham and Mary Mackinnon (eds.), *Labour Market Evolution* (London, 1994) pp. 39–63.

to Balasore, Chapra,[59] Dhaka, Karriemabad, Kasimbazar, Patna, Singia, and Bettiah.[60] Table 4.1 compares wages for coolies in these towns for four benchmark periods.[61] The table shows that wages differed significantly between towns in Bengal and those in Bihar, but that within those regions the labour market was relatively well integrated. This is also the point of Jan Lucassen's observation that the workforce of a gunpowder factory at Ichapur, near Calcutta, consisted largely of migrants coming all the way from Chittagong (500 km east of Calcutta) and Bishnupur (130 km to the north-west).[62] At the beginning of the century, wages for unskilled coolies in Bengal were 0.06 rupees per day and this may have increased somewhat (to around 0.10-012 rupees) towards the end of the eighteenth century. Unskilled wages in towns in Bihar were initially one-third higher, but remained stable over the eighteenth century, and perhaps even declined slightly (see the observation for Patna 1788–89). A similar picture emerges from the nominal wages of skilled craftsmen, which are dealt with further in Appendix A6.1.

While most wage observations for Ceylon refer to Colombo, there are a few years for which we can make some comparisons between wages paid for

TABLE 4.1 *Unskilled daily wages in rupees, various towns in Bengal and Bihar, 1721–1789.*

		1721–31	1742–45	1758–59	1788–9
Bengal[63]	Balasore	–	0.06	–	–
	Chinsurah	0.06	0.06	0.06–0.07	0.10–0.11
	Dhaka	–	–	0.06–0.07	–
	Karriemabad	0.06	0.06	0.08	–
Bihar	Chapra	–	0.09	–	–
	Patna	0.09	0.09	0.09	0.08
	Singia	–	0.09	0.09	–

Sources: VOC archives: statements of costs of repairs and building construction in Bengal; see text and appendix.

59 Sioppra in the sources, situated very close to Patna.

60 Tettua in the sources, assumed to be Bettiah in Bihar. See also Murari Jha. *The Political Economy of the Ganga River. Highway of State Formation in Mughal India, c. 1600–1800* (unpublished PhD thesis, Leiden 2013).

61 Based on data availability.

62 Lucassen, 'Working at the Ichapur', pp. 19, 45–9.

63 There are also observations for the wages of coolies in Kasimbazar, but these could differ significantly even in one year, ranging from 0.06 rupees to 0.21 and even 0.29 rupee per

specific labourers in different towns. Some scattered observations of wages for carpenter's helpers, or *knechts*, are available for the seventeenth century. In Colombo these helpers earned fl. 0.14 per day in 1678 and 1681,[64] while those in Caliture in that same year, and Mannar in 1694, earned only half that amount (fl. 0.06-0.07).[65] However, by 1701 these wages in Mannar had increased to fl. 0.12 per day.[66] Coolie wages reported for Tutucorin in 1678–79 were similarly very low: fl. 0.06-fl. 0.09 per day.[67] The latter wages are dramatically low, and it can be assumed that these are not market-based wages for full-time free labourers, or that these workers received additional remuneration as otherwise they would not be able to sustain themselves at those rates. Coolie wages in Colombo in the period 1762–1790 were consistently fl. 0.18 per day.[68] Only in the years 1789–90 are coolie wages available for several locations: in addition to Colombo, wages are also available for Jaffna and Tutucorin (southern India, but administered from Ceylon). These earnings do roughly correspond, as in Tutucorin coolies earned fl. 0.20 per day,[69] while those in Jaffna (as in Colombo) were paid fl. 0.18 per day.[70] In 1789 a carpenter's helper in Galle earned on average fl. 0.15 per day, but he received additional rice.[71] See Appendix 6 for more details on differences in the wages of skilled workers.

These data are not conclusive, but on the basis of my observations one can hypothesize that the free labour market in Ceylon was relatively underdeveloped in the latter seventeenth century, but that over the seventeenth and eighteenth centuries the labour market matured and the importance of wage labour increased. This is also confirmed by the literature, as will be discussed in Chapter 5. Wages reported for Colombo in the latter seventeenth century are probably not entirely representative for the whole island, but it is likely that the wage-labour market became better integrated in the later eighteenth century.

---

day. Because it is unclear what exactly caused these high wages (especially since the high rates were also higher than those for masons and carpenters), Kasimbazar has been left out of the analysis.

64 fl. 3.60 per month: VOC 1340 f. 1417; 1351 f. 2527; 8902 f. 540.

65 VOC 1340 f. 1417v; 1544 f. 1218.

66 VOC 1643 f. 613.

67 VOC 1340 f. 1418; VOC 1351 f. 2529.

68 fl. 4.80 per month; source: Colombo account books.

69 These were hired for a year for fl. 66.40: VOC 3977, f. 1808.

70 Wages for Jaffna were noted down per day; coolies in Colombo earned 2 rix-dollars per month, which, assuming a 26-day working week and 2.4 guilders per rix-dollar, equals fl. 0.18 per day.

71 This is an average: 36 carpenter's helpers earned fl. 4.95 per month and 2 *parra* of rice, while 16 received fl. 1.83 per month and 1 *parra* of rice: VOC 3922 ff. 1510–1512.

There are almost no comparable data for unskilled coolies across Java before the eighteenth century. The little comparative evidence available suggests that wages in Batavia, as one would expect, were higher than those elsewhere on the island. Around 1686 a coolie in Cirebon made 3 *stuivers* (fl. 0.15) per day, less than half that of a coolie in Batavia, who earned 4 *rix-dollars* per month (fl. 0.37 per day). In the 1740s a coolie in Surabaya earned 6 *stuivers* per day, only slightly below the wage in Batavia of 8 *stuivers* per day. Half a century later, around 1810, coolies in Surabaya earned 8 to 12 *stuivers* per day, while those in Batavia earned 12 to 20 per day. More evidence about wage levels across Java's north-east coast is available for a variety of skilled workers in Appendix 6, Table A6.5. The table shows that wages could differ, not only between occupations (a mason often earned more than a carpenter in Java), but also between cities. Interestingly, wages of carpenters across Java (with the possible exception of Batavia) were roughly equal (fl. 0.30 per day until the 1740s, and fl. 0.60 at the end of the eighteenth century), while those for masons could differ radically. Masons in Demak, Japara, and Rembang could earn as much as fl. 1.20 per day, while those in Surabaya and Semarang got only half that amount, and those in Cirebon earned only fl. 0.30 per day. Because these wage differentials occur only for masons, it seems implausible that this difference was driven by variations in the extent of VOC power in these towns.[72] It is more likely that these wage differentials were in fact driven (as noted above) by market mechanisms of supply and demand: masons were probably more scarce and in higher demand in Demak, Japara, and Rembang than elsewhere.

The data on the spread of wages *within* the various regions is too limited and too heterogeneous to estimate the exact differentials *across* these regions. It is clear, however, that wages in Batavia and Colombo may not be entirely representative for their respective islands. This is not different from what has been observed for other parts of the world. In England nominal wages in Oxford were roughly half the levels in London in the seventeenth and eighteenth centuries,[73] while in the Dutch Republic the daily nominal wage for a master carpenter in Holland (Alkmaar) was about 50 percent higher than those in the eastern provinces (Kampen, Overrijsel) around 1800.[74] Only across Bengal were wage rates very similar, but, again, these differed from those in Bihar. For

72 For example, since the VOC had a less dominant position in Japara than in Cirebon it had to pay a (larger) premium to obtain reliable workers. Also, that would not explain why wages would be higher in Batavia, where the VOC was omnipresent.

73 Allen, 'The Great Divergence', and data on his personal website: http://www.nuffield.ox.ac.uk/People/sites/Allen/SitePages/Biography.aspx.

74 Jan Luiten van Zanden, *Arbeid tijdens het handelskapitalisme: opkomst en neergang van de Hollandse economie, 1350–1850* (Bergen: Octavo, 1991) pp. 136–137; although levels were closer to each other in earlier periods.

the comparisons of real wages I will compare trends and values between the main towns in these regions, so that in the global comparisons I am comparing apples to apples.

2.4 *Estimating a Time Series of Nominal Wages*

In order to be able to compare longer term trends in real wages it is necessary to translate the wage observations from sources into a continuous time trend of wages. To do so, a number of issues had to be resolved. As in the case of prices, wages were reported in different coinages (*rix-dollars*, *guilders*, *rupees*, etc.), and these all had to be converted into grams of silver to make them comparable. Furthermore, the wages found in the sources were reported for a variety of time units (per day, per week and per year); these had to be converted to daily rates in order to make them consistent. Whereas Allen et al. assumed 250 working days per year (21 working days per month) for Europe, the sources for Bengal, Java, and Ceylon suggest that a working month in these areas may have been between 26 and 30 days per month.[75] However, to ensure comparability with Allen et al., and as I wish to compare the purchasing power of wages *ceteris paribus*,[76] to estimate real wages I have assumed in my study that there were 21 working days in a month.

Another problem is formed by remunerations additional to wages in the form of money, such as board and lodging, which are not consistently mentioned in the sources. In the case of the Cape Colony, a report of the Council of Policy from 1717 and two VOC cashbooks (from 1754 and 1786) mention that the lowest ranking VOC employees received an additional 0.75 *reaal* and 31 pounds of wheat per month as board, while skilled craftsmen receive 1.5 to 2 *reaal* extra per month, as well as 3 *mudde* of wheat annually. These additional remunerations were found in separate sources and it can be assumed that all the workers on VOC contracts received similar extras. I have added the monetary value of these additions to the monthly wages.[77] For Ceylon and Java, on the other hand, the data suggest that only those labourers (probably those performing obligatory labour service) who received comparatively low wages received

75 Java: between: 26 and 30 days: Plakaatboek XII, p. 198 (16.1.1796), P. XIV, p. 566–8 (22.1.1808): coolies working 26 days per month; P. XIV p. 699 (3.5.1808). Bengal: 30 days according to differences between daily and monthly wages in VOC 8791 ff. 343–348, VOC 8793 f. 274–6. Ceylon: a month consisted of 30 days as wage notations for 15 days were exactly half the monthly wage: VOC 3204, 3235, 3265, 3323, 3379, 3404, 3434, 3487, 3518 (unfortunately these sources had no page numbers).

76 For Ceylon, this is not a major issue, as most wages were noted down per month, and the subsistence rates were based on annual salaries. For the comparison of nominal daily wages, for Ceylon these were also calculated on the basis of 250 work days per year.

77 Using the wheat price series to convert the 3 *muids* into guilder values.

additional remunerations.[78] Where nothing about additional remunerations was mentioned, no corrections were made.[79]

The problem is more complex for Bengal, as the sources only start mentioning rates with and without board from the 1770s onwards. This means that another assumption had to be made: either that if it was not explicitly mentioned in the sources, then these labourers did not in fact receive any extra income; or they received additional compensation, but this was just not consistently reported. Considering the increase in wages in the 1770s relative to the period before, especially board is included, it may be assumed that workers in the earlier decades of the eighteenth century also received board even though it was not explicitly mentioned. The various series and corrections are reported in Appendix 6, from which it becomes clear that the results reported here are biased against my conclusions (of low living standards in Bengal) as these assumptions result in the highest real wages over the eighteenth century (see Figure A6.1).

Finally, and most importantly, in order to estimate wages over time, one has to deal with missing observations. While these gaps were generally much larger than those in the price series, this is at the same time perhaps less problematic, as, in contrast to prices (which could fluctuate a lot), wages tended to be 'sticky': they remain fixed for long periods, sometimes for more than a century.[80] Furthermore, while they possibly increased from time to time, it seems that in general in pre-modern labour markets nominal wages (almost) never fell.[81]

The data for Chinsurah are relatively complete and the gaps could be linearly interpolated without much risk. The data on the Cape Colony demonstrate, similarly to the other VOC establishments in Asia, that Company wages were fixed throughout the seventeenth and the larger part of the eighteenth centuries;[82] only for 1790 did Du Plessis and Du Plessis find an increase in the wages of soldiers (who represent the lowest ranking VOC employees).[83]

78 Arasaratnam suggests that a *parra* of rice was added to wages in Ceylon in cases of serious labour shortages: Arasaratnam, 'Historical Foundation', p. 17.

79 For details, see Appendix 6.

80 De Vries, 'How did,' p. 40.

81 Ibid., p. 40.

82 LeQuin, *Het personeel*; Matthias van Rossum, 'De intra-Aziatische vaart: schepen, zeelieden en ondergang van de VOC?', *Tijdschrift voor Sociale en Economische Geschiedenis* (2011) 8, pp. 32–69; Claudia Rei, 'Incentives in Merchant Empires: Portuguese and Dutch Labor Compensation', *Cliometrica* 7 (2013) pp. 1–13.

83 Their data from 1756 shows that unskilled building labourers (*fortificatie werkers*) that often represent unskilled labourers in real wage studies earned a monthly wage similar to

As I have already explained, these VOC wages were corrected for underestimation of the average wage level by weighting the shares of free *knechts vis-a-vis* Company employees, which introduces a slightly declining trend in the series because the share of free *knechts* declined over the eighteenth century. Appendix 6 shows that different ways of handling the data do not impact much on the results for unskilled wages. The differences are somewhat larger for skilled workers, which must be kept in mind in the discussion on the 'skill premium' in Section 4.

The data for Ceylon and Java pose greater difficulties. The Colombo account books for the period 1760 to 1790 suggest wages were sticky in this period, but scarcity of data for the period prior to this creates some uncertainty about how well this applies to the entire period. Wages for masons in Colombo confirms that this stability can be projected back into the latter seventeenth century, as suggested by observations from 1681, as well as those from 1738 and 1740.[84] However, a few observations of wages of carpenters and unskilled workers suggest slightly more fluctuation.[85] There are a few ways to deal with this situation. First, one could assume stability over the entire period. Second, one could interpolate between the years for which data is available. A third approach is, using dummies for different levels of skills and ethnicity of labourers, to regress the wages in the database to produce a time trend. All three options are explored in Appendix 6.3.

As Appendix 6.3 demonstrates, the approaches do not lead to dramatically different results. In fact, the regressions suggest nominal wage stability over the entire period. The interpolated series are slightly lower in the latter seventeenth century and a little bit higher for the mid-eighteenth century. For the series presented in this book I use the sticky series. This is also supported by Arasaratnam's observation that in (neighbouring) southern India 'there had been no marked increase in wages from the seventeenth century for over a hundred year period'.[86]

---

that of soldiers. Similarly, the muster roll from 1778 (VOC 12575) suggests *arbeidslieden* (manual labourers) also earn the same wage. There are no data for skilled construction workers for 1790, but there were no increases until 1778 and it has been assumed there were no increases until 1790. This is reasonable as Claudia Rei also shows that craftsman in Amsterdam saw their nominal wage decline, while that of unskilled labourers increased slightly over the eighteenth century: 'Career and wages in the Dutch East India Company', *Cliometrica* 8 (2014) pp. 27–48.

84 VOC 8902 f. 540; VOC 8974 f. 2012; VOC 8978 f. 446.

85 VOC 8939 f. 767, 8974 f. 2012; 8978 f. 446.

86 S. Arasaratnam, 'Weavers, merchants, and company: the handloom industry in South-eastern India 1750–1790', *Indian Economic and Social History Review* 17 (1978) pp. 257–281.

For Java there are more data for the late seventeenth and early eighteenth centuries, but these come from a variety of sources and refer to different types of workers. The same three options described for Colombo again present themselves. Appendix A6.4 discusses the methods for dealing with these missing data, and, as I have already noted, these different methods of dealing with the gaps lead to essentially the same results. As the wages stem from such a variety of sources, the data presented here are far from ideal, but the results seem plausible. While both Boomgaard and Reid have suggested a decline in wages over the seventeenth and early eighteenth centuries,[87] they did not show data on wages for the later eighteenth century, but the evidence I have been able to unearth for this research strongly suggests an increase in nominal wages in the second half of the eighteenth century. This fits with the evidence of high demand for labour in that period, as well as possible increases in productivity in agriculture, which will be discussed in Chapter 5.

Thus, Appendix 6 demonstrates that the different methods of dealing with biases and missing data do not lead to significantly different results. However, it is clear that constructing a continuous time series of wages from these relatively scarce data goes at the expense of some of the interesting details encapsulated in them. The limitations of these procedures, as discussed extensively in the sections above, as well as in Appendix 6, must be kept in mind. New data, perhaps from local archives, may confirm (or refute) the trends sketched in this book. Nonetheless, I consider that creating these series in this manner is still an interesting exercise because it allows the analysis of longer term patterns of living standards from a comparative perspective.

2.5 *Global Wage Comparisons*

Table 4.2 shows the results of inserting the newly estimated wage series into a global context of nominal daily unskilled wages (expressed in grams of silver, to allow international comparisons). These nominal wages provide information on the competitiveness of these regions. One difficulty is that these nominal wages may also reflect differences in the value of silver across the globe.

Table 4.2 to some extent seems to confirm what is known about differences in the relative value of silver. 'Silver wages' were highest in Southern America, where the major silver mines were located and where silver had consequentially a lower value. Silver flowed first to Europe and then on to Asia, and silver wages at first glance also seem to be higher in the former than in the latter. However, looking more closely at some of the developments, the relative value of silver was not the only factor driving global nominal wage differentials. Although the silver mines

87 Boomgaard, 'Why work'; Reid, *Southeast Asia* I.

were located in South America, silver wages in North America were quickly catching up in the eighteenth century. By the end of the eighteenth century, silver wages were higher in Maryland than in Bolivia, Chile and Mexico. This may reflect significant economic development taking place there, but it is also related to the developments in England, as I explain in Section 3 and Chapter 5. While in the sixteenth century most silver came to Europe via Spain, by the early seventeenth century Spain had lost its lead in silver wages.[88] Wages in London, Amsterdam and Antwerp were particularly high in the seventeenth and eighteenth centuries, a possible consequence of the active involvement of these areas in global trade.[89] Furthermore, Allen et al. have shown that industrialization in England also pushed levels in London up above those in Amsterdam in the early nineteenth century. Silver wages in China, where silver was supposedly valued higher than in Europe, were higher than in Spain and on a par with cities in other parts of the European 'periphery'.

The fact that these wage patterns not only depended on variations in the value of silver also corresponds with the observation of converging silver prices in Chapter 3, as well as studies by Flynn and Giraldez suggesting that by the late sixteenth century there was already an integrated global market for silver.[90] Broadberry and Gupta have suggested that levels of silver wages in this period are, thus, already associated to some extent with levels of economic development.[91]

The lower silver wages in China, and especially in India, explain why manufactured goods (like textiles) were transported in great quantities from Asia to Europe, rather than the other way around. The new data assembled for Bengal strongly confirm earlier observations of very low wages there. New data on Surat, taken from Ghulam Nadri, have also been converted to silver values and entered into the global comparison. While those wages are double wages in Bengal, they are still lower than in most parts of Asia and Europe. The low silver wages gave India an important competitive advantage in textile manufacturing, and confirm observations by various contemporaries like Daniel Defoe and Francisco Pelsaert.[92] Wages in Ceylon were similarly low (although still twice the level in Bengal), being only just above those in southern India. Silver wages for unskilled labour were somewhat higher in Batavia

88 Broadberry and Gupta, 'The early modern', p. 5.

89 Allen, 'Progress and Poverty'.

90 Flynn and Giraldez, 'Cycles of Silver'.

91 Broadberry and Gupta, 'The early modern'; Van Zanden notes the strong positive correlation between silver wage and urbanization; J. L. van Zanden, 'Wages and the standard of living in Europe, 1500–1800', *European Review of Economic History* 3 (1999) p. 181.

92 See Parthasrathi, *Why Europe*, pp. 34–38.

TABLE 4.2 *Daily wages across the globe, in grams of silver per day, 1650–1800.*

	1650–74	1675–99	1700–24	1725–49	1750–74	1775–99
Africa						
Cape Town	6.32	6.25	6.07	5.98	5.72	6.92
Gold Coast[93]	–	–	–	1.60	–	–
Asia						
Chinsurah	–	–	0.68	0.73	1.08	1.15
Surat	1.29[94]	1.40[95]	–	2.34	2.08	2.36
South. India	1.15[96]	1.44[97]	–	–	(3.02)[98]	0.86–1.44
Colombo[99]	–	1.77	1.77	1.79	1.93	2.21
Batavia	–	2.31	2.31	2.34	2.63	3.36
Kyoto	–	–	–	2.68	2.68	2.64
Beijing	–	–	–	3.26	3.24	3.20
Suzhou	3.38	3.35	3.31	3.28	3.25	3.22
Europe						
London	9.28	10.02	10.24	10.73	11.17	11.90
Amsterdam	8.34	8.58	8.86	8.99	9.17	9.23
Leipzig	4.32	3.50	3.82	3.53	3.21	3.00
Valencia	2.35	2.58	2.44	2.38	1.91	1.61
Latin America						
Bolivia	12.78	12.78	12.78	12.51	12.43	12.17
Chile	–	9.20	14.42	15.01	15.17	15.96
Mexico	9.98	10.54	11.14	11.41	11.60	11.40
Peru	10.22	10.22	10.22	10.37	11.96	–

93 Observation from K. Rönnbäck, 'Living standards on the pre-colonial Gold Coast: a quantitative estimate of African laborers' welfare ratios', *European Review of Economic History* 18 (2014) pp. 185–202. On p. 197 an annual wage for a free canoe man on the Gold Coast is noted of £3.6. Following Lindert, 'Silver value', the £ was 111.4 grams of silver: (3.6 × 111.4)/250 = 1.60 grams of silver per day.

94 Observation for 1640: Broadberry and Gupta, 'The early modern'.

95 Observation for 1690: Broadberry and Gupta, 'The early modern'.

96 Observation 1600–50.

97 Observation for 1680.

98 Observation by Parthasarathi, 'Rethinking wages'; deemed unreliable by Broadberry and Gupta, 'The early modern'.

99 Calculated on the basis of monthly rates, assuming 250 days per year. As they probably worked more days per month, these figures slightly overestimate the daily wage in Colombo.

TABLE 4.2 *Daily wages across the globe, in grams of silver per day, 1650–1800.* (cont.)

	1650–74	1675–99	1700–24	1725–49	1750–74	1775–99
North America[100]						
Boston	4.70	5.23	5.52	5.97	7.96	11.97
Maryland	–	–	–	8.47	11.05	18.27
Philadelphia	6.43	5.96	6.09	6.69	8.24	–

Sources: Chinsurah, Cape Town, Batavia and Colombo: see text; Gold Coast: Rönnback, 'Living standards'; Surat: Broadberry and Gupta, 'The early modern', Nadri, 'Eighteenth-century Surat'; Southern India: Broadberry and Gupta, 'The early modern', Parthasarathi, 'Rethinking wages'; Kyoto, Beijing, Suzhou: Allen et al., 'Wages, prices'; London, Amsterdam, Leipzig, Valencia: Allen, 'The Great Divergence'; Bolivia, Chile, Mexico, Peru: Arroyo Abad et al., 'Between Conquest'; Boston, Marlyland, Philidelphia: Allen et al., 'The Colonial Origins'.

and these increased even more in the second half of the eighteenth century, thereby surpassing nominal wage levels in China in the final decades of that century.

As a major part of the populations of 'settler' societies came from Europe, wage levels in these colonies are related to those prevailing in *patria*.[101] Consequentially, silver wages were high in Cape Town (and North America) compared with Asia and southern and eastern Europe. This clearly differs from the African Gold Coast, where nominal wages were as low as in Colombo. In the next section, I will explore the question of whether high silver wages also translated into higher levels of material well-being.

3 Real Wages

The nominal wages can be converted into real wages by deflating them by the prices of the baskets calculated in Chapter 3. The prices of the baskets shown in Figure 3.7 fit the nutritional requirements for one adult male. Following Allen et al., the price of these baskets were multiplied by 3.15 in order to cover

100 I thank Bob Allen for sharing these data with me.

101 Robert C. Allen, 'Real Incomes in the English-Speaking World, 1879–1913', in: G. Grantham and M. MacKinnon (eds.), *Labour Market Evolution. The economic history of market integration, wage flexibility and the employment relation.* (London: Routledge, 1994) pp. 107–138; Alan M. Taylor and Jeffrey G. Williamson, 'Convergence in the age of mass migration', *European Review of Economic History* 1 (1997) pp. 27–63; Allen et al., 'Colonial origins'.

the budget for a nuclear family, including the rent.[102] Obviously, such assumptions may be criticized as household sizes were not equal across the world. I investigate this issue in Chapter 5, but for comparative purposes, for now I have accepted the assumption (as one wishes to answer the question of where workers across the globe had the higher purchasing power, *ceterus paribus*, as well as develop a notion about their standard of living relative to subsistence).[103] Dividing full-time, full-year earnings, as estimated in Section 2, by this annual family budget results in so-called 'subsistence ratios'. This ratio allows simple interpretation: a ratio above '1' indicates that the household lived, based on the male wage, above subsistence, which allowed the household to expand consumption and include more luxurious products, or take more time for leisure. A ratio below one suggests that other family members had to work, or households would need to augment their incomes with alternate sources in order to survive, as the costs of a barebones basket cannot be reduced by much.

Figure 4.1 shows that absolute standards of living in the cases studies and compares these with those in Amsterdam, which represents the maritime region of north-western Europe (also including London, and to some extent Antwerp and Oxford), characterized by high living standards. Also included in the comparison are other cities in Asia: Shanghai/Suzhou, situated on the lower reaches of the Yangtze River Delta (reflecting developments in the most advanced region of China), as well as Beijing and Kyoto (representing northern China and Japan, respectively).

Perhaps somewhat surprisingly, subsistence ratios in Cape Town were initially well below those prevailing in Amsterdam; they converged during the eighteenth century.[104] Many of the Cape immigrants came from Holland, Germany, and France and living standards in north-western Europe could have been an alternative.[105] There are a variety of reasons for the relatively low ratios at the Cape. First, living standards in many parts of Germany and France,[106]

102 Allen et al., 'Wages, prices'.

103 But at the same time still being able to get some notion of their 'absolute' standard of living, relative to a poverty line. See Chapter 3 for more on the methodology and see Chapter 5 for an examination of the assumptions on family sizes and their impact on the global comparisons.

104 Not unlike living standards in Boston, as recently shown by Allen et al., 'Colonial origins', p. 878.

105 See the literature on migration and real wages: for example, Allen, 'Real Incomes', and Taylor and Williamson, 'Convergence in the age'.

106 In Stellenbosch in 1704 and 1726, slightly more men came from Germany than from the Dutch Republic: Biewenga, *De Kaap*, p. 32.

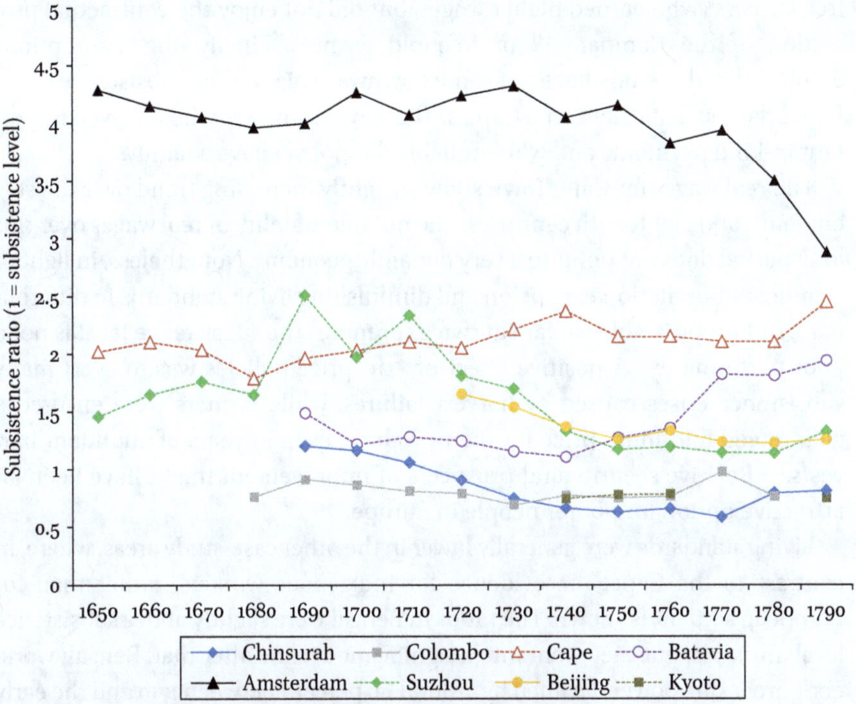

FIGURE 4.1 *Subsistence ratios in Asia and Europe, 10-year- averages.*
Sources: Chinsurah, Colombo, Cape and Batavia: see text; Amsterdam, Suzhou,[107] Beijing and Kyoto: Allen et al., 'Wages, prices'.

although not shown in this figure, were on a par with, or lower than, those at the Cape.[108] Second, many European settlers in Cape Town were either VOC or ex-VOC employees. Europeans enlisting into the lower ranks of the VOC usually came from the bottom ranks of society in Europe.[109] Third, while the VOC paid relatively low wages to its lower personnel, they were ensured a stable income over the long term and there were significant opportunities for climbing the wage ladder within the VOC.[110] Fourth, after the contract with the VOC ended these workers could try to improve their standard of living by either becoming

107 Suzhou is situated, next to Shanghai, in the Yangzi Delta.

108 See Allen et al., 'Wages, prices', and Allen, 'The Great Divergence'.

109 Gaastra, *De geschiedenis van de* VOC, p. 97. Or, as Merle C. Ricklefs put it, 'adventurers, vagabonds, criminals and the unfortunate from throughout Europe took its oath of allegiance' in: *A History of Modern Indonesia since c. 1200* (Stanford: Stanford U.P., 2008) p. 30.

110 Rei, 'Career and wages'.

free *knechts* (who earned higher wages, but did not enjoy the contractual protection of the Company)[111] or freehold farmers. Finally, the assumptions employed in this study have put some downward bias on the subsistence ratios for workers specifically at the Cape as these were workers who received important in-kind payments and who probably did not yet have a family.

The real wages for Cape Town show a slightly increasing trend over the seventeenth and eighteenth centuries. The notable stability of real wages over this long period does not point to a very dynamic economy. Nonetheless, in light of significant population expansion and diminishing living standards in different parts of Europe, stable welfare at twice (or more) the subsistence level is not a poor performance. A positive effect of VOC price policies was to avert many subsistence crises caused by harvest failures, while farmers were ensured a guaranteed minimum price for their produce, even in years of abundant harvests.[112] Relative security and prospects of improvement might have been an attractive option for poorer people in Europe.

Living standards were generally lower in the other case-study areas, where, in contrast to the Cape, the evidence for indigenous workers, rather than for European settlers, is shown. The ratios in Bengal were slightly above subsistence level until 1710, but they went into a significant decline after that. Bengali workers' purchasing power declined by around 60 percent between 1710 and the early 1740s (see Appendix 6, Figure A6.1). Real wages fluctuated around that low level until the drought of 1769–70, when subsistence ratios hit rock bottom. Living standards recovered after that. My research, based on extensive new wage evidence, thus supports the pessimistic view of Bengali living standards. It confirms observations by contemporaries who suggested that the Indian poor 'are poor indeed,'[113] as well as those historians who suggested that the many in India lived in 'great poverty',[114] and it also fits with the evidence of very simple diets there.[115] Furthermore, Figure A6.1 (in the appendix below) also shows the great vulnerability of the region to droughts and famines. Whereas the harvest failures in the Cape Colony in the 1780s did not push subsistence ratios below 1, the drought in Bengal of 1769–1770 reduced those ratios to only one-fifth of the subsistence level (0.2). With up to half of the total crop destroyed, many people perished in the subsequent famine. 'Consensual wisdom' suggests a death toll as high as

111 Shell, *Children of Bondage*.

112 Ross, 'The Cape'.

113 Cited in: Parthasarathi, 'Rethinking wages', p. 80.

114 W. H. Moreland, T. Raychaudhuri, K. N. Chaudhuri, cited in Parthasrathi, 'Rethinking wages'; ibid., *Why Europe*.

115 See Chapter 3, Section 4.

10 million people, or one-third of the total population.[116] These low living standards may also explain the relatively high number of observations for female and children's wages noted in the sources on Bengal (discussed in Chapter 5), as well as the fact that many observations suggest a 30-day working month. Clearly, all stops had to be pulled out for households in Bengal to survive.

Declining real wages were also found in northern (Agra/Delhi) and southern India by Allen, Broadberry and Gupta.[117] Interestingly, India's decline in living standards therefore precedes the nineteenth century, the period mostly associated with colonialism and globalization, which have often been invoked as causes for India's poor economic growth.[118] As argued above, globalization may have started earlier and may thus have led to inflationary pressures in Bengal in the eighteenth century. Nonetheless these trends suggest that other factors also played a role in the declining living standards. Possible alternative explanations are declining agricultural productivity due to increasing warfare, revenue burdens and drought,[119] or population growth leading to labour surpluses.[120]

Standards of living in Ceylon were similarly low, in absolute as well as relative terms. Silver wages were as low as in southern India, while prices were on the same high levels as Amsterdam. This combination led to levels of material well-being almost consistently below subsistence. Workers in southern India could benefit from relatively low food prices, which were either the result of high productivity in rice-growing agriculture or 'an abundance of rice arising from geographical factors and a high proportion of the labour force engaged in agriculture.'[121] Ceylonese labourers, however, seem not to have shared in this benefit of low food prices. In fact, Ceylon was unable to produce enough food for its population, making imports of large quantities of rice from Bengal, Coromandel, and Java necessary (and relatively expensive).[122] The poverty of the indigenous inhabitants of Ceylon around this time was also remarked upon by Governor Jan Schreuder (1757–1761) in his memoirs.[123] Looking more closely at the trends over time in this period, it seems that real wages were

116 Datta, *Society, economy and market*, p. 15.

117 Allen, 'India in the Great Divergence'; Broadberry and Gupta, 'The early modern'.

118 Roy, 'Beyond divergence', p. 58.

119 Clingingsmith and Williamson, 'Deindustrialization'.

120 K. N. Chaudhuri, cited by Parthasarathi, *Why Europe*, p. 38.

121 This is a subject of debate: Broadberry and Gupta, 'The early modern', p. 16; Parthasarathi, 'Rethinking wages'.

122 Arasaratnam, *Dutch power in Ceylon*, p. 130; De Silva, *A history*, p. 171.

123 Jan Schreuder, *Memoir of Jan Schreuder, Governor of Ceylon Delivered to his successor Lubbert Jan Baron van Eck on March 17, 1762*, trans. E. Reimers (Colombo: Ceylon Government Press, 1946) pp. 49 and 67.

stable or even declined in the late seventeenth and early eighteenth centuries, while from the late 1730s/early 1740s real wages increased slightly. These developments are possibly related to demographic trends,[124] which will be discussed more extensively in Chapter 5.

Living standards in Batavia were higher than those in Bengal, Ceylon, and, in the second half of the eighteenth century, China. However, considering the significant gap between Batavia and Amsterdam (roughly four times higher subsistence ratios in the early eighteenth century), these data hardly confirm Reid's suggestion that Southeast Asian's 'lives were no more squalid, their health no more wretched and their physical stature no worse than those of eighteenth century Europeans.'[125] Clearly, at least in terms of purchasing power, Javanese living standards were not on a par with those in north-western Europe.

Reid and Boomgaard have both claimed that real wages declined in the seventeenth and eighteenth centuries. Their claims have been confirmed with regard to 1680–1740. Neither of them showed wage data for the later eighteenth century, however, and as nominal wages increased, while prices declined due to a sustained period of peace and stability, living standards actually improved between the 1740s and the 1790s. Thus, after the crisis of the seventeenth century and the wars of the early eighteenth century, some of the evidence for the later eighteenth century suggests an increase in living standards. This is also corroborated by evidence of increases in production and trade,[126] in monetary exchange,[127] in consumption, and in population growth.[128] Furthermore, various colonial officials remarked upon the increase in production and consumption in the later eighteenth century.[129]

---

124 De Zwart, 'Population, labour'.

125 Reid, 'Economic and Social Change'.

126 Nagtegaal, *Rijden*; Van Niel, *Java's Northeast Coast*; Maddison, 'Dutch Income'; also see: De Zwart and Van Zanden, 'Labor, wages'.

127 Feenstra, 'Dutch Coins'.

128 Peter Carey, 'Waiting for the "Just King"', pp. 89–91; Jacobs, *Merchant in Asia*, p. 241; Lieberman, *Strange Parallels*, Vol. 2, pp. 870–1; Ricklefs, 'Some Statistical Evidence', p. 30.

129 Waterloo to Engelhard (1804): 'one only has to direct one's eyes to those lands which [now] produce rice and which just twenty years ago were still waste and uncultivated' (cited in: Carey, *Power of prophecy*, p. 35), Engelhard to High Government Batavia: 'rice consumption in everyone's household is greater than formerly. [...] the condition of the Javanese is very different from 50 to 60 years ago when they lived in ignorance and were depressed and suppressed by the continual wars' (cited in: Van Niel, *Java's Northeast Coast*, p. 131) and Crawfurd (1812): 'a traveler could now pass a hundred miles in Java without encountering an uncultivated spot' (cited in: Carey, 'Waiting for the "Just King"', p. 91).

Figure 4.1 thus supports the conventional, rather than the Californian, view in the divergence debate. Living standards were generally lower in all parts of Asia (the core, comprising the fertile Ganges and Yangzi river deltas, as well as the periphery, i.e. Ceylon, Japan, and Java).

4 The Skill Premium

One of the reasons for the differences in real wages may be caused by differences in the level of human capital formation, which is related to economic growth. Peter Lindert et al. hypothesised that one of north-western Europe's advantages was in 'the development of non-agricultural productivity concentrated in the capital-goods and knowledge-intensive sectors.'[130] Interest rates were relatively low, but food and other agricultural products were relatively expensive there.[131] Jan Luiten van Zanden has investigated one aspect of this hypothesis by looking at the skill premium. The skill premium can be seen as the market value for skills (human capital) and is calculated by the difference between the wages of skilled craftsmen and those of unskilled labourers.[132]

New growth theory postulates that human capital formation is one of the most important determinants of long-term economic growth.[133] A study by Davin Chor has pointed out that European cities between the sixteenth and nineteenth centuries that had low skill premiums also had higher levels of real wages.[134] Van Zanden finds a strong relationship between the average skill premium during the eighteenth century and GDP per capita growth in the nineteenth century, as well as between the average skill premium and the absolute level of GDP per capita in 1913. He concludes that 'the skill premium is not only a measure of the quality of the institutional framework of an economy, but also appears to be a predictor of growth in the long run.'[135]

130 Peter Lindert et al., 'Preliminary Global Price Comparisons, 1500–1870', Paper presented at the conference *Towards a Global History of Prices and Wages* (IISH Amsterdam, 2004) p. 25.

131 Lindert et al., 'Preliminary Global Price Comparisons'; Van Zanden, 'The skill premium', p. 122.

132 Van Zanden, 'The skill premium', p. 122.

133 See for example: Oded Galor, 'From Stagnation to Growth: Unified Growth Theory', in: Philippe Aghion and Steven N. Durlauf (eds.) *Handbook of Economic Growth* Vol. 1a (Amsterdam etc.: Elsevier, 2005) pp. 171–293; Glaeser et al., 'Do institutions'.

134 Davin Chor, 'Institutions, wages, and inequality: the case of Europe and its periphery (1500–1899)', *Explorations in Economic History* 42 (2005) 547–566.

135 Van Zanden, 'The skill premium', 147.

Van Zanden showed that Europe saw a spectacular decline in the skill premium in the period between 1350 and 1450 (from 140–160 percent to 50–60 percent). Whereas in England and the Low Countries the skill premium remained low and constant at the 50 percent level from 1450 onwards, the skill premium in central and southern Europe again rose to over 70 percent in the sixteenth century. Thus, already before the Industrial Revolution, Western Europe witnessed a greatly increased stock of human capital even though the reward for skill acquisition on the market remained relatively low.[136] The skill premium was much higher in other parts of the world than it was anywhere in Europe. Although data on other parts of the world are scarce, some examples can be given. Data from sixteenth century Russia suggest a skill premium between 100 (carpenter/unskilled labourer) to 167 percent (mason/unskilled labourer). Data from Beijing point to a skill premium of 100 percent during the seventeenth and eighteenth centuries, yet there seems to have been large regional variations in the skill premium in China; some parts even had a skill premium comparable to Western Europe.[137]

Especially in the absence of literacy or numeracy rates for the regions under examination in this study,[138] the skill premium is informative about the spread of human capital there. In the case of the Cape, the assumptions necessary to correct for underestimation in the nominal wage series (see Subsection 2.2), as well as the lack of observations of skilled wages in the later period, affect the calculation of the skill premium in that region. Therefore the skill premium is shown as a range, depending on assumptions. Furthermore, in the case of the Ceylon there is a clear wage gap between ordinary craftsmen and 'master' craftsmen. Table 4.3 shows the results and compares the skill premium in Bengal, the Cape, Ceylon, and Java with Amsterdam between c. 1650 and 1800.

These numbers suggest that the skill premium was indeed the lowest in Amsterdam over almost the entire period. First of all, the early observation of the skill premium in Cape Town is largely influenced by the situation in Europe. This skill premium is slightly higher than in Europe because it was probably harder to find skilled workers to risk their lives to work for the VOC than to find unskilled labourers. During the eighteenth century, the trend in the skill premium is clearly declining at the Cape. The skill premium in Bengal in the first

136 Gregory Clark, 'The condition', p. 1314.

137 The percentages in this paragraph are taken from: Van Zanden, 'The skill premium', 131–33.

138 Except the Cape Colony, where there are data: Jörg Baten and Johan Fourie, 'Numeracy of Africans, Asians and Europeans during the Early Modern Period: New Evidence from Cape Colony Court Registers', *Economic History Review* (forthcoming 2015).

TABLE 4.3 *Skill premium, in percentages, in Amsterdam, Chinsurah, Cape Town, Colombo and Batavia, 1650–1800.*[139]

	Amsterdam	Cape Town[140]	Chinsurah[141]	Colombo	Batavia
c. 1650	59	65–81	-	-	-
c. 1700	51	73–84	81	100[142]	-
c. 1750	52	56–61	91	40–94[143]	130[144]
c. 1800	49	30–57	51	40–94[145]	178[146]

Sources: see text.

of half the eighteenth century is between 80 and 90 percent, which is more than 30 percent below that of the 119 percent for northern and western India in 1637, but higher than the 70 percent noted for southern India in 1680.[147] Towards the end of the century, the skill premium plunges in Bengal as unskilled wages increase more rapidly than skilled wages. In Colombo the premium is also 100 percent or lower. In fact, considering the fact that the 94/100 percent applies to master craftsmen, while only about 40 percent applies to ordinary craftsmen, the skill premium is relatively low there, and on a similar level as that quoted for southern India, although it is hard to discern a clear trend from these observations. The price paid for human capital in Batavia, was, however, relatively high and rising throughout the eighteenth century.

139 Data from the years closely surrounding those benchmarks: the skill premium is calculated by dividing the difference between the skilled and the unskilled wage by the unskilled wage x 100.

140 Ranges depending on assumptions (see appendix). 1650 refers to 1653–6; 1700 refers to 1699–1701, 1750: 1749–1751 and 1800 refers to data for 1789–91.

141 All data refer to the difference between a carpenter's and a coolie's wage in Chinsurah. The figure for 1700 refers to data from 1706/7; 1750 refers to 1745, 1749–51; and 1800 refers to 1788–1791.

142 Refers to 1681.

143 Based on regression 1 in Appendix 6, Table A6.2, range determined by the subdivision between skilled (carpenter) and higher skilled labourers (master carpenter). See Appendix A6.3.

144 Result from regression, see Appendix A6.4.

145 Based on regression 1 Appendix 6, Table A6.2, range determined by the subdivision between skilled (carpenter) and higher skilled labourers (master carpenter). See Appendix A6.3.

146 1797: carpenter and coolies in Batavia.

147 Broadberry and Gupta, 'The early modern', p. 14.

Differences in the skill premium depend on a number of factors.[148] First of all, the skill premium is partly determined by interest rates. The period of decline in the skill premium in Europe coincides with the period in which the Black Death caused an enormous fall in population levels, which resulted in a decline in interest rates from by the rise of wealth per capita, which was in turn the consequence of the more favourable capital/labour and land/labour ratios. Taking England as an example, it has been suggested that interest rates fell from 10–11 percent before 1350 to 4–5 percent in 1450–1500,[149] which then induced households, whose capital increased by about 50 percent,[150] to increase their investments in human capital, leading to the sharp decline in the skill premium in that period. Interest rates were around a low 5–6 percent in Europe in the early modern period. The relatively low and declining skill premium at the Cape may also have been partly the result of similarly low interest rates. The interest rate in 1782 there was 6 percent per annum in 1782.[151] Over the course of the later eighteenth century the interest rate seems to have further declined, to 5 percent in 1793[152] and to only 4 percent in 1797.[153]

Interest rates in other parts of the world were much higher, and may partially account for the higher skill premiums there. In Bengal, interest rates were between 12–18 percent in the mid-seventeenth century,[154] but declined to 10–12 percent on ordinary debts in the later seventeenth-century,[155] and remained at that level during the eighteenth century.[156] Similarly, interest rates were around

148 As discussed by Van Zanden, 'The skill premium'.

149 Gregory Clark, 'The Cost of Capital and Medieval Agricultural Technique', *Explorations in Economic History* 25 (1988) p. 265.

150 Ibid., 267.

151 Or 0.5 percent per month: E. H. D. Arndt, *Banking and Currency Development in South Africa (1652–1927): with an appendix on the rise of savings banking in South Africa* (Cape Town, 1928) p. 5; Rutger Kremers, *On the Colonial Roots of South Africa's Divergence: A Comprehensive Analysis of South African Economic Performance, 1600–1961* (unpublished MA thesis: Utrecht University, 2013) pp. 24–26.

152 Arndt, *Banking and Currency*, p. 167; A. J. Bruwer, *South Africa: A Case National Gold and Banking Policy* (Cape Town: H.A.U.M., 1959) pp. 56–63.

153 G. M. Theal (ed.), *Records of the Cape Colony*, vol. 2 (1905) p. 141.

154 Sushil Chaudhuri, 'The financing of investments in Bengal, 1650-1720', *Indian Economic and Social History Review* 8 (1972) pp. 124–126.

155 Peter Boomgaard, 'Geld, krediet, rente en Europeanen in Zuid- en Zuidoost-Azie in de zeventiende eeuw', in: C. A. Davids, W. Fritchy, L. A. van der Valk and P. W. Klein (eds.) *Kapitaal, ondernemerschap en beleid. Studies over economie en politiek in Nederland, Europa en Azië van 1500 tot heden* (NEHA: Amsterdam, 1996) pp. 483–510.

156 Roy, 'Economic conditions', p. 190.

12 percent in seventeenth-century Ceylon[157] and Coromandel.[158] Yet in Western India (Surat) interest rates were lower: around 8 percent per year in the mid-seventeenth century.[159] Furthermore, while it has been suggested that Southeast Asia was characterized by high interest rates and thin capital markets since as early as the seventeenth century, interest rates in Batavia were relatively low and often only 6 percent per year in the seventeenth century.[160]

However, these are rates charged either by the VOC to European 'freeburghers' or rates paid by the Company itself. Perhaps the risk on these loans was relatively low. Indigenous labourers (those who had to make the investment in human capital) probably had to pay much higher interest. Boomgaard notes that 'the lowest interest rates in the indigenous sphere in Southeast Asia during this period, both in legal texts and in actual practice appear to have fluctuated at between 25 and 35 percent per year.'[161] He even finds annual rates between 40–50 percent charged in Buitenzorg (near Batavia) at the beginning of the nineteenth century.[162] The situation was even more problematic in Ceylon, where peasants paid 10–15 percent interest per month (120–180 percent per year) to Muslim traders,[163] or even 25 percent monthly to 'usurers'.[164] Yet the skill premium was lower in Ceylon and it seems, therefore, that interest rates are not the entire story.

Second, the efficiency of training mechanisms and 'access to the profession in general' are important for the supply of skilled labour.[165] For example, it has been argued that the low skill premium in England was the result of efficient third party (the guilds and the state) enforcement of training contracts, thereby preventing both masters' and apprentices' opportunism, which would have had negative effects on the efficient transfer of skills.[166]

---

157 Lodewijk Hovy, *Ceylonees plakkaatboek: plakkaten en andere wetten uitgevaardigd door het Nederlande bestuur op Ceylon, 1638–1796* vol. 1 (Hilversum: Verloren, 1991) p. 117: edict from 27 May, 1665 in Colombo.

158 Boomgaard, 'Geld, krediet, rente'.

159 Irfan Habib, 'Monetary System and Prices', in: Tapan Raychaudhuri and Irfan Habib (eds.), *The Cambridge Economic History of India* vol. 1 (Cambridge, 1982) pp. 76–93.

160 Boomgaard, 'Geld, krediet, rente': intersest rates in other parts of Java were higher.

161 Peter Boomgaard, 'Labour, land and capital markets in early modern Southeast Asia from the fifteenth to the nineteenth century', *Continuity and Change* 24 (2009) pp. 55–78.

162 Van Zanden, 'The skill premium', pp. 136–7; Peter Boomgaard, 'Buitenzorg in 1805: The Role of Money and Credit in a Colonial Frontier Society', *Modern Asian Studies* 20 (1986) pp. 33–58; ibid., 'Labour, land'.

163 Dewasiri, *The adaptable peasant*, p. 190.

164 Hovy, *Ceylonees plakkaatboek*, 1, p. 234.

165 Van Zanden, 'The skill premium', p. 139.

166 See: S. R. Epstein, 'Craft Guilds, Apprenticeship, and Technological Change in Preindustrial Europe', *Journal of Economic History* 58 (September 1998) pp. 684–713; Jane Humphries,

In India and Ceylon, on the other hand, Acemoglu and Robinson, among others, suggest that the rigid hereditary caste system limited the functioning of markets and the allocation of labour across occupations.[167] However, the relatively low skill premium there (*vis-à-vis* Batavia) may suggest that the caste system, at least in the eighteenth century, was not as detrimental for the transmissions of skills as expected. A possible reason for this is that the caste system was less rigid in the eighteenth century,[168] and the labour market was working relatively efficiently (despite the existence of the caste system). Yet we should not forget that there were also significant amounts of Muslims, one-third of the Indian population, who fell outside of the caste system.[169]

Most of the literature on India seems to suggest that labour markets were functioning quite well. Nadri describes that the labour market for building craftsmen in eighteenth-century Surat was able to respond to mechanisms of supply and demand and that labour mobility was not hindered by the caste system.[170] Similarly Lucassen's detailed case study of a Bengali gunpowder factory in the late eighteenth century also suggests an efficient labour market in which workers were stimulated through monetary incentives.[171] Parthasarathi also provides various examples of 'a great deal of fluidity and mobility': like *parayans* (landless labourers), who were found in a variety of urban (and military) occupations in the eighteenth century, and *kunbis* (cultivators) who turned to weaving.[172] Similarly, in eighteenth-century Ceylon members of the *karāva* caste, ostensibly fishers, were found performing a variety of jobs. For example, the great demand for carpenters in and around Colombo led many *karāva* in the nearby coastal settlement of Moratuwa to turn to carpentry.[173]

'English Apprenticeship: A Neglected Factor in the First Industrial Revolution', in: Paul A. David & Mark Thomas (eds.) *The Economic Future in Historical Perspective* (Oxford: Oxford University Press, 2003) pp. 73–102; Patrick Wallis, 'Apprenticeship and Training in Pre-modern England', *Journal of Economic History* 68 (2008) pp. 832–861.

167 Acemoglu and Robinson, *Why Nations Fail*, p. 118.

168 As suggested by: Parthasarathi, *Why Europe*, p. 59. Caste in India became more rigid in the nineteenth century, as also suggested by the first prime-minister of India, Jawaharlal Nehru, *The Discovery of India* (Delhi, Oxford and New York: Oxford U.P., 1994 [1946]) p. 225: who sees the causes of India's decline as 'the inevitable result of the growing rigidity and exclusiveness of the Indian social structure as represented chiefly aby the caste system'.

169 Shireen Moosvi, 'The World of Labour in Mughal India', *International Review of Social History* 56 (2011) pp. 245–261.

170 Nadri, *Eighteenth-century Gujarat*, p. 48.

171 Jan Lucassen, 'Working at the Ichapur'.

172 Partahsarathi, *Why Europe*, p. 59.

173 Arasaratnam, 'Social and economic change', p. 45; Dewasiri, *The adaptable peasant*, p. 92.

The *karāva* also carried out coastal trading, while demand for inland transport led many to become boatmen on the interior waterways and there also cases of them being employed to assist in the catching of elephants (the task of the *weenawo*,[174] *pannikeas*, and *cornacx*).[175] Rather than impeding the functioning of the labour market, the caste system may have provided additional trust and security in the transfer of skills through caste and kinship relations lacking in Europe. Labour markets will be discussed in greater detail in Chapter 5.

Third, next to these factors influencing the supply of skilled labour, the skill premium also depends the demand for skilled labour. Population growth can lead to an increase in skill premium, for example because it increases demand for skills in the construction industry that are needed to build extra houses (especially since the skilled worker is represented by building craftsmen).[176] Population growth can lead to an increasing supply of unskilled labour, pushing down real wages and productivity, thereby increasing the wage gap between unskilled and skilled labourers. In Chapter 5 I show that in all four case studies there were increases in population during the eighteenth century, although only in Batavia does it seem to have driven up the already high skill premium. In Bengal, on the other hand, the famine of 1770/1771 possibly led to the decrease in the skill premium, as unskilled workers may have been harder hit by the famine than skilled workers.

Thus, looking at the skill premium, it seems that north-western Europe was indeed ahead of not only China, but also of other parts of Asia. But perhaps the most remarkable feature of this discussion is that the skill premium was about 100 percent (or even less) in those areas with a caste system, i.e. Bengal and Ceylon, while it was much higher in Java. While the caste system obviously hinders labour mobility across occupations, apparently it did provide a relatively efficient framework for the transmission of skills through caste and kinship lines.

5 Conclusion

In this chapter I hope to have contributed to the debate on the Great Divergence of living standards during the early modern period. To do so, I have added wage data for Bengal, the Cape Colony, Ceylon and Java to the comparison. Deflated by the price series constructed in Chapter 3, and taking into account

174 Dewasiri, *The adaptable peasant*, p. 203.
175 De Zwart, 'Population, labour'.
176 Van Zanden, 'The skill premium', p. 139.

additional costs for housing and sustaining other family members, these wages have been converted into subsistence ratios that can be compared across time and space. The construction of such series is by no means straightforward, especially when data are as sparse as in the cases presented here. The issues and limitations related to the creation of these series have been discussed at length in this and the previous chapter, as well as in the appendices to this book. The creation of these series nonetheless increases the reliability of these observations *vis-à-vis* observations of specific benchmark years (which could be outliers),[177] and it allows the analysis of trends over time.

The subsistence ratios calculated in this chapter lead to several conclusions. In general, the data support the conventional view in the Great Divergence debate. Living standards in Asia (at the core and in the periphery) were lower than those in the European core (north-western Europe, here represented by Amsterdam). In line with the study by Allen et al., it must, however, be concluded that living standards in Asia were not exceptionally low, but instead that the living standards in north-western Europe were exceptionally high, as living standards in Asia were by and large on a par with those in many other parts of Europe.[178]

In Ceylon real wages were generally just below subsistence, as it suffered from both relatively low wages and high prices. Material well-being, however, slightly improved in the second half of the eighteenth century. Real wages in Bengal were slightly above subsistence c. 1700, but rapidly declined over the first part of the eighteenth century, and recovered only after a significant part of the population had perished in the crisis of 1769–70. Living standards were somewhat higher in Batavia, in line with Reid and Boomgaard's suggestions that living standards declined until the 1740s, after which they recovered as the rise of VOC hegemony over Java's north-east coast brought a long period of peace and stability. Finally, as a society with a significant number of European settlers, the Cape Colony had the highest standard of living of the four cases under investigation. Similarly to cities in North America, living standards at the Cape were to some extent determined by welfare levels prevailing in the countries of origin of their European migrants (why else would they have undertaken the journey?).

Also in terms of the skill premium, it was the Cape that was most strongly influenced by developments in the home region. Interest rates were relatively low and the skill premium converged to European levels in the eighteenth century. The price paid for skill was generally higher in the other case studies, too,

177 As Pomeranz did in *The Great Divergence*.

178 Allen et al., 'Wages, prices'.

but perhaps lower than expected on the basis of the literature.[179] In Bengal and Ceylon, despite relatively high interest rates, the caste system provided a framework for the transfer of skills.

In order to arrive at conclusions about the comparative standards of living, this book has used Allen's method of computing real wages as subsistence ratios. The biggest advantage in this is that it allows us to place real wages in Bengal, the Cape Colony, Ceylon, and Java in an international comparative context, because similar calculations have been made for Europe, China, Japan and other parts of India in this period. The price and wage data for these case studies had to be put in the same model used for estimating subsistence costs and wage income for other societies, even though conditions are clearly different in each country. For example, Allen's approach assumes 250 working days per year, whereas much wage labour in, for example, Java and Ceylon was seasonal. It also assumes that wages were the only source of income for the household involved – again an assumption that was often not so in practice. It is, however, not possible to reconstruct how many days were actually worked by wage labourers during this period in each of the four cases, and thus how much money was earned per household, because the data for such an exercise are missing. Fortunately, we can, however, reconstruct, making use of Allen's framework, the long-term evolution of the purchasing power of the daily wage and put this into international perspective.

However, it is obvious that the relevance of this method depends on one's view of the organization of the labour market. To maintain comparability with other studies, I have used Allen's model and employed the same assumptions about working days, family composition, and structure of the budget knowing full well that they do not entirely fit reality. Nevertheless the method does tell us something about the purchasing power of the wages earned, which is usually considered to be an important determinant of the living standard. In order to shed more light on these issues, in Chapter 5 the labour market, as well as demographic developments in these societies, will be examined. Furthermore, an analysis of the possible causes of developments in living standards is presented.

---

179 Van Zanden, 'The skill premium'.

CHAPTER 5

Population, Households and Labour Markets

1 Introduction

An increase in the number of real wage studies over the past years has made it possible to place the results of the archival research done for this book in an international perspective. As the real wage research has led to 'provoking and interesting results', this new strand of literature has also started to attract some criticism. First, Anne Booth doubts whether, in developing economies prior to the twentieth century, real wages of urban wage labourers can be seen as representative for the standard of living of the vast majority of the population.[1] Large parts of the population were engaged in agriculture and received a significant share of their remuneration in kind (food and housing). Second, scholars such as Joyce Burnette, Jane Humphries, and Elise van Nederveen Meerkerk have argued that a significant part of household income was generated by women and children and that a narrow focus on male earnings may lead to inaccurate conclusions.[2]

Furthermore, especially in the pre-industrial period, real wages were often closely related to demographic developments.[3] In the long run, wages before the Industrial Revolution often followed a Malthusian pattern, the so-called 'Iron Law of Wages', where population growth caused a decline in real wages, and famines and disasters that led to diminishing population numbers allowed wages to rise. At the same time, it is clear that wages are also determined by the functioning of the labour market.[4] To what extent were wages set in a free and efficient market, and to what extent were labourers coerced to perform their

1 Anne Booth, 'Measuring Living Standards in Different Colonial Systems: Some Evidence from South East Asia, 1900–1942', *Modern Asian Studies* 46 (2012) pp. 1145–1181.

2 J. Burnette, *Gender, Work and Wages in Industrial Revolution Britain* (Cambridge University Press, 2008); Jane Humphries, 'The lure of aggregates and the pitfalls of the patriarchal perspective: a critique of the high wage economy interpretation of the British Industrial Revolution', *Economic History Review* 66 (2013) pp. 693–714; Elise van Nederveen Meerkerk, 'From male breadwinner to family wage: suggestions for reconstructing long-term series of wages in pre-industrial and industrializing societies', Presented at the CLIO-INFRA *Real Wage Workshop*, International Institute of Social History (2012).

3 See: Gregory Clark, *A Farewell to Alms: A Brief Economic History of the World* (Princeton: Princeton U.P., 2007); ibid., 'The Condition'; Sevket Pamuk, 'The Black Death and the Origins of the "Great Divergence" across Europe, 1300–1600', *European Review of Economic History* 11 (2007) pp. 289–317; Allen et al., 'The Colonial'; Arroyo Abad et al., 'Between conquest'.

4 See also: Allen et al., 'The Colonial'.

 | DOI 10.1163/9789004299665_006

tasks for relatively little compensation. In this chapter, in order to address some of the concerns of real wage critics, as well as to explain the trends and levels in real wages as they were uncovered in the previous chapter (Chapter 4), I will investigate demographic patterns, labour markets, and labour relations on the basis of secondary literature, as well as a number of new primary documents from the VOC archives.

In Section 2 estimates are made of total population, population growth rates, and population densities over the seventeenth and eighteenth centuries. This shows that population pressure on the land may indeed have had negative effects on real wages in Bengal, but probably not in the Cape Colony, Ceylon, and Java. Section 3 investigates household composition in order to get an idea of how far, or how close, Allen's model of nuclear households across the globe is to the historical truth. In Section 4 this information is combined with evidence on women's and children's wages to see whether it would change the overall conclusions drawn in Chapter 4. In Section 5 I discuss the labour market in order to get some sense of to what extent the living standards of wage labourers may be representative of the population at large and to analyse how mechanisms of labour coercion may have affected wage levels.

2 The Iron Law of Wages

Most studies in the Divergence literature have included demography as an essential variable, yet the precise relationship with economic growth remains contentious. On the one hand, population growth can be interpreted as a sign of a healthy population and economic success, which might stimulate technological progress and specialization. On the other hand, it can be seen as a cause of poverty as the resources in an economy have to be divided among a greater number of people.[5] These opposing views are hard to reconcile and demographic data thus demand cautious interpretation.

Scholars like Eric Jones and John Hajnal have argued that Western Europe benefitted from fertility checks, such as late marriage and small family sizes, which led to moderate population growth.[6] Western Europe thus escaped from the Malthusian cycle in which all increases in production were absorbed by an increase in the population. In China, India and other parts of Asia, on the other hand, cultural values stimulated early marriage and large family sizes. Overpopulation and relative land scarcity have been pointed out as causes of the lack of

5 For further elaboration on Boserupian and Malthusian views, see Massimo Livi-Bacci, *A Concise History of World Population* (Malden, Mass. etc.: Blackwell, 2007) pp. 70–97.

6 Jones, *The European Miracle*, pp. 13–21; Hajnal, 'European marriage'.

economic development and low per capita incomes in Asia.[7] This has been disputed by the revisionists, who suggest that although the Asians did not share Europe's system of late marriage, they tried to regulate fertility within marriage.[8] Through 'delaying pregnancy in marriage and then preventing pregnancy after establishing a family' birth rates per marriage and per woman in China 'were well below those of western Europe throughout the 1550–1850 period.'[9] Japan had similarly low birth rates, while also for Southeast Asia there is evidence of couples trying to limit fertility. Family size in different parts of Asia was kept small through abortion and infanticide, in addition to contraception and abstinence.[10]

In this part of the chapter I will sketch developments in total population and population growth and relate these to the real wage series. In order to do so, I have estimated total population figures for Ceylon for the period 1684–1798 from new source material and employed a variety of secondary sources to sketch population trends in the other regions.[11] The estimation of population for Ceylon is extensively discussed in Appendix 7. To arrive at these numbers, data on the developments in the number of indigenous Christians on the island were related to total population estimates in benchmark years.[12] These estimates depend, therefore, on assumptions about the ratio of indigenous Christians in the population totals, and on assumptions concerning underreporting, as well as very crude estimates of the population of Kandy. As a result, these estimates are fraught with uncertainties, which must be kept in mind.[13]

7 See, for example, Mark Elvin, 'The high-level equilibrium trap: the causes of decline of invention in the traditional Chinese textile industries', in: W.E. Willmott (ed.), *Economic Organization in Chinese Society* (Stanford: Stanford U.P., 1972) pp. 137–172; and: Kang Chao, *Man and Land in Chinese History: An Economic Analysis* (Stanford: Stanford U.P., 1986).

8 Pomeranz, *The Great Divergence*, p. 41; but also: Lavely and Wong, 'Revising the Malthusian'; James Z. Lee and Wang Feng, *One Quarter of Humanity. Malthusian Mythology and Chinese Realities, 1700–2000* (Cambridge, Mass.: Harvard U.P., 2001).

9 Pomeranz, *The Great Divergence*, p. 41.

10 Ibid.; also: Parthasarathi, *Why Europe*, pp. 71–75.

11 For the Cape Colony: Van Duin and Ross, 'The economy'; Fourie and Van Zanden, 'GDP in the Cape Colony', Jeanne Cilliers and Johan Fourie, 'New estimates of settler life span and other demographic estimates from South Africa, 1652–1948', *Econonomic History of Developing Regions*. 27 (2012), pp. 61–86; for Java: Feenstra, 'Dutch coins'; for Bengal: Rama Deb Roy, 'Population of the province of Bengal, 1751–1801', *Population Studies Unit, Indian Statistical Institute*: http://dmo.econ.msu.ru/epc2001_history/Authors/Rama/RamaRoy.htm. Last accessed, July 3rd, 2014.

12 From: Van Goor, *Jan Kompenie*.

13 In this chapter I will employ the estimates that are corrected for underestimation. Please see appendix 7 for different estimates.

However, until research into more detailed sources is completed,[14] the estimates that I will present here are the best evidence available so far.

For Bengal, population estimates are also tentative, especially for the earlier decades of the eighteenth century. Yet there are a range of estimates available for the later eighteenth century that could differ slightly, also because they may include different geographical areas (some include, while others exclude, the territory of Bihar). In one of the more conservative estimates, the population increased from 22 to 27 million between 1789 and 1801,[15] while high estimates put the total number of people at over 39 million at the turn of the century.[16] For this section, on the iron law of wages, we are mostly interested in the growth of the population over time, so whichever estimate we take it is important to be consistent over time. The most consistent estimates for the second half of the eighteenth century are from a recent reconstruction project by Rama Deb Roy.[17] He suggests an annual population growth rate (excluding famines) of 0.8 percent in Bengal and 0.5 percent in Bihar between 1750 and 1800. Extrapolating this growth rate back to 1700 one arrives at a total population of 27.6 million and a total of 42.2 in 1800. Using these high estimates does influence the calculations of population densities that follow.

The population of Java probably declined somewhat during the first 50 years of the eighteenth century as a result of wars and unrest.[18] Relative peace and stability after the Treaty of Giyanti allowed population growth after 1755, yet estimates of the total population size and the extent of population increase vary greatly. Some estimates suggest that the population increased from 2.5 million around the middle of the century to 3.5 million by its end.[19] It is now generally agreed that these numbers are far too low. Reid suggests that at around 1800 the population was about 5 million;[20] other estimates put the number between 7.5 and 8.5 million.[21] Alberto Feenstra suggests that a growth of about 1.1 percent per year between 1755 and 1800 is reasonable.[22]

---

14 Albert van den Belt, Jan Kok and Kees Mandemakers are investigating the *thombos*: see ibid. 'Digital thombos: A new source for 18th century Sri Lankan family history. Research note', *History of the Family* 16 (2011) pp. 481–489.

15 Datta, *Society, economy*, p. 250.

16 Jha, *The Political Economy*, p. 127.

17 Deb Roy, 'Population of the province'.

18 Feenstra, 'Dutch coins'.

19 Van Niel, 'Economic and population changes'.

20 Reid, *Southeast Asia* I, p. 14.

21 P. Boomgaard and A.J. Gooszen, *Changing Economy in Indonesia. Vol. 11 Population Trends, 1795–1942* (Amsterdam: Royal Tropical Institute, 1991); Jan Luiten van Zanden, 'Economic growth in Java 1815–1939. The reconstruction of the historical national accounts of a colonial economy', *Mimeo* (2002).

22 Feenstra, 'Dutch coins'.

In contrast to the paucity of these figures, there is an abundance of relatively good quality data available for the eighteenth-century Cape Colony.[23] These data not only show total population numbers, but also divide them up into men, women, children, slaves, and *Khoesan* over the entire eighteenth century. Those data are much more detailed and reliable than those for the other case studies.[24] The total population within the borders of the Cape Colony increased from 4,300 in 1700 to over 46,800 by the end of the eighteenth century.

The population growth rates in the four VOC cases during the eighteenth century are compared in Table 5.1 with figures for the England, Europe and China taken from the literature.[25]

A few things stand out in Table 5.1. The most remarkable growth rates were clearly achieved in the Cape Colony. In the first decades of the Colony's existence, immigration from Europe was actively stimulated (as the VOC paid for

TABLE 5.1 *Average annual population growth, 1700–1800.*[26]

	England	Europe	China	Bengal	Cape[27]	Ceylon[28]	Java[29]
1700–1750	0.27	0.31	0.72	0.66	2.71	0.44	-0.26
1750–1800	0.81	0.50	0.79	0.15	2.27	0.23	0.76
1700–1800	0.54	0.41	0.76	0.41	2.50	0.33	0.25

Sources: see text.

23 Generously made available to me by Johan Fourie.

24 These data have already been used in a variety of publications: Fourie and Van Zanden, 'GDP in the Dutch Cape'; Fourie and Cilliers, 'New estimates'; P. Patrizio, S. Muller, J. Cilliers, and J. Fourie. 'The transmission of longevity across generations: the case of the settler Cape Colony', *Research in Social Stratification and Mobility* 35 (2014) pp. 105–119. Baten and Fourie, 'Numeracy of Africans'.

25 Europe and China: Lavely and Bin Wong, 'Revising'; England: Wrigley and Schofield, *The Population History*, p. 529.

26 The average annual growth rate was then calculated by the equation $r = \left[\sqrt[t]{\left(\frac{x}{y}\right)} - 1\right] \times 100$

Where r = the average percentage growth rate; t = the difference in years between the first and last count; y = the total population at the beginning of the period; and x = the total population at the end of the period.

27 This includes slaves. 1700 refers to the period 1701/03, 1750 refers to 1749/51 and 1800 refers to the period 1793/5.

28 1700 refers to 1689/91, 1750 to 1739/41 and 1800 to 1787/89.

29 1700 refers to 1701/03, 1749/51 and 1800 refers to 1798/1800.

immigrants' passages), and land was made available to the settlers on a first come, first serve basis. After 1717, however, immigration was no longer encouraged and population growth relied on high fertility rates among the settlers: the white population grew from 1,300 in 1700 to around 15,000 by the end of the century.[30] In addition, significant numbers of slaves were imported and their number increased more than tenfold, from almost 2,000 at the beginning of century to over 21,000 by its end.[31]

Population growth in Bengal in the first half of the eighteenth century was relatively rapid and approaching (the high?) Chinese levels. The famine in Bengal of 1769–1770 clearly depressed growth rates in the second half of the century. The famine and the previously high growth rates suggest a Malthusian pattern, as previous scholars have proposed.[32] Population increase was also relatively rapid in Java in the second half of eighteenth century, yet there is no evidence that this led to what Malthus called 'positive checks' , hunger, disease and war, in either this or subsequent periods. Only in Ceylon – if the numbers are correct – does the rate of natural increase seem to have been limited, and not only as a result of famines and war. The practice of polyandry (where a household consists of one woman and several men) and relatively high death rates may be the causes of this; this will be discussed in Section 3.

How did this population growth relate to the development of living standards? Figure 5.1 shows the relationship between population and real wages over the eighteenth century in the four cases. In the literature, graphs presenting the relationship between real wages and population usually span several centuries,[33] yet, even though I have data only for the eighteenth century, some interesting patterns can still be discerned. First of all, there is a clear difference between Bengal and Ceylon, on the one hand, and Java and the Cape Colony, on the other. The graph for Bengal shows the negative Malthusian relationship between population and wages. Adam Smith already cited Bengal as an example of an economy with an 'overflowing' labour force where wages sank to the 'most miserable and scanty subsistence', and where population pressure meant that:

---

30 In an earlier paper (De Zwart, 'Real wages'), I suggested that it had increased to 22,000, yet new estimates, by Fourie and Cilliers ('New estimates'), put this number somewhat lower.

31 Shell, *Children of Bondage*, pp. 445–448.

32 Jones, *European Miracle*, ch. 2; Smith, *Wealth of Nations*, pp. 103–104; also see the discussion in Parthasarathi, *Why Europe*, p. 71–78.

33 Clark, *Farewell to Alms*, p. 30; Van Zanden, 'The skill premium'; Livi-Bacci, *A concise history*, p. 78.

> Many…would either starve, or be driven to seek a subsistence either by begging, or by the perpetration perhaps of the greatest enormities. Want, famine, and mortality would immediately prevail in [the lowest] class, and from thence extend themselves to all the superior classes.[34]

Only after the famine in 1769/70, when total population numbers were severely diminished, did the real wage move upwards. In Ceylon a slightly negative relationship can be discerned from the graph, especially up until the 1730s, when population growth was relatively strong. Again, this connection was mainly disturbed by an external shock; as many perished in the Dutch-Kandyan war of the 1760s, real wages shot up in the 1770s, only to decline again with population growth towards the end of the century. As population growth was slower in Ceylon, the relationship was weaker than in Bengal and turned out to be statistically insignificant in regressions.

In Java a negative relationship between population and real wages is apparent in the early eighteenth century. It is, however, difficult to discern because the wars that raged on the island both destroyed crops (increasing prices and diminishing real wages) and killed people, yet later in the eighteenth century, population and real wages show similar trends. Here population growth seems to be a sign of economic growth, as also suggested by other researchers.[35] Real wages did not decline in response to this increased labour pool because the demand for labour by the VOC continued to grow (as testified by the various *plakkaten* to raise the number of labourers) and more people were needed to produce the increase in export output.[36]

In the Cape Colony, real wages are very stable in the face of very significant increases in population numbers. There are several reasons for this. At the same time as population grew, the amount of the land brought under cultivation increased, which meant that the man/land ratios remained stable. The land and population increases were therefore also matched by similar increases in production (production per capita thus remained roughly stable, and perhaps even declined slightly) as noted in Chapter 3. In addition, the influence of the VOC in setting wage and price levels meant a relatively stable real wage over long periods of time.

34 Smith, *Wealth of Nations*, pp. 103–104; cited in Geoffrey Gilbert, 'Adam Smith on the nature and Causes of Poverty', *Review of Social Economy* 55 (1997) pp. 274–291.

35 Carey, 'Waiting for the Just King', pp. 89–91; Jacobs, *Merchant in Asia*, p. 241; Lieberman, *Strange Parallels* 2, pp. 870–1; Ricklefs, 'Some Statistical Evidence', p. 30.

36 For increases in export production see: De Zwart and Van Zanden, 'Labor, wages'; Bulbeck et al., *Southeast Asian*.

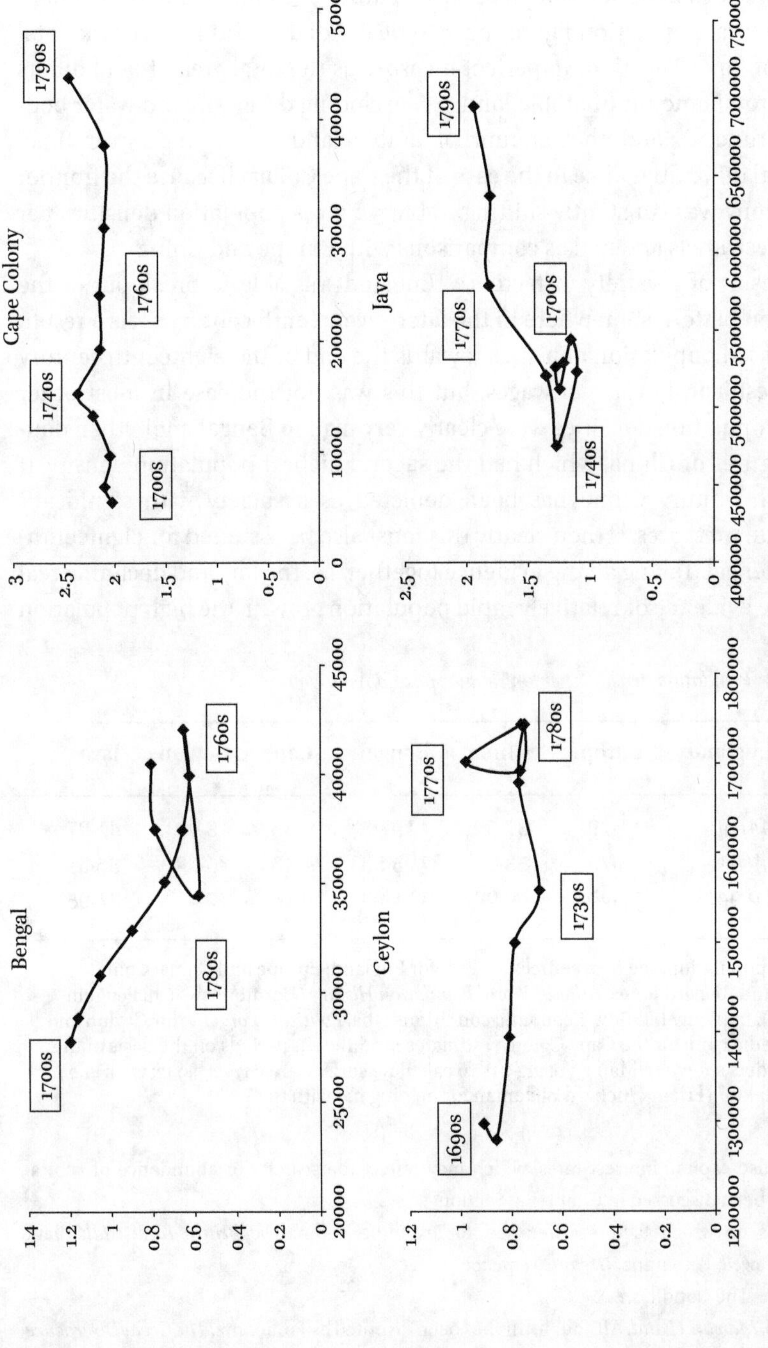

FIGURE 5.1 *Population and real wages in the eighteenth century.*

Sources: see text. Y-axis: Subsistence ratio; X-axis: Total population. Regressing population and real wages demonstrated that the relationship is insignificant in the cases of the Cape Colony and Ceylon, significant (at 1 percent) and negative in the case of Bengal, and significant (at 1 percent) and positive in the case of Java.

The differences in this relationship have to do with the relative scarcity/abundance of labour *vis-à-vis* other factors of production, especially land.[37] This can be seen in population densities. In order to estimate population densities, the total population figures have to be divided by estimates of the total amount of land. This is an imperfect measure as the total area of land differs from the total amount of arable land (i.e. excluding desert, inland water bodies, and tundra), and the amount of arable land can change over time. Additional difficulties arise in the case of the Cape Colony because the frontier of the colony was constantly shifting. Table 5.2 gives population densities per km^2 in these areas and makes comparisons with Europe and China.

As a result of a variety of factors,[38] England was able to break out of the Malthusian pattern somewhere in the later seventeenth century.[39] As a result, the increased population densities towards the end of the eighteenth century did not result in lower real wages, but this was not the case in most other regions. Population densities were clearly very high in Bengal, more than double the figures of China, which had the second highest population density. If eighteenth-century China has been depicted as a society with significant Malthusian pressures,[40] then clearly this must also be assumed for eighteenth-century Bengal. Taking all the evidence together, i.e. the low and declining real wages, the evidence of relatively rapid population growth, the high population

TABLE 5.2 *Population densities per km^2 in Europe and Asia, 1700–1800.*

	England	Europe	China	Bengal	Cape	Ceylon	Java
1700	44.10	11.79	37.50	119.65	0.43	19.86	41.07
1750	46.01	13.75	53.75	165.53	0.42	25.72	35.54
1800	70.94	17.68	80.00	181.22	0.21	27.21	51.95

Sources for population, see text; sources for km^2 for England, Europe and China: Colin MacEvedy and Richard Jones, *Atlas of World Population History* (Harmondsworth: Penguin Books, 1978); for Bengal: T. Roy, 'Economic conditions'; Jha, *Political Economy*; for Ceylon and Java: WikiPedia.com; for the Cape Colony: estimates for different periods on the basis of the shifting borders shown in Map 1.5 using GIS to calculate surface area: 1700: 9,942; 1750: 41,041; 1800: 226,104 km^2 (I thank Richard Zijdeman for helping me with this).

37 But also capital; interest rates, which may reflect the scarcity or abundance of capital, have been discussed in Chapter 4, Section 4.

38 Views on which factors differ: see, for example, Allen, *The British Industrial*; Clark, *A Farewell*; Pomeranz, *Great Divergence*.

39 Clark, 'The Condition'.

40 Chao, *Man and Land*. Although, this has been disputed by Pomeranz, *The Great Divergence*.

densities, and the evidence of the frequent occurrence of major famines,[41] it is hard to discard population pressures as an important factor in Bengal's eighteenth-century decline.[42]

In Java, population densities were lower than those in Bengal, China, and England. Even though Java had the highest population densities in Southeast Asia (generally characterized by low population densities), until the late nineteenth century, when the frontier started to close, it was labour that was scarce rather than land.[43] As a result, wages could continue to increase despite population growth later in the eighteenth century. Densities were even lower in Ceylon.[44] For Ceylon, too, it has been suggested that under-population seems to have been the greater problem, as Arasaratnam notes: 'what was lacking [...] was not land but men'.[45] This explains why the Malthusian pattern was relatively weak in Ceylon. Finally, as is well-known, population densities were very low in the Cape Colony. There were relatively few people within the ever expanding boundaries of the colony, and while the growth of the population may have outpaced the growth of territory; this was and remained a labour-scarce economy. In the Cape, the labour shortage was to be resolved by the use of slave labour. In Ceylon and Java, while there were also slaves, most of the labour shortages had to be resolved by systems of *corvée* labour (see Section 5). It is therefore obvious that population growth only causes wages to decline in situations of labour abundance, when population densities were high, as in the case of Bengal.

3 Households

High birth rates and large family sizes, if not off-set by high death rates, could be the cause of relatively rapid population growth and increasing Malthusian pressures. In this section, a variety of sources will be consulted to gather some information on average household/family sizes, as well as the gender and age distributions of the population. This discussion is relevant methodologically as the cost of sustaining a family is dependent on the number of family members.

41 Datta, *Society, economy*, pp. 240, 243.

42 Parthasarthi attempts to downplay the role of Malthusian dynamics in the Indian case: *Why Europe*, pp. 74–77.

43 De Zwart and Van Zanden, 'Labor, wages'.

44 I have taken the highest estimates here, which are thus biased against the result of low population densities.

45 Arasaratnam, *Dutch Power*, p. 130.

Allen's assumptions of family size have been criticized by, for example, Jane Humphries, who argues that Sir Frederic Eden's Ealing gardener family (used by Allen) is not representative for English families, which were generally larger.[46] She finds that, in the mid-nineteenth century, it was common for seven or eight children to be born into working-class families. Eric Schneider has, however, pointed out that Humphries overestimates family sizes. Schneider's analysis, which employs the detailed Cambridge population data for English parishes in combination with computer simulations, suggests that demography-adjusted real wages are in fact higher than, or match, Allen's original real wages.[47]

While the Allen-series may thus have been reaffirmed for England, this may be different for the cases under discussion, especially since it has been suggested that population growth was particularly rapid in the case of India because of the large family sizes common there. The issue is also important as Rosenthal and Wong have emphasized that the relationship between markets and households differs between nuclear and extended households, and that differences in household size may consequently drive variations in wages.[48]

Yet much of the evidence at hand suggests that families in various parts of Asia were on average not much larger than those in England. For India, Parthasarathi suggests that despite early ages of marriage, Indian family sizes were also fairly small and comparable with Europe, in part due to infanticide, high child mortality, and early widowhood.[49] He cites figures from the early nineteenth century showing that Indian households had similar sizes as those in Europe. However, he also gives data from a 1821 survey of Bengal, Bihar and Orissa that reported an average of 5.14 persons per house.[50] A census of Burdwan (100 km north-east of Calcutta), which includes a total of 40,000 people, suggests an average of 5.27 persons per house.[51] The latter census also provides some more information regarding the age and gender distribution of

---

46 Humphries, 'The lure', pp. 695, 703. Humphries also criticizes the amount of calories in Allen's consumption basket and suggests that Allen underestimates the calorie consumption of women and children. While she may be right and Allen is currently reworking his estimates to new kcal standards (see: Robert C. Allen, 'Poverty Lines in History, Theory and Current International Practice', *Oxford Economics Discussion Paper* 685 (December 2013)), the issue is not relevant here, as it would not change the international comparisons.

47 Eric B. Schneider, 'Real wages and the family: Adjusting real wages to changing demography in pre-modern England', *Explorations in Economic History* 50 (2013) pp. 99–115.

48 Rosenthal and Wong, *Before and Beyond*, pp. 58–64.

49 Parthasarathi, *Why Europe*, p. 74.

50 Ibid.

51 W.B. Bayley, 'Statistical View of the Population of Burdwan, &c', *Asiatick Researches* 12 (1816) pp. 549–574.

this population (shown in Figure 5.2). While it is unclear how representative (or reliable) this census is for Bengal as a whole, there are no reasons to assume it is particularly skewed in terms of gender or age distribution. These data show that the population was not particularly young, as 31 percent could be classified as children (below age 12 for girls, below age 16 for boys), which is similar to England, where also roughly 31 percent of the population was between 0 and 14 in 1696.[52] This suggests either that fertility was roughly at the same level, or that fertility was higher but that more children died before reaching the ages 12–16. As also suggested by another study, the gender ratio in Bengal was relatively balanced (perhaps somewhat surprising considering the existence of female infanticide).[53]

For Ceylon, the data on indigenous Christians used in Section 2 and Appendix 7 to estimate total population also showed on average 4.26 persons per household.[54] Furthermore, the data from 1684 contained additional demographic information on the age and gender distributions of the population.[55] To arrive at the age distribution in Figure 5.2, it is assumed that the 'school age' of boys and girls was roughly the same as in the Dutch Republic in the seventeenth and eighteenth centuries, as these children attended 'Dutch' schools in Ceylon.[56] Based on literature on education in the Dutch Republic, I have

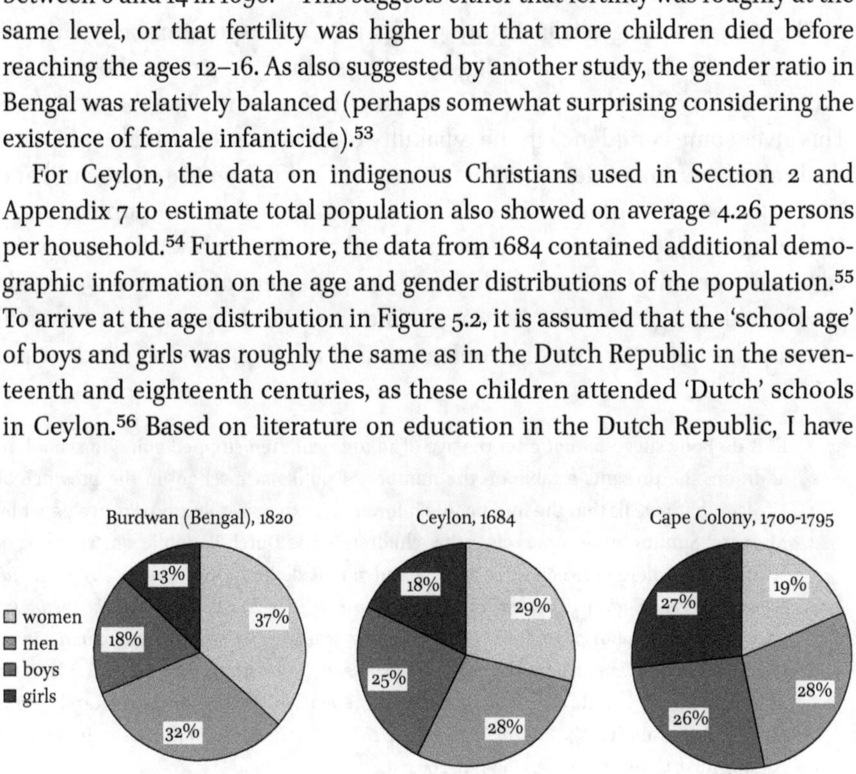

FIGURE 5.2 *Age and gender ratios in Bengal, Ceylon, and the Cape.*
Sources: Bengal: Bayley, 'Statistical View'; Ceylon: VOC 1396, ff. 602–612; Cape Colony: Van Duin and Ross, 'Eighteenth Century'.

---

52 Wrigley and Schofield, *The population history*, p. 528.

53 Bishnupriya Gupta, 'Where have all the brides gone? Son preference and marriage in India over the twentieth century', *Economic History Review* 67 (2014) p. 13.

54 VOC 1506, ff. 1180–1181; VOC 1544, ff 805–806; VOC 1591, ff. 1079–1086; and VOC 1605, ff. 882–888: 'Rolls of baptized indigenous Christians'.

55 VOC 1396, ff. 602–612: '*Sommarium van alle 's Compagnies onderdanen*' [Transl.: 'Summary of all Company's subjects'].

56 Van Goor, *Jan Kompenie*.

estimated that the school-going age in Ceylon was roughly between 5 and 11,[57] with girls leaving school probably somewhat earlier than boys. This is suggested by the smaller number of school girls noted in other literature.[58] It is unlikely that there was a 100 percent enrolment rate among Ceylonese children, but we can assume that those children not going to school have been captured by the numbers of 'young men' and 'young women' grouped in with 'adults'.

The percentages given in Figure 5.2 for 1684 correspond closely with the numbers from the source on indigenous Christians,[59] as well as those arising from a census of Ceylon in 1821,[60] and statistics from the 1830s[61] and 1850s.[62] This gives some confidence in the reliability of these numbers. It also points to the limited amount of demographic change in Ceylon over the eighteenth and early nineteenth centuries. These data demonstrate that the population of Ceylon in the late seventeenth century (and thus, probably also during the eighteenth century) was relatively young, as 43 percent of the total was made up of children aged roughly between 0 and 11, while the group of adults still contained a large number of people classified as 'young'.[63] The gender ratio

57 E. P. de Booy suggests that after the age of 10 to 12 children stopped going to school. In addition, she presents a table on the number of pupils at a school in the province of Utrecht that reveals that the number of children older than 11 is limited. From a paper by Margaret Spufford it becomes clear that children in the Dutch Republic started going to school somewhere between the ages of 4 and 7: E. P. de Booy, *Kweekhoven der Wijsheid. Basis- en vervolgonderwijs in de steden van de provincie Utrecht van 1580 tot het begin der 19e eeuw* (Zutphen, 1980) p. 30; ibid., *De weldaet der scholen. Het plattelandsonderwijs in de provincie Utrecht van 1580 tot het begin der 19de eeuw* (Utrecht, 1977) p. 75; and: Margaret Spufford, 'Literacy, trade and religion in the ommercial centres of Europe', in: Karel Davids and Jan Lucassen (eds.), *A Miracle Mirrored. The Dutch Republic in European perspective* (Cambridge: Cambridge U.P., 1995) p. 260.

58 De Zwart, 'Population, labour'.

59 Ibid.

60 In the 1821 census a total of 595,105 persons were counted; of these 349,917 (59%) were beyond puberty, with 316,059 (53%) of these being male and 279,046 (47%) female. Numbers taken from Robert, *Caste and conflict*, p. 297.

61 Robert Montgomery Martin, *Statistics of the colonies of the British Empire in the West Indies, South America, North America, Asia, Autral-Asia, Africa and Europe. From the official records of the Colonial Office* (London, 1839) pp. 375–6: 1832: total population: 998,259; males: 524,052 (52.5%), females: 474,207 (47.%); 1836: total population 1,229,828; males: 645,492 (52.5%); females: 584,336 (47.5%).

62 *Statistical tables:* 1850: Total population = 1,575,613; Female: 750,010 (47.5%); Male: 825,603 (52.5%), data for 1851–54 reveal a similar picture.

63 Wrigley and Schofield, *The population history*, p. 528.

was skewed towards men (53 percent), although perhaps not as much as one might expect in a society where the practice of polyandry (where one woman has several men) was supposedly widespread.[64] The relatively lower number of school girls and young women, combined with the large number of widows, suggests a significantly lower marrying age for women, which is confirmed by evidence from the *thombos*.[65]

The demography of the Cape Colony is a different story entirely. In recent research, Jeanne Cilliers and Johan Fourie have analysed the demographic composition of the settler population at the Cape. As could be expected from the high growth rates shown in Section 2, average household sizes were much larger than in the other cases. The median number of children per household increased from 7 in the late seventeenth century to 9 in the late eighteenth century.[66] As a result the population at the Cape was even younger than that in Ceylon (again taking children to be aged 11 years or less). In addition, the gender distribution was highly skewed towards men. Rather than being the result of female infanticide,[67] this was due to the fact that many settlers, farmers, or townsmen were former members of the Cape garrison or other Company servants;[68] especially in the early years most of the immigrants from Europe were male.[69] The values shown in Figure 5.2 even underestimate the male bias as these do not include the Company's establishment at the Cape, which also included significant numbers of men (see also Subsection 5.4). Nor does it include the slave population, which also has a clear male bias (75 percent male).[70]

There are several different interpretations regarding households in Java. The common unit of account in Javanese censuses is the *cacah*, sometimes considered as an equivalent of the household. While Governor-General Stamford

---

64 Darshini A. de Zoysa, 'Transformation of customary marriage and inheritance laws of the Sinhalese under British Colonialism', *Dialectical Anthropology* 20 (1995) pp. 111–132.

65 Van den Belt, Kok and Mandemakers, 'Digital thombos', p. 18; Dewasiri, *The adaptable peasant*, p. 91. Also see the research on the marital age gap in Ceylon by Sarah Carmichael: 'Pearls, Girl's best friend? Sri Lankan women's status at the beginning of the 20th century as the roots of their current position'; a paper presented at the *Utrecht Seminar in Social and Economic History* (November 2011).

66 Cilliers and Fourie, 'New estimates', p. 78.

67 The number of girls is higher than the number of boys.

68 Robert Ross, 'The "White" Population of South Africa in the Eighteenth Century', *Population Studies* 26 (1975) p. 222.

69 Ibid., p. 223.

70 Van Duin and Ross, 'The economy'.

Raffles (1811–1816) suggested average household size in Java was 4.16,[71] others have suggested the typical *cacah* had around 5 or, even, 6 members.[72] The consensus, based on more recent numbers, suggests that on average the Javanese household consisted of around 4.5 people.[73] Boomgaard concludes that in Java 'the nuclear family was the rule rather than the exception'.[74] Evidence from the 1920s suggests that family size is correlated with income and that families with higher incomes tend to have more children. Coolies, our main group of interest, had an average family size of 4.[75] In contrast to the other cases, the evidence on Java suggests that, at least in the nineteenth century, there were slightly more females than males. Boomgaard gives a ratio of 47 percent women and 53 percent men in 1802 and these percentages remained roughly the same throughout the rest of the nineteenth century.[76] Numbers given by Raffles suggest even more women: 57 percent.[77] Finally, the nineteenth-century data of Boomgaard suggest the average percentage of children was around 45 percent,[78] while Bosma suggests it was below 40 percent in the eighteenth century.[79]

What does this mean for the real wages calculated in Chapter 4? Regarding three of the regions presented here – Bengal, Ceylon and Java – it can be concluded that these can be reasonably compared with England and other parts of the world, as family size will not drive any significant biases in the results: average

71 Thomas Stamford Raffles, *The History of Java* 2 vols. (Kuala Lumpur [etc.]: Oxford U.P., 1978 [Original: London 1817]), see: Ulbe Bosma, 'Labour Relations in Java 1650, 1800, 1900,' *Global Collaboratory on the History of Labour Relations 1500–2000* (June 2011) p. 10.

72 Van Niel, 'Economic and population changes', p. 300; J. Hageman, 'Geschied- en aardrijkskundig overzigt van Java op het einde der achttiende eeuw,' *Tijdschrift van het Bataviaasch Genootschap* 9 (1860) p. 267; Ricklefs, 'Some Statistical evidence'. The subject is discussed extensively by Boomgaard, *Children*, appendix 1: 'What is a cacah?'

73 Boomgaard finds average households of 4.7 in the nineteenth century; *Children of the colonial*, p. 153. The 1920 and 1930 population censuses identified 4.6 persons per dwelling in Java while another study from 1924–25 suggested 4.3 people per rural household: A. Leigh and P. van der Eng, 'Top Incomes in Indonesia, 1920–2004', in: A. B. Atkinson and T. Piketty (eds.), *Top Incomes: A Global Perspective* (Oxford: Oxford U.P., 2010) pp. 171–219. Bosma, 'Labour Relations', also suggests 4.5 seems a reasonable number.

74 Boomgaard, *Children*, p. 153.

75 Ibid., p. 157.

76 Ibid., pp. 172–175.

77 Raffles, *History of* Java; Bosma, 'Labour Relations', p. 4.

78 Boomgaard, *Children*, p. 154. Boomgaard does not specify until what age people were considered children. Bosma, 'Labour Relations', suggests that adulthood was reached between ages 10 and 12.

79 Bosma, 'Labour Relations', p. 4.

family size in the other areas of the comparisons shown in Figure 4.1 were equal to or on a par with these regions. For example, in pre-modern England the average family comprised 4.8 persons, in Tokugawa Japan it comprised 4.9 persons, and China in the early twentieth century it was 5.3–5.4 persons.[80] Following Schneider's conclusions, this should not lead to significant biases in the comparisons of real wages.[81] In the case of the Cape Colony, however, the large family sizes and skewed gender distribution of the population does perhaps makes comparisons more complicated. These distributions relate to *freeburghers*, who often had their own shop in Cape Town or their own farm in the hinterlands. When they were still working for wages they probably had no, or few, children, and it was only when they set up as *freeburghers* did they extend their families. Furthermore, as Cilliers and Fourie noted, the composition of these families look very similar to those in New England[82] and their real wages also showed similar patterns.[83] Finally, even in the case of the Cape, roughly more than one-quarter of the population consisted of adult men, which fits Allen's model of one male breadwinner feeding three other people. The contribution of women and children to household income might change this picture, however.

4 Family Incomes

Most, if not all, studies on real wages have based their historical reconstructions on male daily wages. Nonetheless, during much of history, women and children have also contributed to household income.[84] Two factors create a bias in the comparison of real wage series based exclusively on male earnings: (1) global variance in the male–female/child wage gap, and (2) differences in the labour participation rates of women and children.

---

80 Boomgaard, *Children*, p. 153: referring to works by P. Laslett, 'Mean household size in England since the sixteenth century', in: P. Laslett and R. Wall (eds.) *Household and family in past time* (Cambridge, 1972) pp. 125–158; C. Nakane, 'An interpretation of the size and structure of the household in Japan over three centuries', in: P. Laslett and R. Wall (eds.) *Household and family in past time* (Cambridge, 1972), pp. 517–543; and: Chi-Ming Chiao, 'A study of Chinese population', *Milbank Memorial Fund Quarterly Bulletin* 11 (1933) pp. 325–341.

81 Schneider, 'Real wages'.

82 Cilliers and Fourie, 'New estimates'.

83 Allen et al., 'The Colonial'.

84 De Vries, 'The Industrial Revolution'; ibid. *The Industrious Revolution*; Burnette, *Gender, work and wages*; Jane Humphries and Jacob Weisdorf, 'The Wages of Women in England, 1260–1850', *Oxford Economic and Social History Working Papers* 127 (2014); Elise van

Concerning the first factor, women's and children's earnings, there are only few observations available for the Dutch Republic,[85] and only recently have more solid wage series for women been constructed for pre-modern England.[86] This research shows that the gender wage gap fluctuated over time and according to location, depending on labour market conditions, type of contracts, and differences between sectors. When labour was scarce in the aftermath of the Black Death, the wage gap narrowed,[87] but it increased again in the period 1500–1800, when demand for labour fell sharply.[88] As a result, women's wages in this period fell from about 80 percent to 40 percent of the unskilled male wage.[89] Recent research suggests that these trends differ somewhat depending on whether women were employed on a casual or permanent basis,[90] while the extent of the gap also differed per sector. Probably as a result of the more physical nature of agricultural work, the wage gap was generally larger in agriculture than in industry.[91]

What matters for international comparisons and any implications for the Great Divergence debate is Pomeranz' suggestion that in eighteenth-century China 'women's earnings more closely approximated men's than in Europe.'[92] Whereas a Chinese male agricultural labourer employed full-time earned about 12 *taels*, a woman spinning and weaving for 200 days per year could earn 14.61 *taels*, slightly more than a man.[93] Allen et al. show, however, that even including these female earnings, living standards in China were far behind those in Europe.[94]

Nederveen Meerkerk, 'Market wage or discrimination? The remuneration of male and female wool spinners in the seventeenth-century Dutch republic', *Economic History Review* 63 (2010) pp. 165–186; Robert C. Allen and Jacob Weisdorf, 'Was there an "industrious revolution" before the industrial revolution? An empirical exercise for England, c. 1300–1830', *Economic History Review* 64 (2011) pp. 715–729.

85 Jan Luiten van Zanden, 'The Malthusian Intermezzo: Women's wages and human capital formation between the late middle ages and the demographic transition of the 19th century', *History of the Family* 16 (2011) pp. 331–342; Van Nederveen Meerkerk, 'Market wage'.

86 Humphries and Weisdorf, 'The Wages of Women'.

87 At least for those women in casual employment.

88 Van Zanden, 'The Malthusian Intermezzo'.

89 Ibid.

90 Humphries and Weisdorf, 'The Wages of Women'.

91 Van Nederveen Meerkerk, 'From Male Breadwinner'.

92 Kenneth Pomeranz, 'Political Economy and Ecology on the Eve of Industrialization: Europe, China, and the Global Conjuncture', *American Historical Review* 107 (2002) p. 432.

93 Allen et al., 'Wages, prices', p. 30.

94 Ibid.

We are now able to include Bengal in this discussion, as I found some female and children's wages in the sources discussed Chapter 4. These women (and children) probably prepared lime-mortar and brought it to masons at work.[95] In the sources, the payment of women and children sometimes specifically stated that only women, or boys, were hired for a certain number of days, but they were also often grouped together. One of the problems with this is that while from the specific series it can be observed that boys generally earned more than women and girls, when they are grouped together the wage differs somewhat, probably depending on the share of each of these groups. For example, the observations for 'boys and girls' in 1721 and 1731 probably refer to a group with more boys than the observation of 1728 in Figure 5.3. In order to increase the number of observations of women's wages, these have been extrapolated using the wages for boys.[96]

The female wage series can now be used to calculate the female wage gap and compare it with that in England. Figure 5.4 shows the English and Bengali

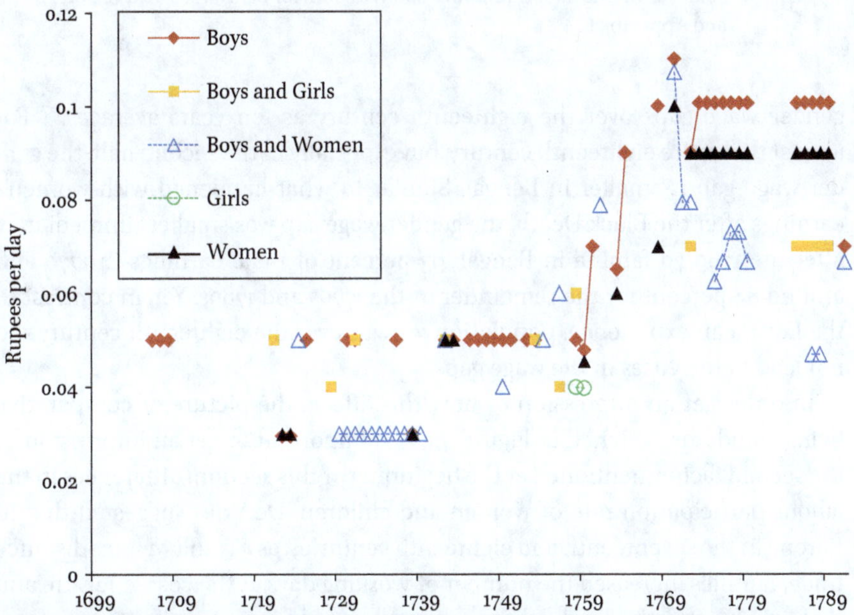

FIGURE 5.3 *Women's and children's wages in Bengal, 1699–1791.*
Sources: various archival sources, see Chapter 5 and Appendix 6.1.

95 Shireen Moosvi, *People, taxation and trade in Mughal India* (Oxford [etc.]: Oxford U.P., 2008) pp. 146–147.

96 FEMALE WAGE = 0.7666 × BOYS WAGE + 0.0101, $R^2 = 0.87$.

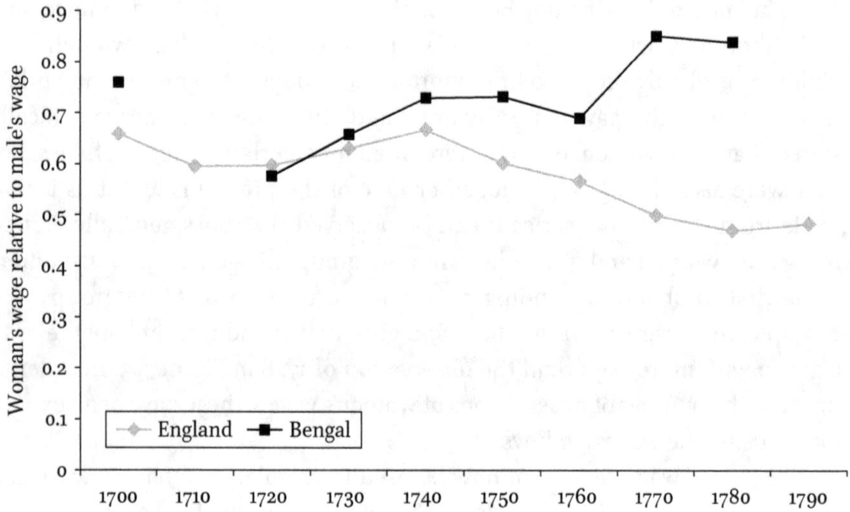

FIGURE 5.4 *Gender wage gap in England and Bengal, 1700–1800*
Sources: for England, Humphries and Weisdorf; for Bengal, see text, Chapter 4, and Appendix 6.

gender wage gaps over the eighteenth century as ten years averages.[97] For almost the entire eighteenth century, but especially in the second half, the gender wage gap is smaller in Bengal. Similar to what happened with women's earnings after the Black Death, the gender wage gap was smallest immediately after the 1769/70 famine in Bengal: 93 percent of male earnings in 1770 and around 84 percent for the remainder of the 1770s and 1780s. Yet, in contrast to the European experience, population growth over the eighteenth century did not lead to increases in the wage gap.

In order get an impression of how this affects the picture of comparative living standards sketched in Figure 4.1, it is important to get an impression of the second factor mentioned at the beginning of this section: differences in the labour participation rate of women and children. De Vries suggested that in Europe in the seventeenth and eighteenth centuries, as a result of long-distance trade, families increased the number of working days at the cost of leisure and that women and children's labour was reallocated from the subsistence sector

97 Humphries and Weisdorf, 'The Wages of Women'. They provide two series of women's wages, those for casual employment and those for fixed employment. Since the wages for Bengal were often paid as daily rates, this probably more closely reflects the casual employment series of Humphries and Weisdorf, which is, therefore, the series I have employed in this analysis.

to the market sector.[98] Research has confirmed the first part of De Vries' thesis, suggesting that the working year in England increased from 257 days in the second half of the sixteenth century to 280 days or more in the latter eighteenth century.[99]

Direct evidence on participation of females and children in the labour market is lacking, but it has been estimated that in England in the late eighteenth and early nineteenth centuries the contribution of women and children to household income among low-wage earners in agriculture was 18.4 percent: women 9.6 percent and children 8.8 percent.[100] In seventeenth-century Zwolle (in the eastern Netherlands) the contribution of just women was 19 percent.[101] Children also contributed to household income, in Europe, as well as in Bengal.[102] However, the research on England and the Dutch Republic suggests that this income substitutes rather than complements women's contribution. In Zwolle, the percentage contribution of women declined from 19 to 12 percent in families where children were also working.[103] In England, women's and children's combined contribution to family income was roughly stable at

98 De Vries, 'Industrial Revolution'.

99 Gregory Clark and Ysbrand van der Werf, 'Work in progress? The Industrious Revolution', *Journal of Economic History* 58 (1998) pp. 830–843, Hans-Joachim Voth, *Time and Work in England 1750–1830* (Oxford: Oxford University Press, 2001); ibid., 'The Longest Years: New Estimates of Labor Input in England, 1760–1830', *Journal of Economic History* 61 (2001) pp. 1065–1082; M. Bell, 'Working hours in East Anglia during the first industrial revolution', University of Oxford Manuscript (2009); Allen and Weisdorf, 'Was there?'

100 Sara Horrel and Jane Humphries, 'Women's labour force participation and the transition to the male-breadwinner family, 1790–1865', *Economic History Review* 48 (1995) pp. 89–117.

101 Elise van Nederveen Meerkerk, 'Couples cooperating? Dutch textile workers, family labour and the "industrious revolution"', c. 1600–1800', *Continuity and Change* 23 (2008) p. 257.

102 Otherwise these wages would not have shown up in the sources. In the literature, Indian women generally show up as spinners (Hossain, *Company Weavers*, p. 39; Prassanan Parthasarathi, 'Cotton Textiles in the Indian Subcontinent 1200–1800', in: Giorgio Riello and Prasannan Parthasarathi, *The Spinning World: A Global History of Cotton Textiles, 1200–1800* (Oxford: Oxford U.P., 2009) p. 29). Although women are also mentioned as performing agricultural tasks and in rice processing and the building industry: Smritikumar Sarkar, 'Social Organization of Artisan Production in India: Changing Role of the Market, Technology, and Merchant-Creditor: 18th to 20th Centuries', in: Binay Bhusan Chaudhuri (ed.), *Economic History of India From Eighteenth to Twentieth Century* (New Delhi: Centre for Studies in Civilization, 2005) p. 269; and as brick-carriers: Moosvi, 'The World of Labour in Mughal India', p. 251–2; ibid., *People, Taxation, and Trade*, pp. 135–158.

103 Van Nederveen Meerkerk, 'Couples cooperating', p. 257. Obviously part of this decline may be that general household income was higher due to this decline, and that the percentage therefore diminishes somewhat.

around 20 percent in the period 1787–1865, while the woman's contribution alone fluctuated between 1.9 and 11.6 percent.[104] It is unclear whether this substitution was also the case in Bengal.

How does the contribution of women and children affect the comparison between England and Bengal (for which we have some data)? Figure 5.5 shows, besides the original series of welfare ratios in England (Oxford, to avoid the high wage bias of London) and Bengal, four additional series to account for the contribution of family members: (1) ENGPlus adds 25 percent to the male income for the England series;[105] (2) BENPlus adds 25 percent to the male wage for the Bengal series; (3) BENWom adds a woman's wage for 250 days per year to the household income;[106] (4) BENWCh adds a boy's and a woman's wage for 250 days per year to the household income,[107] but increases the number of baskets to 3.5 (rather than 3);[108] and (5) BENMax adds 3 boys and a woman's wage for 250 days per year to household income, but increases the number of consumption baskets for the CPI to 5.[109]

Two important conclusions may be drawn from Figure 5.5. First, the contribution of women and children may account for the fact that despite subsistence ratios consistently below the poverty line, the population grew throughout almost the entire eighteenth century. The additional income of a full-time working woman and boy would allow these families to stay out of trouble most years. Still, during the famine of 1769–1770 in Bengal even the most optimistic series plummets below the subsistence level, which fits the evidence of a high death rate in that year. Second, this figure suggests that Allen et al.'s observation for China is also true for Bengal, namely that even taking into account higher earnings and participation rates of women, living standards in Bengal were still behind those in England (and the Low Countries). Figure 5.6 shows the gap between Bengal and a downwardly biased series of English living standards (Oxford wages vs. London prices) without income from other family members. The most optimistic series of Bengali living standards are still on average only about 59 percent of the most pessimistic English series; only during three peaks were they higher. These numbers reflect an unfair comparison: even if the gender wage gap was smaller in Bengal, and Bengali women were

104 Horrel and Humphries, 'Women's labour force'.

105 25 percent increase means 20 percent of household income is generated by women (and children).

106 These series were constructed using linear interpolation between the observations shown in Figure 5.3.

107 Ibid.

108 As in order to work that many days, the boy probably needs at least one whole basket on which to survive.

109 Ibid.

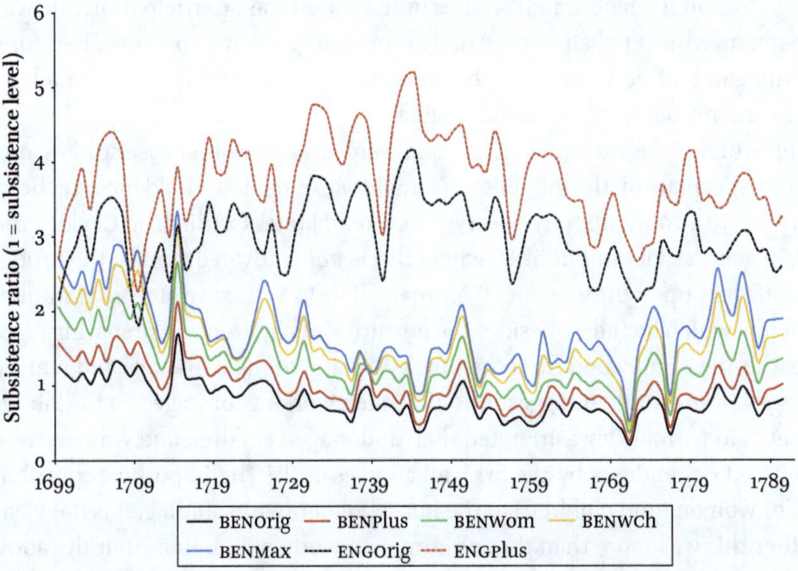

FIGURE 5.5 *Subsistence ratios adjusted with additional family members' incomes, Bengal and England, 1699–1789.*
Sources: see text.

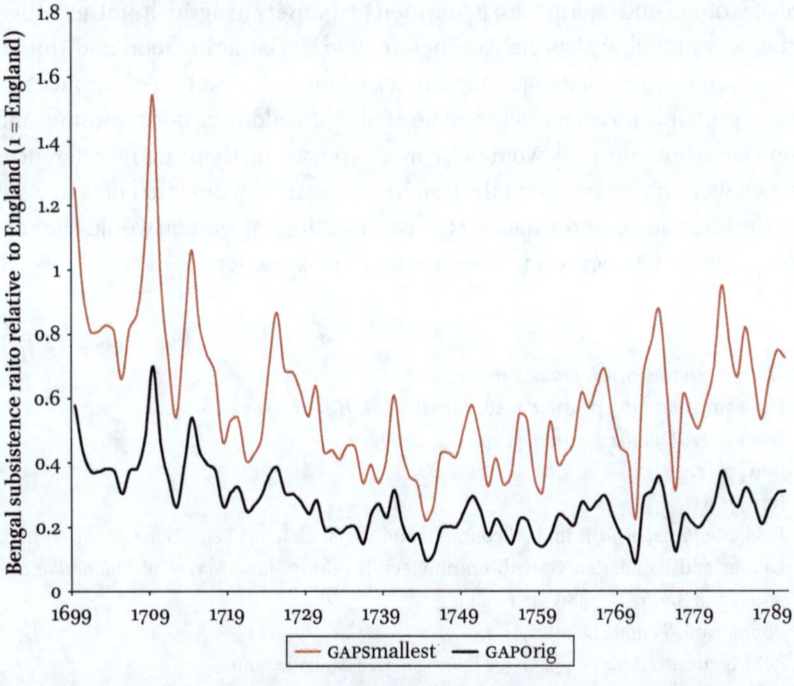

FIGURE 5.6 *Smallest and biggest gap between real wages in England and Bengal, 1699–1789.*
Source: Figure 5.5.

more active on the labour market, it is unlikely that their participation rate was 100 percent, while English women had a 0-percent participation rate. Therefore, the true gap will be somewhere between the original and the "GAPSmallest" series (and probably closer to the original).

Unfortunately, as no female wage data were found for other case studies, one can only speculate on the influence of female wages on household income there. According to a contemporary observer, Reverend James Cordiner, in Ceylon: 'the men, in general, labour but little, where rice is not cultivated; and all the drudgery of life falls upon the women'.[110] A variety of tasks was associated with women in Ceylon, which included, besides the nurturing of children and preparing food, the gathering of firewood from the jungle,[111] going to the market,[112] and rearing cattle.[113] I have found no suggestions of women working for wages on the labour market, and Nirmal Dewasiri noted that 'under-aged children and women were considered dependents by the Sri Lankan peasant'.[114] The important contributions of women (and children) to the household notwithstanding, it is not clear whether this was more than that of European women and, thus, that the additional income generated by these women would fill the significant gap in living standards shown in Chapter 4.

The literature on Southeast Asia in general, and Java in particular, suggests a strong position of women in society.[115] For the nineteenth century there is evidence of women and children assisting men in a variety of agricultural activities, and this was probably also the case before 1800.[116] Gathering food and timber from the woods was a mixed-gender activity, while the marketing of surplus produce was probably an exclusively female affair.[117] In addition, both spinning and weaving were both done by women in Java.[118] Yet, again, there are no references to women working for wages (in the building industry). In order to know to what extent the inclusion of more data on the contributions of women would alter the picture presented in Figure 4.1, more information is needed.

---

110 Cited in: Dewasiri, *Adaptable peasant*, p. 18.

111 Dewasiri, *Adaptable peasant*, p. 18, Robert Knox, *Historical Relation*, p. 147.

112 Dewasiri, *Adaptable peasant*, p. 29.

113 Ibid., p. 18.

114 Ibid., p. 63.

115 Reid, *Southeast Asia* I; ibid., 'Economic and social change'; Peter Boomgaard, 'Female Labour and Population Growth on nineteenth century Java', *Review of Indonesian and Malaysian Affairs* 15 (1981) pp. 1–31.

116 Boomgaard, 'Female Labour'.

117 Reid, *Southeast Asia*, II, pp. 91–93; Boomgaard, 'Female Labour'.

118 As noted by Crawfurd and Raffles, see: Boomgaard, 'Female Labour'.

For the Cape Colony, it is clear that part of the labour force consisted of female slaves and *Khoe* women.[119] It is, however, unclear to what extent women of European descent also contributed to the household income. Considering the relatively large families, and the general scarcity of women, it is likely that most spent significant amounts of time taking care of children and performing domestic duties, rather than performing wage labour.

To conclude, a few conclusions can be drawn from this section. In all these regions, just as in Europe, women (and children) made important contributions to the household. In the literature on Ceylon and Java, women are mentioned performing domestic tasks or as being active in textile production. It is only in Bengal that women are mentioned as being active in the building industry, which explains why it is only for Bengal that several observations of women's and children's wages were found scattered across the eighteenth century. The gender wage gap in Bengal was smaller than in England and decreased over the eighteenth century. There is, of course, the possibility that the non-wage contribution to household income was larger in Asia than in Europe, and this would be an interesting field for further research.[120] For now, however, it seems that including women's and children's contributions in the comparison of living standards does not alter the basic conclusions drawn in Chapter 4.

5 Labour Markets

The relationship between population, wages and living standards also depends on the functioning of the labour market. The prevalence of systems of coerced labour and slavery can affect the level of wages.[121] A discussion of the structure and functioning of the labour markets is important not only for analytical, but also methodological, reasons. Critics of real wages as a measure of living standards have suggested that in many parts of the pre-modern world, most people's lives were unaffected by the level of wages as they were subsistence or small peasant farmers. What part of the population depended on wages as their household income, and what part of the household income came from wages?

In a famous contribution to development economics, W. Arthur Lewis launched his theoretical model of development 'with unlimited supplies of

119 R. Elphick and V. C. Malherbe, 'The Khoisan to 1828', in: Elphick (eds.) *The Shaping*, pp. 28–29; J. C. Armstrong and N. A. Worden, 'The slaves, 1652–1834', in ibid., pp. 109–183.

120 Also see: Van Nederveen Meerkerk, 'From male breadwinner'.

121 As also demonstrated in: Allen et al., 'Colonial Origins'.

labour'.[122] Lewis proposed a two-sector model of reallocation from a low productivity 'subsistence sector' to a high productivity 'capitalist sector'. The subsistence sector is characterized by households or communities in which the members are willing to share the total output among all members. Because there is a surplus of labour and a scarcity of capital in this sector, many of the individual labourers receive a reward for their labour that surpasses the value of the actual output they produce. There, thus, exists 'disguised unemployment' and part of the labour force can be withdrawn from the subsistence sector without affecting total output. This surplus labour will move into the capitalist sector, because productivity is significantly higher there and wages are therefore higher than for the subsistence level. If productivity in the subsistence sector does not increase, while employers in the capitalist sector are able to consistently pay higher wages, the latter sector is said to enjoy 'unlimited supplies' of labour in the sense that practically everyone in the subsistence sector is prepared to enter wage employment.

In this section, I will first argue that there is evidence of widespread commercialization in all areas under scrutiny and that in these regions there were already a considerable number of people working outside agriculture. These people's living standards could thus be influenced by developments in wages, especially as some were landless wage labourers. Furthermore, even many farmers' living standards could be influenced by wages, as many of them were possibly engaged in non-farm activities, including wage labour, outside the farming season. Following Lewis' theory, wages rates in the capitalist sector (i.e. wages paid by the VOC) are related to those in the subsistence sector: the wage at which surplus labour becomes available 'may be equal to the average product per man in subsistence agriculture, plus a margin'.[123]

It can thus be argued that real wages are a reasonable proxy for the average incomes of a substantial part of the populace, 'as well as the marginal productivity of labour in the economy as a whole'.[124] This, however, also depends on the functioning of the labour market: were wages determined in the context of a free labour market responding to demand and supply, or were they influenced by systems of forced labour?

5.1 *Commercialization and Monetization*

To get some sense of what part of the population was affected by the market (in particular the labour market), and thus the activities of the VOC, and what

---

122 W. Arthur Lewis, 'Economic development with unlimited supplies of labour', *Manchester School of Economic and Social Studies* 22 (1954) pp. 139–191.

123 Lewis, 'Economic development', p. 190.

124 Allen et al., 'Wages, prices', p. 29.

part was focussed exclusively on subsistence farming, it is appropriate to briefly discuss the extent of commercialization and monetization in these areas, as it is clear that the spread of wage labour requires a reasonable degree of monetization and commercialization.[125] Following Jan Lucassen, one may assume a close relationship between the circulation of coins and the availability of wage labour.[126]

There is hardly any doubt about the high degree of commercialization of eighteenth-century Bengal. In the seventeenth century, the amount of money in circulation in India as a whole increased roughly threefold.[127] For Bengal specifically, both Datta and Mukherjee suggest that over the eighteenth century a remarkable process of commercialization took place in the countryside.[128]

Similarly, Reid famously pointed to the period 1400–1650 as the 'Age of Commerce' in Southeast Asia. Geoff Wade recently extended on this work, suggesting that 900–1300 should already be seen as an early age of commerce, characterized by population growth, the development of ceramic and textile industries, cash-cropping, booming maritime trade, and monetization.[129] Although the monetization of Java had already started in the eighth or ninth century,[130] it was only 'when Chinese cash came to be used for monetary purposes [during the twelfth and subsequent centuries] that coinage could function at virtually all levels of the Javanese economy, for both commercial and administrative purposes, ultimately allowing for the full development of the Javanese market system'.[131] Over the eighteenth century, commercialization and monetization spread across Java, as both silver and copper coins were

125 Ravi Ahuja, 'Labour relations and labour intermediaries in early colonial India: Four provocations and one case study on the city of Madras', Paper prepared for the *Workshop on Labour Relations in India 1500–2000* (New Delhi: Indian Council of Historical Research, 2011) p. 2.

126 Jan Lucassen, 'Introduction: Wages and Currency, 500 BCE–2000 CE', in: J. Lucassen (ed.), *Wages and Currency. Global Comparisons from Antiquity to the Twentieth Century* (Bern: Peter Lang, 2007) pp. 9–58. See also, Feenstra, 'Dutch coins'.

127 Habib, 'Monetary System and Prices'.

128 Datta, *Society, economy*, p. 17; Mukherjee, 'Markets in eighteenth century'.

129 Geoff Wade, 'An Early Age of Commerce in Southeast Asia, 900–1300 CE', *Journal of Southeast Asian Studies* 40 (2009) pp. 221–265.

130 Robert S. Wicks, *Money, markets and trade in early Southeast Asia: The development of indigenous monetary systems to AD 1400* (1992); Kenneth R. Hall, 'Coinage, trade and economy in early South India and its Southeast Asian neighbours', *Indian Economic and Social History Review* 36 (1999) pp. 431–459; Robert S. Wicks, 'Monetary developments in Java between the ninth and sixteenth centuries: a numismatic perspective', *Indonesia* 42 (1986) pp. 42–77.

131 Wicks, 'Monetary developments', p. 64.

imported into the island on a large scale.[132] Feenstra found that over a billion small copper coins were sent to the island by the VOC. It seems likely that these spread not only through coastal parts of the island under Dutch control: over half of these coins were sent to Semarang, which served as a cross-road to Mataram.[133] The spread of wage labour throughout the island is also supported by the fact that I have found evidence of smiths working for wages in Cartasura (situated in the interior of Mataram) in 1739.[134]

Ceylon has often been described as a predominantly agricultural society with the majority of the people engaged in subsistence agriculture, paddy cultivation being its central feature.[135] However, also in the case of Ceylon, there are indications of widespread commercial exchange. First of all, it is clear that the traditional peasant settlements were not completely self-sufficient: some consumer commodities came from distant areas (rice was imported from Bengal, Coromandel, and Java),[136] as well as across Ceylon.[137] There is also evidence of the existence of local markets and shops used by perhaps 'hundreds of Sinhalese' every day.[138] Such commercial exchange was facilitated by the circulation of a wide variety of coins, and this took place not only among the higher levels of society but also among 'ordinary working people.'[139] As early as the sixteenth century 'there was a substantial circulation of money'[140] and this

---

132 Nagtegaal, *Rijden*, pp. 196–7.

133 Feenstra, 'Dutch coins', p. 4.

134 VOC 7838 ff. 62–65.

135 Da Silva, *A History*, p. 171.

136 Arasaratnam, 'Dutch commercial policy'; and Arasaratnam, 'The rice trade'.

137 Those parts of Dutch ruled south-west Ceylon that had a surplus of paddy traded with parts that did not produce enough. For example, the cinnamon peeling caste, the *Salāgama*, did not produce sufficient rice themselves and thus had to purchase it in Matara: Kotelawela, 'Agrarian policies', p. 13. Dewasiri (*Adaptable peasant*, p. 29) notes that other essential articles and services made or provided by specialist castes were sometimes unavailable in a village, 'as the caste-based division of labour extended beyond one single village settlement.'

138 As previously noted, it was one of the tasks of the women to go to the market. In addition, Robert Knox wrote that there were shops in the cities, 'which sell cloth, rice, salt, tobacco, limes, drugs, fruits, swords, steel, brass, copper, &c.' While Knaap claims that as early as the 1690s 'hundreds of Sinhalese came into Colombo every day to sell rice, cattle and other food in the market': Gerrit Knaap, 'Europeans, mestizos and slaves: the population of Colombo at the end of the seventeenth century', *Itinerario* 5 (1981) p. 85.

139 Arasaratnam, 'Historical foundation', p. 6.

140 Chandra R. de Silva, 'The first Portuguese revenue register of the Kingdom of Kotte–1599', *Ceylon Journal of Historical and Social Studies* 5 (1975) pp. 71–153.

was 'certainly not confined to trading centres on the coast.'[141] S.B.D. de Silva has demonstrated the existence of 'a complex system of commercial relations facilitated through monetary exchange' in the Kandyan regions.[142]

The situation in the Cape Colony was somewhat peculiar. The Cape Town area and its immediate surroundings were clearly highly commercialized. There were many inn-keepers to serve the many ships' crews who called at the Cape. In addition, there were many people working in production and other services. Outside Cape Town there were many commercial wheat farms and vineyards whose production was directly influenced by the ebb and flow of the internal and external market.[143] Living further away from Cape Town were the famous *trekboers*, who were pastoral farmers, many of them existing on a subsistence level.

5.2 *Occupational Structure*

What part of the population worked in agriculture? Parthasarathi presents occupational data from Bengal that suggest various villages enjoying a relatively small, but highly productive, agricultural sector that fed a large non-agricultural population.[144] For example, a 1775 survey of the region of Rangamati suggests only 39 percent of 256 households were cultivators, while the remainder of the households were weavers, coolies, officials and a variety of other non-agricultural occupations. Similarly, a survey of the village of Sibpur in 1791 suggests that only 25 percent of 419 households were agriculturalist in nature, while some 15 percent were artisans. Tirthankar Roy, however, determined that some 80 percent of the total population in Bengal was dependent on agriculture,[145] and that only in a few textile districts of lower Bengal the proportion was smaller. His agricultural figure may, however, be somewhat high when taking into account the significant deindustrialization of the later eighteenth and nineteenth centuries,[146] while for India as a whole it has been suggested that between 1857 and 1900 approximately 73 percent of the male workforce was employed in agriculture.[147]

141 Chandra R. de Silva, 'Sri Lanka in the early sixteenth century: economic and social conditions', in: K. M. de Silva (ed.) *University of Peradeniya History of Sri Lanka* (Peradeniya, 1995) p. 50.

142 S. B. D. de Silva, *Political Economy of Underdevelopment* (London, 1982) p. 211.

143 Boshoff and Fourie, 'The significance'; Ross, 'The Cape'.

144 Parthasarathi, *Why Europe*, p. 70.

145 Roy, 'Economic conditions', p. 184.

146 Clingingsmith and Williamson, 'Indian deindustrialization'.

147 Alan Heston, 'National Income', in: Dharma Kumar (ed.), *Cambridge Economic History of India, vol. 2, 1575–1970* (Cambridge: Cambridge U.P., 1983) pp. 376–462.

In this subsection, a variety of data will be employed to get some idea of the occupational structures of Ceylon, Java, and the Cape Colony. Most attention will be given to Ceylon, as its data were gathered and constructed from archival sources. The population estimates for Ceylon in Section 2 were based on proto-censuses, probably compiled because the people were obliged to perform services either to the Kandyan King or, in the Maritime Provinces, to the VOC, in return for *accommodessans* (land grants). This system was known as *rājakāriya*. What these services encompassed depended on one's caste, hence the existence of an occupational caste system. The farming castes, the *Goyigama* in the Sinhalese part and the *Vellale* in the northern Tamil areas, who formed both the largest and the highest castes, were exempted from these services. Other castes, such as the fisher, washer, carpenter, barber, and silversmith castes (etc.), had to perform the specific duties attached to their caste.

First, using literature on castes in early modern Ceylon, the many occupations and caste names reported in the census have been classified into 13 groups based on the HISCO tree of occupational groups.[148] For example, the *Careas* were part of the *Karāva*, the fisher caste, and have thus been classified as fishermen.[149] Second, these groups have been categorized per sector, following the PST system of classification as developed by the Cambridge project on occupational structures.[150] This implies that all the *Karāva* have been put in the primary sector. The problem that arises is that, as discussed in Section 4 of Chapter 4, not all *Karāva* were fishermen: many of them were carpenters (secondary sector) or boatmen (tertiary). Similar difficulties arise with other groups as well. Also problematic for putting these occupations/castes into an occupational structure is that, as Alicia Schrikker notes, the occupation caste system 'does not mean that all members of the castes actually performed this labour, as most people on the island were involved in subsistence agriculture.'[151]

These problems are, however, not confined to Ceylon: many early modern European farmers were at the same time employed as weavers in the putting-out system.[152] Thus, while some groups in the primary sector were engaged in

---

148 Marco van Leeuwen and Ineke Maas, *HISCO. A historical international standard classification of occupations*, (Leuven, 2002).

149 Michael Roberts, *Caste conflict and elite formation. The Rise of a Karava Elite in Sri Lanka, 1500–1931* (New Delhi, 1995) p. 20;

150 The University of Cambridge project: *The occupational structure of Britain 1379–1911*: http://www.geog.cam.ac.uk/research/projects/occupations/categorisation/pst.pdf Consulted: 18-01-2012.

151 Schrikker, *Dutch and British*, p. 17.

152 E.A. Wrigley, 'The PST system of classifying occupations', p. 3. Wrigley also goes into more details on other problems that arise when constructing an occupational structure of census data.

labour associated with the secondary and tertiary sectors, various groups in the these sectors devoted part of their time to traditional subsistence agriculture. If this approximately evens out, Table 5.3A should provide some indication of the occupational structure occurring in the Dutch-controlled Maritime Provinces of Ceylon.[153]

These are tentative numbers that most likely understate the size of the primary sector. Keeping these limitations in mind, Table 5.3A shows that in 1684 approximately two-thirds of the labour force in maritime Ceylon was engaged in agriculture, 13 percent in the secondary sector and 19 percent in the service sector. If the census had included the interior kingdom of Kandy, the primary sector would have been larger: data from the 1830s show that while in the Maritime Provinces 73 percent of the population worked in agriculture, this was more than 97 percent in Kandy.[154] Data for the entire island for the 1830s and 1850s show that the primary sector accounted between 75 percent and 80 percent, respectively, of the labour force.[155] These figures also point to the limited amount of structural change over the eighteenth century.

Employing tentative figures collected by Ulbe Bosma, it is also possible to give some estimates of the sectoral distribution of the workforce in Java of c. 1650 (in Table 5.3B).[156] These data show an economy dominated by the

TABLE 5.3A *Occupational structure, Ceylon (Dutch parts), 1684.*

	n	%
Primary	52,000	67
Secondary	9,900	13
Tertiary	14,700	19
Unknown	1,400	2
Total	78,000	100

Source: De Zwart, 'Population, labour'.

153 Household heads were counted because the problem of side-line employment in the subsistence and household sector is more acute in the case of women and children: Kumar, 'The forgotten sector', p. 389.

154 Montgomery Martin, *Statistics*, p. 375.

155 Montgomery Martin, *Statistics*, pp. 375–6: 1832: primary 73%, secondary 9%, tertiary, 18%; 1836: primary 78%, secondary 12%, tertiary 10%; *Statistical tables:* 1850: primary 75%, secondary 11%, tertiary 14%; 1851: primary 80%, secondary: 10%, tertiary 10%; 1852: primary 80%, secondary 9%, tertiary 11%, 1853: primary 78%, secondary 12%, tertiary 10%.

156 Bosma, 'Labour relations'.

TABLE 5.3B *Occupational structure, Java, c. 1650.*[157]

	n	%
Primary	2,862,200	85
Secondary	198,200	5
Tertiary	300,800	10
Total	3,361,200	100

Source: Bosma, 'Labour relations'.

TABLE 5.3C *Occupational structure, the Cape Colony, 1732.*

	n	%
Primary	5,764	78.9
Secondary	114	1.5
Tertiary	1,105	15.1
Unknown	326	4.5
Total	7,309	100

Sources: Fourie, 'The remarkable'; and Fourie and van Zanden, 'GDP in the Dutch'.

primary sector. Nonetheless, the secondary and tertiary sectors were not entirely absent, and, as I shall argue below, many of those in the primary sector may have been engaged in secondary and tertiary sector activities through non-farm employment[158] Furthermore, Bosma suggests that these numbers may underestimate the number of people in construction and the shipping industry. Among those in the secondary sector are people working

157 I took Bosma's figures from Table 4, column II, and used the percentages in column III to calculate the total number of people in the primary sector, which, therefore, differ slightly from Bosma's approach. Also included in the primary sector are those for fishing. Slaves were put in the secondary sector.

158 De Zwart and Van Zanden, 'Labor, wages'; B. White, 'Economic diversification and agrarian change in rural Java, 1900–1990', in. P. Alexander, P. Boomgaard and B. White (eds.), *In the shadow of agriculture. Non-farming activities in the Javanese economy, past and present* (Amsterdam: Royal Tropical Institute, 1992); Peter Boomgaard, 'The non-agricultural side of an agricultural economy, Java, 1500–1900', in: Alexander et al. (eds.) *In the shadow*, p. 36.

in textiles, and[159] construction, as well as slaves (based on the literature, these were assumed to be artisans, most likely in the shipbuilding industry). The tertiary sector is somewhat larger than the secondary, as it includes shipping (5 percent), in addition to administrators, shopkeepers, priests and teachers.

Slightly more detailed data are available to sketch sectoral employment in the Cape Colony around 1732 (shown in Table 5.3C). This is done by combining figures on the free burgher population from the Cape Town, Stellenbosch and Drakenstein districts[160] with additional estimates on Company employees and the number of *Khoesan* within the Colony borders.[161] Unsurprisingly, these data show a large primary sector, and the economy was clearly dominated by crop and stock farming. The secondary sector is almost non-existent according to these numbers, possibly as a result the Company's policies prohibiting manufacturing.[162] These data may underestimate this sector as many farmers could have been engaged in trades (e.g. as 'blacksmiths, wagon-builders, tailors, boot-makers, carpenters, and thatchers').[163] In Cape Town district alone 23 percent of the workforce was engaged as artisans, bakers, brewers or millers. The tertiary sector was possibly somewhat larger, as there were many innkeepers, barbers and others providing services to the ship crews calling at the Cape. Furthermore, the tertiary sector includes Company personnel (providing military 'services').

These figures, generally estimates based on scarce data, show that these economies, with between 70 and 85 percent of the population working in agriculture, did not consist exclusively of small peasant farmers. In comparison with north-western Europe, the degree of occupational specialization was perhaps not very impressive. In the Province of Holland already in 1514 only 39 percent of the population worked in the primary sector,[164] while in England in c. 1700 about 32 percent of the labour force was active in agriculture.[165]

---

159 This includes women working as spinners and/or weavers, as suggested in Section 4 of this chapter.

160 Fourie, 'The Remarkable'.

161 Data employed in Fourie and Van Zanden, 'GDP in the Dutch'; figures received from Jan Luiten van Zanden. It was assumed all Khoesan were in the primary sector.

162 Fourie, 'The Remarkable', pp. 423–424.

163 Ibid., p. 424.

164 Jan Luiten van Zanden, 'Taking the measure of the early modern economy: historical national account for Holland in 1510/4', *European Review of Economic History* 6 (2002) pp. 131–163.

165 Mokyr, *The Enlightened Economy*, p. 15.

5.3 *Labour Relations*

What part of these populations was working for wages and to what extent were these influenced by systems of labour coercion? While accurate quantification of labour relations and their shifts over time in these regions in this period is not feasible, the information above can be put in the context of what is known about labour markets and labour relations from the secondary literature.

5.3.1 Bengal

For India as a whole, it has been suggested that as a result of the high degree of monetization, in towns (perhaps 15 percent of the population was living in them),[166] 'money wages were universally in vogue for both skilled and unskilled labour'.[167] While some received payments in kind, Shireen Moosvi suggests that payments of money wages were the rule in Indian towns in the seventeenth century. Similarly, Prakash claims that the VOC had no problem finding sufficient labour at prevailing market wage rates as the supply of labour was very flexible.[168] This is in line with Nadri's finding that in Surat 'beyond some conventional caste or ethnic influences or restrictions on mobility, the labour market was free and any employer could find workers if he wanted to'.[169] For Bengal specifically, there is further evidence of the widespread existence of wage labour. The VOC silk reeling unit in Kasimbazar, established in the 1650s, employed perhaps as many as 4,000 reelers in 1715.[170] In addition, Lucassen gives a detailed sketch of labour at the Ichapur Gunpowder Factory (near Calcutta) that in the 1790s employed as many as 2,000 to 2,500 skilled labourers, making it 'one of the world's largest factories'.[171] While no concrete figures are given, the number of workers in Mughal royal mints was probably also large.[172] Next to these manufacturing centres, there were many wage labourers involved in many building projects, constructing forts, other buildings and ships (from which the wage data in this book were also taken). There could be more than a thousand of workers involved in any one project.[173]

166 Irfan Habib, 'Potentialities of Capitalistic Development in the Economy of Mughal India', in ibid., *Essays in Indian History* (Delhi, 1995) p. 201.

167 Moosvi, 'The World of Labour'.

168 Prakash, *The Dutch East India Company*, p. 238.

169 Nadri, *Eighteenth-Century Gujarat*, p. 37.

170 Prakash, *The Dutch East India Company*, p. 117.

171 Jan Lucassen, 'Working at the Ichapur'.

172 Prakash, *The Dutch East India Company*, p. 117.

173 Morleand, *India at the Death of Akbar*, pp. 173–174.

Labour coercion seems to have been limited in Bengal. Yet, *zamindars* (aristocrats allowed to levy taxes) in Birbhum, some 180 km northwest of Calcutta:

> [c]ould demand the attendance and labour of the Blacksmiths, Carpenters, Goldsmiths and Florists, and each artificer of this description when called was obliged to attend and work for the space of ten or fifteen days in the year, so that no one attended twice in the same year, and assist in the *zamindari* buildings and other works receiving only a small daily allowance and diet money.[174]

But Datta suggests that such *zamindari* claims were absent in the rest of the province and the *zamindars* were never accused of using *corvée* labour for production on their lands. Moosvi argues that forced labour was generally considered unethical in Mughal India.[175] Nonetheless, in neighbouring Bihar, slave labour was widely used for the cultivation of *zamindari* lands.[176]

5.3.2 The Cape Colony

Between 1658 and 1838 the Cape was a slave-based economy; slaves formed almost half the entire population in the eighteenth century. European settlers constituted about 40 percent of the population, with the remaining 10 percent being *Khoesan*.[177] The numbers of *Khoesan* declined after 1713, when an epidemic took the lives of 9 out of 10 *Khoesan*.[178] The shortage of labour led to the indenture of many of the remaining *Khoesan*. From 1721 onwards, the children of male slaves and *Khoesan* women, as well as the children of *Khoesan* who worked for farmers, were indentured for periods of 18 years. While I found a few scattered notations of *Khoesan* wages and prices for slave hire were found,[179] my wage analysis has inevitably focussed on the European population.

The Europeans were either free burghers or Company employees. From 1657 onwards, some of the European settlers became farmers as the Company started to hand out large stretches of land in order to increase agricultural production. The rest of the European population consisted of wage-earning

174 Cited by Datta from English colonial documents.: Data, *Society, economy*, p. 160.

175 Moosvi, 'The World of Labour', p. 251.

176 Datta, *Society, economy*, p. 160.

177 Van Zanden and Fourie, 'GDP in the Dutch Cape Colony': this estimate concerns only those Khoesan participating in the Cape economy, the total Khoesan population was probably much larger.

178 Biewenga, *De Kaap*, p. 107.

179 Khoesan wages were generally relatively low: Elphick and Malherbe, 'The Khoisan'.

Company employees and *knechts* ('servants'). There were two types of *knechts*, Company *knechts* and free *knechts*, who worked without contract. Company *knechts* were VOC soldiers or sailors hired out to a settler. They signed a renewable one-year contract with the head of a household and received a monthly cash wage. After 1692 all contracts between Company *knechts* and settlers had to be in written form and, until 1795, wages were fixed. The free *knechts* (which included free blacks) did not enjoy institutional or contractual protection from the VOC, but their wages were significantly higher (as noted in Chapter 4, Subsection 2.2).[180] Figure 5.7 plots the shares of VOC employees, farmers and free *knechts* among the free male population. The figure shows that while Johan Fourie and Jan Luiten van Zanden have suggested that wage labour formed only a minor part of the labour force at the Cape,[181] until the 1750s the number of wage labourers exceeded that of farmers.

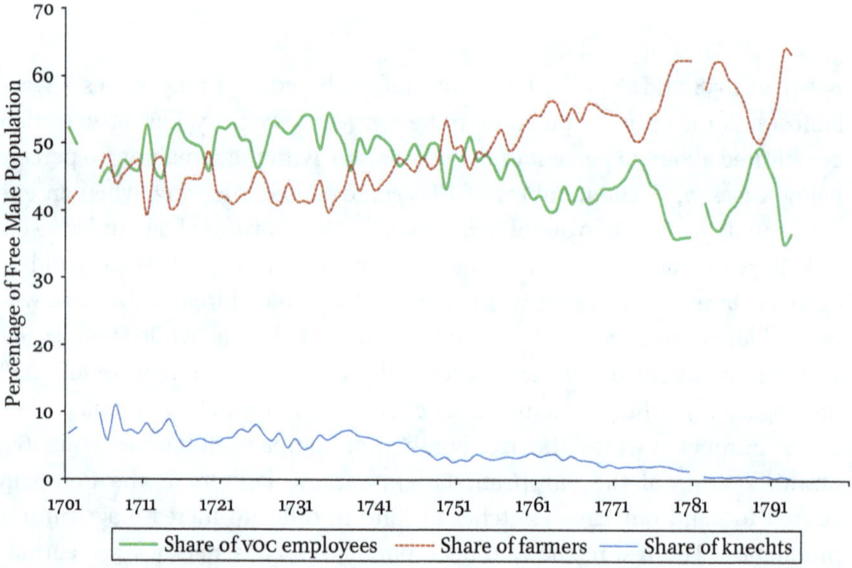

FIGURE 5.7 *Shares of VOC employees, farmers and* knechts *among the free male population of the Cape Colony, 1700–1795.*
Source: Van Duin and Ross, 'The economy'.

180 Shell, *Children of Bondage*, p. 13.

181 Fourie and Van Zanden, 'GDP in the Dutch Cape Colony', p. 471; Fourie, 'The remarkable wealth', p. 425.

5.3.3 Ceylon

It is difficult to quantify the number of wage labourers in Ceylon. Fortunately we can relate some of the figures on the occupational structure with what is known about the labour market from the literature. First of all, following the discussion on commercialization it is clear that wage labour existed in various forms in the Maritime Provinces, as the Reverend Phillippus Baldaeus mentioned wages of carpenters and masons in Jaffna,[182] and thousands of observations of wages for Ceylonese workers are to be found in the VOC documents, as discussed in Chapter 4. Wage labour was not only limited to those parts of Ceylon ruled by the Dutch, as S.B.D. de Silva mentions the existence of 'hired labour, i.e. labour working for money wages' in Kandy prior to the arrival of the English.[183]

Although many of the service and manufacturing castes practiced subsistence agriculture alongside their caste occupation,[184] Nirmal Dewasiri suggests that the Company's high demand for labour also affected its supply, thereby inducing a change of labour relations. Especially in the expanding urban areas, 'there was a growing tendency for caste-based occupations to be transformed into exclusive sources of livelihood'.[185] This seems to especially have been the case among toddy-tappers, artisans, washers, and barbers.[186] At the same time, the *rājakāriya* system was transformed into a 'sort of quasi wage-labour system'.[187] Governor van Gollenesse notes that a variety of workers 'for example carpenters, sawyers, hawkers etc.' did not get *accomodessans*, but received money payments.[188] In late seventeenth-century Jaffna, the required services in the *rājakāriya* amounted to only 'three days in every three months, or twelve days in a whole year',[189] and it was possible for people to buy themselves out of their service by paying a fine, which was then only 2 *stuivers* per day. This was significantly below the daily wage and in 1695 as many as 24,641 people paid

182 Baldaeus, *Nauwkeurige beschrijvinge*, p. 188.

183 De Silva, *The Political Economy*, p. 223.

184 Schrikker, *Dutch and British*, p. 17.

185 Dewasiri, *The adaptable peasant*, p. 62.

186 Dewasiri, *The adaptable peasant*, p. 62; Arasaratnam, 'Social and economic change', p. 48; and: Schreuder, *Memoir*, p. 52.

187 Dewasiri, *The adaptable peasant*, p. 222.

188 Van Gollenesse, *Memoir*, p. 63.

189 Hendrick Zwaardecroon, *Commandeur of Jaffna. Memoir for the guidance of the council of Jaffnapatnam, During his absence at the coast of Malabar, 1697*, transl. by Sophia Pieters (Colombo, 1911) p. 22.

their fines in Jaffna alone.[190] The resulting labour shortage in various construction projects of the Company had to be resolved by hiring wage labourers.[191] By 1762 the fine had increased to 6 *stuivers*, but the service remained only 12 days per year.[192] To put this in perspective, in the 'first modern economy',[193] the seventeenth-century Dutch Republic, the average labourer had to work 17–18 days per year for the 'taxman'.[194] However, according to Arasaratnam, 'feudal relations' in the south were far more pronounced and release from service by the payment of fines was less common.[195]

To what extent labour relations changed and how time was divided between caste-related labour for the *rājakāriya*, wage labour and subsistence agriculture, differed per caste, time period and region. It is outside the scope of this book to examine this for each caste group. Instead, I will illustrate the issue with two cases: the *Salāgama* and the *Karāva* (these were introduced earlier). While the *Salāgama*, or *chalias*, produced the most lucrative item on the island, cinnamon, their economic and social position was dire. Cinnamon peeling was part of their traditional obligation in the *rājakāriya*. Starting at the age of twelve with a delivery of one *pingo* (62 pounds), the amount a peeler had to deliver increased annually to a maximum of 11 *pingos*, which

> they must deliver until they are judged to be beyond a state where they can deliver this through old age or sickness; then they can be relieved by the yearly reduction of a *pingo* until they come to one *pingo* where they remain till they die.[196]

The peeling was an arduous task and workers frequently failed to deliver the obligatory amount, which steadily increased during the Dutch period until it came to a point where the *chalias* had to leave their villages and spent more than eight months per year peeling cinnamon in the forests.[197] In order to avoid the burden, the *chalias* occasionally resorted to violent insurgencies or deserted to Kandy.[198]

190 Zwaardecroon, *Memoir*, p. 22.

191 Ibid., p. 59.

192 Schreuder, *Memoir*, p. 60.

193 De Vries and Van der Woude, *The First Modern*.

194 Maarten Prak, *Gouden Eeuw. Het Raadsel van de Republiek* (Nijmegen: SUN, 2002) p. 90.

195 Arasaratnam, 'Social and economic change', p. 47.

196 Van Gollenesse, *Memoir*, p. 74.

197 Arasaratnam, *Dutch power*, p. 186.

198 Dewasiri, *The adaptable peasant*, p. 79. Similarly, other groups also protested against the high pressure put on labourers by the Dutch, as becomes clear from a rebellion in Matara in 1790; see: Schrikker, *Dutch and British*, pp. 70–71.

The *Karāva*, on the other hand, seem to have been a highly mobile and flexible group. Although *Karāva* people were classified in Dutch records as fishers, they were not only fishermen. Those engaged in fishing did so as a full-time occupation.[199] They were, of course, obliged to deliver part of their catch to the Company as their *rājakāriya*. Yet, the *Karāva* diverted to other forms of employment when this was profitable and they could thus be found in a variety of occupations: as noted in Subsection 5.2 there is evidence of *Karāva* becoming carpenters, elephant catchers or boatmen. Also, Dewasiri found an inland village where 29 *Karāva* families owned substantial patches of paddy fields.[200] The contrast between the *Salāgama*, caught up in an increasingly repressive system of obligational labour, and the flexible *Karāva* is striking.

This discussion suggests that many workers in the secondary sector (a total of 13 percent of the labour force; see Table 5.2a), comprising craftsmen and coolies, may have been working for wages at least part of the time. Next to these, fishers (somewhat less than 9 percent)[201] and a variety of workers in the service sector, such as washers, teachers, and bookkeepers (around 4 percent of the total; see Appendix 8, Table A8.1), could be employed for wages (see Appendix 8 for more detailed numbers).

5.3.4 Java

There has been significant debate on the existence of free wage labour in Southeast Asia in general, and in Java in particular. In much of the older literature on labour in Southeast Asia there has been a general agreement that free wage labour hardly existed before 1880.[202] Boomgaard was the first to dispute this consensus and from his work a different picture emerges.[203] Clearly a significant part of the labour force consisted of bonded labour, of which three types can be distinguished: slavery, *corvée* and debt bondage.[204] It seems that slavery was largely restricted to urban areas on the coast as non-noble entrepreneurs and commercially-oriented rulers in ports of trade had insufficient access to *corvée* labour. Merchants from China, India and Malaysia brought their own slaves with them, while the VOC employed slaves from India or other parts of the Indonesian archipelago. Slaves from Java itself were not allowed in

199 Dewasiri, *The adaptable peasant*, p. 62.

200 Dewasiri, *Adaptable peasant*, p. 87.

201 The 9 percent also includes hunters.

202 Anthony Reid, 'Introduction: Slavery and Bondage in Southeast Asian ', in: ibid. (ed.). *Slavery, bondage and dependency in Southeast Asia* (St Lucia, 1983).

203 Boomgaard, 'Why work'.

204 Peter Boomgaard, 'Human capital, slavery and low rates of economic and population growth in Indonesia, 1600–1910', *Slavery and abolition* (2003) p. 87.

Batavia and other urban centres.[205] Many of the VOC slaves were artisan-slaves who were paid a wage and some of them could, after a given amount of time had elapsed, buy their freedom. Such non-indigenous slavery was rare in the countryside, and according to Boomgaard about 1.5 percent of the total population were slaves.[206] Javanese could become bonded through debt. While this was a widespread phenomenon in Southeast Asia,[207] their total number in the Dutch-governed parts of Java was probably limited, and on several occasions the Dutch tried to abolish debt-peonage.[208] Many people in Java could, however, be subject to *corvée* obligations, as a form of taxation.

Next to those subject to these forms of more or less bonded labour, there was also a group of free labourers. From early on, Chinese migrants were an important source of free labour.[209] Around 1670 the term *coolie* first appeared in the sources, associated with (indigenous) unskilled wage labourers. While some coolies could also be coerced, many were free wage labourers. As well as coolies, there were also *bujang*, who were temporary or seasonal workers, which was the main difference between them and the coolies, the latter resembling a permanent proletariat. In 1750, *bujang* were found as free wage labourers on the sugar estates in the environs of Batavia.[210]

From research by Nagtegaal it becomes clear that the VOC employed free coolies and *bujang* next to *corvée* labourers.[211] The Company mainly used *corvée* labourers for large and irregularly organized operations, such as dredging canals or unloading large ships. These workers almost always received some food,[212] as well as received monetary compensation, even though it was part of their *corvée* service. Free wage-labourers often worked as domestic servants

205 P. H. van der Brug, *Malaria en malaise. De VOC in Batavia in de achttiende eeuw* (Amsterdam, 1994) p. 33.

206 Boomgaard, 'Human capital,', p. 84.

207 Reid, *Southeast Asia* I, p. 131.

208 Hoadley suggests that in the Cheribon-Priangan region around 1700 less than 5 percent of the total population was in debt-peonage (see Mason C. Hoadly, 'Slavery, Bondage, and Dependency in Pre-Colonial Java: the Cirebon-Priangan Region, 1700', in: Anthony Reid (ed.). *Slavery, bondage and dependency in Southeast Asia* (St Lucia, 1983) pp. 90–117), while in the Batang regency in the early nineteenth century this was less than 1 percent: Boomgaard, *Children*, p. 66.

209 Boomgaard ('Why work', p. 41) gives early examples from 1604/5, when the English in Banten hired a Chinese bricklayer, and from 1617, when the Dutch hired Chinese shipwrights.

210 The 'Ommelanden'; Boomgaard, 'Why work'.

211 Nagtegaal, *Rijden*.

212 Nagtegaal gives an exception to this rule; the VOC had to pay so much money to hire 9 *batur* in Surabaya in 1685 that they had to supply their food themselves: *Rijden*, p. 193.

or craftsmen.[213] There is also evidence from the early eighteenth century of labour migrants: inhabitants of Banyumas (in south-central Java) came to the northern coast during the dry season to work as caulkers, while from across the entire island people came to Batavia to work in the sugar mills, or, from the 1720s onwards, on the coffee plantations in the Priangan. In Semarang, men came to the *alun-alun* (central square) every morning to hire themselves out as day labourers.[214]

It seems that the size of the free labour market increased during the eighteenth century as a result of population growth between 1750 and 1850,[215] which may have led to an increase in the absolute number of wage-dependent workers. Finding sufficient workers remained problematic by the end of eighteenth century even though the number of both *corvée* labourers and free wage labourers increased over the seventeenth and eighteenth centuries.[216] A number of *plakkaten* (edicts) were issued to raise the number of labourers by issuing requests between 1750 and 1811 for the supply of *corvée* labourers to work in construction and the sugar mills, or to dredge canals. In addition, several edicts were issued to raise the level of wages in order to attract more free labourers.[217]

5.4 *Labour Markets and Wages*

Considering the degree of commercialization and monetization, the living standards of many people in the case-study areas could be influenced by the wages paid by the Company. In theory, the living standards provided by these wages were slightly above those in the subsistence sector. However, this mechanism could be influenced by systems of labour coercion: how would the differences in the functioning of labour markets influence levels and developments in real wages? To summarize the analysis, the regions under discussion had four different labour markets: (1) Bengal had a large free wage-labour market, where mobility was perhaps hindered by the caste system, (2) Java had a smaller free wage-labour market, supplemented by a larger amount of coerced labour, (3) for Ceylon roughly the same applies, but with an additional occupational caste system limiting mobility, and, finally, (4) the Cape Colony had a labour market with substantial amounts of imported slave labour.

As a result of the high population density and the Malthusian pressures this put on wages in Bengal, there was no need for additional institutional

213 Nagtegaal, *Rijden*, pp. 194–5.

214 Ibid., pp. 195–6.

215 Boomgaard, 'Why work'; ibid., 'Labour, land', Feenstra, 'Dutch coins'.

216 Nagtegaal, *Rijden*, p. 196; Boomgaard, 'Land, labour', p. 62.

217 De Zwart and Van Zanden, 'Labor, wages'.

interventions in the labour market to influence the level of wages. In the other regions, however, various degrees of coercion were introduced into the labour market. This is best explained by the Nieboer-Domar thesis on the causes of slavery and serfdom.[218] This thesis holds that in land-abundant but labour-scarce economies, land is available to all and in the absence of technology leading to profits from economies of scale, there is no wage profitable 'both for a prospective employer to pay and for a prospective worker to accept, as opposed to working for him- or herself.'[219] In this situation coercion has to be used to acquire labour, which explains the introduction of slavery or serfdom in such economies.

In the Cape Colony, labour scarcity (and high European wages) may have induced the VOC to import slaves in large numbers. But, as Allen et al. have argued in the case of eighteenth-century North America, slavery did not influence white real wages or discourage European immigration, because 'white' labour (i.e. free wage labour) and slave labour were complements rather than substitutes. They suggest that while increased numbers of slaves may have raised European wages in the short run, the growth of the European population would keep wages stable in the long run. This is probably also what happened at the Cape: as both the slave and settler population increased tenfold, real wages for Europeans remained stable.[220]

But what of the effects of the systems of *corvée* labour on free wages in Ceylon and Java? As already noted, while quantification is not feasible at the moment, it seems that significant numbers of *corvée* workers were present in both these areas. The regressions in Appendices A6.3 and A6.4 show that this *corvée* labour could be obtained at much lower wages than that paid in the free market; coerced workers in Ceylon and Java earned 70 and 55 percent, respectively, below that of free labourers.[221] Due to the coercion involved in *corvée* work, these wages are not a good index of the relative productivity of alternative activities (in agriculture), nor a good proxy for the standard of living of the workers involved, as most *corvée* work was only seasonal, and these people also

---

218 Evsey Domar, 'The causes of slavery or serfdom: a hypothesis', *Journal of Economic History* 30 (1970) pp. 18–32; H. J. Nieboer, *Slavery as an industrial system: ethnological researches* (The Hague: M. Nijhoff, 1900).

219 Gareth Austin, 'Resources, techniques and strategies south of the Sahara: revising the factor endowments perspective on African economic development, 1500–2000', *Economic History Review* 61 (2008) p. 609.

220 Of course, this is also partly the result of VOC intervention in the market, stabilizing wages and prices.

221 Ceylon: the wage for free unskilled workers was fl. 0.23 per day, coerced workers earning fl. 0.16 less; in Java the free wage was fl. 0.27 per day, while coerced workers earned fl. 0.15 less.

relied on other sources of income.[222] However, the existence of *corvée* labour may have satisfied part of the labour demand of the Company, perhaps also lowering the demand for free labour and, thus, wages in the free market sector. At the same time, *corvée* labour may also have diminished the supply of free labour, thereby putting upward pressure on free wage levels. As this happened in the same labour market, it is possible that these two developments partly cancelled each other out, and that the effects on free wages were limited. In that case, we could still follow Lewis' suggestion that the free wage is related to productivity in the subsistence sector.

6 Conclusion

This chapter served two purposes: (1) to explain trends in real wages in the context of two key variables influencing wages: demographic developments and labour markets; and (2) to engage with some of the critiques that have been raised against the real wage as an appropriate indicator of the standard of living in pre-modern colonial societies.

First of all, including estimates of total population, population growth, and population densities explains part of the developments in real wages. In Bengal it is clear that population growth went hand in hand with declining real wages and only after the great famine of 1769–70 did real wages rise again. This relationship, while not entirely absent, was much less pronounced in Ceylon. The difference is driven by the fact that whereas population densities were high in Bengal, and labour was abundant, densities were much lower in Ceylon. It was still a society with an abundance of land that could be cleared from jungle. Similarly, in Java the frontier would not be closed until the late nineteenth or early twentieth century. In the settler society of the Cape densities were famously low. As a result, in these latter two cases the Malthusian relationship between population and real wages was nearly absent. Both in Java and the Cape, in the face of rising population numbers they experienced increases in living standards in the second half of the eighteenth century.

Second, monetary and non-monetary incomes of other family members may explain that even in areas where the real wage was often below subsistence levels, as in Bengal and Ceylon, there was still population growth, rather than decline.[223] Including wages of women and children in the calculation of household income for Bengal, the only region for which these data were

222 De Zwart and Van Zanden, 'Labor, wages'.

223 Although these areas were more vulnerable to famines.

available, leads to an increase in the average subsistence ratio from 0.8 (in the male breadwinner model), to 1.3 (including full time women's earnings) or even 1.6-1.7 (plus 1–3 children's wages). At the same time, it is unlikely that including such earnings for all areas in the comparison would change the overall picture of the gap in living standards in the early modern world. Similarly, the data on household sizes in Bengal, Ceylon, and Java generally show these to be not significantly different from other regions/countries in the comparison.[224] Only at the Cape were relatively large family sizes the norm rather than the exception. Yet, even there, looking at the gender and age distribution of the entire population, adult males made up slightly more than a quarter of the population, as in other areas, suggesting that the assumptions in the Allen's model hold.

Third, these population figures were also employed to shed some light on the economic structure of these societies. It is clear that the majority of the populations in these societies were engaged in agriculture (some 70–85 percent). Evidently, some of these people were subsistence farmers, whose interaction with the market was negligible. In addition, wage labourers constituted a minority. Nonetheless, I have emphasized that as a result of the existence of significant degrees of commercialization and monetization in these areas it may be assumed that real wages and the living standards of a substantial part of the agricultural population were correlated. Next to a significant body of people working outside of agriculture, often for wages, many agricultural households had at least some sort of relation with the market.[225] Members of these households could have been engaged in wage labour through side-line employment.[226]

Finally, this chapter discussed the functioning of the labour market. Following the familiar Nieboer-Domar thesis on the causes of slavery and serfdom, where labour was abundant, labour markets were relatively free, but where labour was scarce large parts of the population were coerced into working for low wages during part of the year, or slaves were imported from other parts of the Indian Ocean region. At the Cape, slavery did not cause a decrease in wages for the European settler population, as wage and slave labour were complements rather than substitutes. In the cases of Ceylon and Java, there probably was no bias in the real wages for those outside the forced-labour sector. Following Lewis, the analysis of the labour market has also shown that real wages calculated in Chapter 4 may to an extent reflect living standards for a substantial part of the population at the lower branches of the income ladder.

224 In Bengal, mean household size was slightly larger than 5, but, as already noted, this is not out of line with pre-modern England, Japan or early twentieth-century China with, respectively, 4.8, 4.9 and 5.3–5.4 persons per household.

225 Rosenthal and Wong, *Before and beyond*, p. 44.

226 De Zwart and Van Zanden, 'Labor, wages'; White, 'Economic diversification', Boomgaard, 'The non-agricultural side', p. 36.

CHAPTER 6

Conclusion

1 Globalization

The question of when globalization began has been a contentious issue among economic and world historians for over a decade. The stakes in this debate are high because the answer to this conundrum not only puts new perspectives on one of the most important processes of the last quarter of a century, but it can also redirect the search for explanations for that other great puzzle: when and why did the Great Divergence take place?

Circumventing extensive discussions about the definition of globalization, I have focussed in this study specifically on economic globalization: the integration of world markets and, in this case, more specifically on the markets for goods. Price convergence can be seen as a sign of market integration taking place. While it has become commonplace in recent years to view the nineteenth century as the first age of economic globalization, I have tried to make the case for earlier indications of the same developments in the centuries prior to 1800 and the role played by the VOC – then the most important player by far in the Euro-Asian trade – in this process.

New data unearthed in the VOC archives on prices paid for sixteen articles traded by the Company in the Euro-Asian trade (together representing around 90 percent of the total turnover) show that there is sufficient evidence of price convergence, and thus the integration of Euro-Asian commodity markets, taking place. This process was aided by maritime rivalry among the European trading companies, especially between the Dutch and English. Both trends and absolute price gaps varied considerably between the various commodities, however. Rather than the simple dichotomy between monopoly goods and competitive goods (customary in the literature to date), these trends were to a large extent affected by the specific institutional settings of the different markets. I have proposed four different categories of goods that go a long way in explaining some of the variation in the trends observed. In the first category are the four monopoly spices (cinnamon, cloves, mace and nutmeg) that were obtained in areas where the VOC held considerable political power. The Company stipulated the conditions under which they purchased these goods, determining both the total quantities produced, as well as setting the prices for which they bought these goods. As the VOC was the sole supplier of these goods on European markets, sales prices were notoriously high. The second

 | DOI 10.1163/9789004299665_007

category comprised goods purchased, again, in markets where the Company had complete control over purchasing conditions, but where it lacked a monopoly position on European markets as similar commodities were brought to Europe by other companies, sometimes also from other parts of the world. The third category includes goods that were acquired at relatively low cost through contracts negotiated with Asian potentates. In contrast to the first two categories, the Company was unable to influence the quantities of these commodities it could obtain, nor could it one-sidedly set the price for which it bought these goods. It was thus to a large extent depending on the cooperation of the Asian rulers, while on the European markets the Company held no monopoly over the sales of these goods. The fourth, and last, category covers those goods that the Company purchased in competitive markets, especially in India and China, where the VOC competed with other European companies, as well as European and Asian private merchants.

Price convergence could mainly be observed in the latter two categories of goods, while in the first two divergence was the norm. There were two exceptions to this observation as both sugar and cloves (where the VOC controlled production) showed convergence. In the case of sugar, this was the result of the large quantities brought into Europe and the protection of the industry in Java. In the case of cloves, it was a consequence of the loss of monopoly in the later part of the eighteenth century. Despite the few instances of divergence in this period, however, it is clear that in the bulk of the Dutch-Asiatic trade, price convergence was the rule, suggesting that globalization may have taken off earlier than is commonly assumed.

Yet, it is not the exact starting date of globalization that matters, but rather the trends over time. From as early as Roman times (or perhaps even earlier) the world has gone through phases of globalization. The period around the thirteenth and fourteenth centuries, with the *Pax Mongolica*, constitutes one phase, which paradoxically was concluded with the spread of the Bubonic Plague, itself the epitome of globalization in this period. The period immediately following the European 'Voyages of Discovery' of the late fifteenth century constituted yet another phase. These voyages, through the circumvention of Venetian and Arabic monopolies, directly increased the number of suppliers of spices on European markets and, as a consequence, consumers benefitted from lower prices. In the sixteenth century, the Portuguese alone were the main beneficiaries of this global trade, but they were not a strong enough force to have significant effects on Asian trading systems. It was only with the advent of northern European chartered companies that this phase of early-modern globalization achieved maturity. Not only did the breaking of the Portuguese monopoly further decrease European sales prices, the entry of these companies in Asian markets also started to have more profound effects on the societies of the East. These effects were not only the result of the large amounts of bullion being poured into these economies, but were also a consequence of the increasingly aggressive introduction of colonial institutions. Colonialism became, therefore, one of the most manifest consequences of early-modern, as well as nineteenth-century, globalization. In areas where the VOC had colonial power, it hindered the development of 'free' commodity markets, incapacitating indigenous societies to reap the benefits of increased global demand for the goods they produced. In addition, the VOC kept in place, or extended, systems of forced labour in order to satisfy its increasing demand for labour, which again altered the distributional effects of globalization in local societies: those eligible for forced labour suffered, while free labourers could benefit.

Colonialism was an anti-globalizing force in the mercantile period, as it was meant to capture rents rather than to aid the integration of markets. As competition among the companies intensified in the eighteenth century and the VOC steadily lost its dominant position, four o'clock tea became a national tradition in England, while in French coffee houses intellectuals started to prepare willing minds for revolution (we find again that the effects of globalization contributed to its temporary downfall, since the period of French Revolutionary and Napoleonic wars is generally considered an era of de-globalization).[1] When globalization picked up again in the nineteenth century, it did so in full force: steamships, railroads, and canals aided globalization as never before. Planes, the United Nations, and the internet further transformed globalization in the twentieth century. One must take note of the fact that the entering of a new phase of globalization, as revolutionary as it may seem, does not alter the reality of the globalization that came before. Thus, while it may be the case that price convergence was more rapid and consistent in the nineteenth century, this does not alter the reality of globalization in the seventeenth and eighteenth centuries. This study thus emphasizes the earlier origins of this process and stresses the continuity between globalization in eighteenth and nineteenth centuries. Nevertheless, it is clear that each phase of globalization had its own causes, characteristics, and rules.

Thus, without suggesting that seventeenth- and eighteenth-century globalization was more or less important than other phases, I would argue that it was very real and that it could have had effects on global income distribution, or the 'Great Divergence'. I have shown that the process of globalization in the early modern period constituted more than just the advance of technology and the crumbling of barriers to trade. Most of all, the process seems to have

1 Findlay and O'Rourke, *Power and Plenty*, pp. 365–378.

been influenced by the creation and adaption of institutions that varied according to local conditions across the globe. Then, and now, it is clear that with globalization came rules, and as Rodrik noted: '[w]hat they are, who imposes them, and how – those are the only real questions.'[2] The difference between these institutions (rules) affected the way the benefits of globalization, as well as its detriments, were distributed between regions, within regions and among social groups.

2 The Great Divergence

As there are already strong signs of 'hard globalization' in the centuries prior to 1800, it may have had more profound effects on the Great Divergence between Western Europe and the rest of the world. While some scholars have downplayed the effects of long-distance trade for the European economy before the nineteenth century, most recent research has re-emphasized the role of globalization in the ascent of Europe: it gave rise to institutions more conducive to economic growth, led to urbanization, stimulated the growth a work ethic, and gave higher wages and living standards, and as such it played an instrumental role in industrialization. For revisionist scholars in the Great Divergence debate like Pomeranz and Parthasarathi, the divergence would not have taken place without globalization, as Britain would not have benefited from the production of land-intensive goods in the New World, nor would it have felt the pressure to mechanize textile production as a result of the influx of Indian calicos. Yet they suggest that globalization, while important in the eighteenth century, led to divergence only in the nineteenth century, as average incomes were still on a par in the preceding centuries. If incomes were, however, already much lower in Asia (as I have argued) it is possible that globalization also played its part in this. What happened in Asia before the nineteenth century is subject to much uncertainty as a result of the limited availability of reliable quantitative data. This book has filled part of this lacuna with new data on several regions skirting the Indian Ocean. As I have mentioned, these data are not perfect and may be further improved upon by future research in local archives. Nonetheless, by combining data from various sources, and placing them in their proper context, as well as employing various methods of dealing with gaps in the data, it appears that the possible errors and biases most likely do not affect the overall conclusions of this comparative analysis in relation to the Great Divergence.

2 Rodrik, *The Globalization Paradox*, p. 9.

I will summarize the main conclusions here. It seems that, in contrast to Adam Smith's generalization, the cost of subsistence was not generally lower in Asia.[3] Price levels were shaped partly by local conditions and partly by global developments. In the middle of the seventeenth century, prices were relatively high in the Cape Colony, but trends over the following century-and-a-half show a downward trend, partly resulting from agricultural expansion. In Ceylon, indigenous rice production generally did not suffice to meet local demand and the cost of living was consequently relatively high. This was in contrast to Bengal and Java, where the cost of living was generally lower than in north-western Europe during most of the period. Bengal initially profited from its relatively productive agriculture, but this advantage was slowly lost over the course of the eighteenth century. The opposite happened in Java, where wars in the late seventeenth and early eighteenth centuries pushed up the cost of living, with peace and stability leading to an expansion of agriculture and declining prices in the later years of the eighteenth century. Thus, in contrast to current ideas about the relation between prices and development, price decline in this period does not point automatically to economic stagnation. Indeed, it could also have resulted from expanding production and had a positive impact on real wages.

The global gap in nominal silver wage levels was initially much larger. As a result, the standard of living, as measured by real wages, was significantly below that of north-western Europe. These results largely confirm the conventional view in the Great Divergence debate. In line with the study by Allen et al., however, the results suggest that living standards in Asia were not exceptionally low, but instead that living standards in north-western Europe were exceptionally high, as living standards in Asia were largely on a par with those in many other parts of Europe. However, in contrast with Allen et al., as well as the trends in GDP per capita, in terms of real wages the advantage of north-western Europe was not increasing over the eighteenth century. Considering the general European decline in real wages in the eighteenth century and possibly stable or increasing well-being in South and Southeast Asia (with the exception of India), living standards converged towards 1800. Through the investigation of household sizes and the possible contributions of other family members to household income it has been shown that these results can stand up against the criticisms made of the male breadwinner model often applied in comparative real wage studies.

The trends in real wages can in part be explained by demographic developments. Especially in Bengal, the relationship between population and real

3 In line with the conclusions by Allen et al., 'Wages, prices'.

wages is manifest. Population growth went hand in hand with declining real wages and only after the great famine of 1769–70 did real wages rise again. This relationship, while not entirely absent, was much less pronounced in Ceylon as a result of differences in population densities. Bengal had notoriously high population densities and was labour abundant, and consequently wages were low. Densities were much lower in Ceylon, where there was an abundance of land that could still be cleared from the jungle. In Java (despite higher densities than in Ceylon) and the Cape Colony, the Iron Law of Wages was largely absent: in both cases, real wages increased in the face of rising population numbers in the second half of the eighteenth century.

Following the Nieboer-Domar thesis, these difference in population densities and thus varieties in the relative scarcity or abundance of labour led to different interventions in the labour markets. Both Pomeranz and Parthasarathi suggested the existence of well-functioning (neo-classical) labour markets in China and India, yet in the Cape Colony, Ceylon, and Java (where labour was scarce) unfree labour played an important role. While in the Cape Colony, free white labour was complemented with large amounts of Asian and African slave labour, in Ceylon and Java indigenous *corvée* labour was exploited in an attempt to satisfy the VOC's high and growing demand for labour. These interventions in the labour market possibly had only limited effects on the level of wages in the free labour market.

The discussion of demography and labour markets also shows more complex societies than the cliché picture of pre-modern Asian societies entirely dominated by subsistence farming, as depicted in some of the older literature. Agriculture clearly constituted an important part of these economies, but there is also sufficient evidence of widespread monetization and commercialization in these regions. Considering this coexistence of subsistence and a commercial sector in these economies, we can follow W. Arthur Lewis who suggests that the living standards in the subsistence sector were related to those in the commercial sector. Indeed, there is evidence of people from the subsistence sector working for wages in the capitalist sector for part of the year, as well as indications of workers earning wages in a full-time capacity. Data on occupational structures suggest that while a majority of these societies were employed in agriculture (between 70 and 85 percent), there was also a large group depending on the commercial sector for their livelihood, with many farmers even employed in the wage labour sector as seasonal workers. Nonetheless, in comparison with early modern occupational structures in England and Holland, these occupational structures (an indication of the level of specialization and efficiency of institutions in a society) are not very impressive. Thus, such results again support conventional views in the Great Divergence debate.

Another clue regarding the functioning of Asian labour markets can be found in the discussion on the premium paid for skilled labour. While the skill premium was the lowest in Amsterdam (roughly 50 percent), the premium at the Cape converged towards that same low level over the eighteenth century. The skill premium was also lower than expected in Ceylon and Bengal: never higher than 100 percent, and with indications of much lower figures. While the caste system in these societies may have hindered mobility between different occupational groups, apparently it did provide a relatively efficient framework for the transmission of skills through caste and kinship lines. Only in Java was the skill premium consistently above 100 percent.

That this is the result of the functioning of the labour market is suggested by the discussion on interest rates, which is generally considered an important determinant of the skill premium. Interest rates in England and the Dutch Republic were around 5–6 percent, while in Bengal and Ceylon the Company paid, or received, rates of around 12 percent. In Batavia (where the skill premium was high), as well as in Cape Town, interest rates were at European levels of 6 percent (or below). These rates concern probably low-risk official rates: there is evidence that the indigenous people in Java and Ceylon paid extremely high rates – rates as high as 25 percent monthly were reported in Ceylon. Not only do these rates suggest that capital could be very expensive in these areas, such discrepancies in interest rates show that while commodity markets were becoming more intertwined in the seventeenth and eighteenth centuries, financial globalization was still a long way off.

This begs the question as to what extent the developments I have just sketched were influenced by globalization. In general, it seems that globalization contributed to increased commercialization and monetization. Furthermore, as silver flowed from West to East in substantial quantities, there is some evidence of convergence of price levels towards the middle of the eighteenth century. For the Cape Colony (its existence already a direct result of globalization), another study has demonstrated how agricultural production and prices responded to shipping.[4] The long-term decline in prices towards levels more in line with the world market may be a consequence of this, and thus trade may have had beneficial effects on the development of living standards there. The inflation in Bengal could have been caused by the 'bullion for goods' trade. Yet, considering the relative price decline of cotton textiles – the main article of interest in global trade – *vis-à-vis* rice, it is more likely that these price increases were determined by local conditions, possibly a consequence of declining agricultural productivity, resulting from climatic changes and increased rent-seeking

4 Boshoff and Fourie, 'The significance'.

following the Mughal decline. Prices in Ceylon were correlated with those in Java because much rice was imported from there; the VOCs intra-Asian trade thus affected price trends. However, Ceylon's main article in global trade, cinnamon, was monopolized and the increased demand for it did not, therefore, have any effects on price levels. Javanese prices were also to a large extent driven by local conditions, mainly wars. In the absence of inflation, increased exports through global trade may have benefitted parts of the Javanese commercial economy.

While its connection with prices is the most obvious and direct, globalization affected these economies in other ways too. Although, as emphasized earlier, the manner in which societies were affected by globalization depended on the institutions that were locally prevalent or that came with globalization.

3 Colonialism

The effect of globalization in the early modern period, driven by the European quest for Asian commodities, was significant not only through its impact on domestic (relative) price levels, but also because it ultimately led to the opening of Pandora's box of colonialism. It has been suggested that, for the nineteenth century, state-led colonialism became one the main drivers of economic globalization. The paradox of colonialism in the age of mercantilism, when it was in the hands of private companies whose most important goal was maximizing profits, was that it was both a product of globalization and an obstacle to its further development. In the mercantile colonial system, territorial control was a means to capture rents and thereby hindered the process of commodity market integration. The extent to which it hindered further globalization, and how it affected societies around the Indian Ocean and in Asia, differed substantially in the regions I have discussed in this book. The reason is that colonialism in this period was very heterogeneous, perhaps much more so than in the nineteenth century. Colonialism was so diverse because of its driver: the European quest for exotic commodities. It was, therefore, determined partly by initial geographic conditions (the place and spread of specific crops),[5] partly by the strength of initial indigenous institutions, or the level of political centralization, and partly by chance.

The Moluccas suffered from a specific mix of these elements – and paid the price for it. This was the only area of the world producing nutmeg and mace, and as the islands were also small and lacked a strong centralized state, they

5 Engerman and Sokoloff, 'History Lessons'.

were easily taken over and controlled by just a few forts and well-armed men.[6] In the Banda Islands, the VOC killed or expelled virtually the entire indigenous population and set up a plantation system in which slaves worked the nutmeg tree gardens, leased from the Company by a handful of European plantation holders (*Perkeniers*, former VOC servants who had served out their contracts).[7] On the Ambonese islands, the Company did not introduce a plantation system, rather it thought it more effective to let the indigenous population work their own clove gardens as a secondary activity (next to food production for subsistence).[8] Interestingly, several Dutch historians have suggested that this system was generally beneficial to the Ambonese population, who could fairly easily earn some surplus income, while it also offered them a conduit through which to complain to the VOC about fraud and misconduct by village heads.[9] Ceylon was the sole production area of one of the most highly demanded products of the early modern era: cinnamon. In contrast to the Moluccas, however, political centralization was much stronger as this vast area was also home to the Kingdom of Kandy. In order to obtain the cinnamon monopoly the VOC first ousted the Portuguese in the first half of the seventeenth century and fought several wars with Kandy over the remainder of the seventeenth and eighteenth centuries. In the process, Ceylon developed into one of the Company's largest possessions, requiring an extensive military and administrative apparatus to control it. In Java, although the production of a specific monopoly product was lacking, the VOC came to control two-thirds of the island in the latter part of the eighteenth century. This territorial expansion was largely the result of it being dragged into various Javanese power struggles, rather than active expansion to safeguard a monopoly (although, of course, it actively defended its headquarters and main harbour at Batavia). It is for this reason that Femme Gaastra has described the VOC as a reluctant imperialist.[10] It is clear that the effects of the Company's conduct in these areas moved beyond the mere increase in demand, and its possible effect on prices, as these effects also depended on the institutions implemented (or adapted).

---

6 The Banda Islands were controlled by two forts (Belgica and Nassau) on Banda Neira.

7 Willard A. Hanna, *Indonesian Banda: Colonialism and Its Aftermath in the Nutmeg Islands* (Philadelphia: ISHI, 1978) pp. 59–60.

8 Based on: Gerrit Knaap, *Kruidnagelen en Christenen. De VOC en de bevolking van Ambon 1656–1696* (Leiden: KITLV, 2004).

9 Van Goor, *De Nederlandse Koloniën*, p. 136; Piet Emmer and Jos Gommans, *Rijk aan de rand van de wereld. De geschiedenis van Nederland overzee 1600–1800* (Amsterdam: Bert Bakker, 2012) p. 52.

10 Gaastra, *De Geschiedenis*, pp. 64–71.

In contrast to nutmeg and cinnamon, areas of pepper production were very extensive, and it was clear that no single company would ever be able to monopolize its production. When no monopoly would be obtainable through the use of force, the Company generally refrained from expensive military operations, but instead tried to establish contracts with local rulers. This was the case on Sumatra, Kalimantan, and the Malay Peninsula. Only in Malabar, the Indian 'pepper coast', did the Company's involvement became more extensive as it was thought to be instrumental in safeguarding its possessions on Ceylon. Political and economic conditions in Mughal India, Qing China, and Tokugawa Japan meant that the Company fulfilled the role of being merely one among many merchants there. In these areas the effects of the Company's long-distance trade was mainly felt through the additional demand for local produce. However, as these areas were vast and populous, the effects were limited. Om Prakash has suggested that in Bengal the growth of trade resulting from the European companies entry in the market led to the creation of up to 110 thousand new jobs. This represented, however, less than one percent of the total population. As a result, domestic forces (e.g. population growth, climatic change, Mughal disintegration, and changes in agricultural productivity) were probably more important determinants of the development of living standards in Bengal. Similarly, trade probably had negligible effects on real wage trends in China, Japan, and other Indian regions.

Thus, both geography and the level of initial political centralization influenced the form colonization took in the mercantile period. In order to understand its effects on global income distribution, we must therefore move beyond the settler-extraction dichotomy and proceed towards a more complicated framework than that suggested by Acemoglu et al. As expected, real wages were highest in the settler society of the Cape, but considering the consensus in the historiography on the lack of capital investments made by the VOC there, as well as the negative effects of the Company's mercantilist policies, it remains questionable to what extent this 'success' was the result of 'inclusive institutions'. Following Allen et al.'s analysis of real wages in the Americas,[11] it is more likely that high wages were driven by immigration from Europe. Furthermore, real wages in Java (a 'concession', or 'exploitation' colony) were surprisingly high (and rising) throughout the eighteenth century. Here, increased commercial and employment opportunities may have had positive effects for some parts of the population. It is thus not clear whether colonial institutions (mainly interfering with the labour market, the market for goods, and the capital

11 Allen et al., 'The Colonial Origins'.

market) were more inclusive, and more conducive to economic growth, in settler rather than concession colonies in this early period of colonialism.[12]

Neither Acemoglu et al., nor the picture I have just sketched, take into account variance within specific regions. For example, the interior of the Cape Colony was probably poorer than the area around Cape Town, while for Java, it may be noted that the rise of Batavia (Jayakarta) happened at the expense of Banten. The latter had been the main commercial centre in the fifteenth and sixteenth centuries, but nowadays it constitutes one of the poorer parts of Java.[13] Various social groups were also affected by colonialism in a variety of ways. No evidence on the living standards of the *Khoesan* and slaves within the Cape Colony's borders is available, but we can safely speculate that their well-being was substantially below that of the European workers. Yet, as I have already explained, the availability of slave labour in the Cape may have sustained the higher wages for European labourers. In Ceylon, the *Karāva* fishers, among other groups, could benefit from increased employment opportunities generated by the Company, while at the same time the pressure on the *Salagama* cinnamon peelers consistently intensified under Dutch rule. In Java, free coolies and *bujang* could also profit from the high demand for labour by the Company, as well as the increased agricultural productivity due to the peace after the Treaty of Giyanti (1755), which led to increases in their wages in the later eighteenth century. At the same time, those people subject to *corvée* duties probably saw their labour obligations intensify as a result of the Company's conduct (and thus as a result of globalization and colonialism). Both in settler and concession colonies, interferences in the labour market may have led to increased inequality between different social groups, as some could benefit, while others suffered. Unfortunately, gauging living standards for these separate groups was not feasible for this investigation, but perhaps it provides a fruitful area for research in the future. Although such explorations would certainly be rewarding, finding proper sources will present a formidable challenge.

Finally, colonialism, and its effects, differed not only across space, but also over time. What happened after the Company left the scene? For Bengal, it has been suggested in the traditional historiography, and in more recent econometric work, that British colonialism had further negative effects on the economy.[14] Yet, real wage evidence on the latter nineteenth and early twentieth centuries shows a slight improvement *vis-à-vis* the latter eighteenth century.[15] Both in Java

12 Interest rates in Cape Town and Batavia were on a par, as discussed in Chapter 4, Section 4.

13 De Zwart and Van Zanden, 'Labor, wages'. I thank Melissa Dell for pointing this out to me.

14 See: Roy, 'Economic History and Modern India'; Banerjee and Iyer, 'History, Institutions'.

15 Allen, 'India in the Great Divergence'.

and Ceylon, forced cultivation of cash crops started relatively late in the eighteenth century and became much more important in the nineteenth century. According to Schrikker, the colonial transition on Ceylon was marked by, among other processes, a shift from being a trading colony to an exploitation colony.[16] Future research into nineteenth-century living standards in Ceylon will have to show what happened after the British takeover. In Java, forced cultivation of cash crops was implemented in the 1830s though the infamous Cultivation System. Living standards in Java did not improve much over the nineteenth century,[17] but, in contrast to what has been suggested in the historiography on Java, there was no systematic decline in Javanese living standards, as measured by real wages, until the latter nineteenth century. Europeans in the Cape Colony saw their wages steadily increase over the eighteenth century, and, as I have shown elsewhere,[18] probably benefitted from institutional changes implemented by the British in the early nineteenth century. Over the course of the nineteenth century, further increases in 'white' European wages went at the expense of increasing inequality between the European and the 'coloured' population.[19] It may, thus, have been only in the nineteenth century that colonialism developed more in line with what has been suggested in much of the theoretical literature.

In sum, this book shows that globalization had earlier origins than often suggested and that it affected the economies involved in this global trade in various ways. Indeed, the effects of globalization in the early modern world were heterogeneous; they differed between and within continents, countries and regions. The effects were partly determined by neo-classical dynamics of supply and demand, but also by institutional variations resulting from different forms of the colonialism that accompanied early modern globalization. These colonial institutions affected – hindered – the development of labour, commodity, and capital markets. The kinds of institutions implemented depended on a more complex mix of factors than has been suggested hitherto, and the immediate effects were therefore not as straightforward as to be expected. In both settlement and concession colonies, some groups and regions could have benefitted from the VOC's presence, while other groups or regions within the same colony may have suffered. Variations in colonization were influenced by the European quest for exotic commodities. Early modern colonialism and globalization affected patterns of economic development across the globe and thus played a role in the Great Divergence.

16 Schrikker, *Dutch and British*, p. 212.

17 De Zwart and Van Zanden, 'Labor, wages'.

18 De Zwart, 'Real wages'.

19 De Zwart, 'South African'.

APPENDIX 1

Weights and Measures

A1.1 Weights and Measures

In order to create the price series, various old weights and measures had to be converted to metric equivalents, so that prices could be compared over time and space. Various sources have charted the old Dutch weights and different weights and measures used in the various Dutch East India Company's territories.[1] Data from the datasheet 'Weight vs. Volume' by Peter Lindert were used to convert litres into kilograms: 1 litre wheat, or beans, is 0.772 kilograms.[2]

A1.2 Difficulties

Due to the lack of uniformity in these measures over time and across regions, converting these weights and measures is not without problems. A *last* is equal to 3000 *pond* according to the literature and the VOC Glossary. However, a VOC note from 1764 comparing the different weights in Asia suggests that a *last* in Batavia consists of 3066 1/3 *pond*,[3] which is equal to 1515 kg. The *gantang* was 12 *pond* (in West and Middle Java, as well as Ceylon),[4] but in Batavia was 13 1/3 *pond* or 6.6 kg.[5] While only the Java price series mentioned the *koyang*, it is not clear what its weight/volume was. Talens notes that the *koyang* is equal to 3000 *pond* (like the *last*).[6] It is clear that the *koyang* could

---

1 Employed here: Bulbeck et al., *Southeast Asian*, Jacobs, *Merchant in Asia*; Nagtegaal, *Rijden*, Souza, *Survival of Empire*, J. Talens, *Feodale samenleving in koloniaal vaarwater. Staatsvorming, koloniale expansie en economische ontwikkeling in Banten, West-Java (1600–1750)* (Hilversum: Verloren. 1996); Verhoeff, *De oude Nederlandse*; VOC Glossarium; An., 'Verhandelingen der munten, maten en gewigten van Neerlandsch Indië,' *Verhandelingen van het Bataviaasch Genootschap van Kunsten en Wetenschappen* 4 (1824) pp. 281–358, and VOC 3127, ff. 1032–1058.

2 Peter Lindert, 'Weights vs volume', *Global Price and Income History Group* website and the University of California-Davis: http://gpih.ucdavis.edu/Datafilelist.htm#Asia. Last update: April 9, 2006.

3 VOC 3127 f. 1304.

4 VOC Glossary.

5 VOC Glossary.

6 Talens, *Een feodale*, p. 64.

 | DOI 10.1163/9789004299665_008

TABLE A1.1 *'Old' units of measurement and metric equivalents.*

"Old" unit of measurement	Equivalent metric value	Metric unit	Source
Aam	153.6	litre	VOC Gloss.
Bahar	215	kg	Souza/Bulbeck et al.
Bag	30.9	kg	Meilink-Roelofsz
Gantang	6.6	kg	VOC Gloss.
Halfaam	76.8	litre	VOC Gloss.
Kan	1.51	litre	VOC Gloss.
Kati Banda	2.7	kg	VOC 1071, f. 295
Kist	27.9	kg	Own estimate[7]
Koyan	1482–1667	kg	Talens/VOC 3127
Last	1482–1515	kg	VOC Gloss./VOC 3127
Legger	921.6	litre	Verhoeff
Maat	37	kg	VOC 3127
Mengel	1.2	litre	Verhoeff
Mudde	111.5	litre	Verhoeff
Parra	19.8	kg	VOC Gloss.
Pikol	60	kg	VOC Gloss.
Pond	0.49409	kg	Verhoeff
Quintal	59	kg	Souza 1986
Schepel	27.9	litre	Verhoeff
Vadem	2.9–8.5	m^3	Verhoeff/BG 1824
Vracht	1.58	m^3	Own estimate
Vat	155	litre	Verhoeff

Sources: see Column 4.

differ per time, place and product.[8] Focussing on rice alone (as its prices are the only ones that were reported in *koyang*), we find that c. 1750 the *koyang* was around 3000 *pond*, but in the second half of the eighteenth century a weight of 3400 pond was generally assigned to the *koyang*. In the VOC Glossary different weights are also given for

7 Based on observations in the Cape Colony on prices for soap per *pond* and per *kist*; I have assumed that the *kist* was similar to the *schepel*.

8 Alberto Feenstra, 'Kisten met Koper. De opmarks van de Nederlandse duit in het Javaanse geldverkeer 1720–1850' (unpublished MA thesis: Free University Amsterdam, 2012); Jacobs, *Merchant in Asia*.

the *koyang*; ranging from 23 *pikol* in the seventeenth century to 30 or 32 *pikol* in later periods. Nagtegaal mentions *koyangs* of both 3000 and 3500 *ponden*.[9] The VOC note from 1764 suggests that the *koyang* is 3375 *pond* (1667 kg), which has been adopted in this study as all observations of the *koyang* are from around that date.[10]

It is thus clear that the exact volume or weight of a measure might have differed over time and place. Considering the lack of information on the exact date of changes in weights and measures per region, Table A1.1 above, as well as the conversions used to create the price series, might not be always equally accurate. However, only in the case of the *koyang was* the range of weights relatively large. In general, the problem does not seem to affect overall conclusions, although it is important to keep these limitations in mind.

---

9 Nagtegaal, *Rijden*, pp. 176–177.

10 VOC 3127, f. 1034.

APPENDIX 2

Coins and Silver Values

A2.1 Coins

There were several coins with different guilder values circulating in the Dutch East India Company areas in southern Africa and Asia. Following W. G. Wolters, who made a more extensive study of VOC coins, I have assumed for the entire period the following guilder value per coin: *rial* = 3; *rix-dollar* = 2.4; *dubbeltje* = 0.10, *stuiver* = 0.05; and *duit* = 0.0125.[1] In addition, especially in the Cape Colony, the *schelling* was also circulating. I follow Van Duin and Ross, who suggest that these were valued at 6 *stuivers*, or 0.30 guilders.[2]

There is some confusion regarding the value of the rix-dollar in Asia. Some suggest it should be valued at 3 guilders in Asia, while others suggest 2.4/2.5 guilders. In fact, these values could differ according to time and place, depending on whether it concerns 'light' or 'heavy' money. When not specifically mentioned otherwise, I assume 2.4 guilders,[3] which implies the assumption that both guilder and rix-dollar were noted down in 'light' or 'heavy' money at the same time. It seems that rix-dollars are only valued at 3 guilders when it concerns heavy rix-dollars and light guilders. While there is evidence that this is sometimes the case, unless otherwise stated in the sources I follow the periods shown in Table A2.1.

For the data on Bengal, wages were often reported in rupees, *anas* and *ponies*. While the *ana* is always 1/16 of a rupee, the value of the *pony* could fluctuate. While I could not find any other reference to the *pony* in the literature, the sources fortunately always stated how many *ponies* were in a rupee, which was most often 60, but this could fluctuate between 56 and 64 *ponies*. A few of wage observations in the sources on Ceylon (and southern India) were noted in *pagodas*: 1 *pagoda* = 3.2 rupees, except for the period 1678–1705, when it was four rupees equalled 1 *pagoda*.[4] In order to combine the wages for Bengal that were reported in guilders with those reported in rupees and *ponies*, it was assumed that rupees consistently constitute 31.5 *stuivers*, and a guilder 20 *stuivers*.[5]

1 Wolters, 'Heavy and light'.
2 Van Duin and Ross, 'The economy', p. viii.
3 Yong, *The Dutch*; Boomgaard, 'Buitenzorg in 1805', Van Duin and Ross, 'The economy', also suggest a rix-dollar of fl. 2.40.
4 Broadberry and Gupta, 'The early modern', p. 14.
5 VOC 3127 f. 1043.

 | DOI 10.1163/9789004299665_009

TABLE A2.1 *Value of one Asian guilder.*

Period	Equivalent in Dutch Guilders	Equivalent in Grams of Silver
1652–1680	0.80	7.84
1681–1742	0.80	7.69
1743–1768	0.84	8.04
1769–1795	1	9.61

Sources: Van Zanden, 'Prices and wages'; Jacobs, *Koopman in Azië*, pp. 225–228.

A few notations from the literature on Bengal note wages in *dam* or *pice* (or *paisa*).[6] There are some issues regarding the changing value of these copper coins against the rupee (silver). According to Moreland 1 *dam* equals 2 *pice*, at least in Akbar's time,[7] although Najaf Haider suggests that this is a misreading on Moreland's behalf and suggests that 1 *dam* is equal to 1 *pice*.[8] He suggests that in Surat around the middle of the seventeenth century, the value of the *dam* vis-à-vis the rupee fluctuated between 47 and 32 *dam* per rupee.[9] Mukerjee also notes 18th century exchange rates. He finds that in the late 18th century there were 40 *dams* per rupee, but suggests a significant difference between the *dam* and the *pice*: 1 *pice* = 25 *dams*. Mukerjee reports wages in 1729 in *pice*, but converted them to rupees (assuming 1 *pice* = 1 *dam* and 40 *dam* = 1 rupee). However, as these wages are more than six times lower than wages in rupees observed in 1723, and four times lower than wages in rupees observed in 1739, they are considered to be unreliable. For wage data of non-VOC Bengal, see Allen and Studer, 'Prices and Wages'.

A2.2 Silver Values

Silver values per guilder were: 9.8 grams of silver up to 1680; and 9.61 grams of silver from 1681 onwards.[10] The value of the guilder used by the VOC in Asia was lower than

6 Mukerjee, *Economic History*, p. 49; Najaf Haider, 'Structure and Movement of Wages in the Mughal Empire, 1500–1700', J. Lucassen (ed.), *Wages and Currency. Global Comparisons from Antiquity to the Twentieth Century* (Bern: Peter Lang, 2007) p. 318.

7 Moreland, *From Akbar*, pp. 194–5.

8 Haider, 'Structure and Movement', pp. 306–307; Najaf Haider, 'The Quantity Theory and Mughal Monetary History', *Medieval History Journal* 2 (1999) pp. 309–348.

9 Haider, 'Quantity theory', p. 343.

10 Jan Luiten van Zanden, 'Prices and wages and the cost of living in the western part of the Netherlands, 1450–1800', website *Historical Prices and Wages* of the *International*

the guilder in the Dutch Republic and its Asian currency was therefore referred to as 'light money'. The value of the Asian relative to the Dutch guilder fluctuated throughout the seventeenth and eighteenth centuries. According to Els Jacobs one Asian guilder was worth 20 percent less than the Dutch guilder prior to 1743; 16.35 percent less between 1743 and 1768; while after 1768 value differences disappeared (see Table A2.1).

Silvers value per rupee were: 10.78 grams of silver for the entire period under discussion, according to Allen[11] and also Broadberry and Gupta;[12] but 11.54 grams of silver according to Haider.[13] Since I have not found any other evidence of the rupee being worth 11.54, I will use the former equivalent.

Institute of Social History: http://www.iisg.nl/hpw/brenv.xls. Last update: December 11, 2009.

11 Allen, 'India in the Great Divergence', p. 14.

12 Broadberry and Gupta, 'The early modern', p. 14.

13 Haider, 'Structure and Movement', p. 293.

APPENDIX 3

Kcal and Protein

Since the consumption baskets are based on kcal and protein intake, it is important to have information on the caloric and protein values of the foodstuffs included in the various baskets discussed in Section 4 of Chapter 3. The values shown in Table A3.1 have been derived from Allen et al.,[1] as well as the United States Department of Agriculture's (USDA) National Nutrient Database.[2]

TABLE A3.1 *Caloric and protein contents.*

	Metric unit	Kcal per unit	Protein per unit (g)	Source
Rice	kg	3620	75	Allen et al.
Wheat	kg	3420	113	USDA NND
Oats	kg	3890	169	USDA NND
Rye	kg	3380	103	USDA NND
Barley	kg	3450	105	Allen et al.
Millet	kg	3780	110	Allen et al.
Sorghum	kg	3390	113	USDA NND
Beans/peas[3]	litre	3383	213	Allen et al.
Meat	kg	2500	200	Allen et al.
Fish	kg	1301	192	Allen et al.
Butter	kg	7268	7	Allen et al.
Oil	litre	8840	1	Allen et al.
Sugar	kg	3890	0	USDA NND

Sources: see Column 5.

1 Allen et al., 'Wages, prices'.

2 Their search engine can be found at http://ndb.nal.usda.gov/ndb/search/list [Last accessed March 3, 2014].

3 Allen et al., 'Wages, prices' distinguish between European and Asian beans. The Asian beans have been used here, otherwise the figures in the basket would not fit.

 | DOI 10.1163/9789004299665_010

APPENDIX 4

Creating the Price Series

By employing the information found in Appendices 1–3 it is possible to compute time series of prices from the sources introduced in the text. As several ships departed for the Republic every year, and for every ship the value and quantity of products was recorded, there were often several observations of prices for the same good in the same year. In such cases I took the arithmetic mean of several price observations. These prices were not weighted with the amount of goods transported, as this would entail a lot of extra work without leading to any substantial differences in the prices (as these were generally the same throughout the year). Only in the case of data for the *rendementen* (for Ceylon) were the price observations weighted for the total volume sold, as some of the sales concerned very limited amounts of a certain product, which would influence the results too much.

In addition, both the data from the Bookkeeper-General, and those from the *rendementen* were ordered per accounting year: between 1677 and 1694 this period started on March 1st and ended with the last day of February;[1] while in the eighteenth century the accounting year ran from September 1 to August 31. In his database on prices in Ceylon, Van Bochove assigned observations to the initial year of the accounting year: for example, if the accounting year was 1701/1702, the data were entered in year 1701. While the Bookkeeper-General database does contain information on the exact dates of departure or arrival, these cannot be extracted from the database using the standard Excel output offered, and would thus have to be linked manually to the data. Considering the thousands of observations involved, this would be a daunting task, and one that would not lead to any significant changes in the results. For these reasons I have also assigned the prices to the first year, as done by Van Bochove.

I will now give more information regarding the creation of time series of prices of the various commodities used in the chapter on globalization, as well as for the creation of the consumer price indices for the various regions.

A4.1 Globalization

For each product, two price series were computed: one reflecting sales prices in Amsterdam, and one reflecting purchasing prices in Asia. As the VOC always noted down the purchasing price from where it acquired a product, purchasing prices in

1 Van Bochove, 'Prices in Sri-Lanka'.

 | DOI 10.1163/9789004299665_011

Batavia actually reflect prices for different parts of Asia; for example in the case of cloves, it reflects the purchasing price on Ambon.

1 Cinnamon

Asia: Barbosa notes that cinnamon cost 10 *cruzados* per *quintal*.[2] Following George Souza: 1 *quintal* = 119.3 *pond* and 1 guilder = 0.32 *cruzados*.[3] 1 guilder = 16.32 grams of silver in 1563.[4] For 1608: In VOC 603 it is noted that the VOC purchases 1 *picol* (125 *pond*) cinnamon for 4 real (2.5 *guilders*). In 1631 15.3 guilder was paid for a *picol*.[5] All other observations are noted in guilders per *pond*. Considering the stability of the prices, the years 1664–5, 1667–8, 1670–4, 1676–88, 1690–9, 1709, 1727, 1729–30, 1741–51, and 1790–99 were linearly interpolated.

To compare this price with a European price, I took the Antwerp price for 1563 of 333 Brabant *groats*.[6] 1 Brabant *groat* = 0.27 grams of silver.[7] For the period 1609–1800 prices from the VOC auctions were interpolated according to Posthumus:[8]

$$P_{VOC} = 0.8374\, P_{Posthumus} + 0.1854 \qquad R^2 = 0.95$$
$$N = 88$$

2 Cloves

Asia: Bulbeck et al. provide some data for the sixteenth century,[9] namely in *reals* per tonne. On page 32 they suggest 1 Spanish Dollar = 1 real. On page 174 they suggest 1 Spanish Dollar = 2.65 guilders. I have also used these equivalents for my conversions. Additional data were found in reals/*cruzados* per *bahar*.[10] These were converted on the basis on a *bahar* = 436 *pond*, a real = 2.5 guilders and 1 *cruzado* = 1.25 *reals*, which leads to similar prices as Bulbeck et al. For the remainder of the period, all prices from the VOC accounts were noted in guilders per *pond*. These were combined with the prices taken from Bulbeck et al. to fill some gaps. These price series are largely similar, although whereas Bulbeck et al. find prices increased after the 1770s, the VOC data

2 Barbosa, *The Book*, pt. 2, p. 112.
3 Souza, *Survival of empire*, pp. xv–xvii.
4 Van Zanden, 'Prices and the cost'.
5 VOC 1099.
6 Van der Wee, *The growth* I, pp. 314–317.
7 Ibid., pp. 125–129.
8 Posthumus, *Nederlandsche Prijsgeschiedenis*.
9 Bulbeck et al., *Southeast Asian*.
10 Pires, *Suma Oriental*; Barbosa, *The Book*, Meilink-Roelofsz, *Asian Trade*; Souza, *Survival of Empire*; Om Prakash, 'Restrictive trading regimes: VOC and the Asian spice trade in the seventeenth century', in: R. Ptak and D. Rothermund (eds.), *Emporia, commodities and entrepreneurs in Asian maritime trade, c. 1400–1750* (Stuttgart: Franz Steiner Verlag, 1991).

suggest, on the other hand, that prices declined from fl. 0.40 per *pond* to fl. 0.30–33 in the period 1770–1800. No interpolation was needed here.

For European prices in the sixteenth century I used those of Herman van der Wee.[11] For the seventeenth and eighteenth centuries, I averaged prices taken from VOC sales accounts by Glamann and Posthumus.[12] These series were very similar to each other, but all showed some gaps which could thus be filled.

3 Coffee

Asia: All prices were given in guilders or *rijksdaalders* (2.4 *rijksdaalders* per guilder) per *picol* or per *pond*. Prices for coffee were also available from Mason Hoadley, but these diverged from those found in the VOC accounts (they were very similar before 1750, but were much higher thereafter).[13] I have used only the VOC figures. Considering the stability in price (which was fixed by the VOC) the following years were linearly interpolated: 1713, 1715-8, 1719–20, 1729, 1732–3, 1743–5, 1757, 1764, 1769–70, 1785, 1787–8, 1790, and 1793–99.

Amsterdam: the prices paid at VOC auctions were interpolated with data from Posthumus:

$$P_{VOC} = 0.9491\, P_{Posthumus} + 0.0051 \qquad R^2 = 0.68$$
$$N = 55$$

4 Copper

Asia: copper prices were noted in guilders per *picol*, *pond* or *kati*. 1 *kati* = 1/100 picol = 1.25 *pond*.[14] One outlier (1747) from the *rendementen* was discarded as the price was (supposedly) given in *rix-dollars*, but it was more than twice as expensive as the surrounding observations. The series was supplemented by data from the *rendementen* from Surat, as assembled by Nadri.[15] No interpolation was needed.

Amsterdam: copper prices were taken only from the VOC auctions as Posthumus does not offer a price series for Japanese copper. Probably as a result of the small markups, Japanese copper was sold in Amsterdam only for a short period.

---

11 Van der Wee, *The growth*.

12 Glamann, *Dutch-Asiatic*; and Posthumus, *Nederlandsche Prijsgeschiedenis*.

13 Mason C. Hoadley, *Towards a feudal mode of production: west Java, 1680–1800* (Singapore: Institute of Southeast Asian Studies, 1994) pp. 220–1. In his review of this book, Peter Boomgaard is highly critical and laments the lack of accuracy and Hoadley's general carelessness with the sources, therefore it seems justified to trust the primary materials more than the series of Hoadley (review in: *Copgenhagen Journal of Asian Studies* 9 (1994) pp. 109–111.

14 VOC Glossarium

15 Nadri, *Eighteenth-century Gujarat*.

5 Cotton yarn

Asia: all prices were in guilders per *pond*. There were a number of different varieties of raw cotton: that from Bengal, Broach/Cambay/Surat, Coromandel, and Java; some other observations only stated that it concerned white cotton or a variety of cotton. There is not enough data to say anything about price differentials between these varieties, but they seem to be in a similar price range. In fact, the Amsterdam sales only noted down 'cotton yarn', with no specifications regarding the variety, which suggests that, as with pepper, they threw the different varieties together. Therefore, I built just one series of average prices. Purchasing prices from the *rendementen* later in the eighteenth century were consistently below those from the Bookkeeper-General in Batavia (BGB). These observations were dropped from the analysis. Doing so does not affect the conclusions, while including them would only strengthen the observation that there was no price convergence (lowering prices in Java would lead to an increased price gap). As with coffee, Hoadley offers a diverging price series for cotton that I have not included in my calculations. No interpolations were needed.

Amsterdam: the series from the VOC auctions and that of Posthumus could differ somewhat. I have used only the prices from the VOC auctions. However, in order to fill a significant gap (1761–1770) in them, Java cotton prices from Posthumus were interpolated via the equation:

$$P_{VOC} = 0.2666\, P_{Posthumus} + 0.8123 \qquad R^2 = 0.44$$
$$N = 46$$

6 Indigo

Asia: All prices for indigo were stated in guilders per *pond*. As is the case with cotton, there were different varieties and the average price was used. Hoadley again offers a competing price series that has not been used. The outlier of 1761 is based on 13 observations (reflecting a total of 124,884 *pond* of indigo shipped to the Republic) and is therefore assumed to be genuine.

Amsterdam: the VOC series were extrapolated according to Posthumus:

$$P_{VOC} = 0.7395\, P_{Posthumus} + 0.1296 \qquad R^2 = 0.48$$
$$N = 51$$

7 Mace

Asia: Some early price evidence was available in reals per *bahar*.[16] For some of the seventeenth century observations from the VOC accounts, prices could be noted as

16 1515: Pires, *Suma Oriental*; 1599: Keuning, *De Tweede Schipvaart*, p. 204; 1603: De Jonge and Deventer, *De Opkomst*, vol.3, p. 157; 1608: VOC 652; 1603–1615: Meilink-Roelofsz, *Asian Trade*, pp. 275–276, p. 401 note 74.

including or excluding expenses for 'sockels', i.e. the baskets in which the mace was transported. The difference in price was negligible (0.003 guilder per *pond*). Prices for mace could also be noted per *kati Banda*, which was equal to 5.5 *pond*.

Amsterdam: The VOC auctions were interpolated using the Posthumus series:

$$P_{VOC} = 0.855\, P_{Posthumus} + 0.7027 \qquad R^2 = 0.96 \qquad N = 87$$

8 Nutmeg

Asia: early observations were given in reals per *bahar*.[17] Conversion was based on 2.5 guilders per real and 436 *pond* per *bahar*. The remaining observations were in guilders per *pond*. Prices could be the same for years on end, which allowed interpolation.

Amsterdam: see mace. Interpolation was done employing the Posthumus data:

$$P_{VOC} = 0.9715\, P_{Posthumus} + 0.023 \qquad R^2 = 0.97 \qquad N = 108$$

9 Pepper

Asia: 1 real = 0.4 guilders. Unless stated otherwise, according to Bulbeck et al. 1 *bahar* of pepper = 180 kg = 364 *pond*.[18] A *quintal* = 1/4 *bahar* = 91 *pond*. I created a time series using all observations for pepper from different locations (Palembang, Banten, Priaman, Banjarmasin, etc.) and varieties (but excluding white pepper and long pepper – for which there are separate data in the Amsterdam sales). In order to get the average price each year, the data (2618 observations) were regressed on year dummies.

Amsterdam: gaps in the VOC price series were interpolated using the Posthumus data:

$$P_{VOC} = 0.934\, P_{Posthumus} + 0.0166 \qquad R^2 = 0.84 \qquad N = 88$$

10 Saltpetre

Asia: all prices were stated in guilders per *pond*. Prices for the 17th century could be given for a few variants: refined, unrefined, Bengal or Agra. Refined saltpetre from Bengal was the dominant variant and it can be assumed that if no further specification was given, it concerned refined Bengal saltpetre. For the few years when prices were completely stable, gaps were linearly interpolated (1685-6, 1688, 1691-4, 1696-9, 1707 and 1713-7).

---

17 1515: Pires (1515); 1596–7: Rouffaer and IJzerman, *De Eerste Schipvaart*; 1599: Keuning, *De Tweede Schipvaart*, p. 204; 1612: Meilink-Roelofsz, *Asian Trade*.

18 Bulbeckt et al., *Southeast Asian*, p. 182.

Amsterdam: gaps in the VOC price series were extrapolated according to Posthumus (excluding the outlier of 1745):

$$P_{VOC} = 0.7577\ P_{Posthumus} + 0.0049 \quad R^2 = 0.78$$
$$N = 67$$

11 Silk

Asia: prices were noted in guilders or reals (fl. 0.4) per *pond* or *kati* (1.25 *pond*). There were three different varieties of silk: Persian, Bengal and Chinese. There were so few observations for Persian silk that the mark-up ratio could be only be calculated for one year, so this was omitted from the analysis. No interpolation were necessary.

Amsterdam: we have prices for the same three varieties of silk from the VOC auctions and Posthumus. In the earliest auctions, however, there is a price series for silks that have no further specification. These prices were used to extrapolate the Bengal silk series:

$$P_{Silk\ Bengal} = 0.9024\ P_{Silk} + 0.8633 \quad R^2 = 0.91$$
$$N = 17$$

The VOC Chinese silk series were extrapolated with the Posthumus data:

$$P_{VOC} = 0.6608\ P_{Posthumus} + 2.4509 \quad R^2 = 0.81$$
$$N = 49$$

Data from both series were used to generate an average series for silk comprising as many observations as possible.

12 Sugar, Candy

Asia: all prices given were in guilders per *pond.* Hoadley also gave sugar prices, but these were not used because they were slightly higher at the end of the eighteenth century and including them would, therefore, only strengthen the picture of price convergence.

Amsterdam: price series for sugar are available from the VOC sales and Posthumus. Only Posthumus noted that these concerned *kandijsuiker* or candy sugar. Considering the fact that the prices at VOC auctions were much lower than his prices, it can be assumed these applied to *poedersuiker* (icing sugar or castor sugar). For this reason I have interpolated Posthumus' series with the *kandijsuiker* series (rather than the other way around):

$$P_{Posthumus} = 2.5744\ P_{VOC} + 0.0213 \quad R^2 = 0.60$$
$$N = 69$$

13 Sugar, Castor (not included separately in the analysis, similar trends as Sugar, Candy).

Asia: *poedersuiker* all prices given were in guilders per *pond*. For the seventeenth century, different specifications could be given, such as 'white', 'diverse', 'from Japara' or 'from Batavia'. Price differentials were negligible and due to limited observations I have used them all to create a single price series (taking the arithmetic average in case of multiple observations in one year). To fill gaps in the eighteenth century, the series from the Bookkeeper-General were extrapolated with Nadri's data on Surat:[19]

$$P_{VOC} = 0.7742\, P_{Nadri} + 0.0178 \qquad R^2 = 0.65 \quad N = 46$$

Amsterdam: see Sugar, Candy. The VOC series are now interpolated employing the Posthumus series.

$$P_{VOC} = 0.2324\, P_{Posthumus} + 0.1022 \qquad R^2 = 0.60 \quad N = 69$$

14 Tea

Asia : all prices were noted in guilders per *pond*. There were several types of tea: *bohea*, *bing*, and white. Some early observations were only refer to tea as 'Chinese'. Since all teas were Chinese and the price differences in the VOC data between them were not very big, I averaged the prices of the different varieties (in cases of multiple observations). The price series were merged with data from Souza,[20] which also seems to include different varieties, as well as the average price taken from the data on *bohea* tea by Yong.[21] No interpolations were necessary.

Amsterdam: I combined Posthumus' series and that of the VOC auctions. In cases where prices from both series were available in one year, I used the arithmetic average. The correlation was weak, but the differentials small (average CV = 0.25).

15 Textiles

Asia: the VOC traded in a variety of textiles: *baftas*, *guinea cloth*, and *salempuris* of different colours, sizes and qualities. I took average prices of the guinea cloth (average quality, bleached) from the Coromandel Coast as found in the *rendementen*, invoices and BGB. Qualities and specific sizes could differ per batch, but this is not specified in the sources. These series are therefore tentative.

19 Nadri, *Eighteenth-century Gujarat.*
20 Souza, *Survival of Empire*, p. 144.
21 Yon, *The Dutch*, pp. 212–222.

Amsterdam: in the VOC auctions 'because of lack of acquaintance with a number of textiles' the VOC accountants put the information for textiles in the 'undeterminable category' of *catoene lijwaten* (see Glamann).[22] I have linked this to the price level of guinea cloth from Glamann using the equation (thus increasing the prices, no influence on trends):

$$P_{\text{Guinea}} = 0.3057\, P_{\text{Catoene lijwaten}} + 4.886 \qquad R^2 = 0.27,\; N = 43$$

These figures are clearly not ideal, yet, considering the importance of textiles in the Euro-Asian trade I believe it is still worthwhile to give some estimates of general trends: it seems quite certain that over the period 1650–1800 prices for textiles in Amsterdam fluctuated around the same level, while in India prices increased (see also the article by Bishnupriya Gupta).[23] According to Hossain, sales prices in London were stable or declined in the latter eighteenth century.[24]

16 Tin

Asia: All prices were stated in guilders per *pond*. There were observations for three types of tin, Bancas, Malaysian, or Siamese tin. Price differentials were generally small or non-existent, and since for Europe it was not defined which of these varieties was sold, it is assumed that, as in the case of pepper and cotton yarn, these varieties were mixed. These series were therefore combined; in cases of multiple observations in a single year, the arithmetic mean price was used. Note: there was only one observation for a purchasing price for tin in 1746 from a *rendement* for China.[25] As it is an outlier, this data point is of questionable reliability and representativeness and I have therefore omitted it from the analysis. This has no effects on the observed trends or conclusions based on these series.

Amsterdam: the VOC auction prices were extrapolated according to Posthumus:

$$P_{\text{VOC}} = 0.8164\, P_{\text{Posthumus}} + 0.0207 \qquad R^2 = 0.82,\; N = 38$$

17 Porcelain

Margins from Jörg.[26] No interpolation was necessary.

---

22 Glamann, *Dutch-Asiatic Trade*, p. 143.

23 Gupta, 'Competition and control'.

24 Hossain, *Company weavers*, p. 68.

25 VOC 2710, ff. 1208–1263.

26 Jörg, *Porcelain*, pp. 221–223.

A4.2 Bengal

The Bengal price series were taken from Allen and Studer, 'Prices and Wages'.

A4.3 The Cape Colony

1 Wheat

For the Dutch period, prices of wheat were found in several sources, in addition to those in the VOC archives (expense bills and *Scheepssoldijboeken*): i.e. the Cape Archives and the MOOC inventories. The works of A. J. Du Plessis, Van Duin and Ross and Du Plessis and Du Plessis also contain wheat prices.[27] In the event that multiple prices were found in one year, an arithmetic mean of these prices was calculated and used.

2 Beans and peas

Prices were all noted in guilders or rix-dollars per *mudde*. In the years 1784–1786, several sources listed prices, so the arithmetic mean price was used.[28]

3 Meat

Prices were given in guilders or rix-dollars per *pond* or *vat*. It is assumed that a *vat* consisted of 400 *pond*, which would fit with purchasing prices per *pond*. Both prices for just 'meat', as well those explicitly stating it concerned 'fresh meat', were included in the price series. For the latter eighteenth century, observations came from the Cape Archives,[29] as well as from publications by George Theal and S.D. Neumark.[30] The arithmetic mean was taken in cases of several observations in one year.

4 Butter

Butter prices were stated in guilders or rix-dollars per *pond* or *ton*. Since it was unclear how much a *ton* of butter was, these prices were not used in the series. Prices from the VOC and the Cape archives were combined with some observations from the MOOC inventories and Neumark.[31]

---

27 Du Plessis, *Die Geskiedenis*, Van Duin and Ross, 'The Economy', Du Plessis and Du Plessis, 'Happy in the service.'

28 CP 2739; CP 2734

29 CP 2739; CP 2734; BRD 40.

30 Theal, *Records*, vol. 1, p. 216; vol. 3, pp. 195 and 397; S.D. Neumark, *The South African Frontier. Economic influences, 1652–1836* (Stanford, 1956), pp. 110 and 189.

31 Neumark, *South African*, p. 110; CP 2739; MOOC 8/3.9, MOOC 8/3.10.

5 Soap

Prices were recorded in guilders and rix-dollars per *pond* or *kist* (crate). It was assumed that a *kist* was 27.9 kg (similar to the *schepel*). Next to the various VOC sources, prices were found in MOOC inventories and Neumark. For the period 1747–1775, sales prices were taken from the *rendementen*. In cases of multiple observations in one year, the arithmetic mean of prices was used.

6 Cotton

A number of different types of cotton cloths were found in the sources for the Dutch period, such as *salempoeris*, *baftas*, and *ginghams*. For the Cape, most prices were for *baftas*, and because the *bafta* was one of the cheaper varieties, these prices were used to create price series for cotton. A *bafta* had a length of 19 *gaz* and a width of 1 *gaz* and 9 *tussus*; one *gaz* was 67.31 cm and a *tussus* 2.8 cm.[32] Thus, a *bafta* was 12.78 meter in length and 0.93 meter in breadth. The price per m² cotton could thus be calculated:

$$P_{\text{Cotton (m}^2\text{)}} = P_{\text{Bafta}}/(12.78 \times 0.93)$$

Prices, noted in guilders and rix-dollars, from the VOC, MOOC, and the Cape Archives were combined in the series.

7 Candles

Prices were noted for 'wax', 'wax candles' or 'candles' per *pond* or *picol*. There seemed to be no structural difference in prices between these different notations and therefore all were combined to create the price series.

8 Lamp oil

Prices for *klappus* oil, lamp oil, and traan, taken from the VOC and Cape Archives,[33] were combined to create the price series. Prices were given per *aam*, *halfaam*, *mengel* and *kan*. Some gaps were imputed using the prices for candles:

$$P_{\text{Lamp oil}} = 0.0884\,P_{\text{Candle}} - 0.1258 \quad R^2 = 0.16$$
$$N = 52$$

9 Fuel

Firewood prices were written down in guilders per *vadem* or per *vracht*. A *vadem* is 2.9 m³ and from the price differences between the *vadem* and the *vracht* in 1671–1672

32 Hariharan, *Cotton* textiles, pp. 270, 306.

33 From the Cape Archives only two observations for 1784 and 1785: CP 2739.

and 1676–1677, I calculate that a *vracht* of firewood is 1.58 m^3.[34] For the baskets, the price per MBtu was needed. The amount of MBtu's delivered per m^3 of firewood depends on the type of wood. For the Cape Colony, White Oak was used,[35] which delivers 25.7 MBtu per cord.[36] One cord is 128 cubic feet, and 1 cubic foot is 0.028 m^3:[37] this converts to 3.62 m^3 per cord, delivering 25.7 MBtu = 3.62/25.7 = 0.14 m^3 per MBtu. Thus, the price per MBtu was calculated as:

$$P_{MBtu} = (P_{\textit{vracht}\ \text{Firewood}}/1.58) \times 0.14$$

Larger gaps in the price series for firewood were imputed using the prices for lamp oil:

$$P_{\textit{vracht}\ \text{Firewood}} = 0.2083 + 2.62\,P_{\text{Lamp Oil}} \qquad R^2 = 0.7533 \qquad N = 11$$

10 Further gaps

All further gaps were filled by linear interpolation.

A4.4 Ceylon

1 Rice

Rice prices were generally reported per *parra* or per *pond*. In order to impute gaps in the sales price series, I used prices for several towns other than Colombo (see Figure 3.5), as well as the purchasing prices from the following equations:

$$P_{\text{Colombo}} = 0.4767\,P_{\text{Jaffna}} + 0.7467 \quad R^2 = 0.53\ (N = 19)$$
$$P_{\text{Colombo}} = 0.6182\,P_{\text{Kalpitya}} + 0.6958 \quad R^2 = 0.25\ (N = 44)$$
$$P_{\text{Sales}} = 0.4907\,P_{\text{Purchasing}} + 1.0221 \quad R^2 = 0.16\ (N = 30)$$
$$P_{\text{Colombo}} = 0.3886\,P_{\text{Galle}} + 1.0187 \quad R^2 = 0.15\ (N = 49)$$

2 Beans and peas

Prices of both beans and peas were found, expressed per Dutch *pond*, equal to 0.494 kg, or per *parra*, equal to 40 Dutch *ponden*. There were, however, big gaps in the price

34 Please note that this *vadem* is different from the one in Batavia.

35 A.J. Böeseken, *Nederlandsche Commissarissen aan de Kaap, 1657–1700* (The Hague, 1938) p. 31.

36 Information from website: http://mb-soft"m/juca/print/firewood.html. Last visited 11 July 2011.

37 Information from website: http://www.asknumbers.com/CubicFeetToCubicMeter.aspx. Last visited 11 July 2011.

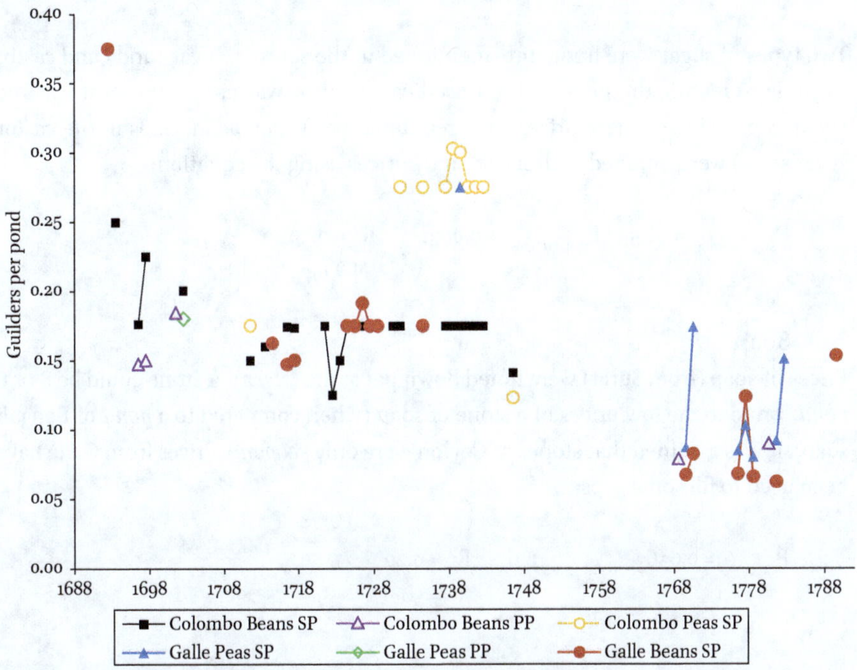

FIGURE A4.1 *Sales and purchasing prices of beans in Colombo and Galle, 1688–1788.*
Sources: Van Bochove, 'Prices'; VOC archives (see text)

series of beans and peas and no correlations could be discovered. However, prices from the various sources and from Colombo and Galle did not differ greatly (see Figure A4.1), therefore I have taken the average of all these price series. In addition, there were a few prices available for *cadjang* in Galle, which was the general word for legumes (VOC Glossary). These prices were significantly lower (one-tenth) and since it is more likely that the local population consumed these, rather than the extremely expensive beans, the beans prices series were corrected for this (divided by 10). Do note that this is an important adjustment to the price index, biasing it downwards (and real wages upwards, against my conclusions).

3 Butter

Prices for various types of butter (Bengal, Cape, and Mannar) could be found in the sources. The butter from Mannar, located in Ceylon, was the cheapest and therefore preferred in the price series. Gaps in the Mannar butter series were filled with prices of Bengali butter via the equation:

$$P_{\text{Butter (Mannar)}} = -0.2186\, P_{\text{Butter (Bengal)}} + 0.337 \qquad R^2 = 0.51$$
$$N = 17$$

4 Sugar

Two types of sugar were frequently mentioned in the sources: sugar candy and castor sugar. For creating the price series, I used castor sugar was used because it was the cheaper of the two. These prices were registered per Dutch *pond*. Gaps in the castor sugar series were imputed with sugar candy prices using the equation:

$$P_{\text{Sugar (Castor)}} = 0.2592\, P_{\text{Sugar (Candy)}} + 0.0831 \qquad R^2 = 0.23,\; N = 64$$

5 Soap

Prices of soap (from Surat) were noted down per stone (*steen*). A stone could be 8 or 6 *pond*;[38] due to the low prices of a stone of soap (when compared to a *pond* of Bengali soap), it was assumed that stones in Ceylon were only six *pond*. Prices from Galle have been used to fill some gaps:

$$P_{\text{Colombo}} = 0.6563\, P_{\text{Galle}} + 0.1126 \qquad R^2 = 0.20,\; N = 30$$

6 Salt

Prices for salt were given per *parra*. Prices from Galle were used to impute a few gaps:

$$P_{\text{Colombo}} = 0.8637\, P_{\text{Galle}} + 0.0741 \qquad R^2 = 0.81,\; N = 59$$

7 Cotton

As in the case of the Cape Colony, a number of different types of cotton cloths were found in the sources, e.g. *salempoeris*, *baftas*, and *ginghams*. Yet Van Bochove focussed his data collection on the *ginghams*,[39] and I therefore used these to create price series for cotton. A *gingham* had a length of 17 gaz and 18 tussus, and a width of 22 tussus; one gaz was 67.31 cm and a tussus 2.805 cm.[40] Thus, a *gingham* was 12.1329 m in length and 0.6171 m in width. The price of cotton per m^2 could thus be calculated:

$$P_{\text{Cotton }(m^2)} = P_{\text{Gingham}}/(12.13 * 0.62)$$

Prices for two types of *ginghams* were found: the normal quality *gingham* and the fine *gingham*. The normal quality *gingham*, which was the cheaper of the two, was used to

38 Van Bochove, 'Prices in Sri Lanka', p. 6.

39 Van Bochove, 'Prices in Sri Lanka', p. 5.

40 Hariharan, *Cotton textiles*, p. 302.

create the time series. Nevertheless, the fine gingham, for which more prices were available, was useful for imputing the normal quality gingham series, using the following equation:

$$P_{Gingham\ (Normal)} = 0.2342\ P_{Gingham\ (Fine)} + 3.7685 \quad R^2 = 0.15, \ N = 35$$

In addition, prices for *gingham* in Galle were used to impute the Colombo prices series:

The fine *gingham*: $P_{Colombo} = 0.8186\ P_{Galle} + 2.0549 \quad R^2 = 0.79, \ N = 37$

The normal quality *gingham*: $P_{Colombo} = 0.8021\ P_{Galle} + 1.0902 \quad R^2 = 0.59, \ N = 23$

8 Lamp oil

Prices of lamp oil were recorded per *kan*. Because the sources stated that *klappus* oil served for illumination at night, prices of both types of oil were compiled together in one price series for lamp oil. In addition, coconut oil prices from Galle were exploited to impute gaps in the series and extrapolate the series back into the seventeenth century:

$$P_{Colombo} = 0.4547\ P_{Galle} + 0.1326 \quad R^2 = 0.33, \ N = 20$$

There was insufficient overlap to estimate the relationship between purchasing and sales prices of lamp oil, or the difference between *klappus* and lamp oil. However prices were generally of the same order of magnitude (see Figure A4.2), and therefore I have simply used all three series to compute an annual series (taking the arithmetic mean in cases of multiple observations in a single year).

9 Candles

All prices for candles and wax were given per Dutch *pond*. In order to fill gaps in the candle sales-price series, I employed purchasing price data from Colombo, as well as purchasing and sales prices from Galle:

$$P_{Colombo\ (sale)} = 3.0796\ P_{Colombo\ (purchase)} - 1.0875 \quad R^2 = 0.90\ (N = 7)$$
$$P_{Colombo\ (sale)} = 0.1961\ P_{Galle\ (sale)} + 0.6602 \quad R^2 = 0.30\ (N = 12)$$
$$P_{Colombo\ (sale)} = 0.9233\ P_{Galle\ (purchase)} + 0.4318 \quad R^2 = 0.48\ (N = 3)$$

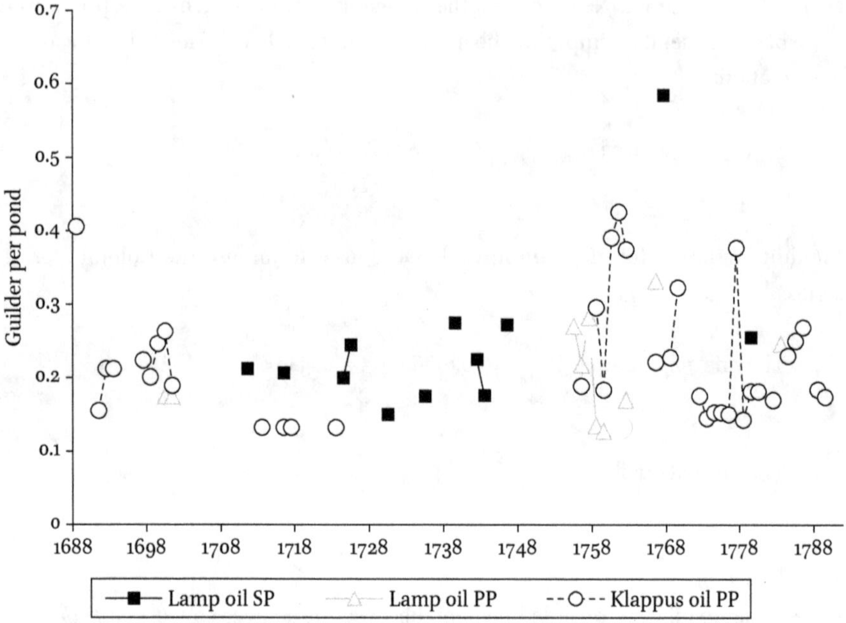

FIGURE A4.2 *Sales and purchasing prices of lamp oil in Colombo, 1688–1788.*
Sources: Van Bochove, 'Prices'; VOC archives

10 Further gaps

All further gaps were filled through linear interpolation.

A4.5 Java

1 Rice

Rice prices were found expressed per *pond*, *last*, *gantang* and *koyang*. Often, there were multiple observations per year (in the same unit of measurement, but sometimes also in different units of measurement). All these prices were converted into prices per kilogram (also from the different sources) and the arithmetic mean of these prices was calculated for each year. For those years in which there are sales prices available from the *rendementen* these prices were favoured over prices from other sources. Some gaps in the price series were imputed using Nagtegaal's price series for Tegal:[41]

$$P_{Batavia} = 1.2206\ P_{Tegal} + 18.436 \qquad R^2 = 0.47$$
$$N = 31$$

41 Nagtegaal, *Rijden*, p. 177. This concerns prices per *last*.

2 Beans

Prices for beans and *cadjang* were found in the sources, both prices being written down per *last*. *Cadjang* can be translated as beans and peas, and it was the general word for legumes.[42] Bean prices were only found in bills of expenses for the periods 1692–1703, 1712 and 1740 and records of the Bookkeeper-General in Batavia (BGB) for 1708 and 1709. In a number of cases the price for beans is exactly the same as the price for *cadjang*, yet in most cases the price for beans was somewhat lower. In the case of both bean and *cadjang* prices being available, I have taken a simple average of the two. In contrast to the prices for Ceylon, there was no great difference in prices for beans and peas and those for *cadjang*.

3 Meat and fish

Prices for meat and fish were sometimes reported in the sources. There were significantly fewer prices for fish. Since the price of fish was almost constantly around 1.77 times lower than those of meat, meat prices were used to extrapolate the price series for fish. There is no evidence to support the use of mark-ups on these data.

4 Sugar

Prices for castor sugar were noted per *pond*. As there were only three observations, an average mark-up of 11 percent was chosen to allow for the difference in purchasing and sales prices.

5 Soap

Prices for soap were expressed per *pond* and *kist*. As in the case of the Cape Colony, it was assumed that a *kist* was 27.9 kg, which roughly fits with the price observations for a *kist* of soap in 1793 (fl. 23.60) and a *pond* of soap in 1801 (fl. 0.37): 23.60/(27.9/0.494) = 0.42.

6 Salt

Prices were recorded per *maat* or *last*. Assuming a similar *last* as for rice, a *last* of salt was 3066 1/3 *pond*, or 1515 kg. A *maat* zout was 75 *pond* at Rembang, but 125 *pond* at Surabaya (VOC 3127). On the basis of only three observations, the relationship between sales and purchasing price was calculated to be:

$$P_{Sales} = 0.9762\ P_{Purchasing} + 0.0016 \quad R^2 = 0.97$$
$$N = 3$$

7 Cotton

For the seventeenth and eigtheenth centuries, I have assembled prices for *baftas* of cotton. Since black and white *baftas* were in the same price range, I have combined

42 VOC Glossary

series of the two to increase the number of observations. In order to go from pieces of *baftas* to cotton per m², some conversions had to be made. A *bafta* had a length of 19 gaz and a width of 1 gaz and 9 tussus; one gaz was 67.31 cm and a tussus 2.8 cm.[43] Thus, a *bafta* was 12.78 m in length and 0.93 m in breadth. The price per m² cotton could thus be calculated:

$$P_{Cotton\ (m^2)} = P_{Bafta}/(12.78 * 0.93)$$

The sales prices were calculated from purchasing prices via the relationship between sales and purchasing prices of *baftas* in the *rendementen*:

$$P_{Sales} = 1.18\ P_{Purchasing} + 0.2943 \qquad R^2 = 0.83$$
$$N = 34$$

8 Lamp oil

Prices for lamp oil and *klappus*, or *klapper*, oil, were stated in the sources. The average of both series was taken. Prices were given per *kan* of 1.51 litres (VOC Glossary), which were converted to price per litre. There is no evidence to suggest the use of mark-ups.

9 Candles

Prices were found for 'wax' and 'wax candles'. Gaps in the prices for wax candles were imputed from those of wax:

$$P_{Wax\ candle} = 0.59\ Pw_{ax} + 0.3511 \qquad R^2 = 0.18$$
$$N = 19$$

10 Fuel

Prices for firewood were noted down per *vadem*, which was 8.495 m³.[44] According to the website of the University of Wisconsin at Stevens Point, and the Wisconsin Energy Education, a standard cord of wood delivers between 21 MBtu on average.[45] One

43 Hariharan, *Cotton textiles*, pp. 270 and 306.

44 According to a note on weights and measures, the *vadem* in Batavia was different from that in Holland, as well as in the rest of Java. The price for a Batavian *vadem* of firewood in the VOC accounts (6–8 guilders) roughly corresponds with the price given in the note (3.25 rix-dollars.). In Batavia a *vadem* is 12 feet long and 5 feet high. In order to arrive at volume in cubic metres we can assume it is also 5 feet wide: $(12 \times 5 \times 5) \times 0.3048 = 8.495$ m³. Source: An., 'Verhandeling der munten'.

45 UW-Stevens Point: http://www.uwsp.edu/cnr/wcee/keep/Mod1/Whatis/energyresource tables.htm. The most common wood on Java was *jati* or teak wood (Van Niel, *Java's Northeast Coast*, p. 183), but no MBTU value could be found for that particular hard wood. Therefore I used the standard average of 18–24".

cord = 3.62 m^3 (128 × 0.028) = 21 MBTU: 3.62/21 = 0.17 m^3 per MBtu. The price per MBtu could thus be calculated:

$$P_{MBtu} = (P_{\textit{vadem}\ \mathrm{Firewood}}/8.495) * 0.17$$

No mark-ups were used.

11 Further gaps

All further gaps were filled using linear interpolation.

APPENDIX 5

An Alternative Method for Dealing with Gaps in the Price Data

For the prices of the main staple (the driver of the CPI), gaps were generally limited and small, yet for some of the other products gaps could be substantial. Where possible these gaps were imputed with other price series that correlated with the prices concerned. However, this was not always possible, and as those other price series also contained gaps, this method was not sufficient to impute all gaps. Remaining gaps were, therefore, linearly interpolated. Consistently decreasing or increasing prices over many years may not be entirely realistic. Therefore a second method of interpolation was employed, following the method of Arroyo Abad et al.:[1] they estimate a budget using the average shares of the products in the basket on the basis of years with sufficient data. The cost of a basket is then calculated on the basis of the available prices (with small gaps still interpolated) and increased by the percentage of missing product(s).

On the basis of information of years with enough data (and scattered over the period) the following shares were estimated:

- For the Cape: wheat 54.8 percent, beans 11.5 percent, meat 7.9 percent, butter 10.7 percent, soap 2.9 percent, cotton 3 percent, candles 4.7 percent, lamp oil 0.41 percent and firewood 4.2 percent.
- For Ceylon: rice 59 percent, beans 3 percent, butter 11 percent, sugar 3 percent, lamp oil 1 percent, soap 0.5 percent, salt 0.5 percent, candles 12 percent, and cotton 10 percent.
- For Java: 42.5 percent rice, beans 8.2 percent, fish 15.5 percent, sugar 2 percent, cotton 9.8 percent, lamp oil 2.2 percent, candles 12.9 percent, soap 6.9 percent, firewood 2.9 percent and salt 0.3 percent.

Gaps smaller than 5 years were still linearly interpolated.

Figures A5.1–A5.3 show that differences between the two methods are in general relatively small. The 'weights' series are generally somewhat bumpier (as they depend less on linear interpolation and more on trends in rice or wheat prices). In the main text of this book, I used the interpolated series.

---

1 Arroyo Abad et al., 'Between conquest'.

 | DOI 10.1163/9789004299665_012

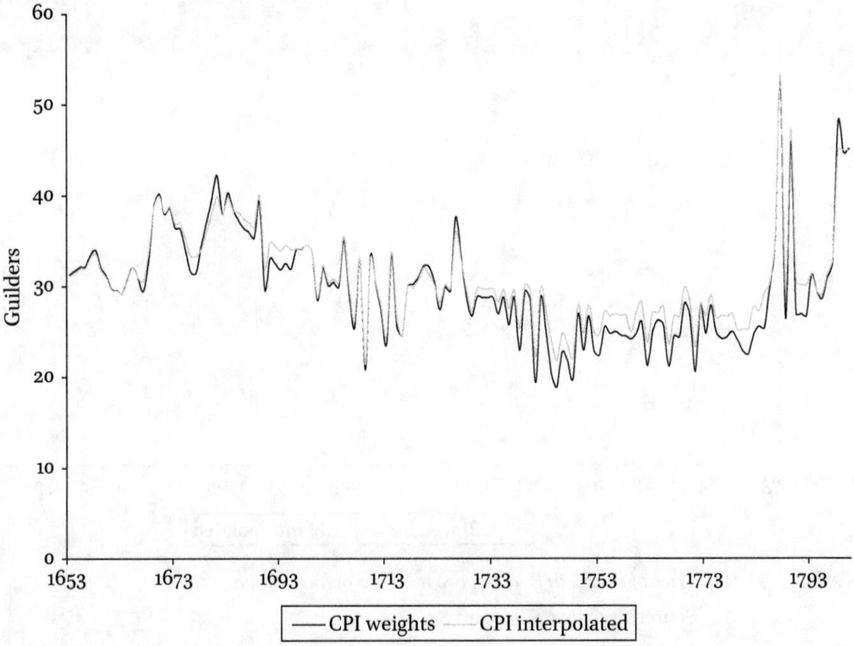

FIGURE A5.1 *Price of a basket in Cape Town, two methods of imputation.*
Sources: see text, Chapter 3.

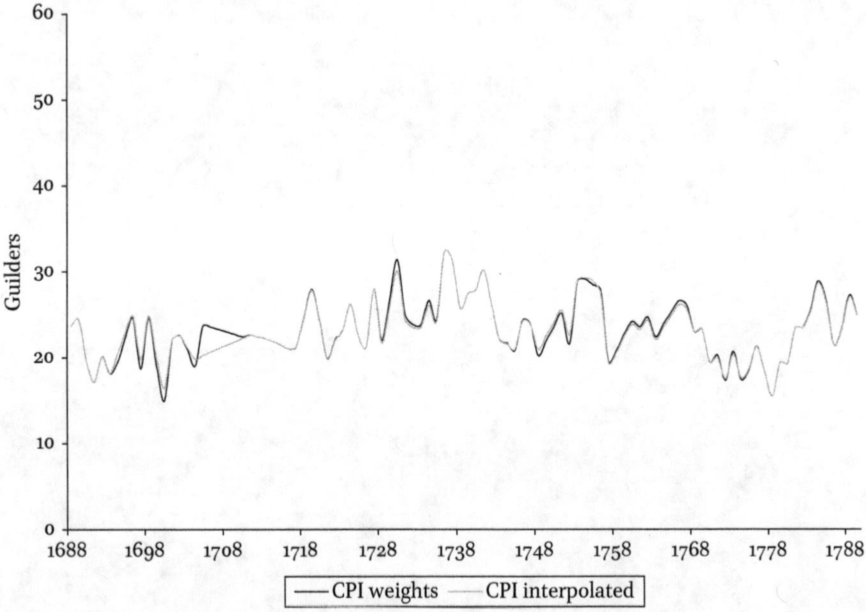

FIGURE A5.2 *Price of a basket in Colombo, two methods of imputation.*
Sources: see text, Chapter 3.

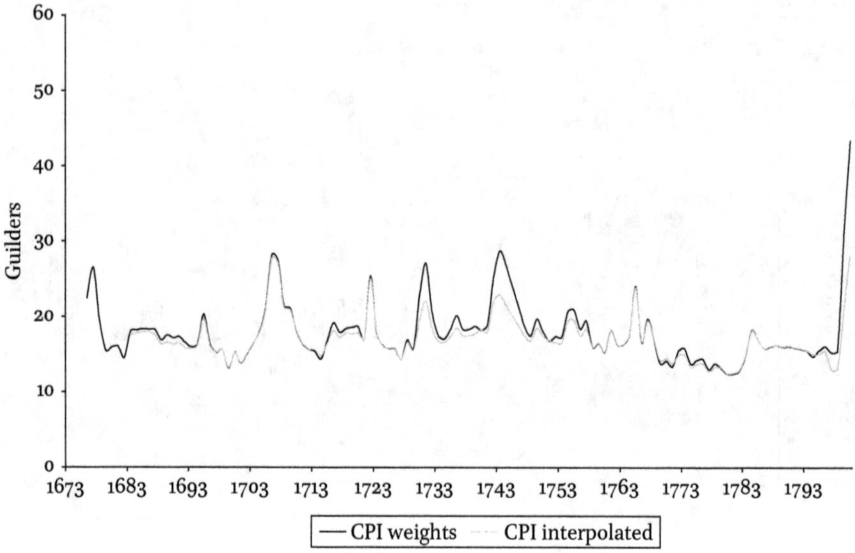

FIGURE A5.3 *Price of basket in Batavia, two methods of imputation.*
Sources: see text, Chapter 3.

APPENDIX 6

The Wage Data

A6.1 Bengal

By far the most abundant and consistent data were found for Bengal. These data were taken from the statements of costs for buildings and repairs. These data permitted simple linear interpolation between observations, as gaps were relatively limited (compared with the gaps in the series to be discussed below). For the years 1770–1789 there are nine years of data for both wages with and wages without board. These data suggested that board amounted on average to an additional 15 percent of the wage. However, an assumption had to be made on whether or not to add board throughout the entire period. Figure A6.1 shows three real wage series for Bengal: (1) where no board was added over the entire century, (2) where only board was added in the period 1770–1790, and (3) where board was added for the entire century. Obviously, the differences between the series did not amount to more than 15 percent, thus this would have no influence on the global comparisons. The third of these series was used in the analysis in the main text.

In addition, as discussed in Chapter 4, Subsection 2.3, Table A6.1 shows the wages of masons in Bengal and Bihar, which reveals a similar pattern as the wages for unskilled workers.

A6.2 The Cape Colony

Wage data from the muster rolls, collected by myself and Du Plessis and Du Plessis, were augmented by the monetary value of board as found in the cashbooks (see Chapter 4, Subsection 2.4). These sources suggested that VOC employees received additional remuneration: unskilled labourers 0.75 *reaal* and 31 pounds of wheat per month as board, while skilled craftsmen received 1.5 to 2 *reaal* extra per month, as well as 3 *muids* of wheat annually. The monetary value of these additions was added to the wages.

Furthermore, as noted in the main text, these wages of unskilled and skilled labourers were corrected for underestimation, as 'free *knechts*', no longer under Company contract, seem to have earned significantly more than those in VOC service. Using the shares of free *knechts* and servants vis-à-vis Company employees, an average wage was calculated, thereby assuming that free unskilled *knechts* consistently earned 1.5 times more than the wage of a VOC servant, while free skilled workers were assumed to earn twice the wages of VOC counterparts. As Figure A6.2 shows, this introduces a slightly

 | DOI 10.1163/9789004299665_013

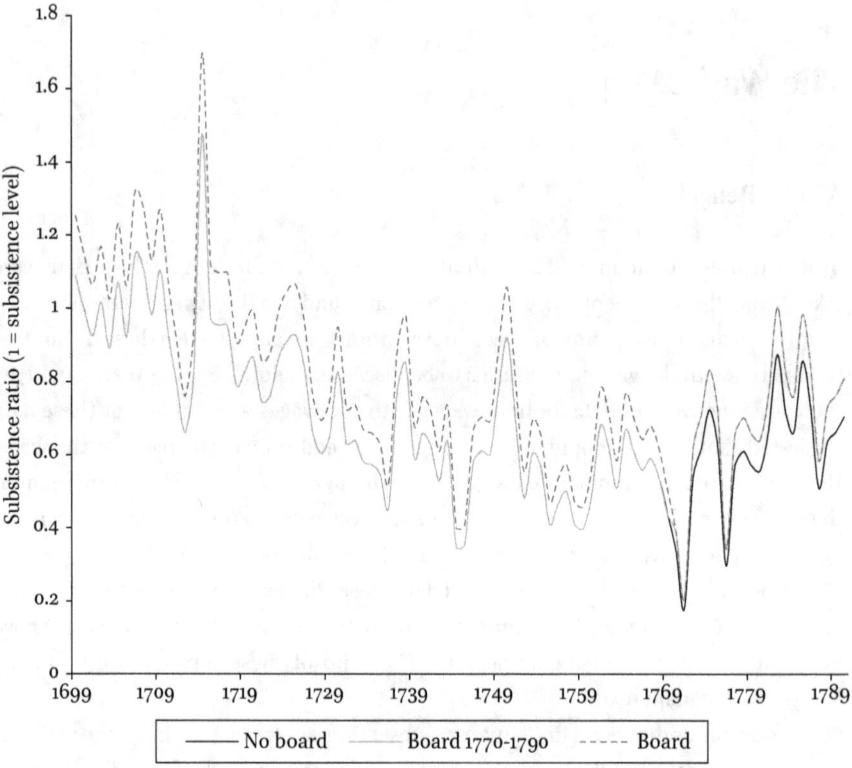

FIGURE A6.1 *Subsistence ratios in Bengal, 250 working days per year, with and without board.* Sources: see text, Chapter 4 and Appendix 6.1

TABLE A6.1 *Mason's daily wages in rupees, various towns in Bengal and Bihar, 1721–1789.*

		1721–31	1742–45	1758–59	1788–89
Bengal	Balasore	–	0.09	–	–
	Chinsurah	0.09	0.09	0.10	0.17
	Dhaka	–	–	0.10	–
	Karriemabad	0.07–0.13	0.08	–	–
	Kasimbazar	–	0.09	0.09	0.12–0.15
Bihar	Bettiah	0.16	0.16	0.17	–
	Chapra	–	0.17–0.19	–	–
	Patna	0.16	0.16	0.17	0.16
	Singia	–	0.19	0.17	–

Sources: see text, Chapter 4 and Appendix 6.1.

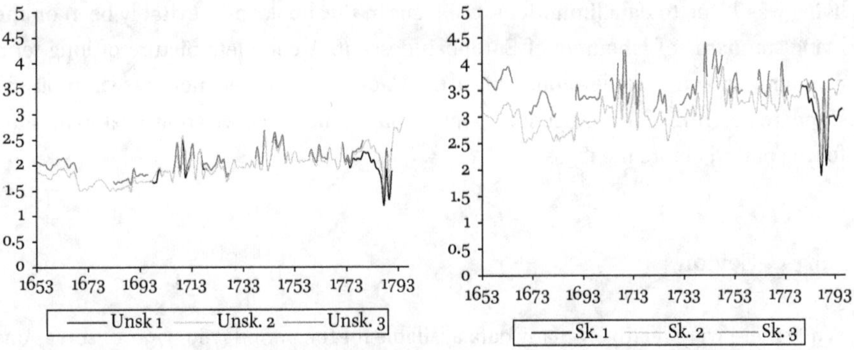

FIGURE A6.2 *Subsistence ratios in the Cape Colony for unskilled and skilled labourers, three methods of correction.*
Sources: see text, Chapter 4 and Appendix 6.2

declining trend in the nominal wage series as the share of free *knechts* declined vis-à-vis VOC servants. While salaries paid by the VOC seem to have been generally stable, Du Plessis and Du Plessis find an increase in soldiers' wages towards the end of the eighteenth century. There are no data for skilled construction workers for 1790, which means one has to assume that either there was a similar increase in wages for skilled workers, or that there was not. The series were interpolated between the benchmarks years for which there are data. Figure A6.2 shows the real wage series with and without corrections for underestimation, as well as with and without the increase in the later years of the eighteenth century.

From Figure A6.2 it becomes clear that for the unskilled wages especially (where the correction is smaller), the differences between the real wage series are relatively small and will have no significant effect on the global comparison of unskilled wages. For skilled workers, the correction is larger, and thus the difference between the series, especially in the second half of the seventeenth century, is significant. In both cases, the third series were used in the analysis, as I believe that in this case correcting for underestimation due to the focus on VOC employees makes sense,[1] and there is evidence of increasing unskilled wages towards the end of the period. For skilled workers, this increase is also in line with evidence of wages paid in the early years of British rule.[2]

Finally, while there are a few observations for the payment of slaves, it is unclear what part of this money went into the pockets of the slave owner and what part the slaves could keep themselves. It therefore remains unclear what their standard of

1 See especially: Shell, *Children of Bondage*, ch. 1 and the other literature cited in chapters 4 & 5 above.

2 See: De Zwart, 'Real wages'.

living was.[3] Due to data limitations, the focus in this book has inevitably been on the living standards of labourers of European descent. A complete picture of long-term economic growth and development at the Cape also requires more research on the standard of living of the indigenous population, about which we know next to nothing for the period before the 1850s.

A6.3 Ceylon

While there were relatively many data available for the period 1760–1790, observations for the earlier years were scarce. As noted previously, there are a few ways of dealing with this. First, one can assume stability over the entire period. This stability can be confirmed by regressing the wages in the database on a time trend; this will be discussed in Section A6.3.1. Second, one can linearly interpolate between the years for which data are available. However, as wages are often sticky, rather than showing a long-term increasing or declining trend, a different method of interpolation may also be used: nearest-neighbour interpolation, where gaps are assigned the same value as the nearest observation. Figure A6.3 plots these various series. Again, the difference between the series is not very large in a comparative global perspective and would not have an influence on the results presented in this book. Nonetheless, in terms of analysing the trends within Ceylon over the eighteenth century, there are some slight differences. The sticky wages show a decline until the late 1730s and growth in living standards after that, while the others series are stagnant until the late 1730s and increase after that. In the main text of the book, the sticky/regression series are shown.

A6.3.1 Regression

The database contains a total of 3,116 observations, all from original VOC accounts (in contrast to the database on Java, where the observations are taken from a variety of sources). By far the most of these data refer to Colombo (2,357 observations). Furthermore the data are very unevenly spread over time (2,255 observations refer to the period 1759–1790). All cities have been assigned a dummy, but due to the uneven spread of observations over time, and across occupations and cities, regression analysis seems unsuitable for estimating wage differentials across the island. In the regressions below, only observations for Colombo have been used. The wages, furthermore, refer to a great variety of occupations, from coolies and carpenters to bookkeepers and translators. These have been assigned dummies for unskilled work, skilled work and highly skilled work. Furthermore, a number of jobs associated with service obligations, such as the washers and the *lascarins*, received very low wages and have been assigned

3 Also see: De Zwart, 'Real wages'.

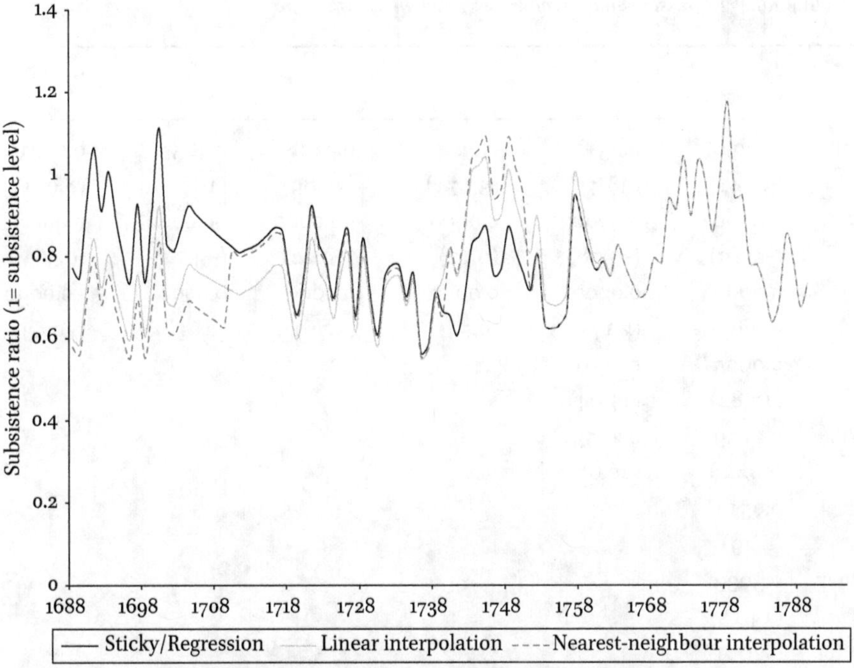

FIGURE A6.3 *Subsistence ratios in Ceylon, three methods of interpolation.*
Sources: see text, Chapter 4 and Appendix 6.3

a dummy. In addition, while most of the data refer to Sinhalese workers (named either simply *inlands*, indigenous, or Sinhalese, specifically), there are also observations for Moorish, Toepasse, Mallabar, and Southeast Asian workers. The regressions only include Sinhalese labourers. All wages were assumed to be male wages, as it is never mentioned otherwise. In Table A6.2 below the observations are regressed with a time trend (a variable called trend = the year minus 1750), as well as the trend squared.

The dependent variable is the daily wage (assuming 21 working days per month). These regressions exclude workers that received additional board, as well as wages for a variety of military occupations and chiefs.[4] Highly skilled denotes master craftsmen, craftsmen 'bosses' and doctors/surgeons. Regression 1 shows the results including all the remaining observations (for Colombo only). Regression 2 excludes teachers, messengers, interpreters and bookkeepers, as these were highly specialized jobs and wages seemingly fluctuated depending on personal merit. As can be seen, excluding these wages leads to roughly similar results, but with a much larger percentage of the variation in wages explained (the R^2 increases by 0.26).

4 Since their remuneration could fluctuate drastically, and, especially in the case of various chiefs, it seems unlikely that it constitutes their entire remuneration.

TABLE A6.2 *Regression analysis of wages in Colombo, 1679–1790.*

	1	2	3	4	5	6
Constant	0.2296***	0.2311***	0.2273***	0.3128***	0.4855***	0.0731***
	(30.41)	(38.41)	(33.71)	(37.89)	(16.22)	(8.07)
Trend	−0.0002	−0.0003*	0.0000	−0.0000	−0.0022***	0.0001
	(−1.19)	(−1.78)	(0.12)	(−0.22)	(−3.14)	(0.36)
Trend^2	0.0000*	0.0000**	0.0000	0.0000	0.0000	−0.0000
	(1.69)	(2.17)	(0.54)	(1.76)	(0.05)	(−0.53)
Skilled	0.0905***	0.0901***	–	–	–	–
	(17.82)	(17.94)				
High Skill	0.2159***	0.2153***	–	–	–	–
	(20.20)	(20.61)				
Teacher	0.0511***	–	–	–	–	–
	(4.29)					
Messenger	0.3033***	–	–	–	–	–
	(14.15)					
Interpreter	0.2021***	–	–	–	–	–
	(18.21)					
Bookkeeper	0.1098***	–	–	–	–	–
	(5.52)					
Service	−0.1596***	−0.1599***	−0.1575***	–	–	–
obligation	(−35.44)	(−35.11)	(−31.87)			
R^2	0.49	0.75	0.70	0.03	0.27	0.01
F	423.28***	652.12***	682.08***	1.55	7.25***	4.21**
N	1761	1116	636	358	122	314

Note: ***, **, * Denote significance at the 1, 5 and 10 percent levels, respectively. Robust standard errors. T-ratios are in parentheses.
Sources: see text.

Regressions 3, 4, 5 and 6, refer only to unskilled, skilled, highly skilled and coerced work, respectively, to see if these share the same trends as the entire sample. Regression 3 confirms the results of regressions 1 and 2 for unskilled workers. The constant is more or less similar and there is no trend over time. The regression for only skilled workers does not explain much. As becomes obvious from regressions 1 and 2, wages were roughly 9 cents higher than of those of unskilled workers. This puts the skill premium at 41 percent, which is surprisingly low. A possible reason for this is that, in contrast to other studies, I have put highly skilled occupations in another category.

Highly skilled workers earn 17 cents more than skilled workers, and over 21 cents more than unskilled workers (a premium of almost 100 percent). The regression on the wages of those workers possibly performing work as a part of their service obligation does not explain a lot of variation. However, it is clear that these earn a lot less, only 7 cents per day, rather than the standard 23 cents for unskilled workers. These labourers, however, probably had their own plot of land and did not perform this service for the entire year.

A6.4 Java

As I noted in Chapter 4, wages for Java were taken from a variety of sources and refer to a wide variety of workers. In order to estimate a time series of wages for unskilled workers there are three options: (1) assume stability over the late seventeenth and early eighteenth centuries and interpolate between observations of unskilled coolies from the 1760s onwards, (2) interpolate between the scarce observations for coolies from the earliest available observations (which introduces more variation), and (3) regress the data on a time trend. The third option is explored in greater detail below. Figure A6.4 shows the real wages for unskilled labourers calculated according to the three options just described. Again, these three approaches for dealing with missing data do not lead to dramatically different results that influence conclusions to be drawn. The regressed series were used in the analysis in the main text.

In addition, Table A6.3 shows the wages of skilled craftsmen in various cities along Java's north-east coast, as discussed in Chapter 4, Subsection 2.3.

A6.4.1 Regression

The database contains in total 633 observations for the period 1630–1820. When constructing the database, all wages stated in the sources and literature were put into one Excelfile. If they were monthly or yearly wages, these were converted to daily wages assuming 250 working days per year. The information on the original wage/time has been retained and the Excel sheet shows the conversion. When the source mentions, for example, that '63 coolies received 6 *stuivers* per day on the wharf'[5] this counts as 1 observation and not as 63. The reason for this is that otherwise the observations explicitly stating how many labourers the wage concerns would get disproportionate weight against observations that that do not specify the number of workers. In the database, when explicitly stated in the source, the number of workers that received the wage is also noted, allowing future calculations that might include this information.

5 Plakaatboek VIII 9.8.1765.

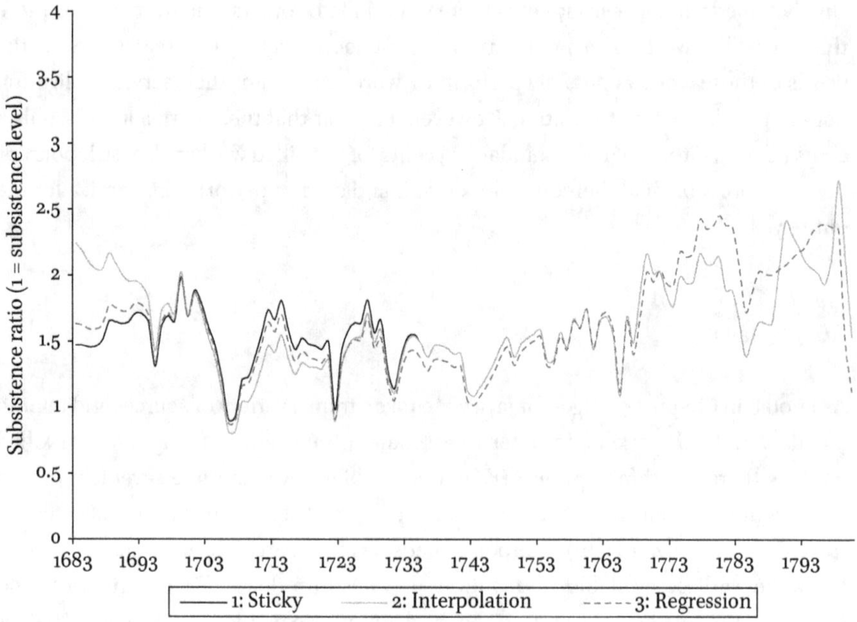

FIGURE A6.4 *Subsistence ratios in Batavia, three methods of interpolation.* Sources: see text, Chapter 4, Appendix 6.4, Table A6.3

Regarding the difference between free, bonded and slave labourers, it was often explicitly mentioned in the source what kind of work they performed. Otherwise I had to rely on what is known from the literature: so if a wage referred to *batur*, I assumed this was about bonded workers, while *coolies* or *bujang* (when not explicitly mentioned that they were unfree) were assumed to be free. Also, wages for occupations known to be related to *corvée* services, such as *modderaars* (dredging the canals) and *grassnijders* (grass cutters), were assumed to be for bonded workers.

Skill dummy: all types of craftsmen are skilled, but this also includes 'bosses' or foremen, as well as those denoted by, for example, Boomgaard as 'semi-skilled'.[6] The dummy thus does not capture differences between various skill levels (a blacksmith usually earned more than a carpenter, see, for example, Plakaatboek VII. 24.3.1797). Furthermore the database contains observations for both Javanese and Chinese labourers. A dummy was given a value of 1 whenever it was explicitly mentioned that Chinese workers were concerned.

The dataset thus constructed for Java contained a great variety of observations for different types of workers from various places across Java and from a great variety of sources (see Figure A6.5). In contrast to the other cases, as a consequence of the great

6 Boomgaard, *Children*.

TABLE A6.3 *Daily wages, various skilled labourers on Java's north-east coast, in guilders.*

		1727	1728	1730	1732	1733	1734	1735	1736	1737	1738	1739	1741	1742	1779	1788	1789	1791	1792
Mason	Cirebon	0.30	0.30	–	0.30	–	–	–	–	–	–	–	–	–	0.60	–	–	–	–
	Demak	–	–	–	–	1.20	1.20	–	–	–	–	–	–	–	–	–	–	–	–
	Japara	–	–	–	–	–	1.20	–	–	1.20	1.20	–	–	–	–	–	–	–	–
	Pasuruan	–	0.60	–	0.60	–	–	–	–	–	–	–	–	–	–	–	–	–	–
	Rembang	–	–	1.20	–	–	1.20	–	–	–	–	–	–	–	–	–	–	–	–
	Surabaya	–	–	0.60	0.60	–	–	–	–	–	0.60	–	–	0.60	–	–	–	–	–
	Tegal	–	–	–	–	–	0.60	–	–	–	–	0.60	–	–	–	–	–	–	–
Smith	Cartasoura	–	–	–	–	–	–	–	–	–	–	0.30	–	–	–	–	–	–	–
	Pasuruan	–	0.60	–	0.60	–	–	–	–	–	–	–	–	–	–	–	–	–	–
	Rembang	–	–	–	–	0.30	–	–	–	–	–	–	–	–	–	–	–	–	–
	Surabaya	–	–	–	0.60	–	–	–	–	–	0.60	–	–	0.60	–	–	–	–	–
Carpenter	Cirebon	0.30	–	–	0.30	–	–	–	–	–	–	–	–	–	0.60	–	–	0.60	0.60
	Demak	–	–	0.30	–	0.30	–	–	–	–	–	–	–	–	–	–	–	–	–
	Gresik	–	–	–	–	–	–	–	–	–	–	–	–	–	–	–	0.75	0.75	–
	Ìndramayen	–	–	–	–	–	–	–	–	–	–	–	–	–	0.60	–	–	–	–
	Japara	–	–	–	–	–	0.30	0.30		0.30	0.30	–	–	–	–	–	–	–	–
	Djoana	–	–	–	–	–	–	–	–	–	–	–	–	–	–	–	0.25	0.25	–
	Rembang	–	–	0.30	–	0.30	–	–	–	–	–	–	–	–	–	0.30	–	–	–
	Tegal	–	–	–	–	–	–	–	–	–	–	–	–	–	–	–	0.60	–	–
	Semarang	–	–	–	0.30	–	–	–	–	0.30	–	–	–	–	–	0.50	0.50	–	–
	Surabaya	–	–	0.30	0.30	–	–	–	–	–	0.30	–	–	0.60	–	0.75	0.75	–	–

TABLE A6.3 *Daily wages, various skilled labourers on Java's north-east coast, in guilders.* (cont.)

		1727	1728	1730	1732	1733	1734	1735	1736	1737	1738	1739	1741	1742	1779	1788	1789	1791	1792
Caulker	Cirebon	–	–	–	–	–	–	–	–	–	–	–	–	–	–	–	–	0.60	–
–	Gresik	–	–	–	–	–	–	–	–	–	–	–	–	–	–	0.50	0.50	–	–
–	Japara	–	–	–	–	–	0.30		0.30	–	–	–	–	–	–			0.60	0.60
–	Djoana	–	–	–	–	–	–	–	–	–	–	–	–	–	–	0.25	0.25	–	–
–	Rembang	–	–	–	–	–	–	–	–	–	–	–	–	–	–	0.30		–	–
–	Semarang	–	–	–	–	–	–	–	–	–	–	–	–	–	–	0.50	0.50	–	–
–	Surabaya	–	–	–	–	–	–	–	–	–	–	–	–	–	–	0.50	0.50	–	–

Sources: Statements of expenditure on the construction and repair of various buildings, see text, Chapter 4.

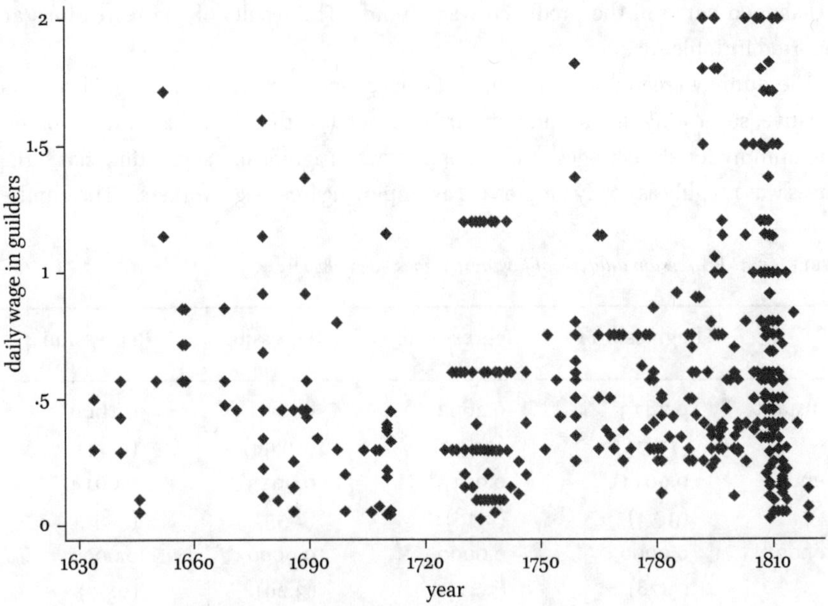

FIGURE A6.5 *Wages observations in Java, 1630–1820.*
Sources: see text, Chapter 4

variance in the database, a consistent time trend for the Javanese wages was estimated using regression analysis (following studies by Allen on India and Allen et al. on China).[7] This includes male wages from different towns and regions across Java, for Chinese as well as Javanese labourers, for free and coerced work and for a variety of occupations. These were all assumed to be male wages, as it is never mentioned otherwise. Because I found a considerable amount of wages for the period 1800 and 1820, these were also included in the regression (although outside the scope of the real wage analysis in Chapter 4). In order to predict a continuous time trend of wages from the scattered observations, dummy variables were included in the regressions for differences in ethnicity (Javanese or Chinese) and free, *corvée* or slave labour. The regressions also include a time trend (called Trend) equal to the year minus 1750.[8] The time trend in all regressions is significant and positive, indicating slight wage inflation over time. Trend2 is the square of the trend and is also significant, which leads to

7 Allen, 'India in the Great Divergence'; Allen et al., 'Wages, prices'.

8 Similar procedures were applied in Allen, 'India in the Great Divergence', and Allen et al. 'Wages, prices'. In the period before 1750 the trend has a negative value, allowing the U-shaped curve in the predicted wage trends.

a U-shaped curve in the predicted wage trend.[9] The results of the regressions are reported in Table A6.4.

The dummy created for the wages of *corvée* labourers was highly significant and negative, suggesting that around 1750 they earned less than half that of free workers. The dummy for slave 'wages' was almost always insignificant, suggesting that hiring slaves was roughly as costly for the VOC as employing free wage workers.[10] The number

TABLE A6.4 *Regression analysis of Javanese wages, 1630–1820.*[11]

	Regression 1	Regression 2	Regression 3	Regression 4
Constant	0.2873***	0.2692***	0.5991***	0.1600***
	(10.71)	(10.33)	(19.54)	(9.84)
Trend	0.0011***	0.0015***	0.0015**	0.0014***
	(3.54)	(2.48)	(2.55)	(3.88)
Trend2	0.00003***	0.00004***	0.00003***	0.0000
	(3.76)	(3.42)	(3.20)	(0.97)
Corvée	−0.1865***	−0.1506***	–	–
	(−7.35)	(−5.68)		
Slave	−0.0504	−0.0193	−0.0269	–
	(−0.77)	(−0.45)	(−0.21)	
Skilled	0.3357***	0.3371***	–	–
	(11.86)	(12.50)		
Chinese	0.7332***	0.6914***	0.7868***	–
	(11.43)	(8.74)	(7.94)	
R^2	0.48	0.48	0.30	0.18
F	101.35***	106.47***	21.04***	7.56***
N	581	357	304	62

Note: ***, **, * Denote significance at the 1, 5 and 10 percent levels, respectively. Robust standard errors. T-ratios are in parentheses.
Sources: see text, Chapter 4.

9 I also included the trend cubed in the regressions, but this always proved statistically insignificant.

10 Only 16 observations for slaves. These are non-Javanese artisan slaves rather than those in debt-bondage.

11 The regressions exclude the data on European wages paid in Java. 14 outliers of wages or more than 2 guilders per day were also excluded from the regression. Regression 2 excludes data after 1800, regression 3 excludes data for unskilled labourers, and regression 4 excludes data for free labourers and slaves.

of observations for slaves is small and, as it is unclear what part of the money paid for slaves went into the pockets of the slave owner and what part the slave could keep himself, I am unable to say anything about their standard of living. The premium for skilled labour is significant: over 130 percent, which is significantly higher than that paid for skilled labour in Europe and China, though more or less on a par with India.[12] Finally, it is shown that Chinese labourers earned much more than indigenous workers, which according to the *Plakaatboeken* was due to their higher productivity.[13]

Considering the price inflation after 1800 (see Figure A5.3), as well as the cluster of data between 1800 and 1820, regression 2 excludes those years. As the coefficients do not change drastically, this suggests that the rise in wages is not only caused by the post-1800 inflation. Regressions 3 and 4 test whether the wages of skilled and *corvée* labourers follow similar trends as free unskilled labourers. Clearly the square of trend becomes insignificant in regression 4, and whereas the wages of free workers (both skilled and unskilled) increased more rapidly towards the end of the eighteenth and beginning of the nineteenth centuries, wages of *corvée* labourers followed a linear trend. So far these regressions have included wages from different places in Java, yet there were some differences between wages in different areas. Unfortunately many observations do not explicitly mention the regional origin of the observation, and are, as well, too unevenly spread across time.[14] It should therefore be kept in mind that we thus perhaps understate the wage rate in Batavia, which seems to have been generally somewhat higher than elsewhere.[15]

While the wage data presented here are far from ideal, the results seem plausible. Both Boomgaard and Reid have suggested a decline in wages over the seventeenth and early eighteenth centuries.[16] They did not show data on wages for the later eighteenth century, but the evidence unearthed for this paper strongly suggests an increase in nominal wages in the second half of the eighteenth century.

---

12 Van Zanden, 'The skill premium'; Broadberry and Gupta, 'The early modern'.

13 Plakaatboek xv", pp. 545–7: '[…] *daar het bewezen is, dat de Chineezen veel beter als de inlanders voor het werk geschikt zijn*'. My translation: '[…] as it has been demonstrated that the Chinese are more capable of the work than the indigenous workers'.

14 Those observations explicitly stating that they refer to Batavia are concentrated towards the end of the period: almost half the observations are for the period after 1800.

15 However, interpolating between observations for only unskilled coolies in Batavia leads to roughly similar wage series as those estimated here. Since those observations are few, I prefer to use the thus estimated average unskilled-wage trend for calculating real wages in the main text.

16 Boomgaard, 'Why work'; Reid, *Southeast Asia* I.

APPENDIX 7

Estimating Population Trends for Ceylon

There are relatively few estimates of the total population of Ceylon during the Dutch period.[1] A crude estimate puts the total Sinhalese population in the mid-seventeenth century in the region of 550,000 to 600,000.[2] Prior to that, in 1505, a traveller estimated that the population in the South (Galle and Colombo) did not exceed 350,000, and the population of Jaffna was calculated at 120,000 people.[3] This is the same number given by the first Dutch commandant of the Jaffna province immediately after the Dutch conquest in 1658.[4] Jumping forward in time, a census was taken in 1789 that covered all three Maritime Provinces – Colombo, Jaffna and Galle – and the population enumerated was 817,000. According to N. K. Sarkar, because this census was taken for the purpose of taxation, 'serious under-enumeration was suspected.'[5] Common belief at the time was that the population of the whole island (including Kandy) was around 2 million, but more educated guesses suggested this number was closer to 1.5 million. Anthony Bartolaccai estimated the population of the Maritime Provinces was approximately 700,000 in 1809.[6] The first population census of the Kandyan provinces was taken in 1821, and the population was found to be 257,000.[7]

Next to these estimates, Jurrien van Goor has assembled data on the total number of indigenous Christians in Colombo, Galle and Jaffna. These figures (shown in Figure A7.1) were submitted annually by the clergy to the Directors of the VOC or the Synods of the Republic.[8] Figure A7.1 shows that the number of indigenous Christians in Jaffna rose from 160,000 in the late seventeenth century, to around 200,000 a century later. The increase in the Colombo area was more spectacular, as the number of Christians there increased fivefold, from 20,000 in 1693 to almost 100,000 in 1793. This growth seems to confirm the movement of people towards towns, especially towards important administrative centres such as Colombo, because of the economic opportunities they may provide.[9] In Galle, the number of Christians reached its high point of little over

1 This appendix draws on: De Zwart, 'Population, labour'.

2 Roberts, *Caste conflict*, p. 32.

3 P. E. Pieris, *Ceylon and the Hollanders 1658–1796* (Tellipalai, 1918) p. 3.

4 Arasaratnam, 'Historical foundation', p. 2.

5 N. K. Sarkar, *The demography of Ceylon* (Colombo: Ceylon Government Press, 1957) p. 18.

6 Anthony Bertolaccai, *A view of the agricultural, commercial and financial interests of Ceylon* (London, 1817) p. 62.

7 Roberts, *Case conflict*, p. 297.

8 Van Goor, *Jan Kompenie*, p. 121.

9 Arasaratnam, *Dutch power*, p. 217.

 | DOI 10.1163/9789004299665_014

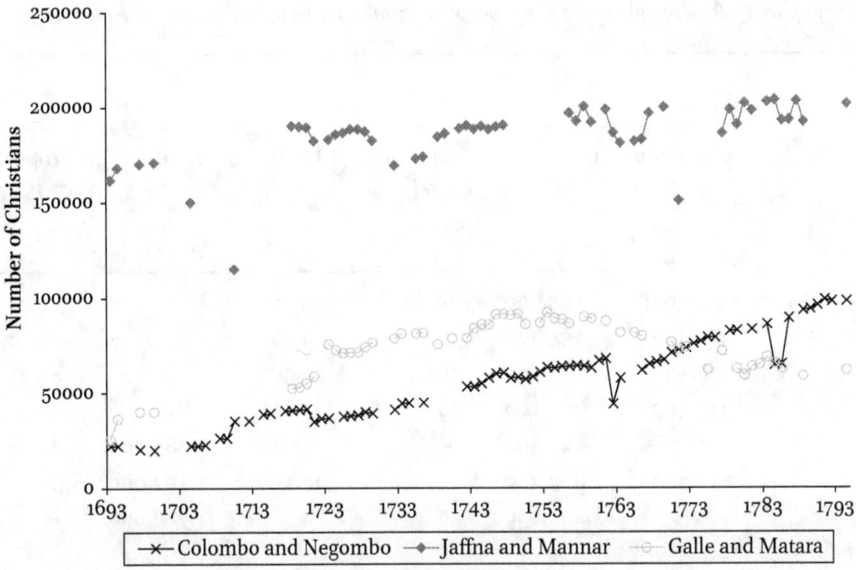

FIGURE A7.1 *Indigenous Christians in Ceylon, 1693–1795.*
Sources: Van Goor, *Jan Kompenie*, pp. 160–161; the numbers for 1694, 1697 and 1699 have been entered by the author from the original source on indigenous Christians

90,000 in the mid-eighteenth century, thereafter declining to 60,000 by the end of the century, reflecting Galle's declining importance as a VOC trade hub.[10]

Van Goor warns that, due to the lack of other demographic studies on Dutch Ceylon, these numbers cannot be related to other data, and that it is impossible to know which part of the population had become exposed to the influence of Christianity.[11] In this book, I attempt to side-step this problem by relating his numbers to population data for two benchmark years: 1684 and 1789 (see Table A7.1). The numbers for 1789 are from the census discussed above (keeping in mind possible under-enumeration), while the numbers for 1684 stem from a newly-found source in the archives of the VOC named 'Summary of all Company's subjects'.[12] Proto-censuses similar to this one have been

10 Femme S. Gaastra, 'Ceylon als "handelscomptoir" van de VOC', in: R. Kromhout (ed.) *Het Machtige Eyland, Ceylon en de* VOC (Den Haag, 1988) pp. 29–36.

11 Van Goor, *Jan Kompenie*, p. 123.

12 VOC 1396, ff. 602–612: '*Sommarium van alle 's Compagnies onderdanen*' for the separate districts; the former Kingdom of Jaffanapatnam, the Island Mannar, the *Dissawany* of Colombo (including Negombo and Hapitagam), and the Commandment Galle, which includes Matara.

TABLE A7.1 *Total population and number of indigenous Christians in Ceylon, 1684 and 1789.*[13]

	1684			1789		
	Christians	Total	Proportion Christians (%)	Christians	Total	Proportion Christians (%)
Jaffna	155,600[14]	155,600	100	193,800	–	–
Colombo	22,400	54,400	41	94,100	–	–
Galle	38,300	68,100	56	59,300	–	–
Subtotal	216,300	278,100	78	347,100	817,000	42
Kandy	–	539,600	–	–	285,000	–
Total	216,300	817,700	26	347,100	1,102,000	32
Total (corrected for underestimation)	–	1,291,100	–	–	1,788,000	–

Sources: see text.

found for other VOC areas in Asia, such as Cochin in Malabar[15] and Ambon.[16] On Ambon, village heads were required to deliver the detailed data each year to the VOC, while schoolmasters and local VOC officials were ordered to keep an eye on the process. Gerrit Knaap, who has worked with these data, warns that 'in reality there seemed to be hardly any control on the part of the VOC.'[17] Since the Ceylon census also contains information on castes, a possible motivation for the population count might be the *rājakāriya* system, in which people had to pay a land tax or to perform services according to their occupational caste. While no unambiguous guarantees can be given regarding the reliability of these censuses, the numbers on, for example, the gender and age distribution of the population, are consistent with data from other

13 Rounded into 100 s.

14 The total number of Christians in 1690 was actually enumerated at 161,863. Therefore assuming some margins of error and growth between 1684 and 1690, it is estimated that this number was equal to the total number of subjects in 1684, which was 155,600.

15 Anajana Singh, *Fort Cochin in Kerala, 1750–1830. The social condition of a Dutch community in an Indian milieu* (Leiden: Brill, 2010).

16 Knaap, *Kruidnagelen en Christenen*; and ibid., 'The Demography of Ambon in the Seventeenth Century: Evidence from Colonial Proto-Censuses', *Journal of Southeast Asian Studies* 26 (1995) pp. 227–241.

17 Knaap, 'The demography', p. 230.

sources.Combined with sources on indigenous Christians, this source suggests that almost the entire population of Jaffna was Christian. In a census in the mid-eighteenth century, the population of Jaffna was found to be 187,599 according to Arasaratnam, who notes that this 'seems to include the total Tamil population.'[18] Most of these people were Christian only in name, and for the vast majority who were baptized (and thus appeared in the statistics), knowledge of the Christian faith and their adherence to it was nominal;[19] Hindu beliefs and practices coexisted alongside Christianity. Many converted to Christianity only because it brought new economic opportunities and material benefits.[20] In the two southern provinces, about one-half of the population seems to have been converted to Christianity (41 percent in Colombo, and 56 percent in Galle). Reliable population estimates for two cities on the eastern coast, Batticaloa and Trincomalee, are lacking. Van Goor's sources suggest less than 1,000 Christians in Batticaloa in the late eighteenth century, and around 2,000 in Trincomalee. It seems unlikely that the total population of these cities together exceeded 10,000.For Kandy we are bereft of any population estimates other than those of the British for the early nineteenth century. Because the territory occupied by Kandy in the seventeenth century was larger than during the late eighteenth century, it is likely that the population exceeded the 285,000 given for 1789 by Sarkar.[21] Baldaeus wrote that the King of Kandy could muster an army of 151,086 men.[22] In Chapter 5, it was shown that in Ceylon approximately 28 percent of the total population consisted of adult men. If we assume that the figure given by Baldaeus constitutes all adult men of Kandy (obviously this is questionable), this would bring the total population of Kandy in the late seventeenth century to 539,592.

Table A7.1 summarizes this discussion. Yet, as I have noted, these numbers are most likely underestimates.[23] Based on growth rates and backward projection from the later nineteenth century, Sarkar estimates that the total population in 1789 was around 1,788,000,[24] which has been adopted by Colin MacEvedy and Richard Jones in their

18 S. Arasaratnam, 'Protestants: the first phase, 1650–1880', Christianity, Traditional Cultures and Nationalism: The South Asian Experience', *Bunker Memorial lectures* (Jaffna, 1978) p. 19.

19 S. Arasaratnam, 'The First Century of Protestant Christianity in Jaffna', *Indian Church History Review* 19 (1985) pp. 39–54.

20 De Silva, *A history*, pp. 196–197.

21 Sarkar, *Demography*, p. 21: 285,000 is Sarkar's estimate for 1789 based on the 257,000 from the census of 1821.

22 Baldaeus, *Naauwkeurige beschryving*, p. 9.

23 The numbers for 1684 are close to estimates by Pieter van Dam, a VOC lawyer, who suggested that the total population of the Maritime Provinces in 1686 was around 278,789. Van Dam, *Beschrijvinge*, Part 2.2, p. 314.

24 Sarkar, *Demography*, p. 22.

Atlas of World Population History.[25] In order to arrive at a corrected figure for 1684, the original number was increased by 62 percent. Compared with total population numbers for Ceylon found for the first half of the nineteenth century, as well as the figure arising from another source, i.e. registers on family composition and landownership, known as *thombos*, for the Colombo province during the 1760s,[26] the corrected figures represent an upper-bound estimate.

Using these data, demographic developments across time can be calculated in four ways. First, take 1684 as the main point of reference and assume that the percentage of Christians in each province remains stable over the eighteenth century. Second, it is possible to project total population numbers backwards from the year 1789. Third, it can be assumed that towards the end of the eighteenth century the 1789 numbers are more reliable, while at the end of seventeenth century the 1684 numbers are more reliable, and use changing weights over the period to reflect this. Fourth, and finally, this combined series can be corrected for underestimation. The results of this are shown in Figure A7.2. While keeping in mind that these numbers are preliminary estimates

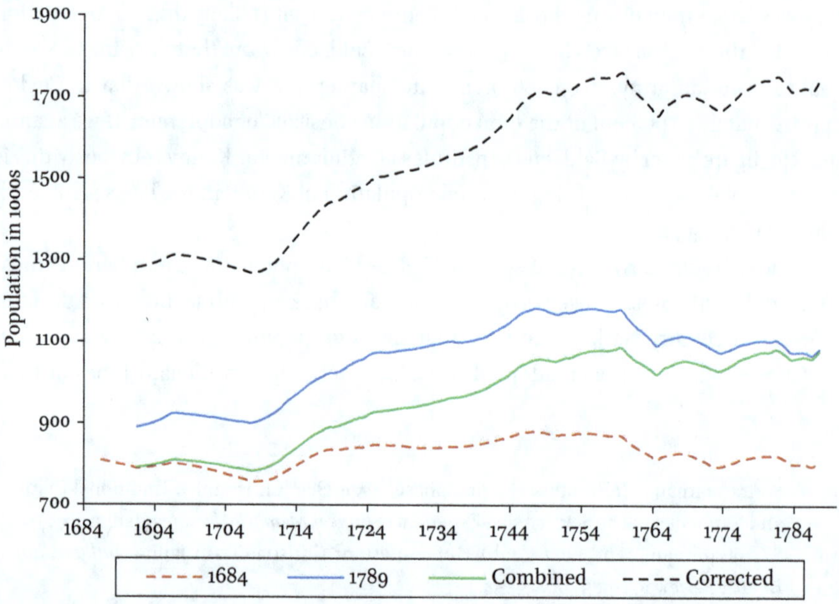

FIGURE A7.2 *Four estimates of the population of Ceylon, 1684–1790.*
Sources: see text

25 MacEvedy and Jones, *Atlas of world*, p. 186.

based on a number of assumptions and a limited amount of evidence, one can consider Figure A7.2 to be a first illustration of demographic developments for eighteenth-century Ceylon. The most notable drops in the graph, between 1700 and 1710, and between 1760 and 1766, coincide with Dutch-Kandyan wars, thus generating some confidence in these series.

APPENDIX 8

Occupational Structure of Ceylon

The occupational groups listed in Table A8.1 are based on the HISCO tree of occupational groups: http://historyofwork.iisg.nl/major.php. This appendix describes which workers (as found in the sources) are included in which groups, and in which sector (according to the PST system).[1]

Primary sector:

6: Agricultural, animal husbandry and forestry workers, fishermen and hunters:

Farmers: *vellala*, *paradesi*, *maddapalli*, and *agamudaiyan* (these were Tamil cultivators' castes),[2] and cattle farmers.

Agricultural workers: *naindes*, *chalias* (cinnamon peelers), durava (headmen of cinnamon peelers) *chiandos* (toddy-tappers), and wood cutters.

Slaves: in Galle and Colombo, these were written down simply as 'slaves', while in Jaffna there were four types of slaves: *nalluas* (slaves), *pallas* ('buijten slaven'/'outside slaves'), *corias* (house slaves), and *heijdense slaven* (non-Christian slaves).

Fishers and hunters: *careas, moeckias*, and *timmulaes* (fishers), *baddas* and *pattangatty* (overseers of the fishers), *barimbas* (sailors), and *paravar* (pearl fishers); hunters, *badamas, marrigares, tammekares* and *pannikias* (elephant hunters), and *cornacx* (elephant riders).

Secondary sector:

7/8/9: Production and related workers, transport equipment operators and labourers:

Various artisans: butchers, carpenters, coppersmiths, masons, painters, potters, shoemakers, silversmiths, smiths, leather workers, lime burners, salt and arrack makers, and weavers.

Labourers: *coolies*, *olias*, *bailedoors* (sources note these 'were used for various services').

---

1 Also see: De Zwart, 'Population, labour'.

2 Van Goor, *Jan Kompenie*, pp. 162–3.

 | DOI 10.1163/9789004299665_015

Tertiary sector:

0/1: Professional, technical and related workers: jurists, accountants (*borrewijs*), priests, teachers, and *merinjos* (assistant teachers).

2: Administrative and managerial workers: *adigars, appuhamy, atta corle, mudaliyar, raalens, vidanes*, and *reformadosse* (all of these were headmen of various positions, high and low).

3: Clerical and related workers: *cannecappuls* (bookkeepers), writers, and messengers.

4: Sales workers: *chetties* (trading-caste, of south Indian origin) and *moors* (Muslim traders from India).

5: Service workers: *tarumbas, hunnewas, maijnatos* (all of these were washers) and *pedias* (overseers of washers), and barbers.

Military service: *mudaliyars* (officers), *arachies* and *canganes* (corporals), *lascarins* (soldiers), *tablinjeros* and *berrewaijs* (drummers), and horn blowers.

TABLE A8.1 *Occupational structure Ceylon, 1684.*

Household heads	*n*	%
Farming	22,538	29
Agricultural workers	11,677	15
Slaves	11,302	14
Fishers & hunters	6,640	9
Total primary	**52,157**	**67**
Artisans	5,992	8
Labourers	3,874	5
Total secondary	**9,866**	**13**
Administration	3,135	4
Military	6,395	8
Professional	626	1
Clerical	355	0
Merchants	1,974	3
Service	2,192	3
Total tertiary	**14,677**	**19**
Unknown	1,394	2
Total	**78,094**	**100**

Source: VOC 1396, ff. 602–612.

Unknown:

For Jaffna, this includes people noted down as cripples, beggars, and *toepasses* (Portuguese speaking peoples). For Colombo, this includes Mallabars, Bengals, Chinese, *toepasses*, and widows. For Galle, this includes babies, widows, free Mallabars, pilgrims and those written down as 'brothers and friends' of other population groups. This is, thus, still a problematic group, as it includes both productive and unproductive peoples and it is unclear what the productive people are doing.

Bibliography

Primary Sources

Dutch National Archives (NA) in The Hague:

- Archives of the Bookkeeper General Batavia (Boekhouder-Generaal Batavia: BGB): 1.04.18.02. General journals: inv. nos. 10751–10809.
- Archives of the Dutch East India Company (VOC): 1.04.02: various documents within the following series:

Chamber Amsterdam

- VOC 602–654: *Facturen van scheepsladingen, rekeningen van inkomsten en uitgaven; rekening, opgemaakt op verscheidene VOC-vestigingen in Indië, 1608–1613* [Bills of ships loads, income and expenditure, made at different VOC-establishments in the East Indies, 1608–1613].
- VOC 1053–3987 *Overgekomen brieven en papieren van Indië aan de Heren XVII en de Kamer Amsterdam, 1607–1794* [Letters and papers received from the East Indies, to the Gentlemen XVII and Chamber Amsterdam, 1607–1794].
- VOC 3988–4366. *Overgekomen brieven en papieren van Kaap de Goede Hoop en Mauritius aan de Heren XVII en de kamer Amsterdam, 1651–1794* [Letters and papers received from the Cape of Good Hope and Mauritius to the Gentlemen XVII and Chamber Amsterdam, 1653–1795].
- VOC 4584–4597: *'Samenvattende staten', overzichten van de boekhoudingen van de verschillende kamers betreffende de verhandelde en onverkocht gebleven goederen [etc.] 1662–1790* [VOC auctions Amsterdam, 1662–1790].
- VOC 5168–5239: *Kopie-generale land- en zeemonsterrollen van de VOC-dienaren in de vestigingen en op de schepen in Indië, 1720–1791* [Copy of general land- and sea muster rolls of the servants in the VOC establishments and ships in the East Indies, 1720–1791].
- VOC 5269–6842: *Scheepssoldijboeken van de opvarenden van voor de kamer Amsterdam uitgelopen schepen, 1633–1795* [Ship's pay-ledgers of the sailors on the ships sailed for the Chamber of Amsterdam, 1633–1795].

Chamber Zeeland

- VOC 7528–9179: *Ingekomen stukken van de Gouverneur-Generaal en Raden bij de Heren XVII en de Kamer Zeeland* [Documents received at the Genlemen XVII and the Chamber of Zeeland].

- VOC 11534–11705: *Kopie-generale landmonsterrollen de VOC-dienaren in de vestigingen in Indië, 1691–1791* [Copy of general land- and sea muster rolls of the servants in the VOC establishments in the East Indies, 1720–1791].
- VOC 12372–12443: *Kopie-generale monsterrollen van de VOC-dienaren in Ceylon, 1694–1778* [Copy of general muster rolls of the VOC servants in Ceylon, 1694–1778].

Western Cape Archives (WCA), Cape Town: various documents within the following archives:

- 1.1. Council of Policy (C)
- 1.82. Burgher Council (BRD)

Published Primary Sources

An., 'Verhandelingen der munten, maten en gewigten van Neerlandsch Indië', *Verhandelingen van het Bataviaasch Genootschap van Kunsten en Wetenschappen* 4 (1824) pp. 281–358.

Bailey, W. B., 'Statistical View of the Population of Burdwan, &c', *Asiatick Researches* 12 (1818) pp. 567–573.

Baldaeus, Philippus, *Naauwkeurige beschryvinge van Malabar en Choromandel, der zelver aangrenzende ryken, en het machtige eyland Ceylon* (Amsterdam, 1672).

Barbosa, Duarte, *The Book of Duarte Barbosa. An Account of the Countries Bordering on the Indian Ocean and Their Inhabitants, Written by Duarte Barbosa and Completed about the Year 1518 AD* [Transl. and ed. by Mansel Longworth Dames] (New Delhi: Asian Educational Services, 1989).

Bertolaccai, Anthony, *A View of the Agricultural, Commercial and Financial Interests of Ceylon* (London, 1817).

Chijs, J. A. van der (ed.), *Nederlandsch-Indisch Plakaatboek, 1602–1811*. Vols. 1–17 (Batavia: Landsdrukkerij, 1885).

Coolhaas, W.Ph. (ed.), *Pieter van den Broecke in Azië. 2 Vols.* (The Hague: Martinus Nijhoff, 1962–1963).

Coolhaas, W.Ph., J. van Goor, J. E. Schooneveld-Oosterling and H. K. s' Jacob (eds.), *Generale Missiven van Gouverneurs-Generaal en Raden aan Heren XVII der Verenigde Oostindische Compagnie* (1960–2007).

Hageman, J. 'Geschied- en aardrijkskundig overzigt van Java op het einde der achttiende eeuw', *Tijdschrift van het Bataviaasch Genootschap* 9 (1860).

Heeres, J. E., H. T. Colenbrander, and J. A. van der Chijs (eds.), *Dagh-register gehouden int Casteel Batavia vant passerende daer ter plaetse als over geheel Nederlandts-India.* Vols. 1–31. (The Hague: Martinus Nijhoff, 1887–1931).

Herklots, G., 'Table Showing the Market Price of Grain &c. in Lower Bengal from the Year 1700 to 1813, Extracted from Authentic Documents of One Month in Each Year, for Which Generally the Month of August was Selected', *Gleanings in Science* 1 (1829) pp. 368–369.

Hovy, Lodewijk, *Ceylonees plakkaatboek: plakkaten en andere wetten uitgevaardigd door het Nederlande bestuur op Ceylon, 1638–1796* vols. 2 (Hilversum: Verloren, 1991).

IJzerman, J. W. (ed.), *Cornelis Buijsero te Bantam 1616–1618. Zijn brieven en journaal. Met inleiding en bijlagen* (The Hague: Martinus Nijhoff, 1923).

Jonge, J. K. J. de, and M. L. van Deventer (eds.), De Opkomst van het Nederlandsch Gezag in Oost-Indië (1595–1811): verzameling van onuitgegeven stukken uit het oud-koloniaal archief. 17 Vols. (The Hague, 1862–1888).

Keuning, J. (ed.), *De tweede schipvaart der Nederlanders naar Oost-Indië onder Jacob Cornelisz. van Neck en Wijbrant Warwijck 1598–1600: journalen, documenten en andere bescheiden.* Vol. 2 (The Hague: Martinus Nijhoff, 1938).

Knox, Robert, 'A Historical Relation of Ceylon', *Ceylon Historical Journal* 6 (1956–57), p. 138 [Original published in 1681].

Merriman, J. X. (ed.), *The Reports of Chavonnes and His Council, and of Van Imhoff, on the Cape. With Incidental Correspondence* (Cape Town: The Van Riebeeck Society, 1918).

Montgomery Martin, Robert, *Statistics of the colonies of the British Empire in the West Indies, South America, North America, Asia, Autral-Asia, Africa and Europe. From the Official Records of the Colonial Office* (London, 1839).

Moodie, D. (ed.), *The Record, or a Series of Official Papers Relative to the Condition and Treatment of the Native Tribes of South Africa* (Cape Town: Balkema, 1960).

Pires, Tomé, *OrientalSuma: An Account of the East, from the Red Sea to Japan, Written in Malacca and India in 1512–1515.* 2 vols. (London, 1944).

Raffles, Thomas Stamford, *The History of Java.* 2 vols. (Kuala Lumpur [etc.]: Oxford U.P., 1978 [Original: London 1817]).

Rouffaer, G. P., and J. W. IJzerman (eds.), *De Eerste Schipvaart der Nederlanders naar Oost-Indië onder Cornelis de Houtman, 1595–1597. Journalen, documenten en andere bescheiden.* Vol. 3 (The Hague: Martinus Nijhoff, 1915).

Schreuder, Jan, *Memoir of Jan Schreuder, Governor of Ceylon Delivered to His Successor Lubbert Jan Baron van Eck on March 17, 1762*, trans. E. Reimers (Colombo: Ceylon Government Press, 1946).

Stein van Gollenesse, *Memoir of Julius Stein van Gollenesse, Governor of Ceylon. For His Successor Gerrit Joan Vreeland on February 28, 1751*, trans. by S. Arasaratnam (Colombo, 1974).

Theal, G. M. (ed.), *Records of the Cape Colony.* Vol. 2 (1905).

Unger, W. S. (ed.), *De oudste reizen van de Zeeuwen naar Oost-Indië 1598–1604* (The Hague: Martinus Nijhoff 1948).

Zwaardecroon, Hendrick, *Commandeur of Jaffna. Memoir for the Guidance of the Council of Jaffnapatnam, during His Absence at the Coast of Malabar, 1697*, transl. by Sophia Pieters (Colombo, 1911).

Literature

Acemoglu, Daron, Simon Johnson, and James A. Robinson, 'The Colonial Origins of Comparative Development: An Empirical Investigation', *American Economic Review* 102 (2001) pp. 3077–3110.

———, 'Reversal of Fortune: Geography and Institutions in the Making of the Modern World Income Distribution', *Quarterly Journal of Economics* 117 (2002) pp. 1231–1294.

———, 'The Rise of Europe: Atlantic Trade, Institutional Change, and Economic Growth', *American Economic Review* 95 (2005) pp. 546–579.

Acemoglu, Daron, and James A. Robinson, *Why Nations Fail. The Origins of Power, Prosperity, and Poverty* (2012).

A'Hearn, Brian, Jörg Baten, and Dorothee Crayen, 'Quantifying Quantitative Literacy: Age Heaping and the History of Human Capital', *Journal of Economic History* 69 (2009) 783–808.

Ahuja, Ravi, 'Labour Relations and Labour Intermediaries in Early Colonial India: Four Provocations and One Case Study on the City of Madras', Paper prepared for the *Workshop on Labour Relations in India 1500–2000* (New Delhi: Indian Council of Historical Research, 2011).

Allen, Robert C., 'Real Incomes in the English-Speaking World, 1879–1913', in: G. Grantham and M. MacKinnon (eds.), *Labour Market Evolution. The Economic History of Market Integration, Wage Flexibility and the Employment Relation* (London: Routledge, 1994) pp. 107–138.

———, 'The Great Divergence in European Wages and Prices from the Middle Ages to the First World War', *Explorations in Economic History* 38 (2001) pp. 411–447.

———, 'Progress and Poverty in Early Modern Europe', *Economic History Review* 56 (2003) pp. 403–443.

———, 'Real Wages in Europe and Asia: A First Look at the Long-Term Patterns', in: Robert C. Allen, Tommy Bengtsson, and Martin Dribe (eds.), *Living Standards in the Past New Perspectives on Well-Being in Asia and Europe* (Oxford: Oxford University Press, 2005) pp. 157–185.

———, 'Pessimism Preserved: Real Wages in the British Industrial Revolution', *Oxford University Department of Economics Working Paper* 314 (2007).

———, 'India in the Great Divergence', in: Timothy J. Hatton, Kevin H. O'Rourke, and Alan M. Taylor, *The New Comparative Economic History. Essays in Honor of Jeffrey G. Williamson* (Cambridge MA: MIT Press, 2007) pp. 111–130.

———, *The British Industrial Revolution in Global Perspective* (Cambridge: Cambridge U.P., 2009).

———, 'Agricultural Productivity and Rural Incomes in England and the Yangtze Delta, c. 1620–1820', *Economic History Review* 62 (2009) pp. 525–526.

———, *Global Economic History: A Very Short History* (Oxford: Oxford U.P., 2012).

———, 'Poverty Lines in History, Theory and Current International Practice', *Oxford Economics Discussion Paper* 685 (December 2013).

Allen, Robert C., and Jacob Weisdorf, 'Was There an "Industrious Revolution" before the Industrial Revolution? An Empirical Exercise for England, c. 1300–1830', *Economic History Review* 64 (2011) pp. 715–729.

Allen, Robert C., Tommy E. Murphy, and Eric B. Schneider, 'The Colonial Origins of the Divergence in the Americas: A Labor Market Approach', *Journal of Economic History* 72 (2012) pp. 863–894.

Allen, Robert C., Jean-Pascal Bassino, Debin Ma, Christine Moll-Murata, and Jan Luiten van Zanden, 'Wages, Prices, and Living Standards in China, 1738–1925: In Comparison with Europe, Japan, and India', *Economic History Review* 64 (2011) pp. 8–38.

Arasaratnam, Sinnappah, *Dutch Power in Ceylon, 1658–1687* (Amsterdam: Djambatan, 1958).

———, 'Dutch Commercial Policy and Its Effects on the Indo-Ceylon Trade (1690–1750)', *Indian Economic and Social History Review* 4 (1967) pp. 109–130.

———, 'Weavers, Merchants, and Company: The Handloom Industry in Southeastern India 1750–1790', *Indian Economic and Social History Review* 17 (1978) pp. 257–281.

———, 'Protestants: The First Phase, 1650–1880', Christianity, Traditional Cultures and Nationalism: The South Asian Experience', *Bunker Memorial Lectures* (Jaffna, 1978) pp. 13–28.

———, 'Historical Foundation of the Economy of the Tamils of North Sri Lanka', *Chelvanavakam Memorial Lectures* (Jaffna, 1982) pp. 1–23.

———, 'The First Century of Protestant Christianity in Jaffna', *Indian Church History Review* 19 (1985) pp. 39–54.

———, 'Elements of Social and Economic Change in Dutch Maritime Ceylon (Sri Lanka) 1658–1796', *Indian Economic and Social History Review* 22 (1985) pp. 35–54.

———, 'The Rice Trade in Eastern India 1650–1740', *Modern Asian Studies* 22 (1988) pp. 533–542.

———, 'Ceylon in the Indian Ocean Trade: 1500–1800', in A. Das Gupta and M. N. Pearson (eds.), *India and the Indian Ocean 1500–1800* (Calcutta: Oxford U.P., 1999) pp. 224–239.

Armstrong, J. C., and N. A. Worden, 'The Slaves, 1652–1834', in: Richard Elphick and Hermann Giliomee (eds.), *The Shaping of South African Society, 1652–1820* (London: Longman, 1979) pp. 109–183.

Arroyo Abad, Leticia, Elwyn Davies, and Jan Luiten van Zanden, Between Conquest and Independence: Real Wages and Demographic Change in Spanish America, 1530–1820', *Explorations in Economic History* 49 (2012) pp. 149–166.

Austin, Gareth, 'The "Reversal of Fortune" Thesis and the Compression of History: Perspectives from African and Comparative Economic History', *Journal of International Development* 20 (2008) pp. 996–1027.

———, 'Resources, Techniques and Strategies South of the Sahara: Revising the Factor Endowments Perspective on African Economic Development, 1500–2000', *Economic History Review* 61 (2008) pp. 587–624.

Banerjee, Abjith, and Lakshmi Iyer, 'History, Institutions, and Economic Performance: The Legacy of Colonial Land Tenure Systems in India', *American Economic Review* 95 (2005) pp. 1190–1213.

Barrett, Greg, 'An Exploration of the Role of Portugal in the Economic Integration of Asia and Europe with a Focus on the Pepper Market', paper prepared for the *Asia-Pacific Economic and Business History Conference* 2012 (Canberra, 2012): http://apebh2012.files.wordpress.com/2011/05/apebh-text-of-paper-barrett.pdf.

Bassino, Jean-Pascal, and Debin Ma, 'Japanese Unskilled Wages in International Perspective, 1741–1913', *Research in Economic History* 23 (2006) pp. 229–248.

Bateman, Victoria N., 'The Evolution of Markets in Early Modern Europe, 1350–1800: A Study of Wheat Prices', *Economic History Review* 64 (2011) pp. 447–471.

Baten, Jörg, and Johan Fourie, 'Numeracy of Africans, Asians and Europeans during the Early Modern Period: New Evidence from Cape Colony Court Registers', *Economic History Review* (2015).

Baten, Jörg, Debin Ma, Stephen Morgan, and Qing Wang, 'Evolution of Living Standards and Human Capital in China in 18–20th Centuries: Evidences from Real Wages, Age-Heaping and Anthrometrics', *Explorations in Economic History* 47 (2010) pp. 347–359.

Baten, Jörg, and Jan Luiten van Zanden, 'Book Production and the Onset of Modern Economic Growth', *Journal of Economic Growth* 13 (2008) pp. 217–235.

Baten, Jörg, M. Stegl, and P. van der Eng, 'The Biological Standard of Living and Body Height in Colonial and Post-colonial Indonesia, 1770–2000', *Journal of Bioeconomics* 15 (2013) pp. 103–122.

Bayly, C. A., *Rulers, Townsmen and Bazaars: North Indian Society in the Age of British Expansion, 1770–1870* (Cambridge: Cambridge U.P., 1983).

———, 'Indigenous and Colonial Origins of Comparative Economic Development: The Case of Colonial India and Africa', *World Bank Policy Research Working Paper* 4474 (2008).

Bell, M., 'Working Hours in East Anglia during the First Industrial Revolution', *University of Oxford Manuscript* (2009).

Belt, Albert van den, *VOC bedrijf op Ceylon. Een voorname vestiging van de Oost-Indische Compagnie in de 18de eeuw* (Zutphen: Walburg Pers, 2008).

Belt, Albert van den, Jan Kok, and Kees Mandemakers, 'Digital Thombos: A New Source for 18th Century Sri Lankan Family History. Research Note', *History of the Family* 16 (2011) pp. 481–489.

Bhagwati, Jagdish, *In Defense of Globalization* (New York etc.: Oxford U.P., 2004).

Bhagwati, Jagdish, and T. N. Srinivasan, 'Trade and Poverty in the Poor Countries', *American Economic Review* 92 (2002) pp. 180–183.

Biewenga, Ad, *De Kaap de Goede Hoop: Een Nederlandse vestigingskolonie, 1680–1730* (Amsterdam: Bert Bakker, 1999).

Blachandran, B., and S. Subrahmanyam, 'On the History of Globalization and India: Concepts, Measures and Debates', in J. Assayag and C. J. Fuller (eds.), *Globalizing India: Perspectives from Below* (London: Anthem Press, 2005) pp. 17–46.

Bochove, Christiaan van, *The Economic Consequences of the Dutch. Economic Integration around the North Sea 1500–1800* (Amsterdam: Aksant, 2008).

Böeseken, A. J. *Nederlandsche Commissarissen aan de Kaap, 1657–1700* (The Hague: Martinus Nijhoff, 1938).

Bodenhorn, Howard, Timothy W. Guinnane, and Thomas A. Mroz, 'Sample-Selection Bias in the Historical Heights Literature', *Mimeo* (2012).

Boomgaard, Peter, 'Female Labour and Population Growth on Nineteenth Century Java', *Review of Indonesian and Malaysian Affairs* 15 (1981) pp. 1–31.

———, 'Buitenzorg in 1805: The Role of Money and Credit in a Colonial Frontier Society', *Modern Asian Studies* 20 (1986) pp. 33–58.

———, *Children of the Colonial State. Population Growth and Economic Development in Java 1795–1880* (Amsterdam: Free University Press, 1989).

———, 'Why Work for Wages? Free Labour in Java 1600–1900', *Economic and Social History in the Netherlands* 2 (1990) pp. 37–57.

———, 'The Non-agricultural Side of an Agricultural Economy, Java, 1500–1900', in: P. Alexander, P. Boomgaard, and B. White (eds.), *In the Shadow of Agriculture. Non-farming Activities in the Javanese Economy, Past and Present* (Amsterdam: Royal Tropical Institute, 1992).

———, 'Geld, krediet, rente en Europeanen in Zuid- en Zuidoost-Azie in de zeventiende eeuw', in: C. A. Davids, W. Fritchy, L. A. van der Valk, and P. W. Klein (eds.), *Kapitaal, ondernemerschap en beleid. Studies over economie en politiek in Nederland, Europa en Azië van 1500 tot heden* (NEHA: Amsterdam, 1996) pp. 483–510.

———, 'From Subsistence Crises to Business Cycle Depressions, Indonesia 1800–1940', *Itinerario* 26 (2002) pp. 35–51.

———, 'Human Capital, Slavery and Low Rates of Economic and Population Growth in Indonesia, 1600–1910', *Slavery and Abolition* (2003) pp. 83–96.

———, 'Labour, Land and Capital Markets in Early Modern Southeast Asia from the Fifteenth to the Nineteenth Century', *Continuity and Change* 24 (2009) pp. 55–78.

Boomgaard, Peter, and A. J. Gooszen, *Changing Economy in Indonesia. Vol. 11 Population Trends, 1795*–1942 (Amsterdam: Royal Tropical Institute, 1991).

Booth, Anne, 'Measuring Living Standards in Different Colonial Systems: Some Evidence from South East Asia, 1900–1942', *Modern Asian Studies* 46 (2012) pp. 1145–1181.

Booy, E. P. de, *De weldaet der scholen. Het plattelandsonderwijs in de provincie Utrecht van 1580 tot het begin der 19de eeuw* (Utrecht, 1977).

———, *Kweekhoven der Wijsheid. Basis- en vervolgonderwijs in de steden van de provincie Utrecht van 1580 tot het begin der 19e eeuw* (Zutphen, 1980).

Boshoff, Willem H., and Johan Fourie, 'The Significance of the Cape Trade Route to Economic Activity in the Cape Colony: A Medium-Term Business Cycle Analysis', *European Review of Economic History* 14 (2010) pp. 469–503.

Botha, G., *General History and Social Life of the Cape of Good Hope* (Cape Town: Struik, 1962).

Botham, F. W., and E. H. Hunt, 'Wages in Britain during the Industrial Revolution', *Economic History Review* 40 (1987) pp. 380–399.

Boven, M. W. van, 'Towards A New Age of Partnership (TANAP): An Ambitious World Heritage Project UNESCO Memory of the World', *VOC Archives Appendix* 2 (2002).

Bowden, Sue, Blessing Chiripanhura, and Paul Mosley, 'Measuring and Explaining Poverty in Six African Countries: A Long-Period Approach', *Journal of Economic Development* 20 (2008) pp. 1049–1079.

Boyer, George R., and Tim Hatton, 'Regional Labour market integration in England and Wales, 1850–1913', in: G. Grantham and M. MacKinnon (eds.), *Labour Market Evolution* (London, 1994) pp. 84–106.

Broadberry, Stephen, and Bishnupriya Gupta, 'The Early Modern Great Divergence: Wages, Prices and Economic Development in Europe and Asia, 1500–1800', *Economic History Review* 59 (2006) pp. 2–31.

———, 'Lancashire, India, and Shifting Competitive Advantage in Cotton Textiles, 1700–1850: The Neglected Role of Factor Prices', *Economic History Review* 62 (2009) pp. 279–305.

Broadberry, Stephen, Bruce Campbell, Alexander Klein, Mark Overton, and Bas van Leeuwen, 'British Economic Growth, 1270–1870: An Output-Based Approach' *Mimeo* (2012).

Broadberry, Stephen, Johann Custodis, and Bishnupriya Gupta, 'India and the Great Divergence: An Anglo-Indian Comparison of GDP per Capita, 1600–1871', *Explorations in Economic History* 55 (2015) pp. 58–75.

Brug, P. H. van der, *Malaria en malaise. De VOC in Batavia in de achttiende eeuw* (Amsterdam, 1994).

Bruijn, J. R., 'Between Batavia and the Cape: Shipping Patterns of the Dutch East India Company', *Journal of Southeast Asian Studies* 11 (1980) pp. 251–264.

———, 'Productivity, Profitability, and Costs of Private and Corporate Dutch Ship Owning in the Seventeenth and Eighteenth Centuries', in: J. D. Tracy (ed.), *The Rise of Merchant Empires. Long-Distance Trade in the Early Modern World, 1350–1750* (Cambridge: Cambridge U.P., 1990) pp. 174–194.

Bruijn, J. R., F. S. Gaastra, and I. Schöffer, *Dutch-Asiatic Shipping in the 17th and 18th Centuries.* Vols. 1–3 (The Hague: Nijhoff, 1979–1987).

Brunt, Liam, 'Property Rights and Economic Growth: Evidence from a Natural Experiment', *CEPR Discussion Paper no. 6404* (2007).

Bulbeck, Davi, Anthony Reid, Lay Cheng Tan, and Yiqi Wu, *Southeast Asian Exports since the 14th Century. Cloves, Pepper, Coffee and Sugar* (Leiden: KITLV, 1998).

Burnette, J., *Gender, Work and Wages in Industrial Revolution Britain* (Cambridge University Press, 2008).

Carey, Peter, 'Waiting for the "Just King": The Agrarian World of South-Central Java from Giyanti (1755) to the Java War (1825–1830)', *Modern Asian Studies* 20 (1986) pp. 59–137.

———, *The Power of Prophecy: Prince Dipanagara and the End of the Old Order in Java, 1785–1855* (Leiden: KITLV Press, 2007).

Carmichael, Sarah, 'Pearls, Girl's Best Friend? Sri Lankan Women's Status at the Beginning of the 20th Century as the Roots of Their Current Position', Paper presented at the *Utrecht Seminar in Social and Economic History* (November 2011).

Chandra, Satish, 'Standard of Living', in: Tapan Raychaudhuri and Irfan Habib (eds.), *The Cambridge Economic History of India. Volume I: c. 1200–c. 1750* (Cambridge: Cambridge University Press, 1982) pp. 458–477.

Chaudhuri, K. N., *The English East India Company; the Study of an Early Joint-Stock Company, 1600–1640* (London: F. Cass, 1965).

———, *The Trading World of Asia and the English East India Company, 1660–1760* (Cambridge: Cambridge U.P., 1978).

Chaudhury, Sushil, 'The Financing of Investments in Bengal, 1650–1720', *Indian Economic and Social History Review* 8 (1972) pp. 109–133.

———, 'Merchants, Companies and Rulers: Bengal in the Eighteenth Century', *Journal of the Economic and Social History of the Orient* 31 (1988) pp. 74–109.

———, 'European Companies and the Bengal Textile Industry in the Eighteenth Century: The Pitfalls of Applying Quantitative Techniques', *Modern Asian Studies* 27 (1993) pp. 321–340.

———, *From Prosperity to Decline: Eighteenth Century Bengal* (New Delhi: Manohar, 1995).

Chiao, Chi-Ming, 'A Study of Chinese Population', *Milbank Memorial Fund Quarterly Bulletin* 11 (1933) pp. 325–341.

Chilosi, David, Tommy E. Murphy, Roman Studer, and A. Coşkun Tunçer, 'Europe's Many Integrations: Geography and Grain Markets, 1620–1913', *Explorations in Economic History* 50 (2013) pp. 46–68.

Chor, Davin, 'Institutions, Wages, and Inequality: The Case of Europe and Its Periphery (1500–1899)', *Explorations in Economic History* 42 (2005) 547–566.

Cilliers, Jeanne, and Johan Fourie, 'New Estimates of Settler Life Span and Other Demographic Estimates from South Africa, 1652–1948', *Econonomic History of Developing Regions*. 27 (2012), pp. 61–86.

Claasens, H. W., *Die geskiedenis van boerekos, 1652–1806* (Pretoria: Protea Boekhuis, 2006).

Clark, Gregory, 'The Cost of Capital and Medieval Agricultural Technique', *Explorations in Economic History* 25 (1988) pp. 265–294, there p. 265.

———, 'The Condition of the Working Class in England, 1209–2004', *Journal of Political Economy* 11 (2005) pp. 1307–1340.

———, *A Farewell to Alms: A Brief Economic History of the World* (Princeton: Princeton U.P., 2007).

Clark, Gregory, and Ysbrand van der Werf, 'Work in Progress? The Industrious Revolution', *Journal of Economic History* 58 (1998) pp. 830–843.

Clingingsmith, David, and Jeffrey G. Williamson, 'Deindustrialization in 18th and 19th Century India: Mughal Decline, Climate Shocks and British Industrial Ascent', *Explorations in Economic History* 45 (2008) pp. 209–234.

Crafts, Nicholas, 'Regional Price Variations in England in 1843: An Aspect of the Standard-of-Living Debate', *Explorations in Economic History* 19 (1982) pp. 51–70.

———, 'The Human Development Index 1870–1999: Some Revised Estimates', *European Review of Economic History* 6 (2002) pp. 395–405.

Datta, Rajat, *Society, Economy and the Market: Commercialization in Rural Bengal, c. 1760–1800* (Delhi: Manohar, 2000).

Deaton, Angus, 'Income, Health, and Well-Being around the World: Evidence from the Gallup World Poll', *Journal of Economic Perspectives* 22 (2008) pp. 53–72.

Deb Roy, Rama, 'Population of the Province of Bengal, 1751–1801', *Population Studies Unit, Indian Statistical Institute*: http://dmo.econ.msu.ru/epc2001_history/Authors/Rama/RamaRoy.htm. Last accessed, July 3rd, 2014.

Dell, Melissa, 'The Persistent Effects of Peru's Mining Mita', *Econometrica* 78 (2010) pp. 1863–1903.

Dewasiri, Nirmal Ranjith, *The Adaptable Peasant. Agrarian Society in Western Sri Lanka under Dutch Rule, 1740–1800* (Leiden & Boston: Brill, 2008).

Dobado-Gonzales, Rafael, Alfredo Garcia-Hiernaux, and David E. Guerrero, 'The Integration of Grain Markets in the Eighteenth Century: Early Rise of Globalization in the West', *Journal of Economic History* 72 (2012) pp. 671–707.

———, 'West versus East: Early Globalization and the Great Divergence', *Mimeo* 2013.

Domar, Evsey D., 'The Causes of Slavery or Serfdom: A Hypothesis', *Economic History Review* 30 (1970) pp. 18–32.

Duin, Pieter van, and Robert Ross, 'The Economy of the Cape Colony in the Eighteenth Century', *Intercontinenta* 7 (Leiden: Centre for the History of European Expansion, 1987).

Dyke, Paul A. van, *The Canton Trade: Life and Enterprise on the China Coast, 1700–1845* (Hong Kong: Hong Kong U.P., 2006).

Easterly, William, and Ross Levine, 'Africa's Growth Tragedy: Policies and Ethnic Divisions', *Quarterly Journal of Economics* 112 (1997) pp. 1203–1250.

Elphick, R., and V. C. Malherbe, 'The Khoisan to 1828', in: Richard Elphick and Hermann Giliomee (eds.), *The Shaping of South African Society, 1652–1820* (London: Longman, 1979) pp. 3–64.

Emmer, Piet, and Jos Gommans, *Rijk aan de rand van de wereld. De Geschiedenis van Nederland overzee 1600–1800* (Amsterdam: Bert Bakker, 2012).

Engerman, Stanley L., 'The Standard of Living Debate in International Perspective: Measures and Indicators', in: R. Steckel and R. Floud (eds.), *Health and Welfare during Industrialization* (Chicago: University of Chicago Press, 1997) pp. 17–45.

Epstein, S. R., 'Craft Guilds, Apprenticeship, and Technological Change in Preindustrial Europe', *Journal of Economic History* 58 (September 1998) pp. 684–713.

Federico, Giovanni, 'When did European markets integrate?', *European Review of Economic History* 15 (2011) p. 93–126.

———, 'How Much Do We Know about Market Integration in Europe', *Economic History Review* 65 (2012) pp. 470–497.

Feenstra, Alberto, 'Kisten met Koper. De opmarks van de Nederlandse duit in het Javaanse geldverkeer 1720–1850' (unpublished MA thesis: Free University Amsterdam, 2012).

———, 'Dutch Coins for Asian Growth. VOC-Duiten to Assess Java's Deep Monetisation and Economic Growth, 1724–1800', *Low Countries Journal of Social and Economic History* 11 (2014).

Feinstein, Charles H., 'Changes in Nominal Wages, the Cost of Living and Real Wages in the United Kingdom over Two Centuries, 1780–1990', in: Peter Scholliers and Vera Zamagni (eds.), *Labour's Reward. Real Wages and Economic Change in 19th and 20th Century Europe* (Aldershot: Edward Elgar, 1995).

———, 'Pessimism Perpetuated: Real Wages and the Standard of Living in Britain during and after the Industrial Revolution', *Journal of Economic History* 58 (1998) pp. 625–58.

———, *An Economic History of South Africa. Conquest, Discrimination and Development* (Cambridge and New York: Cambridge University Press, 2005).

Ferguson, Niall, *Empire: How Britain Made the Modern World* (London: Allen Lane, 2002).

Findlay, Ronald, and Keven H. O'Rourke, 'Commodity Market Integration, 1500–2000' in: Michael D. Bordo, Alan M. Taylor, and Jeffrey G. Williamson (eds.), *Globalization in Historical Perspective* (Chicago: University of Chicago Press, 2003).

———, *Power and Plenty. Trade, War, and the World Economy in the Second Millennium* (Princeton: Princeton U.P., 2007).

Flynn, Dennis O., and Arturo Giraldez, 'Born with a "Silver Spoon"': The Origin of World Trade in 1571', *Journal of World History* 6 (1995) pp. 201–221.

———, 'Cycles of Silver: Global Economic Unity through the Mid-eighteenth Century', *Journal of World History* 13 (2002) pp. 391–427.

———, 'Path Dependence, Time Lags and the Birth of Globalization: A Critique of O'Rourke and Williamson', *European Review of Economic History* 8 (2004) pp. 81–108.

———, 'Born Again: Globalization's Sixteenth Century Origins (Asian/Global versus European Dynamics)', *Pacific Economic Review* 13 (2008) pp. 359–387.

Flinn, M. W., 'Trends in Real Wages, 1750–1850', *Economic History Review*, 27 (1974) pp. 395–413.

Fourie, Johan, *An Inquiry into the Nature, Causes and Distribution of Wealth in the Cape Colony, 1652–1795* (unpublished PhD thesis, Utrecht University, 2012).

———, 'The Remarkable Wealth of the Dutch Cape Colony: Measurements from Eighteenth-Century Probate Inventories', *Economic History Review* 66 (2013) pp. 419–448.

Fourie, Johan, and J. Uys, 'Luxury Product Consumption in Eighteenth-Century Cape Colony Households', *Low Countries Journal of Social and Economic History* 9 (2012) pp. 29–60.

Fourie, Johan, and Jan Luiten van Zanden, 'GDP in the Dutch Cape Colony: The National Accounts of a Slave-Based Society', *South African Journal of Economics* 81 (2013) pp. 467–490.

Frank, Andre Gunder, *AccumulationWorld, 1492–1789* (London: Macmillan, 1978).

———, *Dependent Accumulation and Underdevelopment* (London: Macmillan, 1979).

———, *ReORIENT: Global Economy in the Asian Age* (Berkely: University of California Press, 1988).

Frankema, Ewout, and Marlous van Waijenburg, 'Structural Impediments to African Growth? New Evidence from Real Wages in British Africa, 1880–1965', *Journal of Economic History* 72 (2012) pp. 895–926.

Gaastra, Femme S., 'Ceylon als "handelscomptoir" van de VOC', in: R. Kromhout (ed.), *Het Machtige Eyland, Ceylon en de VOC* (Den Haag, 1988) pp. 29–36.

———, *De Geschiedenis van de VOC* (Zutphen: Walburg Pers, 2002).

Gaastra, Femme S., and Jaap R. Bruijn, 'The Dutch East India Company's Shipping, 1602–1795, in a Comparative Perspective', in: Ibid. (eds.), *Ships, Sailors and Spices. East India Companies and Their Shipping in the 16th, 17th and 18th Centuries* (Amsterdam: NEHA, 1993) pp. 177–208.

Galor, Oded, 'From Stagnation to Growth: Unified Growth Theory', in: P. Aghion and S. Durlauf (eds.), *Handbook of Economic Growth* (Amsterdam 2005) pp. 172–293.

Gilbert, Geoffrey, 'Adam Smith on the Nature and Causes of Poverty', *Review of Social Economy* 55 (1997) pp. 274–291.

Gilboy, Elizabeth W., *Wages in Eighteenth Century England* (Cambridge: Harvard U.P., 1934).

Glaeser, Edward, R. La Porta, F. Lopez-de-Silanes, A. Shleifer, 'Do Institutions Cause Growth?' *Journal of Economic Growth* 9 (2004) pp. 271–303.

Glamann, Kristof, 'European Trade 1500–1750', in: Carlo M. Cipolla (ed.), *The Sixteenth and Seventeenth Centuries* (1974).

———, *Dutch-Asiatic Trade 1620–1740* (The Hague: Nijhoff, 1981).

Goonewardena, K. W., *The Foundation of Dutch Power in Ceylon, 1638–1658* (Amsterdam: Djambatan, 1958).

Goor, Jurrien van, *Jan Kompenie as schoolmaster. Dutch education in Ceylon 1690–1795* (Groningen: Wolters-Noordhoff, 1978).

———, *De Nederlandse Koloniën. Geschiedenis van de Nederlandse expansie 1600–1875* (The Hague: SDU, 1994).

Guelke, Leonard, 'Frontier Settlement in Early Dutch South Africa', *Annals of the Association of American Geographers* 66 (1976) pp. 25–42.

Gupta, Bishnupriya, 'Competition and Control in the Market for Textiles: Indian Weavers and the English East India Company in the Eighteenth Century', in: Giorgio Riello and Tirthankar Roy (eds.), *How India Clothed the World. The World of South Asian Textiles, 1500–1850* (Leiden: Brill, 2009) pp. 281–308.

———, 'Where Have All the Brides Gone? Son Preference and Marriage in India over the Twentieth Century', *Economic History Review* 67 (2014) pp. 1–24.

Haan, Frederik de, *Priangan: de Preanger-regentschappen onder het Nederlandsch bestuur tot 1811* (Batavia: 1910–12).

Habib, Irfan, 'Monetary System and Prices', in: Tapan Raychaudhuri and Irfan Habib (eds.), *The Cambridge Economic History of India*. Vol. 1 (Cambridge, 1982) pp. 76–93.

———, 'Potentialities of Capitalistic Development in the Economy of Mughal India', in: Ibid., *Essays in Indian History* (Delhi, 1995).

Haider, Najaf, 'The Quantity Theory and Mughal Monetary History', *Medieval History Journal* 2 (1999) pp. 309–348.

———, 'Structure and Movement of Wages in the Mughal Empire, 1500–1700', in: J. Lucassen (ed.), *Wages and Currency. Global Comparisons from Antiquity to the Twentieth Century* (Bern: Peter Lang, 2007) pp. 293–321.

Hajnal, J., 'European Marriage in Perspective', in: D. V. Glass and D. E. C. Eversley (eds.), *Population in History* (1965) pp. 101–143.

Hall, Kenneth R., 'Coinage, Trade and Economy in Early South India and Its Southeast Asian Neighbours', *Indian Economic and Social History Review* 36 (1999) pp. 431–459.

Hanauer, A. C., *Etudes economiques sur l'Alsace, ancienne et moderne* (Strasbourg: Hagemann, Librairie, 1878).

Hanna, Willard A., *Indonesian Banda: Colonialism and Its Aftermath in the Nutmeg Islands* (Philadelphia: ISHI, 1978).

Hariharan, S., *Cotton Textiles and Corporate Buyers in Cottonpolis: A Study of Purchase and Prices in Gujarat 1600–1800* (New Delhi: Manak 2002) pp. 298–305.

Harley, C. Knick, 'Ocean Freight Rates and Productivity 1740–1913: The Primacy of Mechanical Invention Reaffirmed', *Journal of Economic History* 48 (1988) pp. 851–876.

Hersh, Jonathan, and Hans-Joachim Voth, 'Sweet Diversity: Colonial Goods and Welfare Gains from Trade after 1492', *Mimeo* (2011).

Heston, Alan, 'National Income', in: Dharma Kumar (ed.), *Cambridge Economic History of India, vol. 2, 1575–1970* (Cambridge: Cambridge U.P., 1983) pp. 376–462.

Hill, Christopher, *The Century of Revolution, 1603–1714* (New York: W. W. Norton, 1966).

Hillmann, Henning, and Christina Gathmann, 'Overseas Trade and the Decline of Privateering', *Journal of Economic History* 71 (2011) 730–761.

Hoadly, Mason C., 'Slavery, Bondage, and Dependency in Pre-colonial Java: The Cirebon-Priangan Region, 1700', in: Anthony Reid (ed.), *Slavery, Bondage and Dependency in Southeast Asia* (St. Lucia, 1983) pp. 90–117.

———, *Towards a Feudal Mode of Production: West Java, 1680–1800* (Singapore: Institute of Southeast Asian Studies, 1994).

Hoffman, Phillip T., David Jacks, Patricia A. Levin, and Peter H. Lindert, 'Real Inequality in Europe since 1500', *Journal of Economic History* 62 (2002) pp. 322–355.

Hopkins, Anthony G., 'The New Economic History of Africa', *Journal of African History* 50 (2009) pp. 155–177.

Horrel, Sara, and Jane Humphries, 'Women's Labour Force Participation and the Transition to the Male-Breadwinner Family, 1790–1865', *Economic History Review* 48 (1995) pp. 89–117.

Hossain, Hameeda, *The Company Weavers of Bengal. The East India Company and the Organization of Textile Production in Bengal 1750–1813* (Delhi, etc.: Oxford U.P., 1988).

Humphries, Jan, 'English Apprenticeship: A Neglected Factor in the First Industrial Revolution', in: Paul A. David and Mark Thomas (eds.), *The Economic Future in Historical Perspective* (Oxford: Oxford University Press, 2003) pp. 73–102.

———, 'The Lure of Aggregates and the Pitfalls of the Patriarchal Perspective: A Critique of the High Wage Economy Interpretation of the British Industrial Revolution', *Economic History Review* 66 (2013) pp. 693–714.

Humphries, Jane, and Jacob Weisdorf, 'The Wages of Women in England, 1260–1850', *Oxford Economic and Social History Working Papers* 127 (2014).

Hunt, E. H., *Regional Wage Variations in Britain 1850–1914* (Oxford: Oxford U.P., 1973).

———, 'Industrialisation and Regional Inequality: Wages in Britain, 1760–1914', *Journal of Economic History* 46 (1986) pp. 935–966.

Hussain, A. S. M. A., 'A Quantitative Study of Price Movements in Bengal during Eighteenth and Nineteenth Centuries' (London: unpublished PhD thesis, 1976).

Irwin, Douglas A., 'Mercantilist as Strategic Trade Policy: The Anglo-Dutch Rivalry for the East India Trade', *Journal of Political Economy* 99 (1991) pp. 1296–1314.

———, 'Strategic Trade Policy and Mercantilist Trade Rivalries', *American Economic Review* 82 (1992) pp. 134–139.

Israel, Jonathan I., *The Dutch Republic: Its Rise, Greatness, and Fall, 1477–1806* (Oxford: Oxford U.P., 1995).

Jacks, David S., 'Intra- and International Commodity Market Integration in the Atlantic Economy, 1800–1913', *Explorations in Economic History* 42 (2005) pp. 381–413.

Jacobs, Els M., *Merchant in Asia: The Trade of the Dutch East India Company during the Eighteenth Century* (Leiden: CNWS Publications, 2013).

Jerven, Morten, *Poor Numbers: How We are Misled by African Development Statistics and What to Do About It* (Cornell: Cornell U.P., 2013).

Jha, Murari, *The Political Economy of the Ganga River. Highway of State Formation in Mughal India, c. 1600–1800* (unpublished PhD thesis, Leiden 2013).

Jones, Eric L., *The European Miracle: Environments, Economies and Geopolitics in the History of Europe and Asia* (Cambridge: Cambridge U.P., 1981).

Jordan, Stacey C., 'Coarse Earthenware at the Dutch Colonial Cape of Good Hope, South Africa: A History of Local Production and Typology of Products', *International Journal of Historical Archaeology* 4 (2000) pp. 113–143.

Kathirithamby-Wells, J., *The British West Sumatran Presidency (1760–85): Problems of Early Colonial Enterprise* (Kuala Lumpur: Penerbit Universiti Malaya, 1977).

Kenny, Charles, 'Why are We Worried about Income? Nearly Everything That Matters is Converging', *World Development* 33 (2005) pp. 1–19.

Kian, Kwee Hui, 'Production, Consumption and Trade of Javanese Cotton Yarn and Textile in the late Seventeenth and Eighteenth Century', Paper presented at *GEHN Conference on Cotton Textiles* (Pune 2005).

Kiewiet, C. W. de, *A History of South Africa. Social and Economic* (London: Oxford U.P., 1972).

Knaap, Gerrit, 'Europeans, Mestizos and Slaves: The Population of Colombo at the End of the Seventeenth Century', *Itinerario* 5 (1981).

———, 'The Demography of Ambon in the Seventeenth Century: Evidence from Colonial Proto-Censuses', *Journal of Southeast Asian Studies* 26 (1995) pp. 227–241.

———, 'Shipping and Trade in Java, c. 1775; A Quantitative Analysis', *Modern Asian Studies* 33 (1999) pp. 405–420.

———, *Kruidnagelen en Christenen. De VOC en de bevolking van Ambon 1656–1696* (Leiden: KITLV, 2004).

———, 'Semarang. A Colonial Provincial Capital and Port City in Java, circa 1775', in: U. Bosma and T. Webster (eds.), *Commodities, Ports and Asian Maritime Trade, c. 1750–1950* (Palgrave/Macmillan 2015).

Knaap, Gerrit, and Luc Nagtegaal, 'A Forgotten Trade: Salt in Southeast Asia 1670–1813', in: Roderich Ptak and Dietmar Rothermund (eds.), *Emporia, Commodities and Entrepreneurs in Asian Maritime Trade, c. 1400–1750* (Stuttgard: Franz Steiner, 1991) pp. 127–158.

Kock, M. H. de, *Economic History of South Africa* (Cape Town: Juta, 1924).

Kotelawela, D. A., 'Agrarian Policies of the Dutch in South-West Ceylon 1743–1767', *A. A. G. Bijdragen* 14 (1967) pp. 3–34.

Kremers, Rutger, *On the Colonial Roots of South Africa's Divergence: A Comprehensive Analysis of South African Economic Performance, 1600–1961* (unpublished MA thesis: Utrecht University, 2013).

La Porta, R., F. Lopez-de-Silanes, A. Shleifer, and R. Vishny, 'Law and Finance', *Journal of Political Economy* 106 (1998) pp. 1113–1155.

Labrousse, C. E., 'Economic Fluctuations and the Individual', in: M. Aymard and H. Mukhia (eds.), *French Studies in History, Vol. 1: The Inheritance* (Delhi, 1989).

Landes, David S., *The Unbound Prometheus: Technological Change and Industrial Development in Western Europe from 1750 to the Present* (Cambridge: Cambridge University Press, 1969).

———, *The Wealth and Poverty of Nations: Why Some are So Rich and Some So Poor* (London: Little/Brown, 1998).

Laslett, P., 'Mean Household Size in England since the Sixteenth Century', in: P. Laslett and R. Wall (eds.), *Household and Family in Past Time* (Cambridge, 1972) pp. 125–158.

Lavely, William, and R. Bin Wong, 'Revising the Malthusian Narrative: The Comparative Study of Population Dynamics in the Late Imperial China', *Journal of Asian Studies* 57 (1998) pp. 714–648.

Lee, James Z., and Wang Feng, *One Quarter of Humanity. Malthusian Mythology and Chinese Realities, 1700–2000* (Cambridge, Mass.: Harvard U.P., 2001).

Leeuwen, Marco van, and Ineke Maas, *HISCO. A Historical International Standard Classification of Occupations* (Leuven, 2002).

Leigh, A., and P. van der Eng, 'Top Incomes in Indonesia, 1920–2004', in: A. B. Atkinson and T. Piketty (eds.), *Top Incomes: A Global Perspective* (Oxford: Oxford U.P., 2010) pp. 171–219.

LeQuin, F., *Het personeel van de Verenigde Oost-Indische Compagnie in Azië, meer in het bijzonder de vestiging Bengalen* (Leiden, 1982).

Leur, J. C. van, *Indonesian Trade and Society: Essays in Asian Social and Economic History* (The Hague: Van Hoeve, 1955).

Lewis, W. Arthur, 'Economic Development with Unlimited Supplies of Labour', *Manchester School of Economic and Social Studies* 22 (1954) pp. 139–191.

Lieberman, Victor, *Strange Parallels: Southeast Asia in Global Context, c. 800–1830* (Cambridge: Cambridge U.P., 2009).

Lindert, Peter H. et al., 'Preliminary Global Price Comparisons, 1500–1870', Paper presented at the conference *Towards a Global History of Prices and Wages* (IISH Amsterdam, 2004).

Lindert, Peter H., and Jeffrey G. Williamson, 'English Workers' Living Standards during the Industrial Revolution: A New Look', *Economic History Review* 36 (1983) pp. 1–25.

Livi-Bacci, Massim, *A Concise History of World Population* (Malden, Mass., etc.: Blackwell, 2007).

Lucassen, Jan, 'Introduction: Wages and Currency, 500 BCE–2000 CE', in: J. Lucassen (ed.), *Wages and Currency. Global Comparisons from Antiquity to the Twentieth Century* (Bern: Peter Lang, 2007) pp. 9–58.

———, 'Working at the Ichapur Gunpowder Factory in the 1790s (Part I)', *Indian Historical Review* 39 (2012) pp. 19–56.

———, 'Working at the Ichapur Gunpowder Factory in the 1790s (Part II)', *Indian Historical Review* 39 (2012) pp. 251–271.

Lucassen, Jan, and Richard W. Unger, 'Labour Productivity in Ocean Shipping 1500–1850', *International Journal of Maritime History* 12 (2000).

MacEvedy, Colin, and Richard Jones, *Atlas of World Population History* (Harmondsworth: Penguin Books, 1978).

MacGillivray, Alex, *A Brief History of Globalization* (London: Constable & Robinson, 2006).

Maddison, Angus, 'Dutch Income in and from Indonesia 1700–1938', *Modern Asian Studies* 23 (1989) pp. 645–670.

Malthus, Thomas, *An Essay on the Principle of Population, as It Affects the Future Improvement of Society with Remarks on the Speculations of Mr. Godwin, M. Condorcet, and Other Writers* (1998 [Original 1798]).

Marshall, P. J., *Bengal – The British Bridgehead* (Cambridge: Cambridge University Press, 1987).

McCants, Anne E., 'Consumer Behaviour in an Early Modern Dutch Orphanage: A Wealth of Choice', *Journal of European Economic History* 22 (1993) pp. 121–142.

———, 'Exotic Goods, Popular Consumption, and the Standard of Living: Thinking about Globalization in the Early Modern World', *Journal of World History* 18 (2007) pp. 433–462.

———, 'Poor Consumers as Global Consumers: The Diffusion of Tea and Coffee Drinking in the Eighteenth Century' *Economic History Review* 61 (2008) pp. 172–200.

Meilink-Roelofsz, M. A. P., *Asian Trade and European Influence in the Indonesian Archipelago between 1500 and about 1630* (The Hague, 1962).

Menard, Russel, 'Transport Costs and Long-Range Trade, 1300–1800: Was There a European "Transport Revolution" in the Early Modern Era?' in: J. D. Tracy (ed.), *Political Economy of Merchant Empires* (Cambridge: Cambridge U.P., 1991) pp. 228–275.

Mitchener, Kris J., and Marc Weidenmier, 'Trade and Empire', *NBER Working Paper 13765* (Cambridge 2008).

Mokyr, Joel, *The Lever of Riches: Technological Creativity and Economic Progress* (Oxford and New York: Oxford U.P., 1990).

———, *The Enlightened Economy. An Economic History of Britain 1700–1850* (New Haven and London: Yale U.P., 2009).

Moor, Tine de, and Jan Luiten van Zanden, 'Girl Power: The European Marriage Pattern and Labour markets in the North Sea Region in the Late Medieval and Early Modern Period', *Economic History Review* 63 (2010) pp. 1–33.

Moosvi, Shireen, *People, Taxation and Trade in Mughal India* (Oxford, etc.: Oxford U.P., 2008).

———, 'The World of Labour in Mughal India', *International Review of Social History* 56 (2011) pp. 245–261.

Moreland, W. H., and P. Geyl (transl.), *Jahangir's India. The Remonstrantie of Francisco Pelsaert* (Cambridge: W. Heffer & Sons Ltd., 1925).

Mukerjee, Radhakamal, *The Economic History of India* (London: Longmans, 1945).

Mukherjee, Tilottama, 'Markets in Eighteenth Century Bengal Economy', *Indian Economic and Social History Review* 48 (2011) pp. 143–176.

Mukund, Kanakalatha, *The Trading World of the Tamil Merchant. Evolution of Merchant Capitalism in the Coromandel* (Chennai: Orient Longman Ltd., 1999).

Myint, Hla, *The Economics of the Developing Countries* (London, 1964).

Nadri, Ghulam, *Eighteenth-Century Gujarat: The Dynamics of Its Political Economy 1750–1800* (Leiden: Brill, 2008).

Nagtegaal, Luc, *Rijden op een Hollandse Tijger. De noordkust van Java en de V.O.C. 1680–1743* (unpublished PhD thesis, Utrecht University, 1988).

———, *Riding the Dutch tiger: The Dutch East Indies Company and the northeast coast of Java, 1680–1743* (Leiden: KITLV Press, 1996).

Nakane, C., 'An Interpretation of the Size and Structure of the Household in Japan over Three Centuries', in: P. Laslett and R. Wall (eds.), *Household and Family in Past Time* (Cambridge, 1972).

Nederveen Meerkerk, Elise van, 'Couples Cooperating? Dutch Textile Workers, Family Labour and the "Industrious Revolution", c. 1600–1800', *Continuity and Change* 23 (2008) 237–266.

———, 'Market Wage or Discrimination? The Remuneration of Male and Female Wool Spinners in the Seventeenth-Century Dutch Republic', *Economic History Review* 63 (2010) pp. 165–186.

———, 'From Male Breadwinner to Family Wage: Suggestions for Reconstructing Long-Term Series of Wages in Pre-industrial and Industrializing Societies', Presented at the *CLIO-INFRA Real Wage Workshop*, International Institute of Social History (2012).

Nehru, Jawaharlal, *The Discovery of India* (Delhi, Oxford and New York: Oxford U.P., 1994 [1946]).

Nieboer, Herman J., *Slavery as an Industrial System: Ethnological Researches* (The Hague: Nijhoff, 1910).

Niel, Robert van, 'Economic and Population Changes in Java, 1750–1850', in: A. Hayami and Y. Tsubouchi (eds.), *Economic and Demographic Development in Rice Producing Societies: Some Aspects of East Asian Economic History, 1500–1900* (Leuven: 1990) pp. 291–315.

———, *Java's Northeast Coast 1740–1840: A Study in Colonial Encroachment and Dominance* (Leiden: CNWS, 2005).

Noques-Marco, Pilar, 'Euro-Asian Globalization in the Early Modern Period (1664–1820s): Trade Boom or Price Convergence?' Paper presented at the conference on *Trade, Poverty and Growth in History* (Madrid 2012).

Nordhaus, William D., 'Do Real Output and Real Wage Measures Capture Reality? The History of Light Suggests Not', in: Robert J. Gordon and Timothy F. Bresnahan (eds.), *The Economics of New Goods* (Chicago: University of Chicago Press, 1997) pp. 29–66.

North, Douglass C., 'Ocean Freight Rates and Economic Development, 1750–1913', *Journal of Economic History* 18 (1958) pp. 537–555.

———, 'Sources of Productivity Change in Ocean Shipping, 1600–1850', *Journal of Political Economy* (1968) pp. 953–970.

North, Douglass C., and Robert P. Thomas, *The Rise of the Western World: A New Economic History* (Cambridge: Cambridge U.P., 1973).

North, Douglass C., and Barry Weingast, 'Constitutions and Commitment: The Evolution of Institutions Governing Public Choice in Seventeenth-Century England', *Journal of Economic History* 49 (1989) pp. 803–832.

Nunn, Nathan, 'The Importance of History for Economic Development', *Annual Review of Economics* 1 (2009) pp. 65–92.

O'Brien, Patrick K., 'European Economic Development: The Contribution of the Periphery', *Economic History Review* 35 (1982) pp. 1–18.

Olsson, Ola, 'On the Institutional Legacy of Mercantilist and Imperialist Colonialism', *Working Papers in Economics* 247 (March 2007).

———, 'On the Democratic Legacy of Colonialism', *Journal of Comparative Economics* 37 (2009) pp. 534–551.

O'Rourke, Kevin H., and Jeffrey G. Williamson, 'When Did Globalisation Begin?' *European Review of Economic History* 6 (2002) pp. 23–50.

———, 'After Columbus: Explaining Europe's Overseas Trade Boom, 1500–1800', *Journal of Economic History* 62 (2002) pp. 417–456.

———, 'Once More: When Did Globalisation Begin?' *European Review of Economic History* 8 (2004) pp. 109–117.

———, 'Did Vasco da Gama matter to European Markets?' *Economic History Review* 62 (2009) pp. 665–684.

———, 'From Malthus to Ohlin: Trade, Growth, and Distribution since 1500', *Journal of Economic Growth* 10 (2005) pp. 5–34.

O'Rourke, Kevin H., Leandro Prados de la Escosura, and Guilaume Daudin, 'Trade and Empire', in: Stephen Broadberry and Kevin H. O'Rourke (eds.), *The Cambridge Economic History of Modern Europe* (Cambridge: Cambridge U.P., 2010) pp. 96–121.

Osterhammel, Jürgen, *Colonialism: A Theoretical Overview* (Princeton: Princeton U.P., 1999).

Özmucur, Süleyman, and Sevket Pamuk, 'Real Wages and Standards of Living in the Ottoman Empire, 1489–1914', *Journal of Economic History* 62 (2002) pp. 293–321, there p. 294.

———, 'Did European Commodity Prices Converge before 1800?' in: T. J. Hatton, K. H. O'Rourke and A. M. Taylor (eds.), *The New Comparative Economic History: Essays in Honour of Jeffrey G. Williamson* (Cambridge, MA: MIT Press, 2007) pp. 59–85.

Pamuk, Sevket, 'The Black Death and the Origins of the "Great Divergence" across Europe, 1300–1600', *European Review of Economic History* 11 (2007) pp. 289–317.

Parthasarathi, Prasannan, 'Rethinking Wages and Competitiveness in the Eighteenth Century: Britain and South India', *Past and Present* 158 (1998) pp. 79–109.

———, *The Transition to a Colonial Economy: Weavers, Merchants and Kings in South India* (Cambridge: Cambridge U.P., 2001).

———, 'Agriculture, Labour, and the Standard of Living in 18th Century India', in: Robert C. Allen, Tommy Bengtsson, and Martin Dribe (eds.), *Living Standards in the Past: New Perspectives on Well-Being in Asia and Europe* (Oxford: Oxford U.P., 2005) pp. 99–110.

———, 'Cotton Textiles in the Indian Subcontinent 1200–1800', in: Giorgio Riello and Prasannan Parthasarathi (eds.), *The Spinning World: A Global History of Cotton Textiles, 1200–1800* (Oxford: Oxford U.P., 2009).

———, *Why Europe Grew Rich and Asia Did Not. Global Economic Divergence, 1600–1850* (Cambridge: Cambridge U.P., 2011).

Patrizio, P., S. Muller, J. Cilliers, and J. Fourie. 'The Transmission of Longevity across Generations: The Case of the Settler Cape Colony', *Research in Social Stratification and Mobility* 35 (2014) pp. 105–119.

Persson, Karl Gunnar, *Grain Markets in Europe, 1500–1900: Integration and Deregulation* (Cambridge: Cambridge U. P, 1999).

Phelps-Brown, E. H. and S. V. Hopkins, 'Seven Centuries of the Prices of Consumables, Compared with Builders' Wage-Rates', *Economica* 22 (1956) pp. 195–206.

Pieris, P. E., *Ceylon and the Hollanders 1658–1796* (Tellipalai, 1918).

Plessis, A. J. du, *Die geskiedenis van die graankultuur in Suid-Afrika, 1652–1752* (Cape Town, 1933).

Plessis, Sophia du, and Stan du Plessis, 'Happy in the Service of the Company: The Purchasing Power of VOC Salaries at the Cape in the 18th Century', *Economic History of Developing Regions* 27 (2012) pp. 125–149.

Pomeranz, Kenneth, *The Great Divergence. China, Europe and the Making of the Modern World Economy* (Princeton: Princeton U.P., 2000).

———, 'Political Economy and Ecology on the Eve of Industrialization: Europe, China, and the Global Conjuncture', *American Historical Review* 107 (2002) pp. 425–446.

Pomeranz, Kenneth, and Steven C. Topik, *The World That Trade Created: Society, Culture and the World Economy, 1400 to the Present* (Armonk: Sharpe, 1999).

Posthumus, N. W., *Nederlandsche Prijsgeschiedenis* (Leiden: Brill, 1943).

Potter, Robert P., Tony Binns, Jennifer A. Elliott, and David Smith, *Geographies of Development* (Harlow: Pearson, 2004).

Prak, Maarten, *Gouden Eeuw. Het Raadsel van de Republiek* (Nijmegen: SUN, 2002).

Prakash, Om, 'Bullion for Goods: International Trade and the Economy of Early Eighteenth Century Bengal', *Indian Economic and Social History Review* 13 (1976) pp.159–187.

———, 'European Trade and South Asian Economies: Some Regional Contrasts, 1600–1800', in: Leonard Blussé and Femme S. Gaastra (eds.), *Companies and Trade* (Leiden: Leiden University Press, 1981) pp. 189–205.

———, *The Dutch East India Company and the Economy of Bengal 1630–1720* (Princeton: Princeton University Press, 1985).

———, 'Restrictive Trading Regimes: VOC and the Asian Spice Trade in the Seventeenth Century', in: R. Ptak and D. Rothermund (eds.), *Emporia, Commodities and Entrepreneurs in Asian Maritime Trade, c. 1400–1750* (Stuttgart: Franz Steiner Verlag, 1991).

———, *European Commercial Enterprise in India* (Cambridge: Cambridge U.P., 1998).

Raben, Remco, and H. Spijkerman (eds.), *De archieven van de Verenigde Oostindische Compagnie/The Archives of the Dutch East India Company* (The Hague: SDU, 1992).

Rei, Claudia, 'Incentives in Merchant Empires: Portuguese and Dutch Labor Compensation', *Cliometrica* 7 (2013) pp. 1–13.

Reid, Anthony, 'The Origins of Southeast Asian Poverty', in: W. E. Willmot (ed.), *Scholarship and Society in Southeast Asia* (Christchurch, 1979) pp. 33–49.

———, 'Introduction: Slavery and Bondage in Southeast Asian ', in: Ibid. (ed.), *Slavery, Bondage and Dependency in Southeast Asia* (St Lucia, 1983).

———, *Southeast Asia in the Age of Commerce 1450–1680. Vol. 1: The Lands below the Winds* (New Haven and London 1988).

———, 'Economic and Social Change, c. 1400–1800', *Cambridge History of Southeast Asia, Vol. 1. From Early Times to c. 1800* (Cambridge: Cambridge U.P., 1992) pp. 460–507.

———, *Southeast Asia in the Age of Commerce 1450-1680. Vol. 2: Expansion and Crisis* (New Haven and London 1993).

Richards, John F., 'The Seventeenth-Century Crisis in South Asia', *Modern Asian Studies* 24 (1990) pp. 625–638.

Ricklefs, Merle C., *Modern Javanese Historical Tradition. A Study of an Original Kartasura Chronicle and Related Materials* (London: SOAS, 1978).

———, 'Some Statistical Evidence on Javanese Social, Economic and Demographic History in the Later Seventeenth and Eighteenth Centuries', *Modern Asian Studies* 20 (1986).

———, *A History of Modern Indonesia since c. 1200* (Stanford: Stanford U.P., 2008).

Roberts, Michael, *Caste Conflict and Elite Formation. The Rise of a Karava Elite in Sri Lanka, 1500–1931* (New Delhi, 1995).

Rodrik, Dani, *Has Globalization Gone Too Far?* (Washington, DC: Institute for International Economics, 1997).

———, *One Economics, Many Recipes: Globalization, Institutions and Economic Growth* (Princeton: Princeton U.P., 2007).

———, *The Globalization Paradox. Democracy and the Future of the World Economy* (New York: W. W. Norton & Company, 2011).

Rogers, J. E. T., *A History of Agriculture and Prices in England.* 7 vols. (Oxford: Clarendon Press: 1866–1892).

Rönnbäck, Klas, 'Integration of Global Commodity Markets in the Early Modern Era', *European Review of Economic History* 13 (2009) pp. 95–120.

———, 'The Speed of Ships and Shipping Productivity in the Age of Sail', *European Review of Economic History* 16 (2013) pp. 469–489.

Rosenthal, Jean-Laurent, and R. Bin Wong, *Before and Beyond Divergence. The Politics of Economic Change in China and Europe* (Cambridge MA: Harvard U.P., 2011).

Ross, Robert, 'The "White" Population of South Africa in the Eighteenth Century', *Population Studies* 26 (1975) pp. 217–230.

———, 'The Cape of Good Hope and the World Economy, 1652–1835', in: Richard Elphick and Hermann Giliomee (eds.), *The Shaping of South African Society, 1652–1840* (Cape Town: Maskew Miller Longman, 1989) pp. 243–282.

Rossum, Matthias van, 'De intra-Aziatische vaart: schepen, zeelieden en ondergang van de VOC?', *Tijdschrift voor Sociale en Economische Geschiedenis* (2011) 8, pp. 32–69.

Roy, Tirthankar, 'Economic History and Modern India: Redefining the Link', *Journal of Economic Perspectives* (2002) pp. 109–130.

———, 'Economic Conditions in Early Modern Bengal: A Contribution to the Divergence Debate', *Journal of Economic History* 70 (2010) pp. 179–194.

———, 'Beyond Divergence: Rethinking the Economic History of India', *Economic History of Developing Regions* 27 (2012) pp. 57–65.

———, *An Economic History of Early Modern India* (Abingdon: Routledge, 2013).

Sarkar, N. K., *The demography of Ceylon* (Colombo: Ceylon Government Press, 1957).

Sarkar, Smritikumar, 'Social Organization of Artisan Production in India: Changing Role of the Market, Technology, and Merchant-Creditor: 18th to 20th Centuries', in: Binay Bhusan Chaudhuri (ed.), *Economic History of India From Eighteenth to Twentieth Century* (New Delhi: Centre for Studies in Civilization, 2005) pp. 107–354.

Schneider, Eric B., 'Real Wages and the Family: Adjusting Real Wages to Changing Demography in Pre-modern England', *Explorations in Economic History* 50 (2013) pp. 99–115.

Schrikker, Alicia, *Dutch and British Colonial Intervention in Sri Lanka, 1780–1815: Expansion and Reform* (Leiden and Boston: Brill, 2007).

Schularick, Moritz, and Solomos Solomou, 'Tariffs and Economic Growth in the First Era of Globalization', *Journal of Economic Growth* 16 (2011) pp. 33–70.

Schutte, Gerrit, 'Company and Colonists at the Cape', in: Richard Elphick and Hermann Giliomee (eds.), *The Shaping of South African Society, 1652–1820* (London: Longman, 1979) pp. 173–210.

Sharp, Paul, and Jacob Weisdorf, 'Globalization Revisited: Market Integration and the Wheat Trade between North America and Britain from the Eighteenth Century', *Explorations in Economic History* 50 (2013) pp. 88–98.

Shell, R. C. -H., *Children of Bondage. A Social History of a Slave Society at the Cape of Good Hope, 1652–1838* (Johannesburg: Wits University Press, 1997).

Shimada, Ryuto, *The Intra-Asian Trade in Japanese Copper by the Dutch East India Company during the Eighteenth Century* (Leiden: Brill, 2006).

Silva, Chandra R. de, 'The First Portuguese Revenue Register of the Kingdom of Kotte – 1599', *Ceylon Journal of Historical and Social Studies* 5 (1975) pp. 71–153.

———, 'Sri Lanka in the Early Sixteenth Century: Economic and Social Conditions', in: K. M. de Silva (ed.), *University of Peradeniya History of Sri Lanka* (Peradeniya, 1995).

Silva, K. M. de, *A History of Sri Lanka* (London: Hurst, 1981).

Silva, S. B. D. de, *Political Economy of Underdevelopment* (London, 1982).

Singh, Anajana, *Fort Cochin in Kerala, 1750–1830. The Social Condition of a Dutch Community in an Indian Milieu* (Leiden: Brill, 2010).

Sivramkrishna, Sashi, 'Ascertaining Living Standards in Erstwhile Mysore, Southern India, from Francis Buchanan's Journey of 1800–01: An Empirical Contribution to the Great Divergence Debate', *Journal of the Economic and Social History of the Orient* 52 (2009) 695–733.

Sokoloff, Kenneth L., and Stanley L Engerman, 'History Lessons: Institutions, Factor Endowments and Paths of Development in the New World', *Journal of Economic Perspectives* 14 (2000) pp. 217–232.

Solar, Peter M., 'Opening to the East: Shipping between Europe and Asia, 1770–1830', *Journal of Economic History* 73 (2013) pp. 625–661.

Solar, Peter M., and Luc Hens, 'The Speed of East India Company Ships', *Mimeo Free University Brussels* (2013).

Souza, George B, *The Survival of Empire. Portuguese Trade and Society in China and the South China Sea 1630–1754* (Cambridge: Cambridge U.P., 1986).

Spufford, Margaret, 'Literacy, Trade and Religion in the Commercial Centres of Europe', in: Karel Davids and Jan Lucassen (eds.), *A Miracle Mirrored. The Dutch Republic in European Perspective* (Cambridge: Cambridge U.P., 1995).

Smith, Adam, *An Inquiry into the Nature and Causes of the Wealth of Nations* (New York: Bantam Classic, 2003 [Original: 1776]).

Srinivasan, T. N., and Jagdish Bhagwati, 'Outward-Orientation and Development: Are Revisionists Right?' *Center Discussion Paper No. 806* (Yale University, 1999).

Steckel, Richard H., and Roderick Floud, 'Introduction', in: Ibid. (eds.), *Health and Welfare during Industrialization* (Chicago: University of Chicago Press, 1997) pp. 1–16.

Steensgaard, Niels, 'Freight Costs in the English East India Trade 1601–1657', *Scandinavian Economic History Review* 13 (1965) pp. 143–162.

———, *The Asian Trade Revolution of the Seventeenth Century. The East India Companies and the Decline of the Caravan Trade* (Chicago and London: University of Chicago Press, 1973).

———, 'The Dutch East India Company as an Institutional Innovation', in: Maurice Aymard (ed.), *Dutch Capitalism and World Capitalism. Capitalism hollandaise et capitalisme mondial* (Cambridge: Cambridge U.P., 1982).

———, 'Asian Trade and World Economy from the 15th to the 18th Centuries', in: T. R. de Souza (ed.), *Indo-Portuguese History: Old Issues, New Questions* (New Delhi, 1985).

Stiglitz, Joseph E., *Globalization and Its Discontents* (New York: W. W. Norton, 2002).

Studer, Roman, 'India and the Great Divergence: Assessing the Efficiency of Grain Markets in Eighteenth- and Nineteenth-Century India', *Journal of Economic History* 68 (2008) pp. 393–437.

Talens, J., *Feodale samenleving in koloniaal vaarwater. Staatsvorming, koloniale expansie en economische ontwikkeling in Banten, West-Java (1600–1750)* (Hilversum: Verloren. 1996).

Taylor, Alan M., and Jeffrey G. Williamson, 'Convergence in the Age of Mass Migration', *European Review of Economic History* 1 (1997) pp. 27–63.

Tielhof, Milja van, and Jan Luiten van Zanden, 'Productivity Changes in Shipping in the Dutch Republic: The Evidence from Freight Rates, 1550–1800', in: Richard W. Unger (eds.), *Shipping and Economic Growth 1350–1850* (Leiden and Boston: Brill, 2011) pp. 47–80.

Topik, Steven, 'The Integration of the World Coffee Market', in: William Gervase Clarence-Smith and Steven Topik (eds.), *The Global Coffee Economy in Africa, Asia, and Latin America, 1500–1989* (Cambridge: Cambridge U.P., 2003) pp. 21–49.

Uebele, Martin, 'National and International Market Integration in the 19th Century: Evidence from Co-movement', *Explorations in Economic History* 48 (2011) pp. 226–242.

Verhoeff, J. M., *De oude Nederlandse maten en gewichten* (Amsterdam: P. J. Meertens Instituut, 1982).

Voth, Hans-Joachim, *Time and Work in England 1750–1830* (Oxford: Oxford University Press, 2001).

———, 'The Longest Years: New Estimates of Labor Input in England, 1760–1830', *Journal of Economic History* 61 (2001) pp. 1065–1082.

Vries, Jan de, 'The Industrial Revolution and the Industrious Revolution', *Journal of Economic History* 54 (1994) pp. 249–270.

———, 'How Did Pre-industrial Labour Markets Work?', in: George Grantham and Mary Mackinnon (eds.), *Labour Market Evolution* (London, 1994) pp. 39–63.

———, 'Connecting Europe and Asia: A Quantitative Analysis of the Cape-Route Trade, 1497–1795', in: D. O. Flynn, A. Giraldez, and R. von Glahn (eds.), *Global Connections and Monetary History, 1470–1800* (Aldershot, 2003) pp. 35–106, there pp. 46–51.

———, *The Industrious Revolution: Consumer Demand and the Household Economy, 1650 to the Present* (Cambridge: Cambridge U.P., 2008).

———, 'The Limits of Globalization in the Early Modern World', *Economic History Review* 63 (2010) pp. 710–733.

Wade, Geoff, 'An Early Age of Commerce in Southeast Asia, 900–1300 CE', *Journal of Southeast Asian Studies* 40 (2009) pp. 221–265.

Wallerstein, Immanuel, *The Modern World System* (New York: Academic Press, 1974).

———, *The Capitalist World Economy* (Cambridge: Cambridge U.P., 1979).

Wallis, Patrick, 'Apprenticeship and Training in Pre-modern England', *Journal of Economic History* 68 (2008) pp. 832–861.

Washbrook, David, 'Eighteenth Century Issues in South Asia', *Journal of the Economic and Social History of the Orient* 44 (2001) pp. 372–383.

Wee, Herman Van der, *The Growth of the Antwerp Market and the European Economy (fourteenth-sixteenth centuries). Vol. I. Statistics* (The Hague: Martinus Nijhoff, 1963).

Weber, Max, *The Protestant Work Ethic and the Spirit of Capitalism* (1905 [2002]).

White, B., 'Economic Diversification and Agrarian Change in Rural Java, 1900–1990', in: P. Alexander, P. Boomgaard, and B. White (eds.), *In the Shadow of Agriculture. Non-farming Activities in the Javanese Economy, Past and Present* (Amsterdam: Royal Tropical Institute, 1992).

Wicks, Robert S., 'Monetary Developments in Java between the Ninth and Sixteenth Centuries: A Numismatic Perspective', *Indonesia* 42 (1986) pp. 42–77.

———, *Money, Markets and Trade in Early Southeast Asia: The Development of Indigenous Monetary Systems to AD 1400* (1992).

Williamson, Jeffrey G., 'Globalization and the Great Divergence: Terms of Trade Booms, Volatility and the Poor Periphery, 1782–1913', *European Review of Economic History* 12 (2008) pp. 355–391.

———, *Trade and Poverty: When the Third World Fell Behind* (Cambridge MA: MIT Press, 2011).

Wilson, Monica, and Leonard Thompson, 'White Settlers and the Origin of a New Society, 1652–1778', in: Ibid. (eds.), *The Oxford History of South Africa. Vol. I* (Oxford: Clarendon Press, 1971) pp. 183–232.

Wrigley, E. A., and R. S. Schofield, *The Population History of England 1541–1871. A Reconstruction* (London: Edward Arnold, 1981).

Yong, Liu, *The Dutch East India Company's Tea Trade with China 1757–1781* (Leiden: Brill, 2006).

Zanden, Jan Luiten van, *Arbeid tijdens het handelskapitalisme: opkomst en neergang van de Hollandse economie, 1350–1850* (Bergen: Octavo, 1991) pp. 136–137.

———, 'Wages and the Standard of Living in Europe, 1500–1800', *European Review of Economic History* 3 (1999) pp. 175–197.

———, 'Economic Growth in Java 1815–1939. The Reconstruction of the Historical National Accounts of a Colonial Economy', *Mimeo* (2002).

———, 'Taking the Measure of the Early Modern Economy: Historical National Account for Holland in 1510/4', *European Review of Economic History* 6 (2002) pp. 131–163.

———, 'Rich and Poor before the Industrial Revolution, a Comparison between Java and the Netherlands at the Beginning of the Nineteenth Century', *Explorations in Economic History* 40 (2003) pp. 1–23.

———, 'The Skill Premium and the "Great Divergence"', *European Review of Economic History* 13 (2009) pp. 121–153.

———, 'The Malthusian Intermezzo: Women's Wages and Human Capital Formation between the Late Middle Ages and the Demographic Transition of the 19th Century', *History of the Family* 16 (2011) pp. 331–342.

Zanden, Jan Luiten van, and Bas van Leeuwen, 'Persistent But Not Consistent: The Growth of National Income in Holland, 1347–1807', *Explorations in Economic History* 49 (2012) pp. 119–130.

Zanden, Jan Luiten van, and Daan Marks, *An Economic History of Indonesia, 1800–2010* (London: Routledge, 2011).

Zanden, Jan Luiten van, and Milja van Tielhof, 'Roots of Growth and Productivity Change in Dutch Shipping Industry 1500–1800', *Explorations in Economic History* 46 (2009) pp. 389–403.

Zoysa, Darshini A. de, 'Transformation of Customary Marriage and Inheritance Laws of the Sinhalese under British Colonialism', *Dialectical Anthropology* 20 (1995).

Zwart, Pim de, 'South African Living Standards in Global Perspective, 1835–1910', *Economic History of Developing Regions* 26 (2011) pp. 49–74.

———, 'Population, Labour and Living Standards in Early Modern Ceylon: An Empirical Contribution to the Divergence Debate', *Indian Economic and Social History Review* 49 (2012) pp. 365–398.

———, 'Real Wages at the Cape of Good Hope: A Long-Term Perspective, 1652–1912', *Low Countries Journal of Social and Economic History* 10 (2013) pp. 28–58.

———, 'Globalization in the Early Modern Era: New Evidence from the Dutch Asiatic Trade, c. 1600–1800', *Journal of Economic History* 76 (2016) pp. 520–558.

Zwart, Pim de, and Jan Luiten van Zanden, 'Labor, Wages and Living Standards in Java, 1680–1914', *European Review of Economic History* 19 (2015) pp. 215–234.

Zwart, Pim de, Daan Marks, Alexandra M. de Pleijt, and Jan Luiten van Zanden, 'Trade and Economic Development: Indonesia in the Long-Run', in: Alicia Schrikker and Jeroen Touwen (eds.), *Promises and Predicaments. Trade and Entrepreneurship in Colonial and Independent Indonesia in the 19th and 20th Centuries* (Singapore: NUS Press, 2015) pp. 61–79.

Online sources

Allen, Robert C., and Roman Studer, 'Prices and Wages in India, 1595–1930', *Global Price and Income History Group* website and the University of California-Davis: http://gpih.ucdavis.edu/Datafilelist.htm#Asia. Last update: September 12, 2009.

Bochove, Christiaan van, 'Prices in Sri Lanka and Southern India', *Historical Prices and Wages Website* of the International Institute of Social History: http://www.iisg.nl/hpw/voc-srilanka-southernindia.pdf. Last accessed: March 4, 2014.

Huygens ING, *VOC Glossarium: Verklaringen van termen, verzameld uit de Rijks Geschiedkundige Publicatiën, die betrekking hebben op de Verenigde Oost-Indische Compagnie*: http://resources.huygens.knaw.nl/vocglossarium. Last accessed: November 13, 2014.

———, *Bookkeeper-General Batavia*: http://bgb.huygens.knaw.nl/. Last accessed: October 25, 2014.

Lindert, Peter, 'Silver in Britain – Mint Prices 1273–1971 and Market Prices 1693–1977', *Global Price and Income History Group* website and the University of California-Davis: http://gpih.ucdavis.edu/Datafilelist.htm. Last update: April 9, 2006.

———, 'Weights vs Volume', *Global Price and Income History Group* website and the University of California-Davis: http://gpih.ucdavis.edu/Datafilelist.htm#Asia. Last update: April 9, 2006.

TEPC Transcription Project (Cape Town), Inventories of the Orphan Chamber: http://databases.tanap.net/mooc/.

United States Department of Agriculture (USDA), *National Nutrient Database for Standard Reference*, Release 26: http://ndb.nal.usda.gov/ndb/search/list. Last accessed: March 4, 2014.

Zanden, Jan Luiten van, 'Prices and the Cost of Living in the Western Part of the Netherlands, 1450–1800', website *Historical Prices and Wages* of the International Institute of Social History: http://www.iisg.nl/hpw/brenv.xls. Last update: December 11, 2009.

Index

www.ingramcontent.com/pod-product-compliance
Lightning Source LLC
LaVergne TN
LVHW010544300926
849162LV00002B/230
* 9 7 8 9 0 0 4 2 9 9 6 5 8 *